Modern American Drama: Playwriting in the 1940s

DECADES OF MODERN AMERICAN DRAMA: PLAYWRITING FROM THE 1930s TO 2009

Modern American Drama: Playwriting in the 1930s
by Anne Fletcher

Modern American Drama: Playwriting in the 1940s
by Felicia Hardison Londré

Modern American Drama: Playwriting in the 1950s
by Susan C. W. Abbotson

Modern American Drama: Playwriting in the 1960s
by Mike Sell

Modern American Drama: Playwriting in the 1970s
by Michael Vanden Heuvel

Modern American Drama: Playwriting in the 1980s
by Sandra G. Shannon

Modern American Drama: Playwriting in the 1990s
by Cheryl Black and Sharon Friedman

Modern American Drama: Playwriting 2000–2009
by Julia Listengarten and Cindy Rosenthal

Modern American Drama: Playwriting in the 1940s

Voices, Documents, New Interpretations

Felicia Hardison Londré

Series Editors: Brenda Murphy and Julia Listengarten

methuen | drama
LONDON • NEW YORK • OXFORD • NEW DELHI • SYDNEY

METHUEN DRAMA
Bloomsbury Publishing Plc
50 Bedford Square, London, WC1B 3DP, UK
1385 Broadway, New York, NY 10018, USA
29 Earlsfort Terrace, Dublin 2, Ireland

BLOOMSBURY, METHUEN DRAMA and the Methuen Drama logo
are trademarks of Bloomsbury Publishing Plc

First published in Great Britain 2018
Paperback edition first published 2021

Copyright © Felicia Hardison Londré and contributors, 2018

Felicia Hardison Londré has asserted her right under the Copyright,
Designs and Patents Act, 1988, to be identified as author of this work.

For legal purposes the Acknowledgements on p. xi constitute
an extension of this copyright page.

Cover design by Louise Dugdale
Cover image © Felicia Hardison Londré

All rights reserved. No part of this publication may be reproduced or
transmitted in any form or by any means, electronic or mechanical,
including photocopying, recording, or any information storage or retrieval
system, without prior permission in writing from the publishers.

Bloomsbury Publishing Plc does not have any control over, or responsibility for,
any third-party websites referred to or in this book. All internet addresses given
in this book were correct at the time of going to press. The author and publisher
regret any inconvenience caused if addresses have changed or sites have
ceased to exist, but can accept no responsibility for any such changes.

A catalogue record for this book is available from the British Library.

A catalog record for this book is available from the Library of Congress.

ISBN: HB: 978-1-4725-7186-1
PB: 978-1-3502-1545-0
ePDF: 978-1-3500-1748-1
eBook: 978-1-3500-1749-8
Pack: 978-1-4725-7264-6

Series: Decades of Modern American Drama: Playwriting from the 1930s to 2009

Typeset by Fakenham Prepress Solutions, Fakenham, Norfolk NR21 8NN

To find out more about our authors and books visit
www.bloomsbury.com and sign up for our newsletters.

*To my mother,
Priscilla Graham Hardison Taylor,
who tried valiantly to protect me from the influence
of unsettling plays like those of Tennessee Williams*

CONTENTS

Acknowledgements xi
Biographical Note and Notes on Contributors xii
General Preface Brenda Murphy and Julia Listengarten xvi

1 Introduction to the 1940s *Felicia Hardison Londré* 1
  Prelude to the Second World War 4
  Leaders of the decade 6
  The Second World War 9
  The war's impact on civilian life 13
  Post-war domestic life and consumerism 16
  Children 18
  Teenagers 20
  Communications, media and transportation 23
  Women and fashion 27
  The culture 28
  Cold War anxieties 32

2 American Theatre in the 1940s *Felicia Hardison Londré* 35
  The late 1930s: Forebodings of war 37
    Idiot's Delight 37
    Influential organizations 37
    It Can't Happen Here 40
    Broadway plays and musicals 41
    Radio drama 43

The 1940–1 and 1941–2 seasons 44
   African-American theatre 44
   Broadway plays and musicals 46
   Lady in the Dark 48
   The American Theatre Wing and other war service organizations 51
   Radio drama 57
The war years, 1942–5 58
   Broadway plays and musicals 58
   This Is the Army 63
   Oklahoma! 66
   The Paul Robeson *Othello* 70
Post-war theatre, 1946–50 73
   African-American theatre 73
   Broadway plays and musicals 74
   Modern dance and theatrical dance 79
   Tributary theatre 80
   Directors and producers 82

3 Introducing the Playwrights *Felicia Hardison Londré* 87

Introduction 87
Eugene O'Neill (1888–1953) 90
Thornton Wilder (1897–1975) 92
Tennessee Williams (1911–83) 95
Arthur Miller (1915–2005) 98

4 Eugene O'Neill: *Zander Brietzke* 101

A Touch of the Poet 104
The Iceman Cometh 109
Long Day's Journey Into Night 114
A Moon for the Misbegotten 119
Conclusion 123

5 Thornton Wilder: Seeing Beyond Dark Times *Felicia Hardison Londré* 125
   Our Town 130
   The Skin of Our Teeth 136
   Shadow of a Doubt 141
   The Alcestiad 145
   Conclusion 149

6 Tennessee Williams: *Thomas Keith* 151
   Early full-length plays 154
   Battle of Angels 156
   Stairs to the Roof 159
   The Glass Menagerie 161
   Summer and Smoke 169
   A Streetcar Named Desire 172
   Conclusion 174

7 Arthur Miller: *Valleri Robinson* 177
   All My Sons 178
   Death of a Salesman 184
   The Crucible 192
   Conclusion 199

Afterword *Felicia Hardison Londré* 201

Documents 207
   For Such is the Ruling of Broadway: *Ann Crisp* 207
   Collecting Eugene O'Neill: *Lamar Lentz* 211
   Acting in *The Skin of Our Teeth*: *Hank Whittemore* 214
   Arthur Miller in Brooklyn Heights: *Stephen Marino* 221

A Retrospective of Influence: *Thomas D. Pawley III* 237

Notes 239
Bibliography 271
Index 287

ACKNOWLEDGEMENTS

Acknowledgements for a book on the 1940s must begin with 'the greatest generation', all who worked and fought with unified purpose to preserve European culture and the values of free people everywhere. That includes my parents, Colonel (USAF) and Mrs Felix M. Hardison, and grandparents, Major General and Mrs Roy C. L. Graham. It was a particular thrill for me when a photograph of my father, taken on 19 November 1942 at Hamilton Field with the B-17e Flying Fortress he piloted, was chosen for the cover of this book. After combat in the South Pacific, Major Hardison had returned to the USA the day before with "Suzy-Q," the first pilot and plane to circumnavigate the globe in wartime. Many people expressed friendly interest in this project and helped me remain focused, beginning with my immediate family: my husband Venne-Richard Londré, son Tristan Graham Londré, daughter Georgianna Londré Buchanan, sisters Suzanne Leighton and Sandra Bartlett, and my mother, to whom this book is dedicated. Others include Sue Abbotson, Martin Buchanan, Stephanie Demaree, Thierry Dubost, Bill and Marge Eckhardt, Angela Elam, John Ezell, Jim Fisher, Ben Fleer, Tom Foral, Gene Friedman, Angela Gieras, Glenda Gill, Greg Mackender, Tom Mardikes, Carla Noack, Sarah Oliver, Sandrine Polomski, Tom Reed, Nell Richardson, Robert Schanke, Cindy Stofiel, Mark Titus, Wayne Vaught and Dan Watermeier. For their ever-prompt and encouraging responses, I thank series editors Julia Listengarten and Brenda Murphy, and Bloomsbury senior commissioning editor Mark Dudgeon, assistant editor Lara Bateman, and editorial assistant Susan Furber. Finally, I want to express special appreciation to all of the contributors whose work appears in this volume; it was a pleasure to work with each one of them.

BIOGRAPHICAL NOTE AND NOTES ON CONTRIBUTORS

Felicia Hardison Londré, Curators' Distinguished Professor of Theatre at the University of Missouri-Kansas City, served a term (2012–14) as Dean of the College of Fellows of the American Theatre, to which she was elected in 1999. She has received two national teaching awards: the ATHE Outstanding Teacher of Theatre in Higher Education (2001) and the ATDS Betty Jean Jones Award for Outstanding Teacher of American Theatre and Drama (2011). Her fourteen books include the George Freedley Memorial Award-winning *The Enchanted Years of the Stage: Kansas City at the Crossroads of American Theater 1890–1930* (2007) and a *Choice* Outstanding Academic Book, *The History of World Theater: From the English Restoration to the Present* (1991). Among her other books are the *Historical Dictionary of American Theater: Modernism* (with James Fisher, 2009), *Words at Play: Creative Writing and Dramaturgy* (2005), *Love's Labour's Lost: Critical Essays* (2000) and *The History of North American Theater: The United States, Canada, and Mexico from Pre-Columbian Times to the Present* (with Daniel J. Watermeier, 1999). Her sixty or so published articles include several on Tennessee Williams and on Eugene O'Neill.

Zander Brietzke is the author of *The Aesthetics of Failure: Dynamic Structure in the Plays of Eugene O'Neill* (2001), *American Drama in the Age of Film* (2007) and *Teaching with the Norton Anthology of Drama* (2009, 2013). He is a former president of the Eugene O'Neill Society and was the editor of the *Eugene O'Neill Review*

(2004–10) at Suffolk University in Boston. His recent essays appear in *Eugene O'Neill's One-Act Plays* (2012), edited by Michael Bennett and Benjamin Carson, *Critical Insights: Eugene O'Neill* (2012), edited by Steven F. Bloom, and *Eugene O'Neill and His Early Contemporaries* (2011), edited by Eileen Herrmann and Robert Dowling. Zander Brietzke has taught at Lehigh University, The College of Wooster and Columbia University.

Ann Crisp graduated from Oneonta High School in 1947 and earned her BA at Murray State College, Kentucky, in May 1950. She married Neil Demaree in June 1950.

David Kaplan is curator and co-founder of the Provincetown Tennessee Williams Theater Festival. He is the author of *Tennessee Williams in Provincetown* (2007) and *Tenn Years: Tennessee Williams on Stage* (2015), and editor of *Tenn at One Hundred: The Reputation of Tennessee Williams* (2011) as well as a college textbook series: *Five Approaches to Acting*. In 2008 he directed the world premieres of Williams's *The Day on Which a Man Dies* (Chicago) and *The Dog Enchanted by the Divine View* (Boston). Internationally, David Kaplan has staged a Russian-language production of *Suddenly, Last Summer* (Gorky Theatre, Samara, Russia), a Spanish-language *Ten Blocks on the Camino Real* (Uruguay) and a Cantonese-language *The Eccentricities of a Nightingale* (Hong Kong).

Thomas Keith has edited over a dozen titles by Tennessee Williams for New Directions Publishing, including three collections of previously unpublished one-act plays: *Mister Paradise & Other One-Act Plays*, *The Traveling Companion & Other Plays* and *The Magic Tower & Other One-Act Plays*, as well as Williams's last full-length play, *A House Not Meant to Stand*. An advisor to the Tennessee Williams/New Orleans Literary Festival and the Provincetown Tennessee Williams Theater Festival, he has written articles and essays for *American Theatre Magazine*, *Tenn at One Hundred*, the *Tennessee Williams Annual Review*, *The Later Plays of Tennessee Williams* and *Tennessee Williams in Europe*, among others. He and Peggy Fox are co-editing *The Selected Letters of Tennessee Williams and James Laughlin* for publication by W. W. Norton. Thomas Keith has taught acting and theatre at the Lee Strasberg Institute and Ohio University, currently at Pace University in New York, and has served as a dramaturg for the Sundance Institute Theatre Lab.

Lamar Lentz is associate managing director of Round Top Festival Institute in Round Top, Texas, where he began his association in 1975. He is also founding curator of the Library and Museum Collections there. He earned his BA in theatre and rare book studies and his MA in art history at the University of Texas at Austin.

Stephen Marino is founding editor of *The Arthur Miller Journal*. His work on Miller has appeared in many journals, essay collections and books. His interviews with Arthur Miller's sister, Joan Copeland; Miller's biographer, Christopher Bigsby; and the playwright David Henry Hwang have appeared in the journal's 'Conversation' series. Professor Marino is the author of *A Language Study of Arthur Miller's Plays, The Poetic in the Colloquial* and the editor of the Methuen critical student edition of *A View From the Bridge*. His new book, *Arthur Miller* Death of a Salesman / The Crucible: *A Reader's Guide to Essential Criticism*, was published by Palgrave Macmillan in September 2015. In October 2015, he chaired the Arthur Miller Centennial Conference at St Francis College, where he teaches.

Thomas D. Pawley III, Curators' Distinguished Professor Emeritus of Speech and Theatre, began his forty-eight-year career (1940–88) at Lincoln University, Jefferson City, Missouri, as instructor of English and director of dramatics, and went on to serve there as department head, division chair, managing director of summer theatre, and dean of the College of Arts and Sciences. He was invested in the College of Fellows of the American Theatre in 1978. In 1987, Professor Pawley was founding president of the National Conference on African American Theatre. His 1970 book, *The Black Teacher and the Dramatic Arts*, co-edited with William R. Reardon, has been called a seminal work in the field. Professor Pawley passed away on 1 August 2016.

Valleri Robinson is Assistant Professor of Theatre History and Criticism at the University of Illinois, Urbana-Champaign. She is author of *Russian Culture and Theatrical Performance in America, 1891–1933* (author listing as Valleri J. Hohman, 2011), and articles and reviews in *Contemporary Theatre Review*, the *Slavic and East European Journal*, *Theatre History Studies*, *Theatre Journal*, *Contemporary Drama* and *The Journal of American Drama and Theatre*. Her essays also appear in *'To Have or To Have Not': New Essays on Commerce and Capital in Modernist Theatre*, edited by James Fisher (2011), and *The Routledge Companion to Stanislavsky*, edited by R. Andrew White (2013). Professor Hohman received a Fulbright award to work with the Kolyada Theatre in Ekaterinburg in 2014.

Hank Whittemore was a university student at Notre Dame when he took time out in 1961 to act on Broadway in *Take Her, She's Mine* with Art Carney. Although he also acted in regional theatre, he became a full-time writer and is the author of ten non-fiction books and one novel. His bestseller *The Super Cops* was made into a movie directed by Gordon Parks. He has written narration scripts for dozens of television documentaries and many magazine articles on varied subjects for *PARADE*, the Sunday supplement. Hank Whittemore has been a lifelong lover of Shakespeare and is deeply involved in the 'authorship' question. His major work on Shakespeare is *The Monument* (2005), offering a radical explanation of the Sonnets.

GENERAL PREFACE

Decades of Modern American Drama: Playwriting from the 1930s to 2009 is a series of eight volumes about American theatre and drama, each focusing on a particular decade during the period between 1930 and 2010. It begins with the 1930s, the decade when Eugene O'Neill was awarded the Nobel Prize for Literature and American theatre came of age. This is followed by the decade of the country's most acclaimed theatre, when O'Neill, Tennessee Williams and Arthur Miller were writing their most distinguished work and a theatrical idiom known as 'the American style' was seen in theatres throughout the world. Its place in the world repertoire established, American playwriting has taken many turns since 1950.

The aim of this series is to focus attention on individual playwrights or collaborative teams who together reflect the variety and range of American drama during the eighty-year period it covers. In each volume, contributing experts offer detailed critical essays on four playwrights or collaborators and the significant work they produced during the decade. The essays on playwrights are presented in a rich interpretive context, which provides a contemporary perspective on both the theatre and American life and culture during the decade. The careers of the playwrights before and after the decade are summarized as well, and a section of documents, including interviews, manuscripts, reviews, brief essays and other items, sheds further light on the playwrights and their plays.

The process of choosing such a limited number of playwrights to represent the American theatre of this period has been a difficult but revealing one. In selecting them, the series editors and volume authors have been guided by several principles: highlighting the most significant playwrights, in terms both historical and aesthetic, who contributed at least two interesting and important plays during the decade; providing a wide-ranging view of the decade's theatre, including both Broadway and alternative venues; examining many historical trends in playwriting and theatrical production during the decade; and reflecting the theatre's diversity in gender and ethnicity, both across the decade and across the period as a whole. In some decades, the choices are obvious. It is hard to argue with O'Neill, Williams, Miller and Wilder in the 1940s. Other decades required a good deal of thought and discussion. Readers will inevitably regret that favourite playwrights are left out. We can only respond that we regret it too, but we believe that the playwrights who are included reflect a representative sample of the best and most interesting American playwriting during the period.

While each of the books has the same fundamental elements – an overview of life and culture during the decade, an overview of the decade's theatre and drama, the four essays on the playwrights, a section of documents, an Afterword bringing the playwrights' careers up to date and a Bibliography of works both on the individual playwrights and on the decade in general – there are differences among the books depending on each individual volume author's decisions about how to represent and treat the decade. The various formats chosen by the volume authors for the overview essays, the wide variety of playwrights, from the canonical to the contemporary avant-garde, and the varied perspectives of the contributors' essays make for very different individual volumes. Each of the volumes stands on its own as a history of theatre in the decade and a critical study of the four individual playwrights or collaborative teams included. Taken together, however, the eight volumes offer a broadly representative critical and historical treatment of eighty years of American theatre and drama that is both accessible to a student first encountering the subject and informative and provocative for a seasoned expert.

Brenda Murphy (Board of Trustees Distinguished Professor Emeritus, University of Connecticut, USA)
Julia Listengarten (Professor of Theatre at the University of Central Florida, USA)
Series Editors

1

Introduction to the 1940s

Felicia Hardison Londré

Decades are often subjected to neatly-packaged characterization, and this may be more true of the United States in the first part of the twentieth century than in any other time or place. In the 1900s our immigrant nation came to awareness of its 'melting-pot' cohesiveness and larger identity in the world. The 1910s were our ragtime decade that segued into jazz along with our involvement in the First World War. Prohibition actually fuelled the free-spirited gaiety of the Roaring '20s until the fun and prosperity came to an abrupt end with the stock-market crash of 1929. Economic depression and social unrest dominated the 1930s, followed by the Second World War's indelible imprint on the 1940s. The 1950s brought rampant consumerism and conformity. The Vietnam conflict and youth rebellion put their stamp on the 1960s. After that, the increasing complexities and fragmented views of life tend to thwart attempts at applying simple labels to the decades.

Yet all historical constructs are more complex than what is readily apparent. The Second World War is indeed the defining feature of the 1940s, but that war and the attitudes it shaped must be tracked back to the second half of the 1930s decade, for the rumblings were heard and feared as early as 1935, as Thornton Wilder noted during his European travels.[1] Thus our inclusion of Thornton Wilder's 1938 play *Our Town* as belonging to the 1940s can be justified. Some effects of the Great Depression of the 1930s also lingered on into the 1940s, even as the wartime stimulus to the economy brought steady progress toward the prosperity of the late 1940s and early 1950s. Psychologically the 1930s left their mark on a generation that distrusted financial institutions and tolerated government expansion. One might describe the 1940s as a two-part decade: war and post-war. Many cultural manifestations discussed here will reflect that dichotomy.

PRELUDE TO THE SECOND WORLD WAR

In retrospect, some significant stepping stones toward the Second World War can be identified in the two preceding decades.

1919: Mussolini's formation of the Fascist party in Italy. Humiliation of Germany at the signing of the Treaty of Versailles.

1920: Adolf Hitler's programme of anti-Semitism adopted by the German Workers' Party.

1921: Excessive war reparations demanded of Germany by the Allies.

1922: Fascist march to Rome culminating in Mussolini becoming prime minister of Italy. French occupation of the Ruhr in response to German failure to pay reparations.

1923: The first National Socialist (Nazi) party congress in January and its failed Munich beer-hall putsch in November.

1926: Decline of the French franc.

1927: Growing power of General Chiang Kai-shek's Nationalist party in China. Arson and looting by communists in Vienna.

1928: Kellogg–Briand Treaty to outlaw war signed by fifteen nations.

1930: Riots in India after Ghandi's arrest. Nazi party's gain of 95 Reichstag seats in German elections, making them the second biggest party, with 107 seats. Widespread starvation in the USSR in the wake of Stalin's farm collectivization.

1931: Closing of German banks. Japanese attacks on China and seizure of Manchuria.

1932: Japanese occupation of parts of China.

1933: Adolf Hitler's accession to chancellorship of Germany. Nazi consolidation of power by blaming Reichstag fire on communists. Japanese withdrawal from the League of Nations, later followed by Germany. Nazi boycott of Jewish-owned businesses. Nazi arrests of labour union leaders. Nazi book-burning.

1934: Riots in Paris following revelations about the Stavisky affair involving French government financial corruption. Worker uprisings and martial law in Vienna. Chancellor Engelbert Dollfuss established as dictator in Austria in April and assassinated by Nazis in July. Heinrich Himmler overseeing concentration camps and executions to suppress opposition to Hitler. Chancellor Hitler's increased power with his accession to the presidency. Assassination of King Alexander of Yugoslavia. Beginning of Mao Tse-tung's 'long march' in China. Continuing Stalinist purges in the USSR. Johnson Act passed by United States Congress to prohibit loans to nations that had not repaid First World War debts.

1935: German violations of the Treaty of Versailles. Nuremburg Laws ending citizenship for German Jews. Italian military build-up and invasion of Ethiopia.

1936: German occupation of demilitarized Rhineland. Italian annexation of Ethiopia. Outbreak of civil war in Spain. German–Italian pact to form Axis.

1937: Nuremburg rally of 600,000 in a show of Nazi power. Japanese full-scale war against China. Italy, Germany and Japan ally in the Anti-Comintern Pact.

1938: Hitler's self-promotion to Supreme Commander of German Armed Forces with control of foreign policy. Show trials and executions in the USSR. German–Austrian 'Anschluss' placing Hitler in power over both nations. British and French acquiescence in transfer of Sudetenland from Czech to German control. Night of terror known as Kristallnacht against Jewish people in Germany.

1939: German advance into Czechoslovakia beyond Sudetenland. Poland assured of British and French aid in case of aggression. German–Soviet non-aggression treaty. Nazi invasion of Poland resulting in British and French declaration of war on Germany. Soviet invasion of Finland. End of American trade agreement with Japan.

1940: Germany's attack and quick defeat of Norway, the Netherlands, Belgium and Denmark. German invasion of France. Disastrous British withdrawal at Dunkirk. Battle of Britain repulsion of German air raids over the English Channel. United States's authorization of peacetime draft and rearmament programme. Tripartite Pact signed by Germany, Italy and Japan.

1941: Beginning of American Lend-Lease programme to aid Britain without violating American neutrality or the 1934 Johnson Act. German advances in North Africa and the Balkans. German invasion of the USSR in violation of the 1939 non-aggression pact. Increasing Nazi submarine attacks on merchant ships. Japanese occupation of Vietnam. Japanese invasion of Indochina. Japanese attack on American fleet at Pearl Harbor, Hawaii.

Prelude to the Second World War

The Great War (1914–18), later known as the First World War, largely unravelled American isolationism. Europe had endured three years of the horrors of trench warfare fought most devastatingly on French and Belgian soil (plus torpedo-launching submarines that menaced Atlantic Ocean passenger liners and commercial shipping as well as battleships) when the United States finally ended its neutrality with a declaration of war against Germany on 6 April 1917. By June the first contingents of American doughboys arrived in Europe to serve under the leadership of General John Jack Pershing, Commander in Chief of the American Expeditionary Forces (AEF). The United States was virtually starting from scratch in its overseas military efforts, but that experience of recruiting, training and transporting soldiers, and supporting them on a foreign front, would serve the nation well when it all had to be done again a quarter of a century later. From the signing of the Armistice on

11 November 1918 until the day German tanks swept into Poland (1 September 1939), the United States mirrored Europe in partying hard to ignore sporadic eruptions of social unrest during the 1920s that by the 1930s could no longer be ignored, as the partying gave way to belt-tightening. With the Bolsheviks entrenched in Russia, communist ideology spread inexorably among disaffected intellectuals and workers in the USA as in Europe. In the United States during the inter-war years there were strikes, anarchist bomb plots and race riots in counterpoint to flappers, bootleggers, lounge lizards, nightclub habitués, silent and talking picture stars, radio personalities and marathon dancers. After 1939 the continuing brazenness of aggression by the Axis powers (Germany, Italy, Japan) began to coalesce American public opinion in favour of the Allies.

Ever conscious of public opinion (which long remained isolationist), President Franklin Delano Roosevelt moved cautiously to find covert ways to aid Britain and to enhance preparedness of the American armed forces even before Germany's conquest of Poland in September 1939. The president's 1940 State of the Union address asked Congress to fund what would amount to the largest peacetime military build-up in American history. Indeed, the United States Army lagged behind 16 other countries in weapons and manpower.[2] On 16 September 1940, Congress passed the first peacetime draft in the nation's history. Potential involvement of the United States in the wars that were engulfing both Europe and Asia was a dominant theme in the presidential campaign that year. The public played it safe with the leadership they knew by electing Roosevelt to an unprecedented third term over Republican Wendell L. Willkie. In March 1941, Congress passed the Lend-Lease Act, which authorized shipment of food, weapons and tanks to Britain by a system of payment that would not negate American neutrality. The American people did not want war, but when the Japanese bombed Pearl Harbor, Hawaii, in a surprise attack on 7 December 1941 that killed 2,403 people, nearly half of them on the battleship *Arizona*, one of eight ships that were sunk or incapacitated, the nation was quick to rally. On 8 December 1941, President Roosevelt spoke to the nation about the hostilities of 7 December, a date that would 'live in infamy'. With over 81 per cent of American homes tuned in, it was radio's largest audience until then.[3] Suddenly the United States was at war on two fronts, one in the Pacific and one in Europe. The next four years would have a profound impact on almost all aspects of American life for the remainder of the decade and beyond: women in the workforce, the rise of the teenager, the baby boom, education, popular culture, consumerism, business and the economy, technology, politics, foreign affairs and atomic energy.

Leaders of the decade

The swing in American public opinion from the isolationism of 1940 to broadly united support for the Allied war effort in 1941 was astonishingly rapid. Among the leaders who effectively articulated the importance of saving Europe from Nazi domination were President Franklin D. Roosevelt with his periodic radio broadcasts to the nation, the British Prime Minister Winston Churchill whose radio addresses and bestselling books like *While England Slept* (1938) captivated Americans, and General George Catlett Marshall who was sworn in as Chief of Staff of the United States Army on the very day German forces invaded Poland, 1 September 1939. General Marshall had been warning for many years about the potential dire consequences of American unpreparedness. Thanks to his efforts, American factories belatedly turned to manufacturing armaments, which had the secondary effect of stimulating economic recovery and pulling the country out of the Depression at last. Ultimately, President Roosevelt and Congress learned to respect and trust General Marshall's vision for first defeating Germany to win the war in Europe and then turning to the Pacific to defeat Japan.

George C. Marshall (1880–1959) was a man of great integrity, honesty and non-partisan patriotism, for he believed that the military should have nothing to do with politics. Asked about his own inclinations, Marshall responded, 'My father was a Democrat, my mother was a Republican, and I am an Episcopalian'.[4] Winston Churchill would later recognize General Marshall as 'the organizer of victory' in the war, and President Harry Truman called Marshall 'the greatest living American'. George Marshall five times graced *Time* magazine's cover, twice as Man of the Year (for the years 1943 and 1947).[5] The 3 January 1944 cover story observed, 'The American people do not, as a general rule, like or trust the military. But they like and trust George Marshall.' The article cited his devotion to duty, 'competence and integrity' and team-building as qualities that would uphold the confidence and morale of the US soldier in combat.[6] The 1947 recognition underscored the importance of the European Recovery Program, better known as the Marshall Plan, a staggeringly generous American contribution of money to bring economic and political stability to war-torn Europe while also generating strong returns for American commercial interests and hedging against Soviet initiatives to spread communism abroad. As reported in *Time*, 'Europe was broke. Unless the U.S. acted, the whole front of Western democracy was about to collapse.' To counter 'starvation and despair in Europe, the cynical and ruthless policies of Joseph Stalin', Secretary of State George Marshall called upon the better instincts of the American people to enforce through strength their will for peace, and it was then 'in 1947 that the U.S. people, not quite realizing the full import of their act, perhaps not yet mature enough to accept all its responsibilities, took upon their shoulders the leadership of the world'.[7]

IMPORTANT ACRONYMS OF THE 1940s

AEC	Atomic Energy Commission
AEF	American Expeditionary Forces (First World War)
CIA	Central Intelligence Agency
FBI	Federal Bureau of Investigation
GI	Government Issue, an informal term for an enlisted man in the American military
HUAC	House Un-American Activities Committee
NAACP	National Association for the Advancement of Colored People
NATO	North Atlantic Treaty Organization
NCO	non-commissioned officer
OPA	Office of Price Administration
OWI	Office of War Information
PTA	Parent Teacher Association

RCA	Radio Corporation of America
RFC	Reconstruction Finance Corporation
ROTC	Reserve Officers Training Corps
UFO	unidentified flying object
UN	United Nations
USAF	United States Air Force, established 18 September 1947
USO	United Service Organizations
USSR	Union of Soviet Socialist Republics (the Soviet Union); in Russian the acronym is CCCP
WAC	Women's Army Auxiliary Corps
WPB	War Production Board
YMCA	Young Men's Christian Association

Among other American leaders of the decade, Harry S. Truman (1884–1972) took the nation by surprise, first as he emerged from his inauspicious early career to run for vice president in 1944, which catapulted him into the presidency after only three months in office under Roosevelt, later as he rose to the job of president while facing serious challenges from both liberals and conservatives on issues of labour and the economy, and most unexpectedly when he won election to a second term by narrowly defeating the very strong Republican candidate Thomas Dewey. During his first term, Truman promoted the Fair Deal, which might be described as a more moderate version of Roosevelt's New Deal, and which managed to curb the spectre of inflation. In 1947 he reached out to African-Americans as the first president to address the NAACP, and 'he was the first president to make civil rights a major part of his program'.[8] Virtually hand-in-hand with the Marshall Plan in 1947 came the Truman Doctrine, stimulated by George F. Kennan's famous 'Long Telegram' that analysed Stalin's ruthless strategy for the USSR. Truman's ensuing hard-line policy of containment of Soviet ambitions in Europe set the long-term course of American foreign policy and was maintained by his successor, President Eisenhower. Dwight D. Eisenhower proved himself a gifted military leader under General MacArthur in the Philippines and as high commander for strategic operations during the Second World War in Europe. He finished the 1940s decade as president of Columbia University. 'Ike' had a sincere common touch and broad vision that made him widely popular. Later he would serve two terms, 1953–61, as president of the United States.

Eleanor Roosevelt (1884–1962) had been a visible and outspoken first lady during her husband's presidency, 1933–45, but it was after Franklin D. Roosevelt's death that she truly came into her own as an activist for women's causes and as a United States delegate to the United Nations from 1946 to 1952, during which time she chaired the UN Commission on Human Rights. From 1936 to 1962, her syndicated newspaper column 'My Day' appeared six days a week. Widely sought as a speaker, she earned huge sums that she gave to charity. Mrs Roosevelt's activism for African-American civil rights is exemplified by her championing of black singer Marian Anderson when the Daughters of the American Revolution denied her the use of Constitution Hall for a concert in 1939. Eleanor Roosevelt invited Anderson to the White House and also sponsored her for an open-air concert that drew 75,000 people at the Lincoln Memorial.

Another American who demonstrated extraordinary leadership on several fronts during the 1940s was Ralph Bunche, the first African-American to earn a doctorate in political science at Harvard University. He began as a scholar, but during the war worked in government intelligence services. In 1944 and 1945 he participated in United Nations preparatory conferences and drafted sections of the charter. From 1947 he served on UN committees working to create separate Jewish and Arab states in Palestine. As chief aide to the Swedish mediator Count Folke Bernadotte, Bunche headed the negotiations after Bernadotte's assassination by Jewish terrorists. Ralph Bunche's success in arranging the cease-fire agreements and creating the state of Israel earned him the 1950 Nobel Peace Prize.[9]

The Second World War

After the attack on Pearl Harbor provoked the American declaration of war against Japan on 8 December 1941, Hitler's Germany and Mussolini's Italy responded on 11 December by declaring war against the United States. Since France had already fallen to

Nazi occupation in June 1940, American troops were sent first to North Africa, to then fight their way north through Italy. In June 1942, Major General Dwight D. Eisenhower became Commanding General of American forces in Europe in charge of the invasion of North Africa. As Supreme Allied Commander from December 1943, he led coalition forces of the United States, Britain, France and Russia through major operations culminating in the D-Day (6 June 1944) landing in Normandy. President Franklin D. Roosevelt did not live to relish Germany's surrender; with Roosevelt's death on 12 April 1945, his vice president Harry Truman succeeded to the presidency. Eisenhower presided over Germany's unconditional surrender in a signing ceremony in Rheims, France, on 7 May 1945, a date known as V-E Day, for Victory in Europe.

Meanwhile in the Pacific, in February 1942, General Douglas MacArthur, commander of US Army forces in the Far East, was ordered to evacuate the Philippines to regroup in Australia. April 1942 brought the daring, morale-boosting Doolittle Raid, the first bombing raid on Japan, when 16 bombers led by Lieutenant Colonel James Doolittle were launched from the deck of US aircraft carrier *Hornet* to fly 800 miles and bomb Tokyo, Kobe, Nagoya and Yokohama. The Pacific campaign covered a vast area with numerous initiatives, among which the February 1945 landing of US Marines on Iwo Jima (where they famously raised the American flag on Mount Suribachi) made the island available as a crucial base for bombers en route to Japan. With the progressive retaking of the Philippines from late 1944 to the end of the war and strategic bombing of Japanese factories, Premier Kantaro Suzuki's declaration that Japan would go down fighting contributed to President Truman's decision to use the atomic bomb as the most expedient way to end the war and save American lives. Bombs dropped on Hiroshima on 6 August and Nagasaki on 9 August resulted in Japan's unconditional surrender on 14 August 1945, V-J Day. General MacArthur presided at the official surrender ceremony on the deck of US battleship *Missouri* at anchor in Tokyo Bay on 2 September 1945, a second date proclaimed as V-J Day.

Americans avidly followed those events as reported in the newspapers and on radio broadcasts. Edward R. Murrow's observations from London via CBS radio brought vivid awareness of the privations endured by the British people even as they were subjected to German air attacks most nights. In the field, Ernie Pyle reported the war from the point of view of ordinary soldiers as they fought their way from North Africa to Sicily and on the beaches of Normandy. Pyle earned a 1943 Pulitzer Prize for his distinguished war correspondence. Then he turned to the war in the Pacific, but was killed in Okinawa in 1945. GI cartoonist Bill Mauldin took his cue from Pyle and focused on the humble infantryman with his creation of two scruffy soldiers named Willie and Joe. Mauldin's cartoons were featured in the Army's *Stars and Stripes* newspaper and later collected in his 1945 book, *Up Front*, which topped the *New York Times* bestseller list. Another popular wartime cartoon figure was 'The Sad Sack', a hopelessly incompetent and beleaguered soldier created by Sergeant George Baker.

While Americans of all social classes rallied to the Allied cause during the war years, some measures became controversial, notably the confinement of Japanese-Americans to internment camps for the duration of hostilities and the decision to drop atomic bombs on the Japanese cities of Hiroshima and Nagasaki. Americans living on the west coast tended to be more fearful of direct attack than were those facing the Atlantic. The Japanese shelling of an oil refinery near Santa Barbara, California, on 24 February 1942, followed by a series of Japanese victories in the South Pacific, along with media-fuelled hysteria directed against Americans of Japanese ancestry, prompted the establishment of the War Relocation Authority by which about 120,000 men, women and children were confined to hastily-constructed relocation centres remote from the coast; schooling was provided for the children, but no radios were allowed in the camps. After 1943 some Japanese-Americans, eventually numbering 17,000, were accepted for military service. Indeed, 'the most decorated unit in U.S. history' was the all-Nisei 442 Regimental Combat Team that fought in Italy and earned a total of '4,667 medals, awards, and citations, including one Medal of Honor, fifty-two Distinguished Service Crosses, and 560 Silver Stars. When many of the soldiers wrote home, the addresses were detention centers.'[10]

The use of the atomic bomb to end the war by destroying two entire Japanese cities gave rise to considerable controversy, which President Truman countered by extolling peaceful uses for atomic energy. Indeed, according to William S. Graebner, 'the bomb was almost immediately incorporated into the iconography of mass consumption'.[11] Not only did images of atoms and mushroom clouds infiltrate advertising but they even inspired songs like 'Atomic Boogie'. To regulate nuclear power, Congress established the Atomic Energy Commission (AEC) in 1946.[12]

However, the Second World War generated many technological advances besides the development of the atomic bomb. Three models of planes from this era have become legendary: the B-17 Flying Fortress, the B-24 Liberator and the B-29 Superfortress. Among the celebrated feats of the era, a B-17 named *Suzy-Q*, piloted by Major Felix M. Hardison, was the first airplane to circumnavigate the globe during wartime.[13] The Army Air Corps (1926–41) and Army Air Forces (1941–7) were aviation branches of the United States Army. Finally, at last fulfilling the vision of the First World War's great advocate of air power, General Billy Mitchell, on 18 September 1947, the United States Air Force (USAF) was established as a separate branch of the military. During the war, German scientists produced powerful, elusive, long-range V-2 missiles. With the end of hostilities, both Americans and Soviets were quick to capture the German rockets as well as the rocket scientists. Dr Wernher Von Braun and Willy Ley were among those brought to the United States where they became instrumental in developing American space flight programmes.

When American GIs liberated Nazi concentration camps in 1945, the American public began to learn about the horrifying atrocities committed against Jewish people in places like Nordhausen, Gusen, Theresienstadt, Bergen Belsen, Treblinka, Belzec, Sobibór, Auschwitz-Birkenau, Dachau and Buchenwald. The shock of those revelations made a profound impact on the American psyche over the decades afterward as the full story was increasingly uncovered; ultimately, the word 'Holocaust' was chosen to evoke the incomprehensible savagery and devastation. In his opening address at the Nuremberg War Crimes Trial on 21 November 1945, the American lead prosecutor, Supreme Court Justice Robert Jackson, said:

> Of the 9,600,000 Jews who lived in Nazi-dominated Europe, 60 percent are authoritatively estimated to have perished. 5,700,000 Jews are missing from the countries in which they formerly lived, and over 4,500,000 cannot be accounted for by the normal death rate nor by immigration; nor are they included among displaced persons. History does not record a crime ever

perpetrated against so many victims or one ever carried out with such calculated cruelty.[14]

Yet it is individual stories more than statistics that best convey the lessons of the past. The 1944 Hollywood movie *None Shall Escape* anticipated the reports of anti-Semitic persecutions. *The Diary of a Young Girl* by Anne Frank, who died in the Bergen-Belsen concentration camp, was first published in Dutch in 1947, and its impact grew as it was soon translated into over sixty languages, became a play in 1955 and a Hollywood movie in 1959. Shirley Jackson's chilling short story 'The Lottery' (1948) dealt allegorically with the wilful blindness of ordinary people to a practice like Hitler's scapegoating of Jewish people.

The war's impact on civilian life

The war somehow touched every aspect of American life, even causing major shifts of population from the agrarian South to the industrial North. Despite a declining number of family farms, agricultural production increased by more than 25 per cent thanks to mechanization and government price supports.[15] Daylight saving time began on 9 February 1942, followed by many additional government-mandated exigencies. Before the war, nylon stockings for women were rapidly replacing silk stockings, but from February 1942 all nylon went to military uses (parachutes, tyres) and women's legs went bare. Other measures included prohibition of steel in many non-military goods, and rationing of gas, coffee, shoes, rubber, meat, butter and sugar. To compensate for food rationing, Americans planted 'victory gardens' that produced great quantities of vegetables. To finance the war, Americans were encouraged to buy War Bonds and were also subject to unprecedented income taxes imposed on moderate-wage earners (whereas only the wealthiest had been taxed on income since 1913). To instil patriotic pride in the idea of paying taxes, Irving Berlin wrote a song, 'I Paid My Income Tax Today' (1941), that got frequent radio air time: 'A thousand planes to bomb Berlin. / They'll all be paid for, and I chipped in.'[16]

To keep the factories going after much of the labour force had volunteered or been drafted for military service, women left the home and worked at manual labour jobs like the one epitomized in the iconic poster of a woman – popularly known as 'Rosie the Riveter' – with her curls tucked under a kerchief, baring a muscular arm, under the slogan 'We Can Do It!'. Whether for blue-collar or white-collar employment, 'one-third of the female population went to work'.[17] With the creation of the Women's Army Auxiliary Corps (later known as WACs) in May 1942, women could serve non-combat roles in the Army; women's branches of the Navy, Marines and Air Forces soon followed. Civilian women contributed to the war effort by writing frequent letters that boosted soldiers' morale. As another well-known morale-boosting phenomenon, 'pin-ups' might be pinned up in soldiers' tents or barracks; these were photographs or posters of glamorous women, notably Betty Grable in a bathing suit, Rita Hayworth in a slinky negligée or Jane Russell in a low-cut blouse.

The importance of live entertainment for the troops had been recognized during the First World War when the YMCA and Broadway's Over There Theatre League had sponsored performers at the front in France. Singer-comedian Al Jolson, whose electrifying voice and magnetic stage presence earned him the sobriquet 'World's Greatest Entertainer', spent his own money to travel and entertain at military encampments in both world wars and in the Korean conflict.[18] With the establishment of the draft in September 1940, the need was clear for a new agency that would bolster the men's morale and offer some off-duty comforts. The United Service Organizations (USO) was created on 4 February 1941 and continues its mission yet today. In May 1941, comedian Bob Hope performed his first of hundreds of USO Camp Shows over the decades, and many Hollywood stars followed his lead, touring shows to training camps in the United States and combat areas abroad. By 1944 the USO operated over 3,000 clubs where volunteer women would listen to men who needed to talk, mend their clothes or jitterbug with them.[19] Similar initiatives were undertaken by the American Theatre Wing, successor to the Great War's Stage Women's War Relief. The Wing operated the beloved Stage Door Canteens, enhanced by the glamour of stage and screen celebrities serving the free coffee or dancing with the soldiers (only enlisted men and NCOs in uniform were admitted). At the original Stage Door Canteen in New York City, the men could enjoy an alcohol-free evening and hobnob with Broadway stars who would come in after their performances. Similarly, the celebrated Hollywood Canteen put movie stars as well as starlets on the dance floor with the men.[20] The decade saw several milestones in the continuing African-American struggle for civil rights, beginning with President Roosevelt's 1941 executive order that established the Fair Employment Practices Committee as a means of averting potential damage to the war effort by a threatened march on Washington, DC, that was organized by A. Philip Randolph, union leader of the Brotherhood of Sleeping Car Porters. Randolph called for an end to racial discrimination in the defence industries, and Roosevelt's order was essentially a symbolic first step. Race riots in northern cities during the summer of 1943, notably in Detroit and New York, stemmed from frustrations over various discriminatory conditions as well as overcrowding due to housing restrictions. In 1944 the NAACP-backed plaintiff won a Supreme Court ruling against exclusion of black citizens from voting in primary elections, and a 1946 decision ended segregation on interstate public transportation. Following President Harry Truman's 1948 executive order that desegregated the armed services came a Supreme Court ruling against 'restrictive covenants' by which white neighbourhoods had prevented blacks from buying homes. All of these important advances could not end discrimination in practice, for the decade still saw separate drinking fountains labelled 'white' or 'colored' and blacks relegated to balcony seating in movie theatres. Singer Paul Robeson made national news when he interrupted his own concert in Kansas City on 17 February 1942 to protest against segregated seating in the auditorium. In 1943, poet Langston Hughes published in the *Journal of Educational Sociology* an eloquent call for the American Negro's full participation in American democracy.[21]

The 1944 passage of the G.I. Bill of Rights had a far-reaching impact as it made college education affordable for returning veterans. The great tide of servicemen who went on to earn degrees after the war benefitted American universities even as it expanded the educated population base of the nation as a whole. One factor that contributed to the widespread zeal for learning after the war was the government-backed programme to publish and distribute small-format, soft-cover Armed Services Editions of a great variety of books that soldiers could easily carry in their pockets. Over

1,300 titles were published between September 1943 and – because American occupation forces still needed books after war's end – June 1947. Putting over 120 million free books in the hands of soldiers created a reading habit in a generation the majority of whom had not completed high school.[22]

Post-war domestic life and consumerism

With the end of wartime rationing and with a soaring economy, Americans were ready to settle down to what they regarded as normalcy. Most women were happy enough to give their factory jobs back to the men and to focus again on housework, shopping, women's clubs and children. Many who had married in haste before the soldiers shipped out were raising 'goodbye babies' who were now toddlers, but the great population bulge known as the 'baby boom' came during the years following the war, setting a new record in 1946 with 3.4 million babies born.[23] Adjusting or readjusting to family life took some effort, but there was help for new mothers with the 1946 publication of Dr Benjamin Spock's *Common Sense Book of Baby and Child Care*, which remained a bestseller well beyond the decade. For a sick child, the attentive mother would prepare milk toast, a soup bowl of warm milk with bite-size pieces of buttered toast floating in it, all perhaps sprinkled with salt and pepper. Milk and other dairy products were delivered directly to homes; milkmen who made their rounds by horse and wagon were soon a rarity as more and more of them drove vans. The milk came in glass bottles, and the housewife left the empties at the back door for the milkman to take and reuse. Butter remained expensive; margarine could be sold only in untreated form, so it came with a yellow capsule that the homemaker could knead into the white substance to make it look more appetizing. Above all, Americans were voracious to eat meat after the privations of the war years: meat consumption rose to a record 155 pounds per person in 1947.[24] Sugar, also liberated from rationing, was sprinkled liberally on breakfast cereal and fresh grapefruit halves. At the same time, there was a growing obsession with vitamins that included a daily spoonful of hated cod liver oil for each child.

Among the food products introduced during the 1940s were

York peppermint patties (1940), M&M's candy-coated chocolate bits (1941), Cheerios cereal (1941), La Choy canned Chinese food (1942), frozen concentrated orange juice (1946), Maxwell House instant coffee (1946), Almond Joy coconut-and-chocolate candy bars capitalizing on the already-popular Mounds bars (1947), V8 juice (1948) and instant cake mixes (1949).[25] Spam (a canned pre-cooked meat product) and Toll House (chocolate chip) cookies were both introduced in 1937 and retained their popularity. From an earlier era, thin discs of candy in various flavours, called Necco wafers, were favoured by soldiers and remained popular with children after the war.

Both automobile manufacture and housing construction had been prohibited during the war, and both became priorities after 1945. The rapid construction of small affordable homes on the outskirts of cities created a new suburban lifestyle made possible by the explosion in new car sales. Noteworthy among businessmen who addressed the post-war housing shortage were brothers Alfred and William J. Levitt, who purchased land on Long Island and built thousands of boxy virtually-identical houses that sold for only $7,900 each in a development called Levittown. While the Housing Act of 1949 brought some government aid to such builders of low-cost single-family homes, the G.I. Bill made home ownership newly possible for a generation of young adults. Family life indoors focused upon a piece of living-room furniture with a radio in it, or after 1948, a television set that provided several hours a day of black-and-white programming. Kitchens were designed with continuous countertop work surfaces, while labour-saving appliances became more and more standard: electric refrigerators with freezer compartments, electric stoves with ovens, blenders and, beginning in 1949, dishwashers. For outdoor family activity, the backyard replaced the front porch of older homes. Indeed, the action of one of the emblematic plays of the 1940s, *All My Sons* (1947), takes place in the backyard of a family home. Clotheslines disappeared from backyards after electric clothes dryers became available in 1946, so Americans re-envisioned that outdoor space as a place for cooking on a grill or hosting neighbourhood cocktail parties.

The family car permitted food shopping at the supermarkets that were replacing neighbourhood butchers, bakers and fresh produce grocers. As automobile sales expanded, so did the phenomenon of drive-in restaurants and movies. The first McDonald's and the first Dairy Queen had opened in 1940, but it was not until after the war that both became nationwide chains with car-hops (cutely uniformed young women) who would bring the food order on a tray that could be propped outside the car window. The tray and car-hop concept had actually been pioneered earlier by A & W Root Beer stands, which expanded to 750 or so franchises after the war. The family could enjoy their hamburgers or soft-serve ice cream cones without ever getting out of the parked car! Similarly, the whole family could watch a movie on an outdoor screen by parking next to a post with a speaker that attached to the car window. Of course, there was a refreshment stand at the centre of the drive-in movie lot, and the father would be expected to fetch popcorn or Cracker Jacks and soft drinks for everyone in the car. Some drive-ins had a playground below the screen to let children expend their energy until the movie began at dusk. As more and more Americans took to the road for family vacations, advertising billboards sprang up everywhere to further promote consumerism. Travel could be uncertain when highways varied greatly from state to state, but one interstate highway (opened in 1926) truly flourished in the 1940s after gas rationing ended: Route 66. Known as 'the Main Street of America' and 'the mother road', Route 66 had been 'almost completely paved' by 1937[26] and allowed relatively easy travel between Chicago and Los Angeles, going through Missouri, Oklahoma, Texas, New Mexico and Arizona. Motor courts were built to encourage tourism, and in the southwest there was a fad for 'wigwam' motels with teepee-shaped units. Nat King Cole's 1946 recording of Bobby Troup's 'Get Your Kicks on Route 66' added to that highway's mystique.

Children

Outdoor playtime for neighbourhood children might encompass old-fashioned jump-roping, roller-skating, marbles, jacks, hopscotch, hide-and-seek and tag. For unstructured fantasy play, little girls would play 'house', while the boys preferred 'cops 'n' robbers' or 'cowboys 'n' Indians'. On a school playground with lots of fallen autumn leaves, the girls would push the leaves together to form outlines of rooms in a house, often relaying the home-owner wisdom of their parents: 'Make the closets bigger' or 'The kitchen window goes over the sink'. The ubiquitous toy for boys was the cap gun, a shiny metal replica of a cowboy pistol. A paper roll of caps (dots of explosive compound) inserted into the chamber produced a sharp gunshot sound as the caps advanced with each pull of the trigger. Toy-makers took advantage of parents' readiness to spend on their children. Slinkys (small metal coils that could move down a flight of steps), first marketed in 1945, quickly became one of the bestselling playthings in American history. By 1949, Silly Putty, Erector sets, Lego and games of Scrabble, Candyland and Clue joined the market. At ten or twelve years of age, a boy might take a job as a paperboy, which was exempt from child labour laws, as 'throwing papers' on a home-delivery route usually involved about an hour on foot or bicycle before or after school.

Elementary school teachers across the land had ultimately succeeded in banning the word 'ain't' from children's vocabulary, but there were additional taboo words that very few children would dare to pronounce on the playground: hell, damn, son-of-a-bitch, pregnant. *Dick and Jane* textbooks had been introduced in 1927 and were still the standard first-grade reading texts in public schools; indeed, the 1940s were the heyday for positive value reinforcement by six-year-old Dick along with his little sisters Jane and baby Sally, and their pets Spot and Puff. While the charming *Dick and Jane* illustrations showed the joys of a happy family at work and play, the teacher herself was restricted by her profession to spinsterhood, as most elementary schoolteachers were expected to resign if they married. Certain Caldecott Medal-winning children's books reflected adult concerns of the decade, according to William S. Graebner: *Make Way for Ducklings* (1941) by Robert McCloskey shows the family unit navigating in a cooperative world to find a home. *The Little House* (1942) by Virginia Lee Burton acknowledges the anxieties of encroaching urbanism that threaten one's accommodation with nature, a concern that would be echoed in Arthur Miller's 1949 play *Death of a Salesman*. *The Little Island* (1946) by Golden MacDonald considers one's relationship to the world at large.[27] The puppet shows aimed at children under the 1930s Federal Theatre Project had shown the educational – and possibly commercial – value of live performances for child audiences; during the 1940s many cities saw the creation of community theatre groups, run by women on a volunteer basis, that took children's plays into the schools. Saturday mornings brought the long-popular *Let's Pretend* radio series; many who were children in the 1940s can still sing the sponsor's jingle: 'Cream of Wheat is so good to eat / That we have it every day / It makes us strong / So we sing this song / And it makes us shout 'Hooray! / It's good for growing children / And grown-ups too to eat. / For all the family's breakfast / You can't beat Cream of Wheat.' *Smilin' Ed's Buster Brown Gang*, sponsored by Buster Brown Shoes, was another radio series for children.

Parents made an effort to see that their children were well dressed in public. Children who did not attend parochial schools that required uniforms would usually wear the same cotton dress or shirt for two days in a row before putting it in the laundry. Little boys loved to dress in cowboy outfits, echoing the adult craze for cowboy songs and movies; Hopalong Cassidy ('Hoppy') was a favourite whose kiddie cowboy boots were widely marketed. When parents took their children to buy shoes, it was common for the parent and salesperson to check the fit by having the child stand on a small platform with the feet inside a boxy fluoroscope; when the device was switched on, the child and the adults could all peer through viewers to see a silhouette of the bones inside the outline of the shoe. Children regarded these unregulated X-ray machines as play equipment, and when the parent was not looking, one might stick a hand in the opening while other children viewed the hand bones. Not until the early 1950s were these sources of potentially-harmful radiation eliminated from shoe stores. Another precaution taken by good parents was to have the pre-school child's tonsils removed; tonsillectomies were routinely performed on children from the 1930s through to the 1970s.

Teenagers

Teenagers began to be recognized during the 1940s as a demographic group to be targeted in advertising and celebrated in popular culture. In 1944, *Seventeen* magazine began publication, dispensing advice about relationships while promoting junior fashions. In 1947, Toni home permanents became available as one solution to maintaining feminine curls in those days before blow dryers; the less-reliable solution was to put one's hair up each night in curlers or bobby-pinned pin curls and hope the next day's weather would not be damp. Teen social life in the decade centred on dating as a way for young people to get to know one another on an individual basis. Typically, a teenage boy would call a girl on the family's home telephone to invite her to go skating or to a movie. On the appointed evening he would come to her house (maybe in a car borrowed from his father, maybe in his own jalopy), meet her parents and agree to a suggested time for her to be home. The outing might culminate with a hamburger at a drive-in. There might or might not be a goodnight kiss at the front door. The girl might well repeat the pattern with another young man the next night. There was considerable conformity in teenage dress and behaviour. Both boys and girls wore loafers or saddle shoes with white socks. The term 'bobbysoxers' referred to clusters of teenage girls swooning over a popular singer. Improbably topping all teen idols of the decade was Frank Sinatra, whose smooth voice compensated for his scrawny physique. When school finished for the day, students might congregate at a soda fountain where they could drink milkshakes and dance or jitterbug to popular numbers from the jukebox.[28]

As consumers, teenagers served as a ready market for the lighter-weight 33-rpm and 45-rpm records that in 1948 were replacing the heavy albums of 78-rpm their parents had enjoyed. Revolutions per minute (rpm) referred to the speed at which the record revolved on the turntable. Many teens owned record-players that accommodated either the long-playing (23 minute-) 12"-diameter 33-rpms or the smaller 45-rpms with one song on each side. One could put a stack of 45-rpms on the central post and each record in turn would drop down to the turntable where the automatic needle arm would swing in and play it. Record sales increased throughout the decade, averaging about 10 million per month![29] Record sales and jukebox selections partially determined which were the 'top ten' songs played each week on radio's long-running programme *Your Hit Parade*.

Popular music encompassed a variety of styles from the large swing bands (Glenn Miller, Tommy Dorsey, Benny Goodman, Duke Ellington, Sammy Kaye) of the early 1940s to boogie-woogie, bebop (developed by trumpeter Dizzy Gillespie and saxophonist

Charlie 'Bird' Parker), cool jazz (notably by Miles Davis) and African-American-influenced blues of the second half of the decade. Songs inspired by the war included, in 1942 alone, Frank Loesser's 'Praise the Lord and Pass the Ammunition' and Irving Berlin's 'This Is the Army, Mr. Jones' and 'I Left My Heart at the Stage Door Canteen'. There were sentimental songs, sophisticated songs, Broadway musical songs including virtually all the numbers from *Oklahoma!* (1943), optimistic songs like 'Zip-a-Dee-Doo-Dah' (1946), nonsense songs like 'Mairzy Doats' (1943), and even songs borrowed from the enemy: 'Lili Marlene' (1944). Crooner Bing Crosby had a great decade with 16 records surpassing one million in sales and with his version of Irving Berlin's 'White Christmas' (1942) becoming the all-time bestselling single. The Andrews Sisters (LaVerne, Maxene and Patty) sang in close harmony to produce hits like 'Boogie Woogie Bugle Boy' (1941), 'Don't Sit Under the Apple Tree' (1942) and 'Rum and CocaCola' (1944). They recorded many numbers with Bing Crosby, including 'Accentuate the Positive' (1945), and some with Danny Kaye, including 'Woody Woodpecker' (1948). Nat King Cole transitioned from instrumentalist to singer and sold three million copies of 'Mona Lisa' in 1949. Roy Acuff and Hank Williams popularized country music, while Woody Guthrie reinvigorated traditional folk songs and composed his own ballads inspired by labouring men. Singing cowboys included Roy Rogers and Gene Autry; the latter's 1949 recording of 'Rudolph the Red-Nosed Reindeer' sold numbers of single copies second only to Crosby's 'White Christmas'. Among singer-composers, Hoagy Carmichael scored with 'Ole Buttermilk Sky' in 1946, as did Frankie Laine with 'That Lucky Old Sun' and 'Mule Train' in 1949. Leading songwriters included the perennially prolific Irving Berlin with 'God Bless America' (introduced by Kate Smith in 1938) and 'White Christmas' (1942), as well as several from his 1946 musical *Annie Get Your Gun*; Cole Porter with 'Don't Fence Me In' (1944); and Frank Loesser with the jukebox favourite 'Baby, It's Cold Outside' (1944). Musical satirist Spike Jones was a drummer who prepared comic arrangements with irreverent sound effects for his City Slickers band; they reached the top of the charts in 1948 with 'All I Want for Christmas Is My Two Front Teeth'.[30]

Communications, media and transportation

Not only did most middle-class homes have telephones by the mid-1940s, but callers could also bypass the operator and enter the numbers through finger-holes on a rotary dial; it was necessary to let the dial rotate back to its original position before dialling the next digit. A tabletop telephone was usually black and had a cord connecting it to a bone-shaped receiver and mouthpiece. Long-distance calls were reserved for emergency business or very special occasions.

Mail was picked up from ubiquitous street-corner mailboxes twice a day in cities, and many homes got twice-daily mail delivery. Letter-writing was the standard form of communication among family and friends who lived in different cities. Commercial greeting cards had been available since the turn of the century, but Hallmark leaped to the forefront of those companies in 1944 with its adoption of the advertising slogan 'When You Care Enough to Send the Very Best', followed by the crown logo in 1949. Hallmark's all-time bestseller had already come out in 1941 – a 'pansies always stand for thoughts' friendship card – and is still sold at a rate of over 750,000 per year.[31] Postcards had been popular for four decades and remained a cheap, casual and fun way to keep in touch even as they provided a visual record of a time and place; the postage was only a penny throughout the 1940s. Most postcards were written with fountain pen, some with pencil.

Keeping up with current events involved listening to the radio, reading the newspapers (with home delivery of both morning and evening papers for most families) and watching the newsreels that – along with animated cartoons and previews of coming attractions – prefaced the showing of feature films in movie theatres. Besides the news, radio programming included daytime serialized 'soap operas' (stories of romantic relationships often sponsored by soap or detergent companies), Saturday children's programmes, and shows anchored by celebrities that offered a vaudeville-like mix of specialty numbers. For example, each weekly half-hour of *The Al Jolson Colgate Show* on CBS (thirty-nine broadcasts, 1942–3) and *The Kraft Music Hall* hosted by Jolson on NBC (seventy-one broadcasts, 1947–9) would feature two or three songs by Jolson, some banter (on the latter show with regular cast member Oscar Levant) and a featured guest, all interspersed with commercial announcements from the sponsor. Jolson's Kraft guests included such luminaries as Bing Crosby, Groucho Marx, Charles Boyer, Dorothy Lamour, Red Skelton, Yehudi Menuhin, Boris Karloff, Lucille Ball, Charles Laughton, Dorothy Kirsten, Judy Garland and many others. During those same years, Al Jolson made frequent guest appearances on shows like *Bing Crosby's Philco Radio Time*, *The Eddie Cantor Pabst Blue Ribbon Show*, *The Bob Hope Pepsodent Show*, *The Jack Benny Lucky Strike Program*, *The Jimmy Durante Rexall Show* and many more.[32] Among the entertainers who transitioned from vaudeville to radio, Edgar Bergen was an unusual case in that his talent as a ventriloquist was more appropriate for a visual medium; however, the dapper and monocled Charlie McCarthy, the most featured of the puppets who sat on Bergen's knee and moved their wooden jaws to banter with him, won loyal audiences with his wit and personality. Harold Peary compellingly voiced the title character in *The Great Gildersleeve* (1941–57), a half-hour weekly comedy series set in a small town. Long popular on radio for his relaxed voice was Arthur Godfrey, who would deliver the requisite commercial announcements extemporaneously and often with a wry personal comment that the public loved. Many commercials of the decade were sung, and those advertising jingles became as casually well known as popular songs.

Television had been invented in the 1920s, but commercial broadcasting did not begin until 1941 when rival companies NBC and CBS each offered several hours of programming a day for the few New York households that had television receivers. Although the new medium had a strong promoter in David Sarnoff, the Second World War necessarily put further development on hold. Sarnoff's company, RCA (Radio Corporation of America), which also owned NBC, began selling television sets with 10"-screens in 1946; 7,000 were sold that year for $375 to $500 (compared to $40 for a radio in a piece of furniture known as a console). By 1949, one could buy a TV–radio–phonograph console for $350.[33] Both sales and programming expanded at the end of the decade, notably with the 1947 broadcast of baseball's World Series face-off between the Brooklyn Dodgers and the New York Yankees. Among the regular series that began broadcasting at the end of the decade were *The Howdy Doody Show* for children, *The Ed Sullivan Show*,

Philco Television Playhouse and *Texaco Star Theatre*; the latter earned its popular host Milton Berle the epithet 'Mr Television'. Just as radio programmes had begun with transfers from vaudeville, so TV programmes continued familiar shows from radio like *Jack Benny* and *The Lone Ranger*.

Motion pictures had enjoyed a peak year in 1939 but – like so many other aspects of life – had limited production during the war years. By 1943, over 27,600 employees of the film industry – actors as well as technicians – had already joined the armed services, and many more would follow.[34] Immediately after Pearl Harbor, director Frank Capra joined the Signal Corps as a major and was soon asked by General Marshall to make a series of documentary films at a level of Hollywood professionalism that would be aimed at both fighting men and the American public to explain America's role in the war. The result was the renowned *Why We Fight* series of one-hour films, the first of which – *Prelude to War* (1942) – won the Academy Award for Best Documentary. Director John Ford joined the US Navy and managed to film *The Battle of Midway* as part of his combat experience; it too garnered an Academy Award.[35] Feature pictures also dealt with themes of war: *Sergeant York* (1941), *Mrs. Miniver* (1942), *Memphis Belle* (1944), *They Were Expendable* (1945); and post-war coping, as in *The Best Years of Our Lives* (1945).

After 1945, the market for war pictures evaporated, and Hollywood went back to the traditional genres that it had never really abandoned: women's pictures like *Mildred Pierce* (1945); detective or *films noir* like *Notorious* (1946); comedies like *Adam's Rib* (1949); feel-good movies like *It's A Wonderful Life* (1946) and *Miracle on 34th Street* (1947); family films like *The Yearling* (1946) and *Life With Father* (1947); westerns like *My Darling Clementine* (1946), *Duel in the Sun* (1947), *Red River* (1948) and *Treasure of the Sierra Madre* (1948); musicals like *The Jolson Story* (1946) and *Jolson Sings Again* (1949); literary classics like *Hamlet* (1948) and *Little Women* (1949); and swashbucklers like *The Adventures of Don Juan* starring Errol Flynn (1949). *Yankee Doodle Dandy* (1942), based upon the life of song-and-dance man George M. Cohan, managed to cover a lot of bases, with its patriotic application of First World War ideals to the current war effort in a nostalgic, upbeat narrative with comedy and musical numbers, not to mention one of James Cagney's greatest roles. Walt Disney's studios built on the success of their first animated feature film, *Snow White and the Seven Dwarfs* (1938), with *Pinocchio* and *Fantasia* in 1940, *Dumbo* in 1941 and *Bambi* in 1942; Disney also branched into live-action features like the long-beloved *Song of the South* (1946). Cartoonist Tex Avery, who had already created Porky Pig and Daffy Duck for Warner Brothers, introduced Bugs Bunny in 1940, and the Looney Tunes animated cartoon series (with many characters voiced by Mel Blanc) dominated movie shorts for the rest of the decade. Also in 1940, *Tom and Jerry* cartoons about a cat and a mouse, created by William Hanna and Joseph Barbera for MGM, made their debut.

Magazine sales and subscriptions burgeoned with the post-war end to paper rationing, and by 1947, 38 magazines could boast circulations of over a million.[36] Movie fan magazines like *Photoplay* and *Modern Screen* boasted subscribers, mostly female, who ranged in years from teen to middle age.[37] Popular mass-circulation magazines included *Life, Time, Reader's Digest, Good Housekeeping, Ladies Home Journal, McCall's, Saturday Evening Post, Saturday Review, Look, Harper's, Atlantic Monthly, New Republic, Science Illustrated, Popular Mechanics* and, beginning in 1946, *Holiday*. Many newspaper comic strips created in earlier decades continued to be favourites: *Bringing Up Father* (Maggie and Jiggs), *Blondie* (with Dagwood Bumstead), *Gasoline Alley, Prince Valiant, Little Orphan Annie, Dick Tracy, Terry and the Pirates, Alley Oop, Nancy* (and Sluggo) and *L'il Abner*. Al Capp's ever-popular *L'il Abner* was mostly about the country boy's relationship with the lovely Daisy Mae along with other denizens of Dogpatch, but in 1948 Capp created the benevolent white smiling blobs known as Shmoos who served themselves up for all kinds of basic human needs. Suddenly Shmoo merchandise was everywhere; one popular toy was a white plastic Shmoo that contained smaller ones like a Russian nesting doll. Among the new strips introduced in the 1940s were *Brenda Starr* (1940), *Wonder Woman* (1944), *Mary Worth* (1944), *Steve Canyon* (1948) and *Pogo* (1949). The 1940s have also been called the golden age of comic books. The Superman character had been created in 1934 but really found an enduring audience in Action Comics of the 1940s; six *Superman* comic books appeared in 1941 and all six presented him 'as a defender of American democracy'.[38]

Despite the popularity of the automobile and the growth of commercial air travel, trains remained the most efficient and luxurious way for most people to travel. Pullman cars had seats that could be converted into curtained berths for sleeping. The dining car seemed luxurious with its white tablecloths and heavy glassware that was unlikely to tip over if the train lurched. Airlines began passenger service in the 1930s, and by 1940, with the advent of pressurized cabins, might carry as many as fifty passengers per flight. Flight attendants were called 'air hostesses' and expected to be registered nurses.

Women and fashion

The need to conserve fabric for military use during the war years had an impact on fashions for women and men. The War Production Board's Order L-85 directed ready-to-wear clothes manufacturers to reduce the amount of fabric by up to 15 per cent per garment without modifying the fashion to the extent that one's wardrobe might seem outdated.[39] The restriction applied also to commercial pattern-makers, for many women sewed their own garments on home sewing machines, using packets of paper cut-out patterns with instructions for assembling the outfit. The look was classic and conservative, dresses with no bias-cut or draping or ruffles, boxy jackets, men's pants without cuffs. For work or casual wear, women adopted slacks and low-heel or wedge-sole shoes. It was a great period for accessorizing with small hats, for ladies' hats required little fabric and could change the look of a basic outfit for different occasions.

Whether a woman ran the household or worked outside the home as a stenographer or other non-factory position, she looked to the movies and the magazines for tips on fashion. A craze for jewellery and hair ornaments of bright, shiny artificial fruit pieces had been inspired by Carmen Miranda's headdresses in movies like *Down Argentine Way* (1940), and this was a fashion, sometimes called 'tutti-frutti', that spanned the decade. The housewife would dress up to go shopping downtown; the rule of thumb was to match shoes and purse, and a second match would be gloves and hat. One liked to dress well for other women, either at a women's club meeting or when hosting a bridge party at home. After the war, women were eager to return to a softer look with full skirts, wide belts, pinafore sleeves, big pockets and higher heels. In 1947, French fashion designer Christian Dior introduced the 'New Look' – a radically different silhouette with rounded shoulders, cinched waists and skirts that flared to mid-calf, worn over petticoats. Perhaps the male equivalent of such extravagance was the brief 1943 fad for zoot suits, particularly among urban Latinos; the look featured draped jackets with wide lapels, high-waisted baggy pants and a long loop of watch chain.

There were women's clubs for many different interests and causes: bridge, cooking, gardening, needlework, books and civic volunteerism. A mother of elementary school children would join the neighbourhood school's Parent Teacher Association (PTA). The earnestness of such women with their bake sales, tea parties and discussion groups made them a target for gentle spoofing in 1940s *New Yorker* magazine cartoons by Helen Hokinson. Alastair Cooke observed in 1949 that 'This plump crusader for tiny causes, this domestic robin pecking courageously at the boundless pastures of culture has a highly developed enough sense of civic duty to hope that a sale of her home-made gingerbread may save Tibet.'[40]

Most adults smoked in the 1940s, and women learned from the movies how to use cigarettes as an accessory; their evening bags would always contain an attractive cigarette case in addition to a mirrored compact for checking lipstick and powdering one's nose. The standard brands were Chesterfields, Old Gold, Philip Morris, Lucky Strike (in green packages until changed to white in 1942) and Camels (with the slogan 'I'd walk a mile for a Camel'). From 1941 until 1966, a famous Camel billboard above Times Square in New York City featured a face that blew gigantic smoke-rings. For men, a pipe (like that of Bing Crosby) or a cigar (like that of George Burns) could be a defining element of the persona.

The culture

For a decade packed with innovations and cultural developments that captured the interest of a largely unified national audience, coverage here must necessarily be selective.[41] Some newsworthy occurrences not previously noted may be summarized chronologically as various aspects of the culture. The year 1940 brought the first American helicopter flight as well as Buckminster Fuller's Dymaxion steel igloo, which would lead to his more famous 1948 geodesic dome. Two important books published in 1940 were Richard Wright's *Native Son* and Ernest Hemingway's *For Whom the Bell Tolls*. John Steinbeck's *The Grapes of Wrath* (1939) won the 1940 Pulitzer Prize; the 1940 movie poster and a deluxe edition featured illustrations by painter Thomas Hart Benton, whose monumental figures in socially-engaged contexts enjoyed wide popularity throughout the 1940s. Boxing continued as a popular spectator sport, and heavyweight Joe Louis dominated most of the decade, although Rocky Graziano would command attention in 1945. Two major constructions were completed in 1941: the National Gallery of Art in Washington, DC, funded largely by industrialist Andrew W. Mellon; and Mount Rushmore in South Dakota, whose sculptor-designer Gutzon Borglum had died only eight months earlier, having worked on the monumental mountainside project since the 1920s. Major movies of 1941 were *Citizen Kane*, by twenty-six-year-old Orson Welles, and *The Maltese Falcon*, starring Humphrey Bogart. Edward Hopper painted what is probably his best-known work, *Nighthawks* (1941), showing a diner in an urban setting. Also in 1941, New York Yankee Joe DiMaggio set a major league record with safe hits in 56 consecutive games. Norman Rockwell's *Four Freedoms* (1943) comprised four compelling paintings that illustrated the 'four freedoms' that President Franklin Roosevelt had extolled in his speech to Congress on 6 January 1941: freedom of speech and expression, freedom from want, freedom of worship and freedom from fear. Also in 1943 in Washington, DC, the Jefferson Memorial was dedicated, and the Pentagon, the world's largest office building, covering 34 acres, was completed. A method of producing penicillin in large quantities enabled medical breakthroughs as the war progressed. A disturbing side to 1943 was a series of so-called Zoot Suit Riots that began in Los Angeles and sparked attacks on Latinos in several other cities. The zoot suit was a fad in male clothing that featured long jackets with broad shoulders, wide pants pegged-in at the ankle and long gold watch chains. Young Mexican-Americans, called *pachucos*, favoured the outfits as a visible defiance of the mainstream even after the War Production Board mandated cutbacks in fabric. Since the military was still segregated, Latinos took wartime factory jobs, yet the zoot suits labelled them in some eyes as unpatriotic or even as hoodlums. May and June of 1943 saw violent street clashes between servicemen and people of colour. Despite obvious racial overtones, the episodes have generated a wide range of interpretations. The establishment of the United Nations proceeded from a 1944 conference at Dumbarton Oaks near Washington, DC, followed by the 1945 charter signing in San Francisco, the 1946 gift of land by John D. Rockefeller Jr for the UN's headquarters in Manhattan, and the laying of the cornerstone in 1949. One of the enduring legacies of the war, the phrase 'Kilroy was here', began appearing everywhere in 1945 as a graffiti assertion of GI presence. It was a great year for book publishers, especially with the vast and growing market for paperbacks. Books published in 1945 include Betty MacDonald's *The Egg and I*, Arthur M. Schlesinger's *The Age of Jackson*, and Canadian author Thomas B. Costain's *The Black Rose*, which launched his many historical fiction bestsellers for an American readership. Most notable in 1946 was Robert Penn Warren's *All the King's Men*. The age of computers was heralded in 1946 by the installation of the 30-ton ENIAC (Electronic Numerical Integrator And Calculator) in Philadelphia. The United States conducted atmospheric and underwater testing of atomic bombs at Bikini Atoll in the Pacific. On 4 July 1946, President Harry S. Truman proclaimed the Republic of the Philippines as an independent nation. Three days later, Pope Pius XII canonized the first American saint, Mother Frances Xavier Cabrini (1850–1917). Americans garnered Nobel Prizes in Medicine, Physics, Chemistry and Peace that year.

In 1947, a Freedom Train departed from Philadelphia on a nationwide tour; it carried 100 important documents of American history for viewing mainly by schoolchildren on field trips in each city where it stopped. Two important firsts in 1947 were twenty-four-year-old Captain Chuck Yeager piloting a Bell X-1 rocket plane to break the sound barrier at 700 miles per hour, and 28-year-old Jackie Robinson becoming the first African-American to play in major-league baseball. Robinson weathered many affronts, yet was voted Rookie of the Year and batted the Brooklyn Dodgers to the National League pennant that season. In 1949, Robinson was the league's Most Valuable Player and an effective advocate for black players on every major league team. Despite those positive achievements, there were signs of general unease during the late 1940s, notably the 'UFO scare' that was sparked in June 1947 when a pilot in a private plane claimed to have seen 'saucer-like' objects in the air near Mount Rainier. Within a month, 'flying saucers' had purportedly been spotted in thirty-five states; Air Force investigations later showed that almost all 'sightings' could be dismissed as natural phenomena, hallucinations or hoaxes. In response to the widespread strikes of 1946, Congress in 1947 passed the controversial Taft-Hartley Act, which scaled back some of President Roosevelt's concessions to labour unions, notably curtailing their ability to call a strike if it would 'imperil the national health or safety'. Inspired by W. H. Auden's Pulitzer Prize-winning poem 'The Age of Anxiety' (1947), Leonard Bernstein composed his second symphony, 'The Age of Anxiety' (1949). Major books published in 1947 were Bernard De Voto's *Across the Wide Missouri*, John Gunther's *Inside U.S.A.* and James A. Michener's *Tales of the South Pacific*. The following year brought General Dwight D. Eisenhower's *Crusade in Europe*, Dale Carnegie's *How to Stop Worrying and Start Living*, Norman Mailer's *The Naked and the Dead* and Dr Alfred C. Kinsey's *Sexual Behavior in the Human Male*.

In 1948, the world's largest telescope was dedicated at Mount Palomar. The end of the decade also saw the phenomenal rise to prominence of golfer Mildred 'Babe' Didrikson Zaharias, named Associated Press Athlete of the Year for three consecutive years (1945, 1946 and 1947) for golf; she had earned that distinction in 1932 for track and field. Didrikson had excelled as an amateur in numerous sports during the 1930s, then decided to focus on golf as a professional, helped found the Ladies' Professional Golf Association and won many tournaments. Another woman whose dazzling career came to full fruition in 1949 was ballerina Maria Tallchief, a Native American of Osage descent. In 1942 she joined the Ballet Russe de Monte Carlo; with the company she danced that year in Agnes de Mille's *Rodeo* and worked under choreographer George Balanchine, whom she married in 1946. In 1947 she was the first American to dance in the Paris Opera Ballet, where her athleticism, technical skill and passion – as well as her ethnic origins – thrilled French audiences. In 1949 it was her brilliant performance of Balanchine's technically challenging choreography in *The Firebird* at New York City Ballet that elevated her to prima ballerina status. Tallchief was America's first internationally renowned ballerina.

Cold War anxieties

Post-war optimism, increasing prosperity and technological advances were countered by widespread anxieties during the later part of the decade. Indeed, technological advances – especially atmospheric testing of atomic bombs – contributed to the general sense of unease. The 1947 'UFO scare' paralleled a 'sex crime' panic that incited parents everywhere to warn their little daughters to run away and scream for help if a man ever offered them candy to get into his car. Hervey Cleckley's bestselling *The Mask of Sanity* (1941) had introduced awareness of the psychopathic personality, one who seemed normal or charming yet could act remorselessly to harm even those close to him or her.[42] All of these factors underlay fears about unseen forces lurking as potential menaces to ordinary American life. Above all lurked a very specific, well-known and frequently reported threat: the Soviet expansionist agenda.

Although the USSR had been an ally during the war, Stalin's anti-capitalist rhetoric could be documented as early as 9 February 1946 in a speech that US Supreme Court Justice William O. Douglas called 'World War III'.[43] As George Kennan reported from Moscow, only a position of greater strength could deter further Soviet westward incursions. When Winston Churchill spoke at Westminster College in Fulton, Missouri, on 5 March 1946, he planted the image of an 'iron curtain' by which Moscow had isolated much of eastern Europe and was installing communist regimes there. Elder statesman Bernard M. Baruch, US representative to the UN Atomic Energy Commission, added the term 'cold war' in a speech (16 April 1947, before the South Carolina legislature) to describe the ongoing hostile rivalry between communist-controlled Eastern Europe and the Western democracies; he warned further of enemies at home as well as abroad. That same year brought a communist coup in Czechoslovakia and Soviet obstruction of ground traffic to the Allied-occupied sectors of Berlin within Soviet-controlled East Germany. As a lifeline to the two million residents of West Berlin, the Western powers instituted massive airlifts of food and industrial supplies, 4,500 tons per day for 11 months, until the Soviets lifted the blockade. The National Security Act passed in July 1947 authorized establishment of the Central Intelligence Agency (CIA) as a means of countering Soviet espionage and other well-documented communist attempts to infiltrate American government and undermine the recovery of Western Europe. President Truman's policy of 'containment', known as the Truman Doctrine, led to such measures as subjecting federal employees to FBI loyalty checks and adopting a hard line that forestalled the attempted Soviet takeover of Greece and Turkey in 1947.

In this climate of fears and uncertainties, the US House of Representatives directed increasing attention to its Committee to Investigate Un-American Activities, which had been formed in 1938 and became generally known as HUAC (House Un-American Activities Committee). Hollywood cooperated by investigating its own industry professionals for suspected communist leanings; in November 1947 the so-called 'Hollywood Ten' were blacklisted. The Committee was further called upon in 1948 when Whittaker Chambers, senior editor at *Time* magazine, testified that Alger Hiss had been passing State Department documents to the Soviets. The hearings on that issue brought to the fore a young California congressman, Richard Nixon, who would later become president of the United States. However, the most infamous era for HUAC investigations, headed by the self-aggrandizing, 'witch-hunting' Senator Joseph McCarthy, would come during the early 1950s.

Increasing aggression by the USSR under Stalin prodded the United States in 1949 to ratify a mutual defence alliance with 11 other nations. The North Atlantic Treaty Organization (NATO) not only pledged military cooperation and assistance in the specified region, as permitted by the United Nations charter, but also approved President Truman's Point Four Program to share technological advances that would aid in the cause of world peace. In August 1949 the USSR detonated a nuclear bomb that was confirmed and announced to the American public on 23 September 1949. One week later, on 1 October, China became the People's Republic of China, led by the Communist Mao Zedong, while the US-supported leader of the Chinese nationalists, Chiang Kai-shek, and his followers settled on Formosa (Taiwan).

To conclude this overview of the decade on a positive note, one could signal the creation a year earlier (June 1948) of a new branch of the CIA: the Office of Policy Coordination (OPC) to conduct covert operations that would counteract Soviet initiatives in the realms of propaganda, economic subversion and political destabilization. It was under this rubric, quietly funded by the Marshall Plan, that 'some of America's finest performers and minds were flown to Europe: Leonard Bernstein and George Gershwin performed and even premiered some of their work, and Eugene O'Neill, Thornton Wilder and Tennessee Williams productions were all put on in freezing European theaters'.[44] Amidst the anxieties of the time, it must have been heartening for Americans to take pride in an arts initiative as a means of winning hearts and minds for the democratic way.

2

American Theatre in the 1940s

Felicia Hardison Londré

At the turn of the millennium and afterward, there was a mania for making lists of 'the best' in various categories, and that included plays. Among the lists of 'fifty best' or 'top one hundred' American plays (and even among all English-language plays) of the twentieth century, four plays almost always appear among the top ten. They are, in roughly the most frequent rank order: *Death of a Salesman* by Arthur Miller, *A Streetcar Named Desire* by Tennessee Williams, *Long Day's Journey Into Night* by Eugene O'Neill and *Our Town* by Thornton Wilder. Moreover, such lists usually include, only slightly farther down in the rankings, *The Glass Menagerie*, *The Iceman Cometh*, *All My Sons* and sometimes *The Skin of Our Teeth*.[1] What is amazing is that all of these great plays were written within the twelve-year period that we might call 'the long 1940s'.

Such 'best play' lists, however, may tell us more about the list-makers of our own time than about the theatre of the 1940s. Not all of these plays that we enshrine as classics were so recognized when they premiered sixty or seventy years earlier. The 1945 Pulitzer Prize for drama went to *Harvey* instead of to *The Glass Menagerie*. No Pulitzer was awarded for drama in 1947, when both *The Iceman Cometh* and *All My Sons* were eligible. A *Time* magazine article reviewing the year 1947 commented:

In the arts, only old limp banners were unfurled. Uncertainty and a lack of confidence came out in nostalgia. Beyond a small epic in frustration called *A Streetcar Named Desire*, the only important Broadway plays were revivals of Shakespeare and Shaw, a rewrite (*Medea*) of Euripides.[2]

One way to understand the theatre of the decade as it was understood in its own time is to proceed chronologically through developments in legitimate drama, musical comedy, dance performance, radio drama, theatre organizations and other trends as they were observed and experienced by the public. This is particularly appropriate for the first half of the decade as the stage reflected evolving American concerns about the war in Europe. Theatrical practices were certainly influenced by the Second World War even more than what is reflected in the literature of the stage, which necessarily lags somewhat in time behind the events that inspired the dramatist. This linear approach to understanding the theatre of the 1940s will encompass commercial (largely Broadway) theatre as well as so-called 'art theatres' and the nationwide network of community theatres that grew out of the Little Theatre Movement of the 1920s.

THEATRE-RELATED ACRONYMS

AFRS	Armed Forces Radio Service
ANT	American Negro Theatre
ANTA	American National Theatre and Academy
ART	American Repertory Theatre, founded by Eva Le Gallienne, Cheryl Crawford and Margaret Webster, 1945–8
CBS	Columbia Broadcasting System
CSI	Camp Shows, Incorporated, as touring arm of the USO
ECEI	Emergency Committee of the Entertainment Industry
FTP	Federal Theatre Project
HUAC	House Un-American Activities Committee
NBC	National Broadcasting Company
NPC	Negro Playwrights Company
WPA	Works Progress Administration

The late 1930s: Forebodings of war

Idiot's Delight

War plays from the 1910s to the early 1930s came out of the experience of the First World War. At some point in the 1930s, plays about war switched from rehashing the past to warning about the future. The rumblings of a future war were most clearly heard on Broadway in the March 1936 opening of *Idiot's Delight*, for which Robert E. Sherwood won his first Pulitzer Prize in drama. While the Great Depression still weighed upon American life, this play may be said to mark the beginning of a transition from the dominance of economic issues to anxieties about ominous developments in Europe. In October 1935, Mussolini's Italian forces invaded Ethiopia, and Hitler began defying provisions of the Versailles Treaty. Sherwood, who had fought in the First World War but then committed himself to pacifism, presciently set the action of *Idiot's Delight* on the eve of the next world war. The play sends mixed signals about what can or should be done in response to a brutal onslaught bent on conquest. Idealism and hope are as ineffectual as wilful ignorance. Those responses – along with collaboration, passive resistance and violent resistance – are embodied in an odd assortment of international guests at a mountain resort hotel near the border between two countries. The action is much enlivened by the presence of a small touring troupe of American chorus girls and their manager Harry Van. Alfred Lunt and Lynne Fontanne brought their star power to the leading roles. Romantic interest in the plot (with hard-boiled language keeping it real rather than sentimentalized) and some lively musical sequences further gratified theatregoers who sought entertainment value, while the attempt to grapple with larger issues earned critical respect. The all-too-accurate forebodings of the Second World War suggest that it is not amiss to incorporate this 1936 play into the rubric of 'the long 1940s'.

Influential organizations

When it produced *Idiot's Delight*, the Theatre Guild was at the apogee of its prestige – within 'its most productive years of 1919–39'.[3] The influential Theatre Guild retained its strong presence in professional theatre of the 1940s along with its power to shape careers and audience expectations. It had originated in the Washington Square Players (1914–18), one of the earliest companies that spawned the Little Theatre Movement of the 1920s. Not long after that company's debts forced its demise, several of its leaders met to form a new organization with guiding principles based upon lessons learned from the previous, semi-professional producing experience. The Theatre Guild would be fully professional at every level and would aim to produce the best of both European and American plays that would not otherwise find a niche in commercial theatre. Under the canny management of Lawrence Langner, with co-founders Theresa Helburn, Philip Moeller, Lee Simonson and others, the Theatre Guild weathered some difficult times but managed to construct its own Guild Theatre on 52nd Street (opened in 1925; leased out to radio in 1943; sold in 1950 to the American National Theatre and Academy and renamed ANTA Theatre; renamed Virginia Theatre in 1981; since 2005, the August Wilson Theatre) and to bring to the fore some outstanding plays in well-mounted productions with outstanding actors. While the early seasons were heavily weighted toward European drama (intentionally chosen as examples of Modernist theatricality in counterpoint to American commercial theatre), the balance began to tip in the 1930s toward American playwrights. For example, in 1928 the Theatre Guild produced the first of seven premieres of plays by Eugene O'Neill, culminating in *The Iceman Cometh* in 1946. Even beyond its first two decades, the Theatre Guild amassed an impressive record of introducing playwrights of lasting interest while garnering Pulitzer Prizes and New York Drama Critics' Circle awards.

The New York Drama Critics' Circle is another important legacy of the 1935–6 season that brought *Idiot's Delight* to the stage. Theatre critics from two dozen New York newspapers and magazines formed the Circle in 1935 as a result of their dissatisfaction with certain Pulitzer Prize decisions. The NY Drama Critics' Circle still meets twice a year and keeps the focus on plays rather than performance. Their very first Best Play award went to Maxwell Anderson's *Winterset*, with Sherwood's *Idiot's Delight* as runner-up. Later years would see the addition of awards for Best Foreign Play and Best Musical. Both Anderson and Sherwood would continue as distinguished playwrights of the 1940s; indeed, Maxwell Anderson won his second Drama Critics' Circle's Best Play Award in 1936–7 for *High Tor*, while the Pulitzer went to *You Can't Take It With You* by George S. Kaufman and Moss Hart. And the following season, 1937–8, Thornton Wilder's *Our Town* won the Pulitzer, but was runner-up for the Drama Critics' Circle Award, which went to John Steinbeck's *Of Mice and Men*.

Awards are indicative but can never tell the whole story. Many long-forgotten plays testify to the tenor of the times. As shown in Albert Wertheim's definitive study *Staging the War: American Drama and World War II*, quite a few plays from the 1930s pointed the way to the war issues of the 1940s: 'Before Pearl Harbor, American plays provide eloquent evidence for the national conflict between American post-World War I isolationism and the voices of those warning that the U.S. must take a stand to stem the aggression and the ideologies of Hitler and Mussolini.'[4] While some war-themed plays of the mid-1930s – Irwin Shaw's *Bury the Dead* (1936), for example – were conceived in response to the First World War, Wertheim sees forward-looking consciousness-raising intent as early as 1934 in Elmer Rice's *Judgment Day* at the Belasco Theatre in September of that year. Rice had followed reporting from Europe about Hitler's manipulation of the German judiciary for his own dictatorial purposes, and *Judgment Day* used the courtroom drama format to warn against allowing political considerations to supersede truth and justice. Clifford Odets's *Till the Day I Die*, which opened in March 1935, embedded sequences of Nazi brutality within an episodic melodrama that proposed the communist ideal of collective responsibility as a means of countering fascism. Some late 1930s plays on Broadway that exposed Nazi ruthlessness and/or anticipated a war that would require American involvement include *The Ghost of Yankee Doodle* (1937) by Sidney Howard, *Waltz in Goose-Step* (1938) by Oliver H. P. Garrett, *Lorelei* (1938) by Jacques Deval, *The American Way* (1939) by George S. Kaufman and Moss Hart, and *Margin for Error* (1939) by Clare Boothe.

It Can't Happen Here

Because of its widespread production by the Federal Theatre Project, the 1936 dramatization of Sinclair Lewis's 1935 novel *It Can't Happen Here* must be signalled. The Federal Theatre Project (FTP) had been chartered by Congress in 1935 as part of the Works Progress Administration (WPA) initiative to put people back to work at the kind of jobs they had held before the Depression. Hallie Flanagan was appointed to head the FTP, and she ran it skilfully enough to employ 10,000 theatre people nationwide at the peak of its four-year existence. Initiatives such as Living Newspapers, the Negro Theatre Project (with 16 regional units), Project 891 for classical theatre, and children's theatres all brought new audiences to experience live performances. However, federal funding for the FTP ended in June 1939 and was not reinstated despite Hallie Flanagan's eloquent testimony for the positive power of art in people's lives. Controversial productions such as *Triple A Plowed Under* (1936) or *The Cradle Will Rock* (1937), whether blatantly left wing or perceived as communist propaganda, undoubtedly contributed to the FTP's demise. *It Can't Happen Here* is an interesting case in the context of the times, as summarized by Albert Wertheim:

> At home there was the specter of Huey Long's demagogic reign in Louisiana, the openly anti-Semitic radio broadcasts from Detroit of Father Charles Coughlin, and the formation of the American Nazi party by Gerald L. K. Smith and Governor Eugene Talmadge of Georgia. Using a rural New England setting and the joblessness of the Depression, *It Can't Happen Here* suggests the myopia of Americans who could witness the rise of Hitler and Nazism in Germany, or even of those homegrown demagogues who would create dictatorship and racism in the U.S. and say, 'It can't happen here'.[5]

The dramatization by Sinclair Lewis and John C. Moffitt opened on 27 October 1936 in twenty-two theatres in eighteen cities plus a Kansas City production opening two weeks later. New York City saw the simultaneous openings of two productions in English and one in Yiddish.[6] The action shows a fascist politician ascending to the presidency of the United States and deploying his private military to suppress dissent; the protagonist is a newspaperman who stands up for free speech. The theatrical trade newspaper *Variety*'s assessment of *It Can't Happen Here* was that 'if viewed as a show selling at $.55 top and for the purpose of keeping unemployed actors from going hungry, it's very good; if viewed as the newest play of a Nobel prize winning writer, it's very bad'.[7] Another show that spun off from the antics of Louisiana Governor Huey Long, Irving Berlin's musical satire *Louisiana Purchase* (1940), would prove more successful with a long New York run and a movie version.

However, *It Can't Happen Here* is interesting in view of what was to come in the 1940s, not only for the script's warning against the spread of fascism, but also because the production contributed to congressional fears that the FTP was promulgating communism. Under the chairmanship of Representative Martin Dies, the House Committee on Un-American Activities in the summer of 1938 launched an investigation of the Federal Theatre Project, which one Dies Committee member called 'a veritable hotbed of un-American activities'.[8] The committee's many misguided charges were deeply draining on Hallie Flanagan and damaging to the FTP. She finally got her long-sought opportunity to testify in December and rebutted the falsehoods with copious documentation.[9] Flanagan testified again six months later to the House Appropriations Committee, but to no avail; funding for the FTP was not renewed. These 1939 Dies Committee investigations strangely presage the more famous HUAC hearings of the late 1940s that would bring the arrests of 'the Hollywood ten' and segue into the 'McCarthyism' of the early 1950s.

Broadway plays and musicals

Beyond the anti-fascist plays of the late 1930s, a rich variety of offerings enlivened Broadway. Comedy, always popular in times of anxiety, included such hits as Clare Boothe's *The Women* and Kaufman and Hart's *You Can't Take It With You* (both 1936) and *The Man Who Came to Dinner* (1939), Philip Barry's *Philadelphia Story*, S. N. Behrman's *No Time for Comedy* and Howard Lindsay and Russel Crouse's *Life With Father* (all 1939). A few of the many musicals from those seasons are Marc Blitzstein's *The Cradle*

Will Rock (1937, a particularly fraught FTP production), Harold Rome's *Pins and Needles* (created by the International Ladies Garment Workers Union, 1937), Rodgers and Hart's *I'd Rather Be Right* (1937) and *The Boys from Syracuse* (1938), Cole Porter's *DuBarry Was a Lady* (1939) and Kurt Weill's *Knickerbocker Holiday* (1938). Shakespeare got two productions of *Hamlet* (John Gielgud and Leslie Howard) and one of *Richard II* (Maurice Evans) in the 1936–7 season, plus the Mercury Theatre's *Julius Caesar* in 1938 and Maurice Evans in an uncut *Hamlet* in 1938. Foreign plays included the French *Amphitryon 38* (1937) by Jean Giraudoux, the Irish *Shadow and Substance* (1937) and *The White Steed* (1939), both by Paul Vincent Carroll.

The Group Theatre, which had spun off from the Theatre Guild to do more politically committed plays, presented plays by Paul Green and Clifford Odets. Maxwell Anderson's late-1930s plays on Broadway were *The Wingless Victory* starring Katharine Cornell (1936), *High Tor* and *The Star Wagon* (both 1937), and *Key Largo* (1939). Already established as a novelist, Thornton Wilder redefined himself as a dramatist during these years, first with his 1937 adaptation of Henrik Ibsen's *A Doll's House* with a successful Broadway run of 144 performances starring Ruth Gordon, and then with *Our Town* (1938), followed by *The Merchant of Yonkers* (1939); moreover, a television production of his one-act *The Happy Journey to Trenton and Camden* was broadcast in New York on 1 February 1937.[10]

Other important productions that rounded out the 1930s decade include John Steinbeck's *Of Mice and Men* (1938), Robert E. Sherwood's *Abe Lincoln in Illinois* (1938), Lillian Hellman's *The Little Foxes* (1939), DuBose and Dorothy Heyward's *Mamba's Daughters* starring Ethel Waters (1939), and William Saroyan's *The Time of Your Life* (Pulitzer and Drama Critics' Circle Awards, 1939). And in the wings, poised to take the stage, were young Arthur Miller, 1937 recipient of the Theatre Guild's Bureau of New Plays scholarship for promising playwrights, and Tennessee Williams, runner-up in the Group Theatre's 1939 competition for young playwrights.

Radio drama

Radio drama began its rise to popularity and influence at the end of this decade. In April 1937 and in a 1939 repeat broadcast on CBS, Archibald MacLeish's *The Fall of the City* took its place as 'the first radio play to deal with the rise of European fascism' and 'also radio's first play written in verse'. Arthur Miller heard it and became convinced that 'radio was made for poetry'.[11] Other radio dramas in verse followed. In a *Theatre Arts* (February 1940) article extolling the possibilities of radio drama, Norman Corwin used examples from *The Fall of the City* and other radio dramas by MacLeish. Corwin wrote: 'Since in radio drama the word has no visual collaboration, it bears the entire burden of communication and therefore assumes far more responsibility and authority than it does in any other dramatic medium. It is a story-teller, image-maker, character-delineator, set-builder.'[12] Because of radio's time constraints and the need to be readily assimilated by the ear with no recourse to repetition, Corwin claimed that 'radio is the greatest disciplining force in modern playwriting' and 'has contributed the greatest stimulation to dramatic techniques since the invention of the movies'.[13] Innovative use of sound effects helped stir a 'you are there' feeling in the radio listener. The long-running *The March of Time*, dramatizations of current news stories, used actors like Orson Welles and Agnes Moorehead who could imitate the voices of prominent figures, among whom Hitler was the most frequently voiced in 1938.[14] Arthur Miller was one of 11 writers for *Cavalcade of America*, a DuPont-sponsored series of 'sanitized' episodes from American history and great lives.[15] Reaching the widest audience, with the most prestigious roster of performers, *Lux Radio Theatre* presented radio adaptations of stage plays, hosted during the war years by Cecil B. DeMille.[16] By 1940 the War Department realized the potential of radio drama to influence public support, which led to its sponsoring service-story series on both CBS (*Spirit of '41*) and NBC (*Wings of Destiny*).[17] The Red Cross too used radio dramas to disseminate examples of its services, as in the 1942 series *Thus We Live*.[18]

The 1940–1 and 1941–2 seasons

African-American theatre

The first two theatre seasons of the decade might still be considered pre-war, since the United States did not declare war until 8 December 1941, and the remainder of that season, running until May 1942, was already well in progress. Nevertheless, there was a drastic drop in the number of shows running on Broadway in 1940–1: only sixty-nine, down from ninety-one in the previous season and down from 187 a decade earlier, in the 1930–1 season.[19] The figure for new plays opening that season is even lower, only forty-eight, compared to sixty-two in the 1939–40 season.[20] The sudden decline in both long runs and new productions might be partially attributed to the military draft, which had become law in September 1939, with the first draftees called in October 1940. Undoubtedly, the box office suffered also from general anxieties about the future during that uneasy transitional phase before the certainty of American involvement could rally spirits to a unified war effort.

Meanwhile, this was a fruitful phase for African-Americans in the theatre, beginning in May 1940 with the formation of the non-profit Negro Playwrights Company (NPC). Its sole production, Theodore Ward's *Big White Fog*, had previously enjoyed a ten-week run in Chicago under the FTP in 1938. The NPC production opened on 22 October 1940 at Harlem's Lincoln Theatre and featured Canada Lee as a Negro nationalist on a futile political quest. Perry Watkins, the first black member of the Union of Scenic Artists, designed the set and lighting. The NPC's *Big White Fog* achieved a run of 64 performances, but also marked the end of that group's idealistic endeavours.[21] On Broadway that season, Ethel Waters continued her rise as a singer and actress; building on her successes in Irving Berlin's *As Thousands Cheer* (1933) and *Mamba's Daughters* (1939), she headlined the all-black cast of *Cabin in the Sky* in 1940, as well as its 1943 movie version. The musical *Cabin in the Sky* by Vernon Duke and John Latouche, with choreography by George Balanchine, also featured dancer Katherine Dunham and Rex Ingram and Arthur 'Dooley' Wilson in major roles. Opening on 25 October 1940, it achieved 155 performances at the Martin Beck Theatre. In 1941, Ethel Waters became the first black elected to the council of Actors' Equity. Canada Lee moved from his leading role in the controversial *Big White Fog* into the role for which he may be best known: Bigger Thomas in Richard Wright's *Native Son* (1941), directed by Orson Welles. Lee's performance was central to the critical acclaim accorded the production. *Native Son* 'played twice on Broadway, first in March of 1941 for 97 performances. It then toured major cities, and reopened on Broadway in October of 1942 for 84 performances', and yet, as shown by historian Glenda E. Gill, 'Lee endured many indignities'.[22]

In June 1940, a small group of African-Americans who had been meeting periodically in Harlem, led by Abram Hill and Frederick O'Neal, announced the creation of the American Negro Theatre (ANT), which went on to build a distinguished record of eleven original productions[23] before its demise in 1950. Abram Hill held a BA in English from Lincoln University in Pennsylvania and had directed plays for teens and young adults under the WPA's Civilian Conservation Corps. During a stint as script reader for the FTP's Negro Theatre Project, Hill began writing his own plays, for which he was awarded a Theresa Helburn scholarship to study playwriting under John Gassner and Erwin Piscator at the New School for Social Research. Hill's social satire *On Striver's Row* was first produced by the Rose McClendon Players (sixteen performances) and later launched the American Negro Theatre with an initial run of 101 performances, and two later revivals.[24] ANT's co-founder Frederick O'Neal had begun his acting career in St Louis, then made his New York debut with the Civic Repertory Theatre in 1936. After ANT's most successful production, *Anna Lucasta* (1944), moved to Broadway, O'Neal won the Clarence Derwent award for his performance in it and had a long, distinguished career as an actor; he became the first African-American president (1964–73) of Actors' Equity Association and he was elected to the College of Fellows of the American Theatre. Another notable ANT production, Theodore Browne's *Natural Man* (1941), had originally been staged under the FTP in Seattle. Despite limited resources, ANT made crucial advances in its training of black actors at its 135th Street Library Theatre in Harlem where it presented plays from 1940 to 1945.

Broadway plays and musicals

The 1940–1 Broadway season began auspiciously with Al Jolson's stage comeback (following a decade in Hollywood) in *Hold On to Your Hats*. The plot's spoofing of radio drama relied upon the audience's recognition of tropes from that medium and also provided a pretext for Jolson to interpolate some of his beloved musical standards within a strong score by Burton Lane and lyrics by E. Y. 'Yip' Harburg. *Hold On to Your Hats* could have settled in for a long run if Jolson had not been eager to take it on the road and used his clout to do so.[25] The 1940–1 season faded out with the closing (31 May 1941) of Jack Kirkland's dramatization of the Erskine Caldwell novel *Tobacco Road*, which had been running since 1933 and had occupied three different theatres with five different actors in the role of Lester Jeeter. Its 3,182 performances set a record for a straight play and it grossed about $1,500,000.[26] Set in rural Georgia, the squalid play with unpleasant characters had in 1939 broken the earlier long-running record held by Anne Nichols's ethnic comedy *Abie's Irish Rose* (1922).

The 1940–1 season saw the final collaboration of George S. Kaufman and Moss Hart, *George Washington Slept Here*, a character comedy that got only 173 performances (in contrast to the 739 performances of their 1939 comedy *The Man Who Came to Dinner*). Kaufman directed the hit comedy *My Sister Eileen* by Joseph Fields and Jerome Chodorov, based upon a *New Yorker* story by Ruth McKenney, and it achieved 866 performances, more than two years on Broadway. Three additional shows running that season originated in *New Yorker* stories: the perennial favourite *Life with Father* (opened in November 1939 for a 3,224-performance run), the cynical musical *Pal Joey* by Richard Rodgers and Lorenz Hart, and *Mr. and Mrs. North*, a murder-mystery comedy by the prolific Owen Davis. Also combining murder and laughter was *Arsenic and Old Lace* by Joseph Kesselring (1,444 performances). Both *Life with Father* and *Arsenic and Old Lace* retained their popularity over the decades in community theatre productions. Rose Franken, a popular writer of light fiction, drew upon her own 'Claudia' novels for her second play, *Claudia*, which she also directed. Claudia is a charming but immature young married woman whose minor misadventures of daily life held audiences through 453 performances on Broadway, a radio series and two movie versions. Lillian Hellman's *Watch on the Rhine* shows Nazi infiltration of a nice home in Washington, DC; it won the New York Drama Critics' Circle Award for Best Play. Robert E. Sherwood won his third Pulitzer Prize (after *Idiot's Delight* and *Abe Lincoln in Illinois*) for *There Shall Be No Night*, a Theatre Guild production that starred Alfred Lunt and Lynne Fontanne. Set in Helsinki during the very recent Russian invasion of Finland, *There Shall Be No Night* urged war's necessity when democracy is threatened. Coming from the formerly pacifist playwright and based upon virtually current events, Sherwood's drama resonated powerfully.

The 1941–2 season was far less interesting and, indeed, midway through it 'most critics had pronounced the year the worst in Broadway history'.[27] By the end of the season, only 12 plays were in the black, 'the fewest since *Variety* began to keep track in the 1923–1924 season'.[28] Even the venerable Maxwell Anderson's *Candle in the Wind*, co-produced by the Theatre Guild and the Playwrights' Company and starring Helen Hayes, warning that Nazi brutality in occupied France would ultimately target 'spoiled and soft' Americans, was harshly dismissed by critics. Noel Coward's *Blithe Spirit* provided an exceptional bright spot. Another English writer, Shakespeare, gave the season its dramatic highlight, as Margaret Webster directed Maurice Evans and Judith Anderson in *Macbeth*. The longest-running (710 performances) American comedy was *Junior Miss* by Jerome Chodorov and Joseph Fields, based upon *New Yorker* stories by Sally Benson, and directed by Moss Hart; the amusing escapades of the teenage protagonist led to a 1945 movie. The best thriller came from London where it had been titled *Gaslight*; Broadway audiences saw Patrick Hamilton's play under the title *Angel Street*. Other offerings of the largely dismal season included Sophie Treadwell's *Hope for a Harvest* and John Steinbeck's dramatization of his novel *The Moon Is Down*, about a Nazi takeover of a town in Norway. The 1941–2 season marked the first year that saw neither a Pulitzer Prize for Drama nor a Drama Critics' Circle Award for Best Play.

Lady in the Dark

If one were to choose a single 1940–1 Broadway show as a highlight of that transitional season, it would have to be *Lady in the Dark*. With an original script by Moss Hart, music by Kurt Weill, lyrics by Ira Gershwin, costumes by Irene Sharaff and gowns by Hattie Carnegie, and Gertrude Lawrence in the title role, this musical play was an attention-getter even before its opening on 23 January 1941. In performance there were additional revelations, notably a breakthrough supporting role by a singer-comedian from vaudeville: Danny Kaye. His fast-paced rendering of the tongue-twisting Russian names in the musical number 'Tschaikowsky' proved a nightly show-stopper. Moreover, audiences were charmed by his portrayal of a gay character as he mined the comic potential of the standard stereotypes of the day.[29] Both the subject matter and form of *Lady in the Dark* presented innovations. The storyline traces the progress of a career woman's psychiatric treatment sessions to rediscover her true feminine nature; psychoanalysis was rapidly gaining recognition among the general public at the time. Indeed, Moss Hart's own psychiatrist, Dr Lawrence S. Kubie (who would later briefly treat Tennessee Williams), gained some renown from his endorsement of the accurate portrayal of the title character's mental condition. Bruce D. McClung, author of a 'biography' of the musical, describes the show:

> Hart based his plot on the Freudian allegory of a woman choosing among three men, representing the roles of father, lover, and husband. Music provided the key to the story: when the heroine is able to remember a childhood song and the events tied to it, her neuroses are brought to light and her tangled love life straightens itself out.[30]

Another innovative feature of the musical was the lack of an opening overture; the first scene, set in a psychiatrist's office, into which the leading lady made a low-key de-glamorized entrance, set the tone of a straight drama. However, when the lady's dreams came to life on the stage with a huge and lavishly costumed chorus that included the Albertina Rasch Group Dancers, the audience was more comfortably watching a musical. The incorporation of 'dream ballet' into the action to stimulate the leading character's self-understanding was a device that would reappear in such musicals as *One Touch of Venus* (1943), *Oklahoma!* (1943), *On the Town* (1944) and, as late as 1957, *West Side Story*; there was even a spoof of the 'dream ballet' in *This Is the Army* (1942). *Lady in the Dark*, in Gerald Bordman's assessment, was

> ... the most imaginative, intelligent and cohesive work of the theatrical year ... [Moss Hart's] dialogue was far more literate than that of the run-of-the-mill Broadway musical book. His characters not only spoke grammatically correct and complete sentences, they often spoke complete paragraphs. Yet his touch was so light, stylish and sure that he dispelled the artificiality and turgidness of the old comic-opera librettos.[31]

The show's box office, with phenomenal advance sales and standing-room-only performances, attested to its artistic and popular success. On a top ticket price of $6 and standing-room tickets as low as $1.65 for matinees, *Lady in the Dark*'s weekly gross came to about $31,500 during its initial Broadway run.[32] *Lady in the Dark* ran for two seasons with a summer break (mandated in Gertrude Lawrence's contract) between seasons for a total of fifty-eight weeks (462 performances), thirty-two of those weeks playing to standing room only.[33] In September 1942 the show began an eight-city tour, again to ecstatic reviews: Philadelphia, Baltimore, Pittsburgh, Cleveland, Detroit, Cincinnati, St Louis and Chicago. The Chicago engagement was held over for a fifth week with record-shattering box-office receipts there.[34] Then the production was brought back to New York for a return engagement, which closed at 83 performances only because an immediate west coast tour had been negotiated. The five weeks in San Francisco and Los Angeles played as well as ever, and yet, as Bruce D. McClung notes, because the title character edits a fashion magazine 'with a staff of single women postponing marriage in favor of careers', by 1943 the show 'no longer fit the national profile'.[35] During all of those engagements totalling 777 performances, Gertrude Lawrence, in a gruelling role with no understudy, had cancelled only eleven times for health problems.

Lady in the Dark gave Gertrude Lawrence 'the greatest vehicle of her career, one that melded her abilities as a dramatic actress and music-hall comedienne'.[36] Shortly after the show's original opening, the English-born star was featured on the cover of *Time* magazine

(3 February 1941), which rounded up such critical accolades as 'the greatest feminine performer in the theatre' (Richard Watts, Jr), 'a goddess' (Brooks Atkinson) and 'a welcome substitute for the Life Force' (John Mason Brown).[37] Gertrude Lawrence's salary, famously one of the highest ever paid to a Broadway actress, included a percentage of the gross receipts and averaged about $4,300 per week. The show required exceptional stamina of its star, for she was on stage almost constantly or else making a whirlwind costume change behind the scenery. And yet she led a double life, for in her discretionary time Lawrence poured her earnings and her energy into war relief activities. Even before she had signed on for *Lady in the Dark*, Gertrude Lawrence spoke of returning to England to serve patriotically: 'cook, scrub, sew, nurse, sing songs and be generally useful'.[38] But her American future husband persuaded her that she could do more by continuing her career and sending financial support than by going home to roll bandages.[39]

Gertrude Lawrence sold British War Relief (BWR) emblems and gave talks at Red Cross events and on the radio. In her curtain speech on opening night of *Lady in the Dark*, 23 January 1941, nearly eleven months before the United States entered the war, she spoke out against American isolationism. The high-fashion dresses and hats she wore in the show generated such interest in women that she created a line of dresses with the profits going to the British War Relief Society, Bundles for Britain, and the British American Ambulance Corps.[40] For Christmas 1941, Lawrence borrowed a theme from her 'My Ship' song in *Lady in the Dark* and organized a Happiness Ship drive to send toys to war-besieged English children with an appeal in the *New York Times*.[41] Pearl Harbor broadened the horizons of her efforts. 'With the United States' entry into the war,' her husband Richard Stoddard Aldrich recalled, 'Gertrude increased her Red Cross activities ... At the first call for volunteers for civil defense, she signed up as an air raid warden and took the course, being tremendously proud of her official helmet and badge.'[42] When the show toured, she spoke in every city and often sold War Bonds in department stores or at a table in the theatre lobby. She donated blood and rallied others to give 15,000 pints in San Francisco.[43] When *Lady in the Dark* finally closed in Los Angeles on 13 July 1943, Gertrude Lawrence moved full-time into war work. In 1944 she performed for soldiers in England and France, followed by a USO tour to naval bases in the Pacific.⁴⁴ As early as April 1942, Lawrence had earned the American Women's Voluntary Services recognition as 'the representative of the stage who had done the most for American Defense'.⁴⁵ Gertrude Lawrence's dedication to the war effort was characteristic of many theatre artists who combined volunteer work with their careers, or even sacrificed their careers, to serve a larger cause. Such devotion was also manifested by the founders – Lawrence among them – of the American Theatre Wing.

As Maxene Andrews observed in *Over Here, Over There: The Andrews Sisters and the USO Stars in World War II*:
But if there was a dark side to those trying years, there was a bright side, too – a sense of national unity, *real* togetherness, a feeling so strong, so exhilarating and so unifying that it did more than help the country to survive. It helped us to win the war.

The American Theatre Wing and other war service organizations

The origins of the American Theatre Wing go back to the First World War. When the war menaced democracy, one of Broadway's most prolific and successful playwrights put aside her own career to rally theatre artists, first to send relief to beleaguered French civilians, and later, after the United States declared war in April 1917, to support American soldiers in American camps and in Europe. Rachel Crothers began by gathering a group of theatre women to discuss what they could do,⁴⁶ and this led to the founding of the Stage Women's War Relief (SWWR), which contributed on various fronts: collecting food and clothing, assembling medical supplies, selling Liberty Bonds, opening recreation centres for servicemen, sending entertainers to military hospitals, and much more.

When asked by the United States government in 1939 to reactivate the organization, Rachel Crothers again gathered a group of theatre women: Gertrude Lawrence, Josephine Hull, Minnie Dupree, Antoinette Perry, Vera Allen, Lucile Watson, Theresa Helburn and Edith Atwater.⁴⁷ In January 1940 they founded the

American Theatre Wing, which today is known for its sponsorship of the annual Antoinette Perry (Tony) Awards that began in 1947 to recognize distinguished work in the theatre. At its founding and until the United States declared war in December 1941, the American Theatre Wing was a subsidiary of the British War Relief Society and focused on aid to civilians in Britain. After Pearl Harbor, the Wing chartered itself as an independent charitable war service organization with Rachel Crothers as president; vice presidents Helen Hayes, Gertrude Lawrence and Vera Allen; treasurer Josephine Hull; and secretary and chair of the board Antoinette Perry. A men's executive committee boasted similarly big names: Gilbert Miller, Brooks Atkinson, George S. Kaufman, Raymond Massey, Brock Pemberton, Billy Rose, Lee Shubert, Max Gordon and Vinton Freedley.[48] The American Theatre Wing ultimately sponsored 54 different initiatives that included 'Lunchtime Follies' (variety numbers performed by celebrities at defence plants to boost morale and productivity),[49] radio broadcasts, entertainments in hospitals, educational performances for civilians by the Victory Players, a speakers' bureau for selling war bonds and, later, educational and theatre training programmes for returning veterans.[50] The American Theatre Wing even raised money for the United Service Organizations (USO) to ensure that legitimate plays would be in the mix of entertainment provided for servicemen abroad.

During the war years, the American Theatre Wing carried out its single most publicized activity: running Stage Door Canteens in several cities. The first and most celebrated of the American Theatre Wing's Stage Door Canteens opened on 2 March 1942 in The Little Club, a space donated by Lee Shubert under the Forty-Fourth Street Theatre in New York. Actresses Jane Cowl and Selena Royle co-chaired that canteen committee, which involved signing up 600 girls to volunteer as junior hostesses (150 to come in each evening) and arranging cars to transport food from donors to the canteen.[51] Everything was volunteered or donated or financed by contributors, and there was never any cost to the men in uniform. Marian Moore, who co-chaired food preparation for the 3,000 or so servicemen who arrived each evening between five o'clock and midnight, tallied what was served free of charge on an average night: '2,000 sandwiches, 3,000 slices of cake or doughnuts, 1,000 half pints of milk, 80 gallons of fruit juice and cider, 25 lbs. of candy, six crates of fruit, and 5,000 cigarettes'.[52] But never any alcoholic drink. Nor were officers or civilians admitted. Unlike the military and many other institutions of the day, the American Theatre Wing's Stage Door Canteens were always racially integrated, welcoming African-American servicemen as well as entertainers, although black junior hostesses were few.[53] According to Carl Van Vechten, who managed the New York canteen two nights a week and saw frequent interracial dancing as well as table-sharing, the policy was for hostesses to 'dance with uniforms, not with colors'.[54]

On the New York Stage Door Canteen's first anniversary, it was estimated that the hostesses had danced a total of 2,184,000 miles with the servicemen.[55] Stars of the Broadway stage volunteered there, some coming in after performances, to serve food, wait tables, wash dishes and dance with the soldiers, sailors and marines. On the New York Stage Door Canteen's opening evening, 2 March 1942, the cast of *Lady in the Dark* actually showed up when the canteen opened at five o'clock and spent two hours before their regular Broadway performance (8.30 p.m. curtain):

> Lawrence's performance of 'The Saga of Jenny' tore the place apart. Afterward, an RAF flyer rushed up, took her into his arms, and began to dance. An American sailor then cut in, and soon the star was besieged with partners. Not one to show any favoritism, Gertie began a conga line.[56]

After her performances also, Gertrude Lawrence would stop in at the canteen, as she did at other service clubs in various cities on the tours. One never knew which Broadway stars one might see on any given night, perhaps Marlene Dietrich at the milk bar or Jane Cowl at work in the kitchen or Alfred Lunt handling the garbage to find out what the men were leaving uneaten.[57] The 1943 movie *Stage Door Canteen* by Sol Lesser shows the configuration of the space, the uniform striped aprons worn by the junior hostesses and numerous performances by stars who really did donate their time and talents there, including Ed Wynn, Ethel Waters, Judith Anderson, Ray Bolger, Ethel Merman, Edgar Bergen and Charlie McCarthy, Harpo Marx, Katharine Hepburn, Helen Hayes, Yehudi Menuhin and many more. In a truly moving sequence in *Stage Door Canteen*, the great Katharine Cornell is serving food to a soldier who recalls having seen her when she toured *Romeo and Juliet*, and they have an impromptu exchange of lines from the balcony scene.

Then Broadway's leading actress hands him an orange, which he vows to keep as a memento. The movie's substantial profits were ploughed back into the operations of the American Theatre Wing. The Wing also authorized a weekly half-hour CBS radio broadcast from the Stage Door Canteen. Given the success of its New York canteen, the Wing opened Stage Door Canteens in Boston, Philadelphia, Cleveland, Newark, San Francisco, Washington, DC, London and, after its liberation, Paris.[58]

The famous Hollywood Canteen in Los Angeles was a separate organization that opened on 3 October 1942, seven months after New York's Stage Door Canteen; it was founded by Bette Davis (who became president and remained tireless in her devotion to it) along with John Garfield and music producer Jules Stein. The Hollywood Canteen's services were very similar to those of the Stage Door Canteens, except that most of the 3,000 volunteers came from the motion picture industry. Many stars of stage and screen, like Marlene Dietrich, appeared at both east and west coast canteens as well as on USO tours.[59] When the American Theatre Wing's New York Stage Door Canteen finally closed on 28 October 1945 after three and a half years, it had entertained 3,250,000 men, and the junior hostesses had danced well over ten million miles.[60] Producer Brock Pemberton, co-chair of the Wing's branch canteens, was there on the last night to announce that 'Wing performers would continue to entertain GI's in local hospitals'.[61]

A full year after the American Theatre Wing began its work in January 1940, the USO was incorporated under its original name, United Service Organizations for National Defense (4 February 1941). This was in response to the first American peacetime draft (the Selective Service Act of 16 September 1940) and the realization that young men called to military camps around the nation would be vulnerable to immoral influences and in need of morale-building diversion. The plan was to organize pooled resources from the YMCA, YWCA, Salvation Army, National Catholic Community Service, National Jewish Welfare Board and National Travelers Aid Association 'to handle the on-leave recreation of the men in the armed forces'.[62] Technically, the USO should also have overseen the American Theatre Wing's war efforts, but the Wing's charter defined it as an independent organization run by volunteers from the theatre, whereas the USO was broadly based. Entertainers at the Stage Door and Hollywood Canteens who also performed under the auspices of the USO included the Andrews Sisters, sometimes accompanying Bing Crosby. Maxene Andrews later recalled, 'The whole country was dotted with USO canteens. They were in every town, either in their own buildings, or in church social halls, train stations, and even bus depots.'[63] Like the Stage Door Canteens, the 3,000 USO centres offered free coffee and snacks as well as volunteer junior hostesses to dance with the servicemen, but on the whole the USO's emphasis tended to be less on entertainment than on providing a 'home away from home' atmosphere for relaxing, letter-writing, talking with local clergymen or with motherly figures who might sew on a button.[64] In sum, the numerous centres and other projects 'that served the needs of America's men and women in uniform' at the same time effectively channelled 'civilian volunteer efforts. By the war's end in 1945, over 1.5 million Americans had contributed their time to the USO.'[65]

Meanwhile, the Army and Navy Citizens Committees had faced organizational problems with their various initiatives to boost the morale of servicemen abroad and finally realized that such efforts would be better handled by civilians from show business. With authorization by the Army and Navy, USO Camp Shows Inc. (CSI) came into being on 8 October 1941.[66] CSI operated on USO funding but drew upon the expertise of entertainment industry professionals for implementation. While relatively unknown entertainers travelled in paid units on modified standard Equity contracts, big-name performing artists got dispensation from their unions to waive payment and to work under less-than normal conditions.[67] Overseas Unit No. 1 left the USA on 1 November 1941 and played a 13,000-mile Caribbean tour that quickly proved its value. By the spring of 1943, there were 119 units performing in different parts of the globe.[68] A soldier stationed in North Burma in 1944 wrote in a letter that the men in his unit 'for the first time in a long time' felt like 'practically normal humans' thanks to a travelling Camp Show in which 'five girls put laughter and memories into the hearts of nearly 500 lonely GIs – GIs who haven't seen a beautiful American girl in two years, some cases longer'.[69]

Among the 7,000 'soldiers in greasepaint' who gave their time and talents were headliners like Bob Hope, Bing Crosby, Fred Astaire, Marlene Dietrich, the Andrews Sisters, Dinah Shore, Edgar Bergen and Charlie McCarthy. They performed in combat areas on what was known as the Foxhole Circuit. According to Maxene

Andrews, 'Like the rest of the USO Camp Shows, the Foxhole Circuit was an enormous undertaking. In its first three years, the circuit presented 40,000 performances for our GIs, totaling 3,818 weeks of entertainment.'[70] Three smaller, specialized circuits complemented the Foxhole Circuit. The Victory Circuit booked road versions of Broadway shows into military bases in the United States where facilities could accommodate the production needs and large indoor audiences. The Hospital Circuit focused on entertaining military personnel in general hospitals in the United States. The Blue Circuit took easily-mobile units of variety entertainers into the smallest military installations.[71] Each of these circuits also had units of all-black entertainers, under the direction of African-American actor-director Dick Campbell; indeed, blacks comprised over one-tenth of all Camp Show entertainers and were paid union salaries. Noble Sissle (of the famed 1920s duo Sissle and Blake) had served with the Harlem Hellfighters in the First World War and now served on the CSI board; he assembled a Negro unit that toured a condensed version of the legendary 1921 musical *Shuffle Along*.[72]

While most CSI entertainment emphasized music and comedy in variety format, there were some legitimate shows. The first of those, the 1941 Broadway hit play *Junior Miss* by Chodorov and Fields, earned much acclaim for its wholesomeness as well as its high-spirited comedy.[73] Other straight plays on the CSI circuit included *Blithe Spirit*, *The Man Who Came to Dinner* and *Our Town*. The renowned Shakespearean actor Maurice Evans toured *Hamlet* in the Pacific. It was through the management of the USO Camp Shows that the American Theatre Wing made arrangements in 1944 to finance a production of *The Barretts of Wimpole Street* starring Katharine Cornell, Brian Aherne and Guthrie McClintic, with a supporting cast of fourteen, for an overseas tour as a high-brow entertainment option for the men at war.[74] As Brooks Atkinson noted: 'In December 1945, there were only thirty productions on Broadway ... But USO had fifty-nine touring companies in the United States and 228 overseas; and it employed 2,200 actors, ninety-seven per cent of whom had to be paid. The three per cent who were able to volunteer included eminent people.'[75] Camp Shows, Incorporated came to an end in 1956, but the USO continued sending celebrities to entertain the troops. Bob Hope, who entertained Americans stationed abroad in war and peace for fifty years, described the USO as an organization that provided 'the military with a "pause" from both the terror and tedium of war', 'an oasis of America to our men and women overseas' and the 'touchstone of our sympathy and support'.[76] Certainly, much was learned and reinforced during the Second World War about the power of the performing arts in perilous times.

Radio drama

Radio also played a major role in disseminating morale-building entertainment along with information for listeners at home and, in expanding initiatives, for American troops. The strength of radio's 'hold on the imagination of America in the '30s and '40s' is powerfully evoked by Terry Teachout in an essay recalling his interview with the legendary Norman Corwin, 'one of the giants' of network radio.[77] Families would schedule time for listening together to favourite programmes, and all remained alert for war bulletins, which could reach the public most quickly via radio broadcasting. The war years marked the apogee of radio drama. Many radio plays on war themes were programmed in serial format; for example, writer Arch Oboler created a series titled *Plays for Americans* in 1942 and another, *Free World Theatre*, in 1943, both for NBC.[78] Norman Corwin, later named 'America's most prominent playwright' in a 1947 *New Yorker* essay,[79] was a prolific writer whose radio series included *Norman Corwin's Words Without Music* (1938), *Pursuit of Happiness* (1940), *26 By Corwin* (1941), *An American in England* with Edward R. Murrow (1942), *This Is War* (1942) and *Columbia Presents Corwin* (1944), all for CBS. Eight days after Pearl Harbor, CBS broadcasted Corwin's programme celebrating the 150th anniversary of the US Bill of Rights, 'We Hold These Truths'. Corwin's most remembered work, 'On a Note of Triumph', was commissioned by CBS to be ready to perform live on radio as soon as Germany's surrender was announced; its 8 May 1945 broadcast is yet regarded as one of the high points in radio history. A recording of 'On a Note of Triumph' became a bestseller, and many of Corwin's radio plays are published in anthologies of his work. Another well-regarded series was NBC's *Words at War* (1943–5), with occasionally-tendentious radio plays on a variety of war themes.

The War Department quickly recognized the reach and power of radio, and launched its Armed Forces Radio Service (AFRS) in May 1942. Most of its programming was aimed at servicemen on military bases at home and abroad, but NBC worked with the AFRS on a series titled *They Call Me Joe*, with plays about American GIs of various ethnic ancestries, and that series went out also to general audiences.[80] Also for both military and home consumption, the *Chaplain Jim* (1942) series on NBC's Blue network arose from a military initiative seeking programmes to reassure families that their sons in the service had a source of spiritual guidance; listeners thought of the title character as a real person and wrote letters to him (all answered by the Adjutant General's office).[81] The future playwriting team of Jerome Lawrence and Robert E. Lee began their long collaboration in 1942 as writers for AFRS for which they created series and wrote numerous radio plays. The rise of network television after 1947 brought an end to the market for radio drama, and indeed to radio itself as a news and entertainment medium. 'Ironically,' according to Ray Barfield, 'the decade of the 1940s, which seemed to solidify the maturing medium's place in American popular culture, would be radio's last decade of uncontested dominance.'[82]

The war years, 1942–5

Broadway plays and musicals

Broadway actually perked up in production quality and in ticket sales once the die was cast that the country was at war. The marquees were dimmed to save electricity, but wartime prosperity kept the theatres going strong even as ticket prices gradually edged higher, up to $4.80 for a straight play by 1945. Audiences craved comedies and – if skilfully handled – patriotic themes. The 1942–3 season, according to Bruce D. McClung, was 'when the theater began in earnest to reflect the war experience'.[83] In a *New York Times* article (16 May 1943), Martha Dreiblatt raised the issue of 'what the theatre should be in wartime' and gathered opinions. Producer John Golden responded that 'people don't want the war in their theatrical entertainment. They want escape.' Actress Helen

Hayes acknowledged the importance of escapist entertainment for war workers. Playwright Elmer Rice wanted to see 'good plays on many themes' especially in a time when the theatre was 'flourishing' again 'because people have more money to spend'. He noted that 'the biggest hits today are by old-timers. Kingsley, Anderson, Wilder.' Director Shepard Traube similarly looked beyond war plays as a category: 'We must find out what we are going to die for or not die for, and state or restate that cogently in the theatre.' Actor Horace Braham, approached by Dreiblatt while he was volunteering at the Stage Door Canteen, spoke eloquently:

> What the theatre should be at all times, as I see it, is the giver of that rare, Dionysiac pleasure which the theatre at its best can give. It is to experience this that people go to the theatre thirty times in the hope of finding it at least once. And having found it once will hopefully return again and again in spite of disappointments. That's its most precious contribution in war or any other time – that enriching of the spirit.

Dreiblatt tallied over thirty plays on war themes on Broadway during the 18 months after Pearl Harbor. Of those 30 plays, she designated eight successes: Irving Berlin's *This Is the Army*, *The Doughgirls* by Joseph Fields, *Janie* by Josephine Bentham and Herschel Williams, Maxwell Anderson's *The Eve of St. Mark*, Sidney Kingsley's *The Patriots* (New York Drama Critics' Circle Award), Thornton Wilder's *The Skin of Our Teeth*, and *Harriet* by Florence Ryerson and Colin Clement, in which Helen Hayes starred as Harriet Beecher Stowe.[84] Wilder's Pulitzer Prize-winning *The Skin of Our Teeth* arrived early in that season, a puzzling work for many, but exuberantly produced; its wartime resonances are discussed in Chapter 4. Apart from the war theme, comedies in the 1942–3 season that achieved or exceeded respectable 100-performance runs included Philip Barry's *Without Love*, starring Katharine Hepburn; S. N. Behrman's *The Pirate*, starring Alfred Lunt and Lynne Fontanne; and F. Hugh Herbert's *Kiss and Tell*, whose teenage protagonist became the basis for the long-running radio series 'Meet Corliss Archer' (1943–56) and even three issues of a comic book series in 1948.

The 1943–4 season again brought a mix of wartime concerns and escapist fare: Moss Hart's *Winged Victory*, produced as a benefit for the Army Emergency Relief Fund; John Van Druten's *The Voice of the Turtle*, which became a long-time staple of community theatres; Ruth Gordon's *Over 21*, starring herself and directed by George S. Kaufman; Maxwell Anderson's *Storm Operation*; Zoe Akins's final Broadway production, *Mrs. January and Mr. X*, starring Billie Burke; and Lillian Hellman's *The Searching Wind*. Broadway was especially thriving in 1944–5, with every theatre booked and a dozen shows sold out long in advance. The American Negro Theatre's production of *Anna Lucasta* by Philip Yordan transferred to Broadway to critical acclaim and a 957-performance run, featuring strong acting by Canada Lee, Rosetta LeNoire and Frederick O'Neal. John Van Druten adapted Kathryn Forbes's memoir as the sentimental comedy favourite *I Remember Mama*. Mary Chase's long-beloved *Harvey* featured vaudeville comedian Frank Fay as Elwood P. Dowd, whose chosen companion is the tall and invisible rabbit Harvey; the droll comedy won the Pulitzer Prize and ran for 1,775 performances. The season also included George S. Kaufman and John P. Marquand's *The Late George Apley*, Arthur Miller's debut, *The Man Who Had All the Luck*, which got four performances, Norman Krasna's *Dear Ruth*, John Patrick's *The Hasty Heart*, Clare Kummer's *Many Happy Returns*, *Dark of the Moon* by Howard Richardson and William Berney, and Tennessee Williams's *The Glass Menagerie*. These and many other plays went on to long popularity throughout a vast nationwide network of community theatres.

Musicals truly came into their own during the decade and contributed to what historians now see as 'the golden age of Broadway'. Because so many early-career composers and lyricists had been lured to Hollywood with the rise of sound pictures and because many of them were drafted, the great musicals during the war years tended to be the work of a relatively small number of established artists: Irving Berlin, Cole Porter, Richard Rodgers, Oscar Hammerstein II, Guy Bolton, Harold Arlen, E. Y. Harburg, Harold Rome, Vernon Duke and Howard Dietz. Because many of them had been tempered by the First World War and the Depression, according to Gerald Bordman, 'these writers and composers had become less optimistic, less flashy. They led the American musical theatre into a more sober, sentimental era' and 'it was the escapist turnback to real or exaggerated joys of a bygone Americana that became the war's impressive and lasting contribution to the lyric stage'.[85] Ethan Mordden attributes the reinvigoration of the musical during this period to the unexpectedly successful pairing of composer Richard Rodgers and the operetta-formed lyricist-librettist Oscar Hammerstein II, who together discovered through *Oklahoma!* (1943) how to foreground story and character, with musical numbers that emerged seemingly naturally from their dramatic moment.[86] The final collaboration of Richard Rodgers with his pre-Hammerstein lyricist Lorenz Hart, *By Jupiter* (1942), had featured dancer Ray Bolger and was poised for a long run but closed after Bolger left on a USO tour; Hart died in 1943. The death in 1942 of Broadway's legendary song-and-dance man, George M. Cohan, also marked the end of the old era.

In *Something for the Boys* (1943), with Cole Porter's music and lyrics in a book by siblings Herbert and Dorothy Fields, Ethel Merman introduced songs that included 'Hey, Good-Lookin'' and other numbers calculated to appeal to the boys in uniform. Then came the phenomenal *Oklahoma!* (1943), to be discussed below. In the 1943-4 season, Mary Martin wore gowns by Mainbocher for her title role in *One Touch of Venus* (1943), which boasted music by Kurt Weill, lyrics by Ogden Nash, book by Nash and S. J. Perlman and choreography by Agnes de Mille. Alan Jay Lerner and Frederick Loewe began their long, fruitful collaboration in 1943 with the relatively unremarkable *What's Up?* Borrowing Georges Bizet's score from the opera *Carmen*, Oscar Hammerstein II created *Carmen Jones* (1943) for an all-black cast and it ran for 503 performances. *Mexican Hayride* (1944) was another success with Cole Porter's songs in a book by Dorothy and Herbert Fields, not to mention big-budget production values and June Havoc in the leading role. *Follow the Girls* (1944), set in a servicemen's canteen, which served as a pretext for lots of specialty numbers, at least touched upon the wartime context.

The 1944-5 season brought *Song of Norway* (1944), which incorporated melodies by Edvard Grieg in episodes from the composer's life, along with plenty of nostalgic Norwegian folk ethnicity. *Bloomer Girl* (1944) by composer Harold Arlen and lyricist E. Y. Harburg clearly took inspiration from *Oklahoma!* in its combination of a nostalgic American historical past and thought-provoking material (women's capacity for more than wifedom), along with ballets by Agnes de Mille and a leading role for Celeste Holm fresh from her triumph as Ado Annie.

Sadie Thompson (1944), on the other hand, was saddled with a protagonist's role that could never resonate with what women wanted to see in wartime, even though its progenitor, the 1920s sex melodrama *Rain*, had successfully shocked and titillated audiences. This musical, composed by Vernon Duke with lyrics by Howard Dietz, could not be saved even with June Havoc as Miss Sadie Thompson. Billy Rose produced a legendarily lavish revue, *The Seven Lively Arts* (1944), studded with big names, to reopen the fabulous Ziegfeld Theatre (a Thomas Lamb/Joseph Urban-designed theatre that had been used for movies since 1933) on the third anniversary of Pearl Harbor, but few of the songs or comic bits sparkled enough to pull it beyond 182 performances and repay the investment. For *On the Town* (1944), composer Leonard Bernstein and choreographer Jerome Robbins expanded the concept of their 1943 ballet *Fancy Free*: three sailors spend their 24 hours of shore leave in New York City looking for girls. Betty Comden and Adolph Green wrote a book for it and shared lyric writing with Bernstein. George Abbott directed and Oliver Smith designed the sets. The fast-paced action with much of the stage time taken over by energetic dancing gave *On the Town* its zany yet ultimately poignant quality. Its songs such as 'New York, New York' and 'Lucky to Be Me' still resonate with audiences.

Sigmund Romberg's musical sensibility based in operetta returned to Broadway after his long absence; for his 55th Broadway score he collaborated with book and lyric writers Herbert and Dorothy Fields on *Up in Central Park* (1945) and it got a substantial run of 504 performances.[87] Rodgers and Hammerstein had another hit with their second collaboration, *Carousel* (1945), using American regionalism as they had in *Oklahoma!*, this time drawing upon New England as evoked in the song 'This Was a Real Nice Clambake'. For all its celebrated innovations in musical comedy, *Oklahoma!* mostly pleased war-weary audiences through its nostalgic glimpse of a specific American not-too-distant past. Possibly that inspired the resurgence of operetta that occurred early in the 1945–6 season: *Marinka*, *Mr. Strauss Goes to Boston*, *Polonaise* and revivals of *The Gypsy Baron*, *Show Boat* and *The Desert Song*. These musical comedy seasons also boasted African-American shows: *Blue Holiday* (1945), starring Ethel Waters and featuring the Katherine Dunham Dancers with the Hall Johnson Choir; *Memphis Bound!* (1945), with the great tap dancer Bill 'Bojangles'

Robinson; *Carib Song* (1945), as another vehicle for the Katherine Dunham Dancers; and *St. Louis Woman* (1946), starring Ruby Hill and Rex Ingram with a score by Harold Arlen and Johnny Mercer.

This Is the Army

Three shows from the war years merit closer study: two are musicals – Irving Berlin's *This Is the Army* (1942) and Rodgers and Hammerstein's *Oklahoma!* (1943) – and the third is a landmark production of Shakespeare's *Othello* starring Paul Robeson on Broadway in 1943. *This Is the Army* recycled elements of Irving Berlin's First World War soldier show, *Yip, Yip, Yaphank* (1918). Berlin had already retrieved an old song he wrote in 1918 but had not used then; when Kate Smith asked him for a patriotic song to sing at the end of her 1938 Armistice Day radio broadcast, Berlin made a few revisions in the words and the melody of 'God Bless America' and gave it to her. The song stirred the public as no song had done since George M. Cohan's 'Over There'. The sheet music sales were phenomenal, and Kate Smith sang 'God Bless America' on her weekly broadcasts thereafter.[88] Berlin soon established a trust that would relay all the revenues from the song to the Boy Scouts and Girl Scouts of America.[89]

By 1942, Irving Berlin was thinking of reviving his earlier soldier show, and the War Department had the same idea. In putting together his new show, *This Is the Army*, Berlin kept the previous format, an all-soldier cast in a series of sketches with even the female roles played by soldiers in drag. However, he wrote ten new songs, notably 'I Left My Heart at the Stage Door Canteen' and 'I'm Getting Tired So I Can Sleep'. From the earlier show, Berlin retained the rousing 'This Is the Army, Mr. Jones' and the song he reserved for himself in a show-stopping moment, the 'eleven o'clock number' near the end of the second act: 'Oh, How I Hate to Get Up in the Morning'. In 1918, Private Irving Berlin had been promoted to sergeant to give him the authority he needed to get the show on. In 1942 the 53-year-old civilian Irving Berlin had his celebrity and the Army's backing to cut through military red tape and make it all work. He chose his own production staff and cast from among enlisted men nationwide who had some performance experience. Staff Sergeant Ezra Stone, who directed *This Is the Army*, had performed on radio and directed on Broadway. Corporal Milton Rosenstock became music director, and Corporal Alan Anderson, with three years of professional stage management experience, was stage manager. Anderson (son of playwright Maxwell Anderson and author of a 2004 memoir about the show) had expected a temporary diversion, but ended up working on the show during its subsequent tours to Europe, the Middle East, the South Pacific and the Philippines: that is, 'every performance for three and a half years as the production stage manager and first sergeant of the Army company'.[90] Irving Berlin, 'Mr B' to the men, stayed in the show for all but the Middle East portion, when he was called to other responsibilities. Some 310 soldiers formed the original company that opened on 4 July 1942 at the large Broadway Theatre. Berlin had insisted upon including African-American performers, whom he featured in a stylish production number titled 'That's What the Well-Dressed Man in Harlem Will Wear'. Thus *This Is the Army* was racially integrated even before the Army was. According to Berlin's daughter Mary Ellin Barrett, the show brought 'blacks and whites together in the first and only integrated division in the US Army'.[91] On Broadway and on tour, 'the company accepted no invitations unless the entire company was included'[92] and presented a unified front in demanding equal accommodations.[93] According to Alan Anderson, 'the biggest star of all our black guys was an incredible comic dancer, Sergeant James A. Cross, known in the vaudeville world as "Stump Cross"'.[94] All proceeds from the show and the songs in it went to the Army Emergency Relief Fund; *This Is the Army* raised funds even as it raised morale.

After playing eight sell-out performances for twelve weeks on Broadway, *This Is the Army* went on the road. The tour began in Washington, DC, at the request of President and Mrs Franklin D. Roosevelt, who attended a special matinee for an enthusiastic all-soldier audience in the second week of the run. At a post-performance White House supper on 9 October 1942, all of the men were charmed by Eleanor Roosevelt, who made a point of sitting at each of the 31 tables in turn. As Alan Anderson recalled, she 'chatted with us about the show, about us, about the war. She was incredible. She took in everything; she responded to everything and to every one of us.'[95] The tour went on to Pittsburgh, Philadelphia, Baltimore, Boston, Cleveland, Cincinnati, St Louis, Detroit, Chicago, Los Angeles and San Francisco. Then the company returned to Los

Angeles for three months while Warner Brothers combined the stage company with some Hollywood actors (including Ronald Reagan to play the stage manager) to produce the movie version. The movie version of *This Is the Army* added over $10 million dollars to the Army Emergency Relief Fund.[96] Then came word from General George C. Marshall that he wanted the show to go to London to bolster ties with Britain. That resulted in the hard task of trimming the company from 300 to 150 and reworking the show for soldier audiences in war zones. The chorus was cut from 171 men to 60.[97] Racially, the international touring company tallied 149 whites and 16 blacks.[98] The renovated show opened triumphantly at the London Palladium on 10 November 1943 and played to celebrity-studded audiences. Then it travelled to Glasgow, Manchester, Liverpool, Birmingham, Bristol, Bournemouth, Belfast and back to London for two performances at Her Majesty's Theatre for military personnel only. After one of the London performances, General Dwight D. Eisenhower appeared and spoke movingly of the importance of the show and his wish to have it seen by every American soldier. And that took the show on to a new phase of touring. They played two weeks to 40,000 troops at the Teatro San Carlo in Naples, which had been liberated by the Allies, then travelled to Santa Maria, near the combat zone. The first performance for men straight from the fighting front was a revelation: the zombie-like men who sat unexpressively before the opening curtain were transformed, refreshed, exhilarated. Beyond his role in the show, Irving Berlin tirelessly entertained in hospitals. *This Is the Army* went to Rome upon its liberation, then Egypt, the Persian Gulf Command and Australia. Between engagements, company members would entertain in hospitals. Anderson recalled:

> We played for thousands of Allied servicemen and women that were stationed all over this east end of New Guinea – US, British, Australian – nurses, Red Cross, WACs. We did short shows and long shows. The audiences were huge and hungry for us – thousands from every imaginable service; 8,000 one day, 10,000 the next. These shows were all unscheduled, arranged within hours, put on just anywhere they could gather an audience.[99]

For five months in the Pacific the company lived on a ship and performed the show on a different island every few days for audiences ranging from 6,000 to 12,000.[100] The final portion of the wartime tour took the show to various ports in the Philippines and the Mariana Islands. It was there that they learned of the death of President Roosevelt and, three weeks later, V-E Day, 8 May 1945. After V-J Day, 2 September 1945, the company continued performing for Americans still stationed in Okinawa, Iwo Jima and finally the Hawaiian Islands. After the closing performance in Honolulu, Irving Berlin spoke movingly of the teamwork by which the men had done their part to win the war.

Oklahoma!

While *This Is the Army* exemplifies wartime spirit in a musical (not to mention the contributions to morale and charitable funds by the USA's greatest songwriter), *Oklahoma!* (1943) stands as a watershed achievement in the development of American musical comedy. As John Lahr observed:

> In its out-of-town tryouts, the show, then titled 'Away We Go!', was billed as a 'musical comedy'; by the time it arrived in New York, with its now indelible brand name, it had become a 'musical play'. With that semantic mutation, the musical's job description changed, virtually overnight ... [It was] an artful marriage of music and lyrics that traded in narrative. Seriousness replaced sass. Big names were no longer needed to carry the show; the show itself was the star.[101]

Theresa Helburn, one of the founders of the Theatre Guild, may be credited with the idea of making a musical version of Lynn Riggs's 1931 play *Green Grow the Lilacs*, set in 1900 in Indian Territory (the future state of Oklahoma) among the simple folk that Riggs had known in his childhood there. Riggs had chosen to keep the story simple in order to expand upon a range of moods from sweetness to a melodramatic irruption of evil: the cowboy Curly loves Laurey, but their happiness as a couple is threatened by the sinister hired hand Jeeter Fry (a name that evoked the loathsome Jeeter Lester of *Tobacco Road* but was changed to Jud Fry in the musical). The Theatre Guild premiered the play in 1931 in a lovely production that could not sustain a run beyond eight weeks as the Great Depression was tightening its grip. Helburn had always believed that the material deserved a wider audience and in 1940 she approached Richard Rodgers, who was enthusiastic but was having difficulties with his long-time collaborator Lorenz Hart. Composer Rodgers and lyricist Hart had first been professionally paired by the Theatre Guild in 1925 for the *Garrick Gaieties* and had a long string of successes leading up to *Pal Joey* (1940) and *By Jupiter* (1942). But Hart's drinking problem led Rodgers to seek out a school friend, lyricist Oscar Hammerstein II, as a potential future collaborator. Hammerstein was best known for his book and lyrics for *Show Boat* (1927), with music by Jerome Kern, but by 1942 had endured quite a few flops and was no longer among the most acclaimed Broadway lyricists. The new team, Rodgers and Hammerstein, was regarded as a risky unknown quantity, but Rodgers and Hammerstein both loved the play *Green Grow the Lilacs*, and their working methods clicked together. Whereas Hart had needed Rodgers's melodies before he could write lyrics, Hammerstein preferred to write the lyrics first and Rodgers would then set them to music.[102] According to Denny Martin Flinn, 'this new method was as large a step as any other toward the greatness of the American musical, for it codified the increasing emphasis on the drama and the ideas'.[103] The method suited both of them and resulted in the greatest collaboration in American musical comedy history. The words and music for each dramatic moment and character fit so seamlessly that, as Stephen Sondheim later observed, in contrast to other musicals, which could readily absorb songs from various sources, you could not 'move songs from *Oklahoma!* to *Carousel*'.[104] As Rodgers and Hammerstein wrestled with staying true to the spirit of the play, they made the conscious decision to defy musical comedy convention that called for an opening number with a fabulously-costumed chorus of pretty girls. Instead, the curtain opened on an older woman working a butter churn and an offstage solo male voice singing 'Oh, What a Beautiful Mornin''.[105] Rodgers warned Alfred Drake, who played Curly, that this song was 'only to set the scene ... it's *not* an applause-getter'.[106]

Complicating the venture was the Theatre Guild's precarious financial condition. The Guild's artistic prestige masked the fact that in 1942 it was verging on bankruptcy. Indeed, the theatre itself was sold that year; thus rehearsals for *Oklahoma!* put a Guild company on that stage for the last time; the show itself went into the St James Theatre. Theresa Helburn struggled valiantly and often fruitlessly to amass the financial backing needed to get the show on. To produce a show about cowpokes with nobody of star stature in the cast seemed irresponsibly risky in the wake of the Guild's recent flops, and the work in progress became known as 'Helburn's Folly'.[107] Helburn sent the script to potential backers and held endless auditions of the songs for them while she hounded MGM to take an option on the film rights. Her persistence in the face of so many rejections and negative reactions to the work in progress is simply remarkable. Finally she persuaded Columbia Pictures producer Harry Cohn and New York producer Max Gordon each to invest $15,000 of their own money. The Theatre Guild needed $100,000 to capitalize the show that would become *Oklahoma!* Helburn eventually reached that goal with only 28 investors,[108] many of whom expected to lose their money.

Having raised the funding to go ahead, Helburn assembled the production team. Rouben Mamoulian had been directing in Hollywood and took a substantial pay cut to direct the Broadway musical. Choreographer Agnes de Mille had worked in Hollywood and in ballet, but was completely untested in musical comedy. Finding the right set and costume designers proved easier, for both Lemuel Ayers and Miles White had designed for the Theatre Guild and were in tune with the material as well as with the budgetary constraints. Ayers used bold colours behind minimalist set props to evoke the bright Oklahoma skies and cornfields in contrast to Jud Fry's dreary smokehouse lodging. Miles White turned to a 1901 Montgomery Ward catalogue to understand what the characters would have aspired to wear.[109] Alfred Drake and Joan Roberts were cast as Curly and Laurey with Howard Da Silva as Jud Fry and Betty Garde as Aunt Eller. For the comedic side, Celeste Holm's Ado Annie played off Lee Dixon as Will Parker and Joseph Buloff as the peddler Ali Hakim. The casting of the dance ensemble became rather fraught as Agnes de Mille insisted on dancers of genuine rigour even if they did not match the kind of pretty faces expected of a Broadway chorus. It was de Mille's idea to create the dance of cigarette-card girls that pulled together the material of the first act and 'introduced a dark suspenseful ominous note' in contrast to the 'innocuous gingham-aprony Sunday-school' tone of the show up to that point. Showing the kind of dance-hall female who possessed Jud Fry's dark dreams gave the story a needed boost to hold the audience beyond intermission.[110] Helburn's great artistic contribution on top of her fundraising was to mention to Hammerstein during the rehearsal period that she wished the show had a song about the land itself; the result was what became the title song in the prime spot – the 'eleven o'clock number' – near the end of the second act. But for the New Haven tryout performances, the show was still titled with a square-dancing call: *Away We Go!*

The split-week New Haven tryout was expensive for the Theatre Guild and did not go particularly well. After the opening night first act, one press representative wired the judgement that famously ran in Walter Winchell's column the next day: 'No Legs, No Jokes, No Chance'. During that same intermission, investor Max Gordon was having serious doubts and welcomed the approach of two audience members who asked to buy in. Gordon elatedly lightened his personal financial burden by $5,000, and the two who each gave him a cheque for $2,500 that night – like other brave investors in the show – eventually reaped a 2,500 per cent return on what they had put in. Tryouts continued at Boston's Colonial Theatre with a heavily cut and much revised show, with changes always geared to the principle of advancing the plot or illuminating a character. Celeste Holm recalled that Hammerstein wrote an encore for Ado Annie's 'I Cain't Say No', and it was the funniest part of the song; she also admired 'the skill with which they knew what to put in and what to take out'.[111] Although Boston audiences and critics were favourably receptive, the show still needed something. The change was complicated, prepared in haste by arranger Robert Russell Bennett and rehearsed by the entire cast on their day off; it involved having the 'eleven o'clock number' sung not in unison but in harmony. The song 'Oklahoma' 'propelled *Oklahoma!* into a smash hit'.[112]

So many obstacles arose during those out-of-town tryouts and even on opening night in New York: the frantic rewrites and elimination of entire well-rehearsed numbers, the unending search for more funding, the measles that swept through the singers and dancers, the snow turning to sleet on opening night, the unsold seats in the St James that were hastily filled by pulling in servicemen from the street, the injured dancers who danced on through pain, the reviews destined to see print on April Fool's Day. The company pulled through and the euphoric audience on the night of 31 March 1943 participated in a historic turning point for American musical theatre history. The hummable melodies, charming lyrics, dazzling dances, golden glow of the visuals and the emotions, the sheer down-home Americanism of it: all added up to the greatest possible respite from the privations of the war's dreariest year and a reinvigoration of the spirit. The advance sales soared. The Theatre Guild was saved. Careers were launched.

A new Broadway musical practice was inaugurated: the original cast album. The company and orchestra recorded all the songs on a set of 78-rpm records, one number per side, and Decca put the heavy, breakable records in sleeves between cardboard covers with production photographs on the endpapers. Sales surpassed one million albums.[113] The sheet music for 'People Will Say We're in Love' sold 9,000 copies a day and the song topped the radio charts in 1943.[114] *Oklahoma!* ran for five years and nine weeks (2,212 performances) on Broadway. The national touring company had ten years on the road and was seen by eight million people. The London company opened at Drury Lane in 1947 for a record-breaking run there, 'the second-longest run in London's theatrical history'. Worldwide there have been over 600 productions each year.[115] *Oklahoma!* is still going strong.

The Paul Robeson *Othello*

Almost seven months after *Oklahoma!*'s opening, legitimate drama could also boast a trailblazing work. The Theatre Guild's 1943 *Othello*, destined to hold the record as the longest-running Shakespeare production on Broadway, starred a black actor in the title role opposite a white actress as Desdemona. The great African-American singer-actor Paul Robeson had first achieved renown as a concert artist with his lifelong accompanist Lawrence Brown. Robeson began acting in the 1920s, notably playing the title role in the 1924 revival of Eugene O'Neill's *The Emperor Jones* and opening ten days later in O'Neill's racially controversial *All God's Chillun Got Wings*. He went on to win extraordinary acclaim in the 1928 London production of *Show Boat* and to play Othello there in 1930 opposite young Peggy Ashcroft. Twelve years after his London Othello, Robeson had matured as an actor and was ready to tackle the role again and to take it to American audiences, this time under the direction of the British actress-director Margaret

Webster. In Robeson's long, distinguished career, Othello would be his only Shakespearean role, but he played it three times (the third in 1959 in Stratford-upon-Avon). 'By all odds,' according to Martin Duberman, 'the Broadway *Othello* was the most distinguished and historic of the three.'[116] However, that success did not come easily.

When Robeson and Webster decided to work together on *Othello*, she approached numerous producers who turned down the project for fear of reprisals against the pairing of a white actress with a black actor portraying a truly black Othello instead of a tawny Moor. Nor could Webster get any big-name actors to take the roles of Iago and Desdemona. The casting difficulty proved fortuitous when Webster signed a husband and wife who were looking for an opportunity to perform together and whose careers were just on the verge of gaining recognition: José Ferrer and Uta Hagen. Margaret Webster herself took the role of Emilia as a matter of expediency. Without a producing organization behind them, Webster and Robeson sought summer theatre bookings and found courageous managers to book them at Cambridge's Brattle Theatre and Princeton's McCarter Theatre. Webster and Robeson's intuition that audiences in university communities might exhibit relative openness toward the provocative venture proved correct. The sweating opening night audience in the Brattle on 10 August 1942 ignored the sweltering heat as they avidly bought into the action on stage. The performance culminated in unbridled applause, stomping feet, bravos, cheering. Although both Webster and Uta Hagen had privately expressed reservations about Robeson's lack of technique as an actor and the seeming artifice of his operatic vocal quality, audiences as well as critics thrilled to his commanding presence and vitality, his 'combined charismatic grandeur and innocence'.[117] The Cambridge run sold out immediately and Princeton continued the momentum. According to the *Variety* critic, no white actor could ever again presume to play Othello.[118]

Now producers clamoured to bring the production to Broadway, and Margaret Webster contracted with the Theatre Guild to remount the production the following year, after Robeson had completed his other commitments – concert engagements and political speaking. After tryouts in New Haven, Boston and Philadelphia, *Othello* opened at New York's Shubert Theatre on

19 October 1943 with the same actors in the principal roles and with settings by Robert Edmond Jones. Robeson took a financial loss to play Othello for $1,500 dollars a week when he could have continued his concert tours at $2,000 or more for each evening; moreover, he claimed that his energy expenditure in a performance of *Othello* was that of three concerts.[119] He worked hard to refine his performance, to find deeper characterization with less reliance on physical and vocal monumentality. 'Magic happened', Webster wrote to her mother about the Broadway opening. The ovations were largely for Robeson, and he got ten curtain calls.[120] Robeson's biographer Martin Duberman cites a Soviet journalist who called that opening 'the moment when "the doors of the American theatre opened for the Negro people"'.[121] Reviewers particularly praised Webster's directing. The box office boomed, and every performance played to standing room only.[122] However, Webster left the cast in March over a disagreement with Robeson, who insisted on star billing for Uta Hagen and José Ferrer. Certainly, it was this production that made celebrities of them, and they remained ever grateful to Robeson for his support.[123]

The 296-performance run that ended on 1 July 1944 set the yet-unsurpassed record for Shakespeare on Broadway. Columbia Records made a cast recording of the play, but those involved later judged it woefully inadequate as a representation of the production. Robeson saw his role as Othello as an opportunity 'to convey the dignity and humanity of his people ... Robeson also used his success as Othello to speak out for racial equality.'[124] In September the production embarked upon a thirty-six-week tour that took the company to forty-five cities in seventeen states and Canada. Since Hagen and Ferrer had become close friends with Robeson, the tour exposed them to the depth and variety of difficulties experienced by a black man travelling in integrated company. Robeson's biographer Martin Bauml Duberman describes Robeson's ability to rise above the indignities or to use his charm to turn the tables or to play one of several social roles he had developed to defuse a situation.[125] The company had played *Othello* 587 times when it opened on 22 May 1945 for another New York engagement, two weeks at the City Center.[126] Paul Robeson would go on to more triumphs and travails, but his 1943 Othello stands as a trailblazing and defining accomplishment for African-Americans in the arts.

Post-war theatre, 1946–50

African-American theatre

Several plays on African-American themes appeared on Broadway after the war and featured integrated casts, although apart from Theodore Ward, the authors were white. José Ferrer moved from playing Iago in *Othello* to directing a mixed-race production of *Strange Fruit* (1945) by Lillian and Esther Smith, in which Jane White made her Broadway debut as a black girl seduced and abandoned by a white boy, and the play achieved a 60-performance run. Arnaud D'Usseau and James Gow's *Deep Are the Roots* (1945), a long-running melodrama – 477 performances plus a London engagement – showed a black war hero's return to his Southern home town where he is falsely accused and beaten. *On Whitman Avenue* (1946) by Maxine Wood focused on the difficulties encountered by a black veteran (Canada Lee) and his wife (Perry Wilson) when they move into a white neighbourhood; it ran for 150 performances at the Cort Theatre. Ossie Davis and Ruby Dee made their debuts in the short-lived *Jeb* (1946) by Robert Ardry. *Our Lan'* (1947), Theodore Ward's post-Civil War historical drama of racial conflict, opened Off-Broadway at the Henry Street Settlement House and moved to Broadway for a brief run.

Alice Childress, an actress in the original company of the American Negro Theatre, made her playwriting debut in 1949 with *Florence*, a one-act play for a Negro woman and a white woman, and it launched her as a dramatist whose major plays include *Trouble in Mind* (1955) and *Wedding Band* (1963).[127] Owen Dodson began writing documentary dramas for radio during his two years in the US Navy (1940–2). That work led to Dodson's commission by the Negro Labor Victory Committee to write and direct a war-rallying pageant that also touched on black and Jewish labour issues; *New World A-Coming* was performed at Madison Square Garden on 26 June 1944 with Canada Lee and Abbie Mitchell heading the cast and an audience of approximately 25,000.[128] Dodson continued writing plays and poetry as a professor at Howard University, where students performed his *Bayou Legend* (1948). In 1949 the State Department sponsored the Howard Players on a ten-week tour to Scandinavia and Germany with their all-black productions of Ibsen's *The Wild Duck* and DuBose Heyward's *Mamba's Daughters*.[129]

Mention must also be made of actor Canada Lee's other work in the decade: a role in Alfred Hitchcock's 1943 movie *Lifeboat*, an acclaimed Othello in a performance on 2 April 1944 – even as Robeson was playing the role on Broadway – at the Studio Theatre of the New School, narrator of thirty-four episodes in the radio series *New World A-Comin'* (1944–45), Caliban in *The Tempest* (1945) directed by Margaret Webster and, using whiteface make-up, Bosola in the Jacobean classic *The Duchess of Malfi* (1946).[130] The latter was not a gimmick but a decision by the producers 'to de-emphasize race, make it less visible, in order to focus on the dramatic narrative and Lee's talent',[131] a purpose with which Lee fully agreed in terms of his quest for recognition as an actor, not as a 'Negro actor', selected by the producer as 'the man he considered the best actor for a role regardless of color'.[132]

The late 1940s also saw continuing efforts to fully desegregate the theatre. Maxwell Anderson, Lillian Hellman and others had earlier worked to draft a set of principles for the Emergency Committee of the Entertainment Industry (ECEI), calling for 'the treatment of blacks as equals in all presentations' on stage, screen or radio, but the ECEI ended in 1944.[133] While rehearsing *Strange Fruit*, José Ferrer published 'The Negro in the American Theatre' in *Variety* (9 January 1946) and pledged never to perform before a segregated audience.[134] Actors' Equity led a push against segregated seating in theatres in Baltimore and Washington, DC. The Washington, DC, performances of *Joan of Lorraine* in October 1946 were picketed because the theatre would not even sell tickets to blacks.[135] By August 1947, Actors' Equity planned to boycott Washington's National Theatre to end its segregated seating.[136]

Broadway plays and musicals

Immediately following the war, new plays were in short supply, but the stimulus of the Theatre Guild's playwriting competitions would eventually pay off as their early support for Tennessee Williams and Arthur Miller led to *A Streetcar Named Desire* (1947) and *Death of a Salesman* (1949) and their many other plays. Meanwhile, there were revivals and classics: Shakespeare's *The Tempest* in 1945, in

1946 the *Hamlet* Maurice Evans had toured for GI audiences, and in 1947 *Antony and Cleopatra* with Katharine Cornell; Bernard Shaw's *Candida* in 1946, *Man and Superman* in 1947, *John Bull's Other Island* and *You Never Can Tell*, both in 1948. The year 1946 brought a mixed bag of revivals: Edmond Rostand's *Cyrano de Bergerac*, Oscar Wilde's *Lady Windermere's Fan*, Ben Hecht and Charles MacArthur's 1928 newspaper play *The Front Page*, J. M. Synge's *The Playboy of the Western World*, and the 1927 tawdry showbiz comedy *Burlesque*. That year also saw Eva Le Gallienne's first attempt to create an art theatre, the short-lived American Repertory Theatre, co-founded with Cheryl Crawford and Margaret Webster; it opened with Shakespeare's *King Henry VIII* starring Victor Jory.

The new plays of the later part of the decade exhibit variety of theme and style, as exemplified by the few highlights noted here. Howard Lindsay and Russel Crouse had two hits in 1945: *The Hasty Heart* and their Pulitzer Prize-winning *State of the Union*. Tennessee Williams also had two Broadway plays in 1945: *The Glass Menagerie* and a minor play, *You Touched Me!*, written with Donald Windham. *The Glass Menagerie* deservedly won the New York Drama Critics' Circle Award in 1945, but the Pulitzer that year went to *Harvey*. In 1946 the Pulitzer went to *State of the Union*, while the Drama Critics signalled *Carousel* as best musical, but found no play worthy of an award. In 1947 Eugene O'Neill's *The Iceman Cometh* was strangely overlooked, as no Pulitzer was awarded for drama; the Drama Critics' Circle Awards went to *All My Sons* for best play, to Alan Jay Lerner and Frederick Loewe's *Brigadoon* for best musical and to Jean-Paul Sartre's *No Exit* for best foreign play. Also in 1947, the American Theatre Wing created the Antoinette Perry Awards, popularly known as the Tony Awards, to honour distinguished achievement in the theatre and to honour the memory of Antoinette Perry (1888–1946), who had led the Wing all during the Second World War.

The Tony Awards expanded recognition beyond the work of the playwright and even encompassed special awards for a variety of contributions. In 1947, Tony Awards for acting went to Ingrid Bergman for *Joan of Lorraine* and Helen Hayes for *Happy Birthday*, and to José Ferrer for *Cyrano de Bergerac* and Fredric March for *Years Ago*; March was the first to win both a Tony and an Academy Award (*The Best Years of Our Lives*) in the same year.[137] *All My Sons* garnered 1947 Tony Awards for both the playwright and for director Elia Kazan. Lucinda Ballard's costumes for five productions that season were recognized with a Tony. In scenic design the Tony went to David Ffolkes for *Henry VIII*. For choreography, Agnes de Mille (*Brigadoon*) and Michael Kidd (*Finian's Rainbow*) each got a Tony. In 1948, *A Streetcar Named Desire* took the Pulitzer and the Drama Critics' Awards, but the Tony Awards for best play, best producer and best director (Joshua Logan) went to *Mister Roberts*. Top acting awards went to Henry Fonda, Paul Kelly, Basil Rathbone, Judith Anderson, Katharine Cornell and Jessica Tandy. Finally, in 1949 all three best play awards clustered on *Death of a Salesman*. The Drama Critics' Circle also recognized Jean Giraudoux's *The Madwoman of Chaillot* as best foreign play and Rodgers and Hammerstein's *South Pacific* as best musical. Because of a discrepancy in timing, the 1949 Tony for best musical went to Cole Porter's *Kiss Me, Kate* and the one awarded in 1950 went to *South Pacific*, as did the 1950 Pulitzer Prize in drama. Indeed, *South Pacific* swept many of the Tony Awards in 1950, alongside a few recognitions for T. S. Eliot's *The Cocktail Party*.

Among other plays were the folk fantasy *Dark of the Moon* (1945) by Howard Richardson and William Berney; Lillian Hellman's period melodrama *Another Part of the Forest* (1946); Ruth and Augustus Goetz's psychological drama *The Heiress* (1947), based on the Henry James novel *Washington Square*; poet Robinson Jeffers's version of Euripides' *Medea* (1947), with Judith Anderson in the title role; Sidney Kingsley's hard-boiled melodrama *Detective Story* (1949); plays on topical issues like *Home of the Brave* (1945) by Arthur Laurents on what we now call PTSD; plays about historical figures or events like Emmet Lavery's *The Magnificent Yankee* (1946) on Supreme Court Justice Oliver Wendell Holmes, Maxwell Anderson's *Joan of Lorraine* (1946), with Ingrid Bergman as both Joan of Arc and the actress who plays The Maid, and Anderson's *Anne of the Thousand Days* (1948), about Anne Boleyn; war plays like *Command Decision* (1947) by William Wister Haines and *Mister Roberts* by Thomas Heggen and Joshua Logan; comedies including Elmer Rice's *Dream Girl* (1945), Garson Kanin's *Born Yesterday* (1946), Ruth Gordon's autobiographical *Years Ago* (1946), Fay Kanin's *Goodbye, My Fancy* (1948) and Moss Hart's *Light Up the Sky* (1948). Eugene

O'Neill appeared on the cover of *Time* (21 October 1946) for his first Broadway play since 1934: *The Iceman Cometh* opened on 9 October 1946, with a four-and-a-half-hour running time. Six weeks later, the curtain time would be moved to 5.30 p.m. to allow for a dinner break.[138]

Quite a few French plays in English translation or in adapted versions had Broadway runs during these years. There were, for example, Jean Anouilh's modernized *Antigone*, starring Katharine Cornell, and Jean Giraudoux's *The Madwoman of Chaillot* (1948). Jean-Paul Sartre had several productions: *No Exit* (*Huis clos*, 1946), starring Claude Dauphin; *Red Gloves* (*Les mains sales*, 1948), starring Charles Boyer; *The Respectful Prostitute* (*La Putain respectueuse*, 1948), transferred from Off-Broadway to Broadway; and *The Victors* (*Morts sans sepulture*, 1948), translated by Thornton Wilder. S. N. Behrman's *I Know, My Love* (1949) was adapted from Marcel Achard's *Auprès de ma blonde* (1946), with a plot that runs backward in time, the five acts set in 1939, 1920, 1918, 1900 and 1889; the Theatre Guild produced it as a star vehicle for Alfred Lunt and Lynne Fontanne, who were also celebrating in real life their 25 years as an acting team.

The 'golden age' of musicals launched by Rodgers and Hammerstein got additional sparkle with Irving Berlin's *Annie Get Your Gun* (1946), in which Ethel Merman consolidated her superstar status in a succession of Berlin's great songs: 'I Got the Sun in the Mornin'', 'Doin' What Comes Natur'lly', 'Moonshine Lullabye', 'You Can't Get a Man with a Gun', 'I Got Lost in His Arms' and 'There's No Business Like Show Business'. Rodgers and Hammerstein produced the show, with a book by Herbert and Dorothy Fields, directed by Joshua Logan. It ran for 1,147 performances on Broadway and 1,304 with the London company beginning in 1947. Mary Martin took the title role for the American tour, and Betty Hutton played it opposite Howard Keel in the 1950 movie version. *Annie Get Your Gun* brought Irving Berlin $2,500 a week at the box office in addition to $100,000 from the original cast album, $500,000 from the sale of sheet music and $650,000 for the movie rights.[139] The year 1947 began well with *Finian's Rainbow*, for which composer Burton Lane and lyricists E. Y. Harburg and Fred Saidy successfully combined fantasy with issues of racism, immigration and nostalgia for Ireland ('How Are Things in Glocca Morra?'). *High Button Shoes* (1947) brought the nostalgia back to the American past with its 1913 setting. Directed by George Abbott, it had music by Jule Styne and lyrics by Sammy Cahn. With *Allegro* (1947) as their third collaboration, Rodgers and Hammerstein did not rise to the heights of *Oklahoma!* or *Carousel*, but the minimal staging requirements of that show gave it a life in community and school theatres; the composer and lyricist-librettist would be back at the top of their form in the 1950s. However, Denny Martin Flinn credits *Allegro* with setting the stage for Postmodernism in the musical, representing 'a significant attempt to play with the form of the musical [as it] took inspiration from Thornton Wilder's *Our Town*, staged nine years earlier'.[140] Rodgers and Hammerstein would triumph again two years later with *South Pacific* (1949), based on James A. Michener's book *Tales of the South Pacific*. Mary Martin washed her trend-setting short hair on stage at every performance when she sang 'I'm Gonna Wash That Man Right Out of My Hair' about the plantation owner played by Metropolitan Opera star Ezio Pinza. Other great songs included the lovely 'Some Enchanted Evening' and 'Bali Ha'i', the socially-conscious 'You've Got to Be Carefully Taught' and the rollicking 'There is Nothing Like a Dame'.

Kurt Weill experimented with an operatic approach to the musical in his *Street Scene* (1947) based on Elmer Rice's earlier play of that title; poet Langston Hughes wrote the lyrics. Weill returned to Broadway in 1948 with *Love Life*, and for his third straight year with *Lost in the Stars* (1949), which had a book by Maxwell Anderson, based upon Alan Paton's *Cry, the Beloved Country*. Perhaps the most significant development in musical comedy of the post-war years was the rise of Lerner and Loewe. Lyricist-librettist Alan Jay Lerner and composer Frederick Loewe had worked together since 1943 and finally triumphed with *Brigadoon* (1947); their great decade would be the 1950s (*Paint Your Wagon*, *My Fair Lady*, *Camelot*). The wealth of new musicals in 1948 and 1949 included Frank Loesser's *Where's Charley?* (1948), a star-studded musical version of the play *Charley's Aunt*, and Cole Porter's *Kiss Me, Kate* (1948), a brilliant musical take-off from Shakespeare's *Taming of the Shrew*, with a libretto by Bella and Samuel Spewak. Marc Blitzstein wrote both the libretto and the score for *Regina* (1949), an operatically musical version of Lillian Hellman's play *The Little Foxes*. Yet another adaptation of a work of fiction was *Gentlemen Prefer Blondes* (1949), based upon Anita Loos's novel of that title. Carol Channing soared to stardom in the role of the gold-digging, *faux*-naive Lorelei Lee, making the most of songs by Jule Styne like 'Diamonds Are a Girl's Best Friend'. With Agnes de Mille's choreography, sets by Oliver Smith and costumes by Miles White, *Gentlemen Prefer Blondes* ran for 740 performances.

Modern dance and theatrical dance

Theatrical dance flourished in the 1940s. George W. Beiswanger had signalled 'the creation of an American theatre dance' in his article for the January 1939 issue of *Theatre Arts*; he noted theatrical structures in works by Martha Graham, Hanya Holm, Doris Humphrey and Charles Weidman.[141] Albertina Rasch had 'created self-contained ballets for revues'.[142] *Oklahoma!* showed that dance could be as integral to a musical comedy's narrative and character as the text and the singing. Dance actually trumped narrative in *On the Town*, which grew out of Jerome Robbins's ballet *Fancy Free* (1944), with dance accounting for 30 minutes of the show's stage time.[143] *On the Town* may be considered the progenitor of 'the dance musical', wherein the dancing conveys the essence of character and situation. Dancer-choreographer Katherine Dunham moved from ballet to modern theatrical dance in the 1930s, and in the 1940s she led her African-American dance company to numerous stage and film engagements: *Cabin in the Sky* (1940), *Tropical Review* (1943) and *Bal Nègre* (1946) on Broadway, with movie appearances in *Carnival of Rhythm* (1931), *Star Spangled Rhythm* (1942), *Stormy Weather* (1943) and *Casbah* (1948). Dunham's activism was ignited in the 1940s when the Katherine Dunham Dance Company encountered segregation and discrimination during its national tours.

Martha Graham, the doyenne of American modern dance, choreographed several major dance dramas in the 1940s: *Letter to the World* (1940), a ballet in which she danced the role of the poet Emily Dickinson; *Deaths and Entrances* (1943); *Appalachian Spring* (1944), which Agnes de Mille saw as 'perhaps the most dearly loved ballet in the Graham repertory';[144] *Dark Meadow* (1946), a masterpiece of abstract art; *Cave of the Heart* (1946), based upon Medea of Greek mythology, with music by Samuel Barber; *Errand into the Maze* (1947), on Ariadne, Theseus and the

Minotaur; and *Night Journey* (1947), on Oedipus and Jocasta; the latter five had scenic designs by Isamu Noguchi.

Agnes de Mille rose to pre-eminence among dancer-choreographers of the decade. She had trained under Marie Rambert in London; she never studied under Martha Graham, but regarded her as a mentor. De Mille had choreographed for American Ballet Theatre, but did not seem to be getting anywhere either as a dancer or dance director until the Ballet Russe de Monte Carlo gave her the chance to create a new work. Aaron Copeland's score for *Rodeo* allowed Agnes de Mille to display her strengths as a choreographer: a sense of humour in an American idiom, based in ballet but exploring theatrical forms that conveyed character psychology. At its Metropolitan Opera House premiere on 15 October 1942, *Rodeo* got twenty-two curtain calls and impelled one audience member, Theresa Helburn, to contact de Mille about joining the production team of the show that would become *Oklahoma!* Agnes de Mille's choreography contributed significantly to that show's triumph, and she went on to choreograph *One Touch of Venus* (1943), *Bloomer Girl* (1944), *Carousel* (1945), *Allegro* (1946), *Brigadoon* (1947), *Fall River Legend* (1948) and *Gentlemen Prefer Blondes* (1949), and to form her own Agnes de Mille Dance Theater.

Tributary theatre

While Broadway remained the focus for the awards and for American theatre as a whole, a vast network of community theatres was building on the foundations of the 1920s Little Theatre Movement, and this 1940s surge in local theatre groups would in turn fertilize the blossoming of regional resident professional companies in the 1960s and afterward. Moreover, through the efforts of pioneers like Brander Matthews, George Pierce Baker, Frederick H. Koch and Thomas Wood Stevens, theatre studies and production were gradually carving out a niche in higher education. In *Theatre Arts* magazine (1916–48), the civic theatres and university theatres of the 1940s were lumped together under the rubric 'Tributary Theatre'. The periodic lists of tributary theatre productions, brief descriptions and news bites in *Theatre Arts* throughout the decade show thriving activity, strong awareness of current Broadway and international fare plus a good dose of world classics: Shakespeare, Ibsen, Strindberg, Shaw. For the February 1940 issue of *Theatre Arts* the repertories of 100 tributary theatres were tabulated; among new plays, *Our Town* was 'far in the lead' with twenty productions, 'twice as many productions as its nearest competitor, *Family Portrait*'.[145] The dozen tributary theatres whose season selections were listed as representative in that issue included the Carnegie Institute of Technology, the Goodman Memorial Theatre (Chicago), the Kalamazoo Civic Theatre, the University Civic Theatre (Denver), Northwestern University and the Virginia State Players Guild (a charter member of the Negro Intercollegiate Dramatic Association). In addition, new theatre construction was reported for the University of Indiana, Stephens College (Columbia, Missouri), Michigan State College (East Lansing) and Allegheny College.[146] A 1940 address by Lynn Riggs to the San Diego Community Theatre, reprinted in *Theatre Arts* (February 1941) as 'A Credo for the Tributary Theatre', urged the importance of maintaining high standards and ideals beyond the amateur basis for such theatres.[147] The Tributary Theatre Directory in the July 1946 issue of *Theatre Arts* lists 106 tributary theatres in the United States with their addresses and names of directors and technical directors.[148]

Already during the 1940s some community theatres were veering toward professionalism. Cleveland Play House was begun by amateurs in 1916 and often floundered in its early years; the hiring of a professional director, Frederic McConnell, helped it to survive numerous setbacks. Cleveland Play House had a saving hit in 1943 with the comedy *Arsenic and Old Lace* even as the play was still running on Broadway, and in 1945 the company reached its long-standing record attendance of 144,000.[149] Other early community theatres that lasted long enough to become professional include the Pasadena Playhouse (founded 1918), Le Petit Théâtre du Vieux Carré (founded in 1919 in New Orleans) and The Pittsburgh Playhouse (founded in 1934). In 1947, Nina Vance founded Houston's Alley Theatre as an amateur venture; years of struggle took it to professional status in 1954.[150] Also in 1947 in Texas, Margo Jones rallied the Dallas community to support her theatre-in-the-round venture, a professional company that opened as Theatre '47 and updated its name at the start of each new year. The Barter Theatre (founded in 1932) in Abingdon, Virginia, started out as a professional theatre for the summer tourist season;

with an impressive record of staging classics and commercial fare, it was named the State Theatre of Virginia in 1941. Its 1948 *Hamlet* was toured to Denmark for a performance at Elsinore's Kronberg Castle.[151] Felix Sper's 1948 book *From Native Roots* further testifies to the richness of American regional drama and theatre throughout the 1940s.[152]

Another indication of the post-war upsurge in theatre 'beyond Broadway' is the *Chicago Stagebill Yearbook 1947*, published to commemorate the 100th theatre season in Chicago's history, which began with the erection of Rice's Theatre in 1847.[153] The Introduction notes that Chicago had boasted '23 legitimate theatres' in 1923, followed by a decline to only four in the late 1930s, and the 'happy augury' of nine in 1947. Chicago's 1946–7 season also saw 50 per cent longer runs than the average for the 1920s, as well as strong improvement in quality.[154] It is true, nonetheless, that these figures do not represent local resident companies but large facilities (Shubert, Selwyn, Erlanger, Blackstone, Harris, Studebaker, Civic, Opera House and Great Northern theatres) that booked in Broadway touring companies. The 1940s was also the heyday of Chicago's all-time most renowned theatre critic, Claudia Cassidy of the *Chicago Tribune*. Beyond her 'sharp-edged writing' that upheld the highest standards, according to Chris Jones, she exhibited 'a particular disdain for any producer intending to send a substandard touring production through her town'.[155] Indeed, there is truth to the theatrical legend that it was Claudia Cassidy above all whose review (27 December 1944) rescued the play that would mark 'a turning point in [Tennessee] Williams's life and career', *The Glass Menagerie*.[156]

Directors and producers

Some producers and directors of the 1940s have been mentioned, but a few merit particular notice. Long regarded as the dean of Broadway directors, George Abbott had been acting on Broadway since 1913. By the 1920s he had branched into directing, producing, play-doctoring and playwriting. 'Mister Abbott' – as he was always respectfully addressed – mastered the mechanics of putting together a legitimate play or musical production and applying 'the Abbott touch'. In 1940 he produced and directed *Pal Joey*; other 1940s shows he directed include *On the Town* (1944), *Billion Dollar Baby* (1945), *High Button Shoes* (1947) and *Where's Charley?* (1948). 'Abbott was particularly supportive of the choreographer – then and later in his career.'[157] He was still at work on Broadway the year before his death in 1995 at age 107.

Jed Harris, the 'boy wonder' of the 1930s, also produced as well as directed and brought promising new works – like Thornton Wilder's *Our Town* – to Broadway; however, he was notoriously ego-driven and unpleasant in his relations with artist-collaborators. Harris continued directing throughout the 1940s but his star had dimmed considerably. In contrast, producer Sam Harris (no relation to Jed Harris) was beloved among theatre people from his long partnership (1904–20) with George M. Cohan, followed by a remarkable string of hits in the 1920s and 1930s and culminating in his last two productions before his death in 1941: *George Washington Slept Here* and *Lady in the Dark*. The jovial producer Brock Pemberton had begun as a drama critic but, mentored by the legendary 1920s producer Arthur Hopkins, turned to producing and occasional directing in 1920. His successes of the 1940s include *Janie* and *Harvey*, both of which were directed by Antoinette Perry, whom Pemberton mentored during her all-too-short directorial career. Perry had become a skilled director and co-producer, but she died during the run of *Harvey*. It was Pemberton who conceived the Antoinette Perry Awards to honour her memory, and it was he who first referred to the award as a 'Tony'.

The 1940s saw three women sustain strong careers as producers and directors. Actress Eva Le Gallienne had been directing and producing since the 1920s with visionary ideas like her Civic Repertory Theatre of the 1920s; she continued acting in productions that she also directed, notably her 1944 *The Cherry Orchard*, which earned 96 performances on Broadway and a tour.[158] Cheryl Crawford emerged from her 1930s association with the Group Theatre to establish herself as an independent producer; her somewhat chequered producing career included notable successes in the 1940s: a revival of *Porgy and Bess*, *One Touch of Venus*, *Brigadoon* and Margaret Webster's *The Tempest*. Webster continued directing classics after her 1944 *Othello* with Paul Robeson. Her acclaimed 1945 staging of *The Tempest* featured Arnold Moss as Prospero, Canada Lee as Caliban, dancer Vera Zorina as Ariel, and Czech comic actors George Voscovec and Jiri Wierich as Trinculo and Stefano. In 1945, Webster, Crawford and Le Gallienne together founded the American Repertory Theatre (ART) with the idealistic aim of employing a permanent company of 30 to perform classic plays in repertory. Webster directed the inaugural production, Shakespeare's *Henry VIII*, with lavish visual elements and music. Over the next few weeks Barrie's *What Every Woman Knows*, Ibsen's *John Gabriel Borkman* and Shaw's *Androcles and the Lion* were folded into the rotating repertory. Unfortunately, unforeseen expenses quickly outran revenues; the company was 'officially dissolved in May 1948', with assets like the electrical equipment obtained by Webster for the touring company she formed that year.[159] The Margaret Webster Shakespeare Company ('Marweb') opened with *Macbeth* and *Hamlet* in New York City and then hit the road. *Julius Caesar* and *The Taming of the Shrew* comprised a second nationwide touring season in 1949–50. Despite the popular and critical success of 'Marweb', mounting debts forced its demise. Another woman producer-director, Margo Jones, has been mentioned for the theatre she founded in Dallas as Theatre '47, successively renamed each year through to Theatre '55, the year of her death. By the end of 1954, Jones's company had 'presented sixty-seven plays, including world premieres of scripts by Tennessee Williams, William Inge ... and Dorothy Parker. Seventy per cent of all the plays produced at the theatre had been new scripts, many by unknown authors.'[160] Of course, Margo Jones will be remembered also as co-director of Tennessee Williams's *The Glass Menagerie*.

Undoubtedly, the most important stage director of the 1940s was Elia Kazan. He had begun his stage career with the Group Theatre of the 1930s and ultimately achieved numerous prizes for his motion picture directing. His stage directing in the 1940s is particularly distinguished by his association with the rising careers of Tennessee Williams and Arthur Miller. As a founder of the non-profit Actors Studio in 1947, Elia Kazan put forth his student Marlon Brando for the role of Stanley Kowalski in *A Streetcar Named Desire*; Kazan also directed Brando in the 1951 movie version. Kazan garnered Tony Awards for his directing of Arthur Miller's *All My Sons* (1947) and *Death of a Salesman* (1949).

Joshua Logan was another director who flourished in the post-war years, mainly for his work on Broadway musicals. Some additional producers who came to prominence include Leland Hayward, whose impressive roster of hits began in 1944 with

A Bell for Adano; Herman Shumlin, who both produced and directed with noted finesse; and Irene Selznick, best remembered as producer of Tennessee Williams's *A Streetcar Named Desire*. While the two halves of the decade – war years and post-war years – were very different in their cultural imperatives and economics, the decade as a whole shows a theatre weathering difficulties and gradually regaining its robustness. The late 1940s ushered in many of the leading artists and trends that would nourish the good times to come in the 1950s.

3

Introducing the Playwrights

Felicia Hardison Londré

Introduction

Four white males. In the 1940s there was no reason to wonder why the four most celebrated American playwrights should all be white males. Although 'diversity' was decades away from being articulated as a value, there actually was significant diversity among the four in terms other than race or gender. Two of the four were homosexual (Wilder remaining closeted, or possibly asexual; Williams evading public acknowledgement until the 1960s). O'Neill and Miller each married three times. Wilder and Williams never married, but Williams had numerous intimate liaisons including one long-term relationship. Wilder maintained various close friendships – both intellectual and emotional – through correspondence. Their formative religious upbringings were Irish Catholic, New England Protestant, Southern Episcopalian and Jewish. Eugene O'Neill focused entirely on writing for the stage, Thornton Wilder supplemented his playwriting with novels and scholarly research, Tennessee Williams dabbled in various genres including poetry and painting, and Arthur Miller made essays his secondary genre. Only Wilder saw active duty in the military. Both Williams and Miller were rejected for military service because of medical conditions. Although O'Neill avidly followed the news of the Second World War, he maintained a cynical attitude toward war and governments as he increasingly isolated himself from political and social involvements. Miller, in contrast, was an outspoken social activist. Williams and especially Wilder kept abreast of current events while focusing primarily on their work and on their circles of friends.

Despite those differences, it is easy to find similarities among the four. The families of all four lived through financial hardship during each writer's childhood (although in Miller's case that did not occur until the Depression, when he was 14). In all four families, the mother represented cultivated manners in contrast to a remote, work-obsessed father. While all four writers were voracious readers throughout their childhoods, none showed any particular academic gift during their school years. Even Wilder, who later gravitated to academia and became multilingual, had difficulties with spelling in his schoolwork; his writing habit can be traced to the detailed weekly letters he was expected to write to his father. O'Neill began writing as a newspaper reporter in his twenties. Williams was in his teens when his mother bought him a typewriter on which he churned out short stories as a kind of escape from feelings of alienation at school as well as a dysfunctional family situation. Miller discovered playwriting as a student at the University of Michigan.

After gaining recognition as a writer – O'Neill in the 1910s, Wilder in the 1920s, Williams and Miller in the 1940s – each struggled to balance private time devoted to writing with the attractions or demands of outside interests and relationships. All four playwrights were peripatetic, unable to settle down for very long in one place. Eugene O'Neill lived during most summers of his teen years from 1900 with his parents and brother at Monte Cristo Cottage, 325 Pequot Avenue, New London, Connecticut; his inclination to wandering might be traced to his shipboard jobs that took him to South America and England in the early 1910s. Later he made successive homes in Bermuda; Tours, France; Sea Island, Georgia; Marblehead, Massachusetts; and Danville, California. His famous deathbed comment is emblematic of that rootlessness: 'Born in a hotel room and ... died in a hotel room.' Thornton Wilder had a permanent address – a house at 50 Deepwood Drive, Hamden, Connecticut, which he built for his family with his earnings from *The Bridge of San Luis Rey* (1927)

– but he was always restless, enjoying frequent travels in Europe or seeking places that would give him the isolation he needed to focus on his writing. Wilder's biographer Penelope Niven traces his 'crazy vagabond life'.[1] During the late 1930s and 1940s, for example, apart from his military assignments, he drifted from Chicago to Hollywood, to France and Austria, Boston, New York, Tucson, Taos, Quebec, South America, England and Scotland, Rome, Belgrade, Mexico and Florida. Tennessee Williams eventually maintained a permanent home address – 1431 Duncan Street, Key West, Florida – but lived most of his life in hotels, and like O'Neill, died in a hotel. Stephen Marino's essay in the Documents section of this book details Arthur Miller's many Brooklyn addresses.

Alongside their high artistic ideals and aspirations, all four dramatists made space for popular culture in their lives. O'Neill enjoyed ragtime music and songs by Al Jolson; a player piano he called Rosie – probably named for Jolson's catchy 'Ma Blushin' Rosie' – gave him particular pleasure during his late years. Wilder (who loved classical music) befriended the flamboyant Texas Guinan and revelled in the cheerful cheesiness of Chicago's 1933 World's Fair, which he visited many times;[2] later he collaborated with filmmaker Alfred Hitchcock. Williams grew up on silent films and submitted his earliest writing to pulp magazines. Miller began his writing career in radio and later wrote the screenplay for *The Misfits* (1961) to feature his second wife, Marilyn Monroe. On the highbrow side, all four borrowed from classical Greek mythology. Examples include O'Neill's trilogy *Mourning Becomes Electra*, with character and plot elements based upon Aeschylus's *The Oresteia*; Wilder's *The Alcestiad*, inspired by Euripedes' *Alcestis*; Williams's *Orpheus Descending*, which draws upon the legend of Orpheus and Eurydice; and Miller's conscious use of elements of Greek tragedy in *A View from the Bridge*. Norwegian dramatist Henrik Ibsen, whose bold themes had shocked American theatre audiences at the turn of the century, can be counted as an influence on these four dramatists along with many other writers of the time who learned economy of means from Ibsen's dramatic structures.

The decade of the 1940s brought the plays that best define each of these four all-time great American playwrights. It is instructive to look briefly at their early struggles and how each arrived at that defining decade in his life.

Eugene O'Neill (1888–1953)

The first internationally-recognized 'great American playwright' was born into the theatre, for he was the son of James O'Neill, a prominent Irish-American Shakespearean actor who won a nationwide popular following for his portrayal of the title role in *The Count of Monte Cristo*, a melodrama based upon the novel by Alexandre Dumas *père*. Until Eugene was sent to boarding school at age seven, he toured with his parents, immersed in backstage life. It is scarcely surprising that Eugene O'Neill's plays – despite their monumental advancement of the art of the drama – evince unmistakable melodramatic qualities in their language and plot elements. He later insisted that his plays needed to be understood in terms of the Irishness that infused them. His mother, Mary Ellen (called Ella) Quinlan O'Neill, was also the daughter of Irish immigrants, but her parents had prospered in Cleveland, Ohio, and gave her a genteel convent-school education. James O'Neill met Ella Quinlan when he played Cleveland, and they married in 1877. Their first son, James, Jr, was born in 1878, and Eugene always looked up to the brother who was ten years older than him, although the older brother would later lead the younger into years of heavy drinking and other dissolute habits. Another son, Edmund Burke O'Neill, born in 1883, died in 1885, and Eugene Gladstone O'Neill, born on 16 October 1888, somehow understood that he was a 'replacement' son. More devastating to his emotional development was the discovery when he was 14 that his difficult birth had prompted the hotel doctor to administer morphine to his mother and thus caused her enduring addiction to the drug, a source of emotional trauma for the entire family, as shown in O'Neill's autobiographical play *Long Day's Journey Into Night*.

As a child, Eugene O'Neill was rarely without a book in hand. Indeed, New London now boasts a sculpture, based upon an early photograph, of the boy seated on a rock overlooking the water and absorbed in a book. The rigid thinking at his Catholic boarding school deeply distressed him, surely contributing to his ultimate loss of faith and profession of atheism. In 1900, he prevailed upon his father to send him instead to the secular Betts Academy. Enrolled at Princeton University in 1906, he wasted his time until bad behaviour led to his expulsion in 1907. Next he took a job as a mail-order secretary at a supply company in Manhattan. According to Robert M. Dowling's biography, it was during this period that O'Neill adopted 'his only self-professed, lifelong worldview: "philosophical anarchism"'.³

O'Neill's sea-going ventures resulted directly from his having secretly wedded Kathleen Jenkins when he learned that she would bear his child. Following a confrontation between their parents, twenty-year-old Eugene sailed off on a banana boat to prospect for gold in Spanish Honduras, where he contracted malaria but gained low-life experience that would later fuel his early one-act plays. In 1910 he embarked again, this time on a sixty-five-day voyage to Buenos Aires, where he lived and worked in foul conditions for nine months. As a seaman for the American Line in 1911, he made his first transatlantic voyage and saw labour unrest among dock workers and coal stokers whose lives would find their way into his 1921 play *The Hairy Ape*.

Having achieved the rank of able seaman, O'Neill returned to New York in August 1911 and took lodgings above a saloon known as Jimmy-the-Priest's. It was there that O'Neill attempted suicide on 30 December 1911. After friends saved his life, his father took him into *The Count of Monte Cristo* touring company. The summer of 1912 saw O'Neill back in New London, writing for the *New London Telegraph*. Diagnosed with tuberculosis that November, O'Neill spent almost seven months in two sanatoriums during which he read a wide selection of world drama while focusing particularly on the plays of August Strindberg. This awoke his desire to write plays. From 1913 until his first full-length play, *Beyond the Horizon* (1920), O'Neill wrote over twenty one-act plays, including his 'sea plays'. During the 1914–15 school year, he studied playwriting under the renowned George Pierce Baker at Harvard, but the greatest impetus to his newly-chosen profession was his summer of 1916 in Provincetown, Massachusetts, where a gathering of artists and bohemians produced his one-act *Bound East for Cardiff* in a makeshift theatre in a fishhouse at the end of a wharf. Calling themselves the Provincetown Players, the group continued producing plays in Manhattan's Greenwich Village as part of what would soon be known as the Little Theatre Movement.

O'Neill's major breakthrough came in 1920 with his first Pulitzer Prize-winning play, *Beyond the Horizon*, as well as the Provincetown Players production of *The Emperor Jones*, with

African-American actor Charles Gilpin collecting accolades in the title role. That decade was O'Neill's most productive and the one that firmly established him as our long-awaited Great American Playwright. He won a second Pulitzer Prize in 1921 for *Anna Christie* and a third in 1928 for *Strange Interlude*. Other important plays of the 1920s are *The Hairy Ape* (1921), *All God's Chillun Got Wings* (1924), starring Paul Robeson, *Desire Under the Elms* (1924) and *Marco Millions* (1927). O'Neill experimented with masks in *The Great God Brown* (1926) and revisited Expressionism (previously tackled in *The Emperor Jones* and *The Hairy Ape*) with *Dynamo* (1929). Meanwhile, the deaths of his father, mother and elder brother in 1920, 1922 and 1923 took a toll on his personal life. His second wife, Agnes Boulton, gave him two children, Shane (1919) and Oona (1926), but he divorced her in 1929 to marry Carlotta Monterey. During a long sojourn at Chateau Plessis near Tours, France, O'Neill wrote *Mourning Becomes Electra* (1931). His only comedy, *Ah, Wilderness!* (1933), starred George M. Cohan. In 1936 he became – and still is – the only American playwright to win the Nobel Prize. While the 1930s look like a dry spell in terms of Broadway premieres of plays by O'Neill, he was hard at work on a projected cycle of 11 plays that would focus on one American family over several generations to show the corrupting effects of materialism. Only two of those plays would survive for release after O'Neill's death: *A Touch of the Poet* (1957) and *More Stately Mansions* (1962). During the 1930s O'Neill was also working on the plays that in the 1940s would constitute a second blossoming of his talent, the mature masterpiece dramas that are discussed in Zander Brietzke's essay.

Thornton Wilder (1897–1975)

Thornton Wilder, an intellectual omnivore, was undoubtedly one of the most erudite American playwrights ever. His wide reading included works in French, German, Spanish, Italian, Latin and a touch of classical Greek. His journals and letters are full of literary allusions from many cultures and epochs. Even as a bestselling author of fiction, he could be distracted from his creative writing to delve into some long-term scholarly investigations. Having collected from childhood articles in German-language publications about the great Austrian director Max Reinhardt, Wilder ultimately experienced the thrill of getting Reinhardt to direct his *Merchant of Yonkers* in 1938. Among the many who delighted in Wilder's conversation or correspondence were Gertrude Stein, Sigmund Freud, Ernest Hemingway, critic Alexander Woollcott, playwright Edward Sheldon, actress Ruth Gordon, University of Chicago chancellor Robert Maynard Hutchins, social activist Mabel Dodge Luhan, interior designer Sibyl Colefax and heavyweight boxer Gene Tunney.

What background could have produced such an exceptional mind and personality? Indeed, Wilder's older brother, Amos Parker Wilder, Jr, and three younger sisters all became prominent in their career fields. They were the children of a controlling and puritanical father, Dr Amos Parker Wilder, and a warm, cultivated, artistic mother, Isabella Niven Wilder, eleven years younger than her husband. Dr Wilder had graduated from Yale University and was regarded as an outstanding orator. In 1894 he married the well-educated daughter of a Presbyterian minister. The Wilders created a home full of books and lively intellectual exchange despite what turned out to be a loveless marriage. Thornton, born on 17 April 1897, was a twin whose brother Theophilus died at birth. He and his sisters Charlotte and Isabel were born in Madison, Wisconsin, where from 1896 to 1906 Dr Wilder was editor and part owner of the *Wisconsin State Journal*. Dr Wilder insisted that his children devote themselves to Bible studies and sign pledges to abstain from alcoholic drink.

Lacking financial stability in the newspaper business, Dr Wilder negotiated a diplomatic appointment as Consul General in Hong Kong. In May 1906 the family sailed for Hong Kong and there Thornton attended a German-language school. Six months later, however, Isabella Wilder and the children returned to the USA to live in Berkeley, California. From this time, each child was expected to write a lengthy weekly letter to their father, a practice that may have given rise to Thornton's lifelong letter-writing habit. Dr Wilder visited his family in 1909 and a fifth sibling, Janet, was born in 1910. When Dr Wilder was promoted to Consul General in Shanghai, the family (except Amos, Jr, at boarding school in Ojai, California) travelled to China, where Thornton and his sister Charlotte were sent to the China Inland Mission School in Chefoo,

Shantung Province, about 450 miles north of Shanghai. The 120 students, strictly segregated by sex – which meant that Thornton and Charlotte rarely saw each other – were mostly children of missionaries; among them was the future founder of *Time* magazine, Henry Luce. In 1911, Isabella Wilder travelled with her two younger daughters to visit her sister in Italy. Besides the weekly letter to his father, Thornton was then writing to his mother in Italy and his brother Amos in California. Dr Wilder closely monitored his children's educations and in 1912 sent Thornton and Charlotte back to California to board at the Thacher School along with Amos, Jr. Dr Wilder also believed in the salutary effects of outdoor labour and arranged for Thornton to spend summers living on farms and doing backbreaking work, which the boy regarded as lost time when he might have been reading or writing.

Thornton had his heart set on following his brother to attend Yale University, but Dr Wilder chose Oberlin College, Ohio, for him instead. Thornton Wilder found a mentor, Dr Charles H. Wager, whose Classics in Translation course proved especially influential and whose continuing encouragement bolstered Wilder's morale long afterward.[4] At last in 1917 Thornton's father allowed him to transfer to Yale, but the USA's entry in the First World War interrupted his studies there when he served three months in the US Coast Guard Artillery. He graduated from Yale in 1920, having published in the *Yale Literary Magazine* and having seen two of his playlets performed by students.

Thornton Wilder realized his long-cherished dream of travel to Europe when he was accepted for a year of study, in 1920–1, at the American Academy in Rome. He honed his Latin, learned Italian, studied archaeology and art history, went on field trips and dined with stimulating new friends. These experiences were seminal for his first published novel, *The Cabala* (1926), and indeed for allusions throughout his works. But Dr Wilder, ever anxious about his son's ability to support himself, got Thornton a job as a French teacher and assistant housemaster at a boys' school in Lawrenceville, New Jersey, a position he held until 1925 and again in 1927–8. While the responsibilities left him little time for writing, Thornton took advantage of the school's proximity to New York and attended the theatre often. He also showed great initiative in making contacts with theatre people and circulating his plays to willing readers.

The 1927 publication of Thornton Wilder's Pulitzer Prize-winning, bestselling novel *The Bridge of San Luis Rey* brought new possibilities, notably a 1928 trip to Europe and the means to support his parents for the rest of their lives in the house he built for the family in Hamden, Connecticut. From 1930 to 1936, Wilder enjoyed what he regarded as his happiest years, when he taught comparative literature part-time at the University of Chicago, where his school friend Robert Maynard Hutchins was president and later chancellor. Wilder enjoyed the intellectual companionship of many, as well as the access to musical events, for music was – like hiking – one of his lifelong passions. He befriended Gertrude Stein when she lectured there in 1934; they maintained a voluminous correspondence, and he often visited her in Paris or at her country home at Bilignin, France. He continued publishing novels and short plays, but gained his foothold in professional theatre through translation and adaptation of foreign plays: *The Rape of Lucrece* (1932), based upon André Obey's *Le Viol de Lucrèce*, for Katharine Cornell, and Henrik Ibsen's *A Doll's House* (1937) for Ruth Gordon. From his youth when he had avidly followed developments in German-language theatre, Wilder admired from afar the work of the acclaimed Austrian 'genius' director Max Reinhardt, one of whose tenets was the importance of suiting the theatrical space and the production style to specific qualities in the play text. Reinhardt's directing of Wilder's *The Merchant of Yonkers* in 1938 may well have contributed to Wilder's obsession with finding a fresh form and language for each new literary subject; as Penelope Niven noted, 'His expression had to be organic to the subject.'[5] And so he was poised to write the 1938 play with which his name will forever be most immediately associated: *Our Town*.

Tennessee Williams (1911–83)

During the first seven years of his life, Thomas Lanier Williams enjoyed an idyllic small-town Mississippi childhood that imbued him with his lifelong Southern accent and sensibilities. He was the grandson of Reverend Walter Dakin and Rosina Otte Dakin, whose daughter Edwina Dakin had married a travelling salesman, Cornelius Coffin Williams. While her husband was on the road,

Edwina lived with her parents and her two children at the Episcopal rectory in a succession of Southern towns: Columbus, Mississippi (where Rose Isabel was born on 19 November 1909 and Tom was born on 26 March 1911); Nashville, Tennessee; Canton and, from 1916, Clarksville, Mississippi. Tom's older sister Rose and his grandparents would figure lovingly throughout his later writing. Also stimulating his imagination during those early years, the children's African-American nanny Ozzie told spellbinding tales of devils and ghosts. Stricken with nearly-fatal diphtheria when he was five, Tom became devoted to books during his long convalescence; the works of Shakespeare and Charles Dickens from his grandfather's library were staples.

In 1918, when C. C. Williams was promoted to manager at the International Shoe Company in St Louis, he moved his wife and children to an apartment there, and the family dynamics changed drastically. Homelife became a living hell, with the incompatible parents often screaming at each other, while Tom and Rose learned to fear their overbearing, hard-drinking father who regarded his son as a sissy while favouring his third child, Walter Dakin Williams, born in 1919. School proved daunting also for Tom and Rose, as the Southern-bred children remained ill at ease among their urban classmates. Tom attended Eugene Field School, Ben Blewitt Junior High, Soldan High School and University City High School in St Louis. He found solace in writing, especially after his mother gave him a second-hand typewriter in 1924. He wrote for the school newspapers, won a $5 prize for an essay published in *Smart Set* magazine (May 1927) and sold a horror story to *Weird Tales* (August 1928). A formative experience was his first trip to Europe, in the summer of 1928, with his grandfather and a church group. They travelled to Paris and to battlegrounds of the First World War in France, as well as to Rome, Cologne, Amsterdam and London; seventeen-year-old Tom Williams wrote about the trip for his school's *U. City Pep* over the next academic year. Besides his sister Rose, his closest friend during those years was Hazel Kramer; he proposed marriage to her when he was eighteen and was devastated when she turned him down.

From 1929 to 1932, Tom Williams majored in journalism at the University of Missouri in Columbia. In campus literary circles, the plays of Eugene O'Neill were much discussed; as John S. Bak notes, 'O'Neill was certainly a major factor in shaping Williams's dramatic voice.'[6] Williams was just beginning to dabble in playwriting alongside his essays and news stories when his father withdrew him from the university and put him to work in a tedious job at the shoe company. By 1932 the Depression was taking a terrible toll on the American work force and C. C. Williams insisted that Tom was lucky to have a job at all. Twenty-one years old and one year shy of his bachelor's degree, Tom Williams would drudge all day for $65 a month, then isolate himself at home to write well into the night. Movie-going provided his only escape from routine until he collapsed of nervous exhaustion in March 1935. That gained him a summer with his grandparents who had retired to Memphis; there he discovered the work of Anton Chekhov, who became an important literary influence along with the poetry of Hart Crane. He also found his vocation as a playwright when he relished the laughter and applause generated by a neighbourhood group's performance of his one-act comedy *Cairo! Shanghai! Bombay!*

Now that Tom Williams saw himself as a dramatist rather than a poet or journalist, he used the second half of the 1930s toward that end, writing plays as he attended Washington University in St Louis (1935–7), where he developed close friendships with future writers Clark Mills McBurney and William Jay Smith, and then completed his BA in English at the University of Iowa in 1938. By 1939 he had adopted his pen name: Tennessee Williams. Thomas Keith's essay in this volume covers the playwriting milestones of that half-decade which prepared the way for Tennessee Williams's great plays of the 1940s.

Brooks Atkinson drew the following comparison of Williams and Arthur Miller in *Broadway* (New York: Macmillan, 1970 397, 399):

The two playwrights who dominated the postwar theatre could not be more unlike. Tennessee Williams is a short man, full of misgivings. Arthur Miller is tall and remarkably self-assured and very articulate. If Williams is always in flight, Miller faces situations head-on ... Although Miller and Williams differ from one another completely, they had a common point of view, in one respect, in the forties. They suspected the social organization of American life of being unreal.

Arthur Miller (1915–2005)

Arthur Miller's childhood was most formatively affected by his family's abrupt change in social status from a position of wealth in Manhattan to economic hardship in Brooklyn. Arthur Asher Miller, born on 17 October 1915, was the second son of Isidore and Gussie Miller. His grandparents had emigrated in the late 1880s from the Jewish town of Radomizl in what is today Poland. His father, Isidore, had been brought at the age of six to New York's Lower East Side, where his parents and older siblings were already earning their livings through a clothing manufacturing business, S. Miller and Sons. Put to work for long days at S. Miller and Sons, Isidore Miller never got a formal education and remained a lifelong illiterate, yet he was good with numbers. Isidore grew up to found his own Miltex Coat and Suit Company, which became 'one of the country's leading manufacturers of women's clothes'.[7] An arranged marriage in 1911 united the enterprising Isidore Miller with Augusta ('Gussie') Barnett, the educated and culturally refined daughter of another Lower East Side garment manufacturer. Their first son, Kermit, was born in 1912, Arthur's younger sister Joan in 1922. They lived well in a spacious sixth-floor apartment at the north end of Central Park, from which Isidore took a chauffeured car to the Garment District. Young Arty was tutored in Hebrew, learned to love classical music and, in the year before the Wall Street crash of October 1929, had his bar mitzvah. Robust business at Miltex had led Isidore Miller to optimistically invest his fortune in the stock market; he lost it all. With the family's move to Brooklyn, Arty was suddenly sharing a bedroom with his grandfather Barnett, getting to know his many cousins who also lived in modest circumstances nearby, and witnessing his mother's cultivated manners become embittered by resentment toward his beleaguered father.[8]

Arty Miller did not do well in his studies at James Madison High School or at Abraham Lincoln High School, but he excelled at sports until a leg injury ended his serious participation in athletics (and would later prevent him from enlisting in the military). He took a job to help the family financially, making early-morning bread deliveries by bicycle. His poor scholastic record made it difficult for him to get accepted into college after graduation in 1932, so he went to work at a warehouse for automobile parts in a slum area where today's Lincoln Center for the Performing Arts has long since reclaimed the area from blight. Experiencing the monotonous drudgery of the lives of manual labourers would fuel his growing social awareness, while he found his own escape by reading Russian novels during each day's hour-and-20-minute subway commute.[9] Miller set his sights on attending the University of Michigan in Ann Arbor, lured by relatively low tuition and living costs, and by the prospect of the awards for writing that were available there. The $512 he was able to save from his two years of warehouse labour barely sufficed for the out-of-state admission that he achieved only by persistence beyond two rejection letters; he pleaded his case in a letter to a dean and was admitted conditionally – depending upon his grades in his first semester. From 1934 to 1938 at the University of Michigan, Miller worked at various jobs, lived frugally and got by academically. Soon he was reporting for the student newspaper, the *Michigan Daily*, and assumed he would continue in journalism. As time allowed, he became politically active, but most importantly – upon referral by his English professor – he took a playwriting class from Professor Kenneth T. Rowe and began writing plays. His first, *No Villain* (1936), won a $250 Avery Hopwood Award; a revised version, *They Too Arise* (1937), brought him a scholarship of $1,250 from the Theatre Guild's Bureau of New Plays and production by the Hillel Players in Ann Arbor. His 1937 play *Honors at Dawn* brought him a second Hopwood Award. For his 1938 entry in the Hopwood competition, Miller wrote *The Great Disobedience* based upon his visits to a nearby penitentiary where he saw the need for prison reform; the play judges ranked it in second place.[10] Having almost no theatregoing experience in his life, Miller took literary models, primarily the plays of Henrik Ibsen and the classical Greeks.

Upon completing his BA in 1938, Arthur Miller returned to live in his parents' home in Brooklyn. With a recommendation from Professor Rowe, he wrote radio plays under the Federal Theatre Project in the final year of its existence. In 1940, still without financial prospects, he married his first wife, Mary Slattery, a fellow social activist from their student days at the University of Michigan. She became their source of support while he tackled various writing projects to little avail. When the US entered the Second World War, Miller took a night-shift job at the Brooklyn

Navy Yard. Meanwhile, he focused increasingly on writing for radio, notably for NBC's *Cavalcade of America* series of weekly patriotic dramas, sponsored by DuPont. In 1941, there were broadcasts of scripts by Arthur Miller on episodes in the lives of Joel Chandler Harris, John Paul Jones and Sacajawea.[11] Radio writing paid moderately well and led to Miller's work on a screenplay, *The Story of G.I. Joe* (1944). That year also brought publication of his first book, *Situation Normal*, a non-fiction work based on what he had observed of military life. And finally, after a long hiatus, he returned to playwriting with a dramatization of his own abortive attempt at a novel, *The Man Who Had All the Luck* (1944). It got Miller his first Broadway production, but negative reviews closed it after only four performances. The play's failure turned him back to writing fiction and he decided to grapple with the anti-Semitism to which he had been exposed when he worked at the Brooklyn Navy Yard; his novel *Focus* was published very successfully in 1945, with several reissues. *All My Sons* (1947), the play that took Arthur Miller back to the theatre and constitutes his breakthrough, is discussed in Valleri Robinson's chapter on Miller.

4

Eugene O'Neill: Love and Loss of the Soul

Zander Brietzke

Eugene O'Neill (1888–1953) wrote his best plays at the end of a long career, but very few people other than he knew it at the time. Secluded in his private study in the remote hills across the bay from San Francisco, he wrote brilliant dramas for the theatre in his mind without any thought of theatrical production.[1] In 1939 he put aside his enormous chronicle of American history that had ballooned from a cycle of four to six, seven, nine and even eleven separate plays and turned attention to what he felt were more manageable projects.[2] He formulated plans for two plays, one about a group of pals he had known and lived with in his youth in New York City, and the other a family play that he had been thinking about for a long time. Working on the New York City play first, O'Neill wrote *The Iceman Cometh* quickly and mostly finished it by the end of the year. He next turned to a more personal play that recalled his youth, *Long Day's Journey Into Night*, with only five characters, which he finished in the first months of 1941.[3] He required no outside validation to confirm the value of either work. To his son, Eugene O'Neill, Jr, he wrote:

> Each achieves my highest aim for it – and my aim was high. *Long Day's Journey Into Night* is the finer drama, but *The*

Iceman Cometh is fine drama, too. They each demanded the best I had to give, and I'm damned happy I didn't let either of them down.[4]

He made final revisions to *A Touch of the Poet* in 1942, the fourth play of the abandoned cycle project and the only one that he completed to his satisfaction; that same year he wrote his one-act play, *Hughie*, the first such short play he had written in over twenty years; and in 1943 he finished *A Moon for the Misbegotten*, an extension of the family story from *Long Day's Journey Into Night*. Although O'Neill lived another ten years, a debilitating and degenerative tremor eventually prevented him from even holding a pencil and he was unable to write using any other means.[5]

While O'Neill set each of his final plays in the distant past, his depression over world conditions, including the outbreak of global warfare (along with his own declining health), informs the pathos as well as the humorous rebellion against inevitable defeat that characterize his works of this period. In the years leading up to the war and through the conflict in Europe and later in the Pacific, O'Neill listened intently to radio broadcasts that confirmed his opinion of barbaric humanity. He complained in letters, too, that he frequently could not write because of his obsession with following devastating news as it was reported. The attack on Pearl Harbor prevented him from completing *A Moon for the Misbegotten* for over a year.[6] The war effort in Europe and Asia eventually claimed all of the professional staff for the house and grounds; this forced O'Neill and his wife Carlotta to sell their property in 1944 and return to a San Francisco hotel. O'Neill withheld production rights for *The Iceman Cometh* during the war years because he thought its dark theme was incompatible with the war effort. After the victory, though, he agreed to let the Theatre Guild produce the play at the Martin Beck Theatre, and he and Carlotta moved back to New York City to oversee and promote the production.[7] Among all his last plays, this was the only one that made it to Broadway during O'Neill's lifetime.

O'Neill's first press conference in 1946 caused quite a stir. He had achieved fame more than two decades earlier, in the 1920s, with a series of plays and productions that scaled dramatic heights in terms of physical size and thematic ambition, but he had not been in New York since the failure of *Days Without End* in

1934. The public had largely forgotten him during the intervening years with the emergence of 'method' acting and a new wave of playwrights such as Clifford Odets, Tennessee Williams and Arthur Miller.[8] O'Neill, by contrast, was old and looked even older than his fifty-eight years. Furthermore, O'Neill was shy and did not speak well in public and his hands shook terribly. No one knew what to say. Finally, someone asked him about the meaning behind the cycle plays, thinking that *The Iceman Cometh* belonged in that series. Very few people knew what O'Neill had been doing for twelve years, so the reporter's confusion was understandable, and O'Neill immediately covered the gaffe with a serious answer that dispelled any awkward embarrassment:[9]

> I'm going on the theory that the United States, instead of being the most successful country in the world, is the greatest failure ... It's the greatest failure because it was given everything, more than any other country. Through moving as rapidly as it has, it hasn't acquired any real roots. Its main idea is that everlasting game of trying to possess your own soul by the possession of something outside of it, thereby losing your own soul and the thing outside of it, too. America is the prime example of this because it happened so quickly and with such immense resources. This was really said in the Bible much better. We are the greatest example of 'For what shall it profit a man if he shall gain the whole world, and lose his own soul?' We had so much and could have gone either way.[10]

O'Neill's analysis of his unfinished history plays, to which he gave the umbrella title of *A Tale of Possessors, Self-Dispossessed*, applies aptly to thematic concerns in earlier works as well as to his final plays, including *The Iceman Cometh*, but powerfully as well to *Long Day's Journey Into Night* and *A Moon for the Misbegotten*. As early as *Desire Under the Elms* (1924), O'Neill dramatized the devastating consequences of greed and covetousness. A year later, *Marco Millions* satirized American materialism in a conflict between Western and Eastern values. Each of those plays, though, is also a love story. In the former, the lovers redeem themselves through confession and commitment even as they face certain prison and possible execution at the conclusion. In the latter, the protagonist, Marco Polo, never recognizes or accepts the responsibility and challenge of an intimate relationship, and his callousness kills the woman who loves him. O'Neill thus offsets his political critique of possessiveness with his personal validation of love as sacrifice.

O'Neill's final plays validate love in a much more equivocal and complex way: how does one maintain equilibrium and even achieve happiness in a human economy of unlimited desires and finite resources? In talking about human greed, O'Neill says it brings the loss of one's own soul as well as of those things one would possess. In personal relationships, however, Nora Melody in *A Touch of the Poet* talks of losing her soul in positive terms as the highest standard of true love in service to her husband. She clings to such loss as a point of pride, but it also creates an existential dilemma for her and for other characters that follow a similar course of action: how much to give of oneself to others? How to maintain a sense of self in service to others? Where does the 'I' begin and end in connection to 'we' and 'us'? Indeed, Nora does not command much respect from either her husband or her daughter throughout most of the play. The undeniably autobiographical nature of O'Neill's plays tends to minimize the autonomy of women at the expense of the playwright's struggle to understand family dynamics that he dramatized throughout his entire career.[11] The female characters, given their due, reveal the most about the subject of love and the problems of committing to and maintaining intimate relationships. Focusing on the leading female characters from Sara Melody to Mary Tyrone and ending with Josie Hogan shows a dialectic progression on the subject of love that makes life worth living but also difficult, painful and even tragic. Revealingly, the question of love appears most bleak in the one play among the final four in which no leading female character appears on stage.

A Touch of the Poet

The poet in this play does not actually appear. Cornelius Melody, the protagonist, repeatedly quotes the refrain from Byron's *Childe Harold* ('I stood among them, but not of them'), but merely spouting poetry, as his daughter Sara points out, does not make him a poet.[12] That role belongs to Sara's beloved, Simon Harford, scion of established Yankee wealth and privilege, who has fallen ill and convalesces throughout the play in an upstairs and offstage bedroom. Both Melody and his wife, Nora, on separate occasions describe Simon as possessing 'a touch of the poet'.[13] O'Neill first used the adjectival phrase in *Beyond the Horizon* to differentiate the poetical brother, drawn to adventure and the sea, from his prosaic brother who dreamed of running the family farm.[14] In this case, though, the split is not between characters but a divide within a single character and the moniker allows O'Neill to explore questions of identity that apply to Harford, certainly, but also extend to Melody, noble war hero and Irish mick, and to his daughter who will follow in his wake.

Although unseen in this play, Simon is the subject of much talk, and his 'presence' in the Melody home incites all of the action. He broke from his rich family and rejected his father's business in order to live apart in a little cabin in the woods that he built for himself on otherwise worthless land owned by Melody. There, according to Sara, he planned on living a Thoreau-like existence and writing a book that critiques American greed and materialism. With her voice raised in opposition, his mother, Deborah, who visits to check on the health of her son, insists that he will never write such a book no matter what he says and that he is destined to go into the family business and succeed with ruthless cunning. To complicate matters further, Sara has fallen in love with the poet in Simon and she is proud of his education and sensitivity and kindness that contrasts evidently with the brash drunkenness of her father. At the same time, Sara perceives those very admirable qualities in Simon as points of weakness that she can exploit to her advantage in terms of dominance and control and even future happiness. She may fall in love with the poet, but she wants to marry the businessman. Emphatically, she tells her mother in the opening act, 'For I'm going to marry him, Mother. It's my chance to rise in the world and nothing will keep me from it.'[15]

Sara, despite loving Simon, also recognizes her opportunity to escape the poverty of an Irish immigrant family and she is willing to seduce Simon and play upon his sense of honour to produce a marriage proposal. Nora tells Melody that Sara loves Simon, and she, too, sees the economic advantages of such a match: 'We'll see the day when she'll live in a grand mansion, dressed in silks and satins, and riding in a carriage with coachman and footman.'[16]

At the end of the play, Melody repeats his wife's words almost verbatim about Sara, and this ironic invocation of the American Dream attacks the heart of O'Neill's entire cycle play project that traces the greed and materialism of one American family from the founding of the United States in the 1770s to the 1930s.[17] While the love story of Sara and Simon remains as the subplot of *A Touch of the Poet*, their relationship is central in the next play of the cycle, *More Stately Mansions*, and the fate of their children is the subject of the unfinished and abandoned plays that were to complete the opus. Central to all of them is the question of love and the splits between desire, greed and possession. Although he intended each one as an independent yet interrelated play, *A Touch of the Poet* best achieves this, perhaps because its hero, Cornelius Melody, like the Byronic hero he emulates, stands apart and alone. Nevertheless, an exploration of this single play catches a glimpse of the whole.

Major Cornelius Melody, late of Wellington's 7th Dragoons, now the proprietor of a down-at-the-heel tavern outside Boston, prepares to celebrate in full uniform on the evening of 27 July 1828, the anniversary of his great victory over Napoleon at the Battle of Talavera in 1809. Unfortunately, Melody later lost his commission in disgrace after trying to seduce a general's wife. He emigrated from England to reinvent himself. There, he quickly fell prey to a real estate scheme that left him owner of an inn that had been recently bypassed by the major highway to Boston. While the native New Englanders look down on his Irish ancestry, Melody, in turn, despises Jacksonian democracy in the new land and aspires to nobility. Indeed, Melody does little to run the actual business of the inn; he leaves all the labour to Nora and Sara, while he rides about the countryside upon his expensive white mare.

When the Harford family lawyer pays a visit the next day, Melody comically and mistakenly assumes that he has come to secure financial arrangements for the marriage between Simon and Sara. The lawyer instead informs Melody that his business is to buy Melody out of the marriage contract and bribe the entire family to move westward as far as Ohio. Enraged, Melody literally kicks the lawyer out of the tavern and then schemes with his cohorts on how to avenge the family honour. In full uniform, Melody exits at the end of Act Three to ride his mare to Harford's house and challenge Simon's father to a duel. He returns in the final act, bruised and bloody, his beautiful red uniform torn and frayed, humiliated from the beating Harford's men gave him under Deborah's gaze. Melody speaks now in an Irish brogue thick enough to require a knife to cut. He vows that the Major is dead and that what is left is only a poor shebeen keeper.[18] His family fears for his life. Instead, Melody shoots and kills his prized mare, the pride of his nobility, an action that proves just as effective as suicide. Melody retreats to the backroom of the bar where he can swill cheap whiskey with his low and common friends and not be forced to put on the airs of a gentleman any longer.

Sara's final line in the play, after she witnesses her father's transformation, asks, 'Why do I mourn for him?'[19] She does not understand her own reactions to what has transpired because they go against her stated wishes. Earlier in the play, she confronted her father with bitter intonations: 'All I pray to God is that someday when you're admiring yourself in the mirror something will make you see at last what you really are! That will be revenge in full for all you've done to Mother and me!'[20] Con's humiliation should be her triumph when he removes himself as the blocking agent to her happiness. She asserts her own pride in telling her father that she did not need him to fight for her honour because she seduced Simon in his absence and the young couple will still marry in spite of the dispute between the parents. In the end, though, Sara identifies with her father and takes up his fight against the Yankees as her own. Indeed, one of her motives for marrying Simon is to avenge herself upon Yankee prejudice against the Irish. Sara has the same pride as her father and pities him for not being able to climb from the hole of oppression as she now has the opportunity to do. To a reporter's question in 1942 about whether she was 'lace-curtain or shanty Irish', O'Neill's real-life daughter, Oona, not yet 17 at the time, responded, 'I'm shanty Irish and proud of it.'[21] O'Neill always thought that his Irishness was a key aspect of his identity as a dramatist and that no one understood that fact or even took notice.[22] Certainly, throughout all of his work, from the earliest one-acts to the later full-length plays, O'Neill always backed and rooted for the underdog, whether he or she be Irish, a prostitute, a coal stoker or an African-American.

Sara's empathy for her father goes well beyond ethnic pride, however, or even solidarity with an underdog. She recognizes in her father's collapse of identity from the hero at Talavera to a dirty shebeen keeper the potential for her own destruction with respect to her marriage conquest of Simon. In the first part of the play she admits that she loves him but she maintains that she will not lose her head or her sense of freedom over the match. She claims, 'I'll not let love make me any man's slave. I want to love him just enough so I can marry him without cheating him, or myself.'[23] She implies that she will only give so much of herself and no more in order to maintain her own unique identity and not merge with that of her beloved. She criticizes her mother, in fact, for having done just that for her father to the extent that her mother has no identity of her own apart from her relationship to Melody. At the end of the play, however, Sara talks about love as if she were her mother and even apologizes to the older woman and confesses that she did not know that her mother was such a wise woman. She speaks of love in personal terms that echo what O'Neill said in political and economic terms about the history of the United States when he spoke to the press in 1946: 'I'd got to the place where all you know or care is that you belong to love, and you can't call your soul your own any more, let alone your body, and you're proud you've given them to love.'[24] How will Sara profit if, by gaining a husband, she loses her own sense of self and individual identity? Within the action of the play, she has changed abruptly from thinking of herself as separate and self-governing to seeking to merge with another in the name of love and sacrifice.

Con Melody's fall, then, stands as a warning to her. Earlier she maintained that his role as the officer and war hero was a false persona. But Con does not shed his skin at the end to reveal his true self as a drunken mick. The grotesque scene can grip an audience emotionally because one persona is just as true and false as the other, and the brilliance of Con's character and key to his charisma lies in his ability to sustain both aspects of his dynamic character. His collapse at the end comes when he tires of keeping multiple sides of the self in play. Sara faces a similar dilemma with respect to love for Simon. How much can she truly love without cheating him or herself? If she is to give everything of herself to him in the name of love, what is left that can still be called hers alone? How can she reconcile all aspects of herself in the name of love and remain recognizable to herself as an individual? In this play of identity, Con Melody shatters. In one of O'Neill's favourite plays of the 1920s, *The Great God Brown*, the titular character declares, 'Man is born broken. He lives by mending. The grace of God is glue.'[25]

The individual challenge is to withstand the complete loss of self through intimacy with others and to emerge in a new relationship with the soul still intact. How does one mend through love and the Grace of God in the face of loss of individual identity and autonomy? That challenge nearly destroys both Sara and Simon in *More Stately Mansions*, and the characters in O'Neill's final three full-length autobiographical plays respond to the same questions in very different, yet interrelated and thoroughly provocative ways.

The Iceman Cometh

There is no love interest in *The Iceman Cometh*. When asked by a reporter if it were true that there were 14 men and four tarts in the play, O'Neill politely countered by asserting that there were four *ladies* in the cast. Upon reflection, he realized that there were only three.[26] Despite the fact, too, that one of the three prostitutes plans to marry her alcoholic beau, love has little to do with the match and she along with her cohorts remains on the periphery of the action. As in *A Touch of the Poet*, absent characters (in this case all women) figure prominently in its meanings.[27] The men who populate New York City's lower West Side dump, Harry Hope's bar, in 1912 choose to live without women, as if in answer to Sara Melody's question from the previous play about how much to love and how much of the self to give to another. They reject intimacy and avoid the kind of pain that comes from deep emotional attachments with others, but their refusal to meet the demands of love results in the reduced way in which they live.

The title combines a popular dirty joke with a biblical allusion. The joke never gets told but refers to the days before modern refrigeration when a block of ice would be delivered to a residence on a weekly basis to preserve food. The actual joke goes something like this: a husband, upon coming home from work, calls upstairs to his wife: 'Honey, has the iceman come yet?' She answers from the bedroom: 'Not yet, but he's breathing hard!' The sacred part of the title plays on the archaic word 'cometh'. The Parable of the Ten Virgins begins with a command, 'And at midnight there was a cry made, Behold, the bridegroom cometh; go ye out to meet him.'[28] Five of the virgins were wise and bought oil for their lamps.

Five were foolish and had none. In the hour that the bridegroom (Christ) came, the latter five were not prepared and came late to the marriage feast only to find the door shut. And the Lord said, 'Watch therefore, for you know neither the day nor the hour.'[29]

In *The Iceman Cometh*, the travelling salesman Theodore Hickman (Hickey) is a kind of false Christ who peddles nothing but the cold touch of death in the name of salvation. All of the derelicts await his arrival at the start of the play to kick off Harry Hope's annual birthday party at midnight. When Hickey does make his entrance near the end of the first act, he claims to have found inner peace; he no longer needs to drink and pretend to be something other than who he is. He suggests that the barflies must confront their illusions, too, but insists that he is only interested in making them happy, only saying this for their own good in order to give them the peace that he has recently discovered for himself. The group bitterly attacks him and suggests that he has fallen victim to the old 'iceman' joke that he used to love to tell. His wife, they agree, must have had an affair with the iceman. Hickey closes the ribbing by informing them that his wife has died.

In Act Three, the next morning, Hickey drives the drunks out of the bar, but they stumble back soon enough after having failed to reclaim their old jobs, or to get married, or to do any of the things that they said that they always wanted to do. Hickey claims that this has all gone according to plan: after having finally confronted their unrealistic illusions and effectively killed them, they should all find peace and an easy conscience with no more false hopes about themselves. Hickey notices, however, that the gang does not seem peaceful and happy as a result of this discovery. To the contrary, they are angry and unpleasant with each other. As a further sign of change that brings no comfort, the group complains that the booze they guzzle no longer has any 'kick' to it and that they cannot get drunk and pass out. Hickey accuses them of being bad sports out to get him, and he confesses that his wife was actually murdered.

In Act Four later that night, Hickey informs the group that he does not have much time left and that he needs to make the time left to him count. In a long speech, Hickey talks about how much he and his wife, Evelyn, loved each other, but how he could not remain faithful to her and could not curb his drinking. Finally, Hickey realized that he was never going to give up his debauched lapses and that he was torturing himself with a pipe dream that he would reform. He decided, ultimately, that he would stop Evelyn from the pain of loving him by killing her – out of love. At the climax of the story, though, he slips and surprises himself by remembering what he said over her dead body: 'Well, you know what you can do with your pipe dream now, you damned bitch!'[30] Horrified, Hickey cannot believe, refuses to believe, that he murdered his wife out of hatred instead of love. He must have been insane! Harry Hope seizes the opportunity by saying that he'll vouch for Hickey's insanity if Hickey will agree that everything he has said previously to the group has been equally insane. The truth vanishes, then, with this pact. All the inhabitants of the bar, including Hickey, reclaim their former illusions about themselves as though nothing had ever happened. As the police officers lead Hickey away, the regulars of the bar discover that the kick of the booze has returned. They begin to get drunk in celebration and forgetfulness again with the lie of the pipe dream newly restored.

Critic George Jean Nathan concluded his final advance article prior to the production in 1946 with a tribute to Evelyn Hickman: 'the most pitifully affecting picture of a woman – the unseen wife of the protagonist – that I for one, have encountered in years of playgoing'.[31] O'Neill described his technique in an earlier letter to Nathan about a proposed series of one-act plays called 'By Way of Obit':

> In each the main character talks about a person who has died to a person who does little but listen. Via this monologue you get a complete picture of the person who has died – his or her whole life story – but just as complete a picture of the life and character of the narrator.[32]

What Hickey says about Evelyn and the way he describes her and their relationship says as much about him and his character as it does about his dead wife. He idealizes her as a way to justify his actions. No verification exists for any of the things that Hickey says about her. Evelyn exists in the play only so far as Hickey creates her. It is entirely likely that she is not the absolute angel that Hickey portrays or that Nathan idealizes in the press. Hickey's monologue about her suggests, rather, that her passive-aggressive reactions to his behaviour motivated his desire to murder her. But, truly, it is just as likely that she quite appropriately expressed her disappointment in him and that he could not tolerate her reproach.

Two other male characters also create idealized portraits of their absent spouses in order to justify their lives of sloth. James Cameron, 'Jimmy Tomorrow', claims that his drinking stems from his wife's unfaithfulness. Later, however, when he attempts to pull away from the pipe dream of the wronged husband, he admits to Hickey, reluctantly, that his wife only left him after he made it clear to her that he preferred drink to her. More dramatically, Harry Hope asserts that he has not left the bar in the twenty years since his wife Bessie's death due to sad remembrance of their life together. But McGloin, the corrupt former cop, calls her a 'bitch' and Mosher, her own brother, adds emphasis: 'Dear Bessie wasn't a bitch. She was a God-damned bitch!'[33] What makes Bessie such a bitch? Once again, what the specialist in graft and the grifter say may reveal as much if not more about them than about Bessie. An objective witness might even conclude that she had every right to dislike such lazy and dishonest men. Hickey lays Bessie's faults on the line for Hope to hear in Act Three, and Hope's silence confirms Hickey's charges: 'You never did want to go to church or any place else with her. She was always on your neck, making you have ambition and go out and do things, when all you wanted was to get drunk in peace.'[34] Seen with a bit of distance, Margaret, Bessie and Evelyn may have tried to build intimacy with their husbands, but the men shirked their marital relationships and escaped to the bar where no demands would ever be placed upon them to do anything at all.

A fourth absent woman, Rosa Parritt, contrasts with the other three in the decisive subplot that comments upon and offsets the main action. Her son, Don Parritt (who parrots Hickey and the main plot), is the newcomer to the bar and a decided outsider. He has none of the ingrained pipe dreams of the other habitués. Instead, he has come to the bar to seek out Larry Slade, whom he knew as a child as his mother's lover, in order to confess his guilt and receive judgement and punishment. His mother led an anarchist movement headquartered on the west coast, and Parritt betrayed the group (and her) to the authorities for a crime that the group committed. Parritt maintains initially that he did it for money, later that he did it for a woman, a prostitute, but in the end he comes clean and says that he did it because he hated his mother. Hate, in this case, is the flip side of love, and Parritt reacted impulsively because he felt neglected by his mother and envied her attention to the political movement rather than to him, her only child. That he seeks Slade to hear his confession suggests that he regrets what he did and feels the need to be punished. Larry Slade, he reasons, is the one other person who truly loved his mother and will demand that he make the ultimate sacrifice of his life in retribution for effectively taking hers. For his part, Larry recognizes early what Parritt wants from him and does everything he can to block the truth from coming out of his mouth. Nevertheless, in the end, Parritt breaks through Larry's pose of philosophical detachment and 'taunts him back into life'.[35] Larry admits that he still has feelings and threatens to strangle Parritt if the young man refuses to take his own life. Unlike Hickey, Hope or Jimmy Tomorrow, Larry Slade truly loved a woman and left her when she broke his heart and refused to remain faithful to him. Larry's genuine emotional ties make him the prized target of Hickey's reform movement and that is why Larry says, ironically, in the end that he is the only real convert to death Hickey actually made. Larry Slade denied his love as an illusion to guard against pain. The illusion for the others, headlined by Hickey, is that they ever did love the women in their lives.

The final stage picture presents the dilemma of how to live in the world by situating Slade alone on one side of the stage and the barflies on the other. The group coagulates around Harry Hope and sings a cacophony of disparate tunes, including, ironically enough, the French Revolutionary *Carmagnole*, to rid the last taint of the departed Hickey and to enjoy once again the reciprocity of shared delusions. The revellers seem to exist happily in denial of truth and time passing. Living in and with truth, on the other hand, is more than Slade can bear. He sits alone and waits for the thud of Parritt's falling body outside the window and then asserts that he, too, is ready to die now, unlike in the past when waiting for death was just a pipe dream. The action of *The Iceman Cometh* dramatizes the painful consequences of emotional attachments and intimacies as it chronicles the hazards of love. At the same time, it is very hard to think that those who refuse to see the truth and form bonds with others live anything more than a half-life of fear and loathing. 'Go out and meet him', directs the parable from Matthew. The challenge seems both awful and awesome.

Long Day's Journey Into Night

Halfway through the play, near the end of the second act, Edmund confronts his mother Mary about her morphine addiction and begs her to stop while it's not too late since she has only just started again. Mary at first feigns having no idea what he is talking about and then implies that his illness caused her relapse. She quickly begs forgiveness and says that his plight is not an excuse for her own behaviour. His bitter reaction prompts her to explain more fully:

> How could you believe me – when I can't believe myself? I've become such a liar. I never lied about anything once upon a time. Now I have to lie, especially to myself. But how can you understand, when I don't myself. I've never understood anything about it, except that one day long ago I found I could no longer call my soul my own.[36]

The last line echoes Sara's in *A Touch of the Poet* and foreshadows O'Neill's later public statement to the press in 1946 about greed and possession. The reference to 'it' ('I've never understood anything about it') reads ambiguously unless tied to the questions of identity and love posed by the preceding plays. If the response in *The Iceman Cometh* to Sara's questions of how much to love and how much of the self to give away is for the men to shrink from intimacy and relationships, then *Long Day's Journey Into Night* takes the direct opposite tack with its focus on Mary as the central figure and prime mover in that play.[37] She, unlike the male lodgers at Harry Hope's bar, suffers from having given too much of herself away to her husband in the name of love.

The male Tyrones try to hold the poisonous drug as the 'it' responsible for the family dysfunction even as they blame each other to varying degrees for Mary's addiction. With respect to the quoted speech above, Mary, too, suggests in an earlier tirade that 'it' refers to the morphine: 'I hate doctors! They'll do anything – anything to keep you coming to them. They'll sell their souls! What's worse, they'll sell yours, and you never know it till one day you find yourself in hell!'[38] Hell is exactly where Mary finds herself in the present action of the play, but how did she get there? Her use of drugs, as frightening and dangerous as it is, actually masks the tragedy that all the characters try to uncover. Mary digs at the root problem a bit earlier when she tries to explain things to her two sons: 'None of us can help the things life has done to us. They're done before you realize it, and once they're done they make you do other things until at last everything comes between you and what you'd like to be, and you've lost your true self forever.'[39] The self is the 'it' in the play and the search for it comprises the journey.

The overt action of the family play is slight, occurring on a single day. The four Tyrones enter the living room after breakfast on a summer morning in 1912 at their summerhouse in Connecticut.[40] The wife and mother, Mary, has recently returned from a stay at a sanatorium to recover from morphine addiction. All the men watch Mary for telltale signs of renewed drug abuse. Compounding their concern over Mary is an expected call from Doc Hardy at noon that confirms his diagnosis of Edmund's illness as tuberculosis. Prior to that revelation, however, the men realize that Mary has relapsed again. Her husband fears a return of the familiar pattern by which Mary keeps injecting the drug until she becomes almost unrecognizable. He complains bitterly that Mary is leaving the family even as his sons head to the doctor's office and he to his club in town where he will drink heavily in response to his wife's condition. Late at night, Mary walks the floors upstairs while James, who is drunk, tells Edmund that the great tragedy of his life was that he turned his back on a promising artistic career as a Shakespearean actor for the certainty of making money in the role of a melodramatic hero. James describes the road not taken as the one he wished he had pursued. What was he looking for all those years, he wonders, when he earned that pile of money? Such sentiments repeat Mary's earlier wishes for an alternative life and prepare the way for her return. She finally descends from upstairs late in Act Four and she appears as a kind of 'mad ghost' in her most intoxicated state. She holds the wedding dress she wore on the day of her marriage to Tyrone. Apparently, that was what she was looking for; she has discovered the first cause of her undoing and unhappiness – her marriage to James Tyrone.

Even as the play moves forward in stages from morning to past midnight, with each successive act occurring at breakfast, lunch and dinner (though significantly no meals are actually served; the dining table remains offstage and only a bottle of bourbon on the table is visible onstage), the action simultaneously moves back in time as the four Tyrones try to recreate history and assign blame for the damage done to the family. Drugs and drink prime the memories of each character to talk endlessly about past events. Why does Mary take morphine and who is responsible for her addiction? In a series of dialogues over four acts, a number of reasons and culprits emerge: Tyrone's stinginess as well as his possessiveness; their older son Jamie's jealousy; Edmund's illness and the circumstances of his birth. As exchanges accumulate between characters who complement or contradict each other in terms of truth, it becomes increasingly apparent that no one true answer will be discovered. As in many plays, the action unfolds as a mystery, and there is anticipation and even expectation raised that the reason behind Mary's drug use and the family's unhappiness will be identified. But the sheer number of competing stories makes such a tidy ending impossible. Each individual story and claim, from first to last, is compelling but incomplete and offers only the subjective perspective of the speaking character who attempts to accept responsibility as well as to shed blame for what happened. In the end, no single character is guilty; but no one is innocent, either.

As the play moves back in time through memories and recollections, the action also moves away in space while Mary pulls away from the family. Morphine provides an escape or refuge for Mary from the male family members. The opening line of the play is telling, as Tyrone says, upon entering the stage with his wife, 'You're a fine armful now, Mary, with those twenty pounds you've gained.'[41] The stage directions indicate that he holds his wife by the waist. From this point forward to the end of the play, Mary 'dispossesses' herself of him and her family physically as well as emotionally. Tellingly, her favourite retreat is to the 'spare' room upstairs that had probably been intended for the second child, Eugene, who contracted measles and died as a baby when Mary was travelling out-of-town with her actor husband. James laments that Mary's drug use means that she literally moves away from him and the family. He refers to her movement as 'drifting' away progressively until she becomes a ghost of herself.[42] Indeed, Mary's desire is to drift away and to disappear. In Act Three she describes the encroaching fog bank outside that addresses her motive behind morphine as well: 'It [fog] hides you from the world and the world from you. You feel that everything has changed, and nothing is what it seemed to be. No one can find or touch you any more.'[43] Edmund, who also rhapsodizes on the virtues of disappearing in the fog, accuses his mother of deliberately trying to get away from the family:

> The hardest thing to take is the blank wall she builds around her. Or it's more like a bank of fog in which she hides and loses herself. Deliberately, that's the hell of it! You know something in her does it deliberately – to get beyond our reach, to be rid of us, to forget we're alive! It's as if, in spite of loving us, she hated us![44]

Love and hate, in the words of the late scholar Michael Manheim, are the rhythm of kinship throughout O'Neill's works.[45] In spite of Mary's withdrawal from the family, the play is essentially a love story between her and James. She does not, as in the case of the men in *The Iceman Cometh*, love too little, but perhaps too well. She fears that she disappears in the relationship, but, at the same time, she does not regret the fact that she married her husband nor would she necessarily live life differently if she had the chance or the choice. She emphatically asserts the bond between them: 'James! We've loved each other! We always will! Let's remember only that, and not try to understand what we cannot understand, or help things that cannot be helped – the things life has done to us we cannot excuse or explain.'[46] Strategically, grammatically, Mary uses the passive voice to gives 'life' agency not only to distance herself from her choices and to make herself a victim, but more importantly to show the irony of fate in which her assertion of choices and even getting her heart's desire still comes at the expense of other choices that ultimately diminished her over time and left her short of where she thought she might be or who she thought she might have become.

Identity, in O'Neill's plays, is made up of a multiplicity of perspectives and dreams and capabilities. The pipe dream, in O'Neill's world, or the hopeless hope, is necessary to live even when the attainment of that same dream is remote or completely impossible. In Mary's case, she dreams of three things: to be a nun, to become a concert pianist and to marry James Tyrone. Now, these three dreams are irreconcilable with one another. One cannot become a nun, say, and also marry a matinee idol! To be sure,

the housemaid Kathleen does not take Mary's desire to become a
nun very seriously. She says, frankly, 'I can't imagine you a holy
nun, Ma'am.'[47] She recognizes the sexual attraction between Mary
and her husband. Tyrone speaks even more bluntly about his
wife's desire to become a nun in conversation in the last act with
Edmund: 'She was never made to renounce the world. She was
bursting with health and high spirits and the love of loving.'[48] As
for her becoming a concert pianist, Tyrone insists that the nuns at
the convent put that notion into her head as a way of flattering
a young girl.[49] Tyrone's guilt, of course, may lead him to dismiss
his wife's dreams as immature, naïve and impossible. He cannot
be considered a completely reliable or an impartial witness. In the
end, though, it does not matter whether he is right or wrong in his
assessment of Mary's talents and desires.

The heart wants what the heart wants. It may be impossible
to be a nun, an artist and the wife of a wildly handsome actor,
but all three of those things sound desirable even if they are not
possible to embody simultaneously. Mary ended up with one of
three (James) and discovers that as wonderful as marriage has
been at times it somehow has not been enough to fulfil and sustain
her for a lifetime. And, the dream of becoming a nun or a concert
pianist, real enough as a dream, exists only as abstract and wishful
thinking. She physically withdraws from the men of the family,
however, from the opening moments of the play through to the very
end. Mary fails spectacularly in her various familial roles. O'Neill
revealed his idealized standard for women with his inscription of
Mourning Becomes Electra addressed to Carlotta in 1931. Written
in France, his thankful tribute concludes, ' – mother, and wife and
mistress and friend! – And collaborator!' His closing adds final
emphasis: 'Collaborator, I love you!'[50] Mary cannot compete with
such a versatile rival in those same roles with the Tyrone men, and
she wilts under the pressure of their collective scrutiny.

The final stage picture is similar to the final stage scene in *The
Iceman Cometh*. Here, Mary enters and stands apart from her
three men, James, Jamie and Edmund, who share the bottle of
bourbon at the table. Mary's gaze – like that of Larry Slade in
the previous play – is directed not at the men but straight ahead,
as if directly to the audience. Three successive stage directions
on the last three pages of the text follow Mary as she '*sits down,
facing front*',[51] then is '*staring dreamily before her*'[52] and then in

the final lines, '*stares before her in a sad dream*'.⁵³ Don Parritt, against Larry's will, pulled the old man back to the world of the living in the previous play. Mary, lost in a haze of morphine, has retreated from the living and appears almost as a ghost of herself.⁵⁴ Each, in his or her way, remembers what it was like to be in love and to be 'so happy for a time'. One tried to run from love; the other succumbed under love's heavy burden. The answer to love's dilemma remains to be solved in O'Neill's very last play.

A Moon for the Misbegotten

O'Neill's last completed play focuses on the final days of Jim Tyrone, the older son in *Long Day's Journey Into Night*, who is based upon the playwright's own brother.⁵⁵ Whereas James O'Neill, Jr drank himself blind and died at Riverlawn Sanatorium in Paterson, New Jersey, in 1923 from alcoholic neuritis, the fictional Jim Tyrone discovers at least one night of peace and spiritual redemption in *A Moon for the Misbegotten*. The epigraph of *Long Day's Journey Into Night*, another inscription by the playwright to his wife, thanks her for allowing him to write it 'with deep pity and understanding and forgiveness for all the four haunted Tyrones'.⁵⁶ It is not always easy to see the forgiveness in that play. Matthew Wikander, for example, challenges the validity of that statement and calls the play a 'testament of rage'.⁵⁷ All the anger that O'Neill may have felt toward his family, however, ebbs away in his last play. It truly is a play of forgiveness that extends not only to his brother, but, just as importantly, to himself as well, and even to his mother in the form of one of his truly unique characters, Josie Hogan.

In the climactic scene at the end of Act Three, Josie plays the part of Tyrone's mother in order to bestow the forgiveness and blessing that the son did not receive from her while she was still alive. This gesture dramatically swings the balance of power and focus between the two characters toward the female part. Steven F. Bloom identifies the dual nature of the play: 'Looked at through a biographical lens, this play seems to be about Jamie O'Neill, the profligate brother who drank himself to death at an early age. Looked at in the context of O'Neill's dramaturgy, however, it is yet another play in which a strong and complex female character becomes the dominant force.'[58] Her complex vitality allows her to don a variety of roles, and she takes over the action of the play as the protagonist. In the wake of questions of love and the responsibilities of one person toward another in loving and intimate relationships posed by Sara in *A Touch of the Poet* and Mary in *Long Day's Journey Into Night*, set further in relief by the absence of female characters in *The Iceman Cometh*, Josie Hogan responds selflessly and compassionately to Jim's most pressing needs. Whereas love is talked about in earlier plays, here, at the end, love becomes the subject of the play through dialogue, certainly, but more importantly through staged action.

All the action takes place on the tenant farm of Josie's father, Phil Hogan. He incites the action by telling Josie that the owner of the farm, James Tyrone, Jr, plans to sell the farm. To get their revenge on him, Phil suggests that Josie invite Tyrone for a date and then seduce him after alcohol incapacitates him. Phil promises to bring witnesses to catch the couple in bed and thus shame Tyrone into a forced marriage that will save the farm for the Hogans. When he shows up early in the day, Tyrone is completely unaware of the anger that Josie harbours toward him and the reason behind it, but he has always liked her, and he agrees to return to see her later that night for a date under the moonlight. Hoping that this night will be different from the ones he usually spends on prostitutes in cheap hotels, Jim eventually unburdens his soul by telling Josie how he defiled himself after his mother's death as revenge against her for leaving him alone. After confessing everything to her, Jim falls asleep with his head on her breast and she holds him through the night. Upon his return in the morning, Hogan does not find things between the two as he had hoped. His story about Tyrone selling the farm was a scheme to get his daughter together with the man she loves. Heartbroken, he hides his disappointment behind Irish banter and blarney once Jim wakes up and walks away for the last time.

The play stages two scenes that are only talked about in *Long Day's Journey Into Night*. First, the confrontation between Hogan and T. Stedman Harder dramatizes Edmund's story of Shaughnessy's pigs and the triumph of the shanty Irish over the Yankee aristocracy. Hogan plays the part of Shaughnessy and Harder is Harker from the earlier play.[59] In a wonderfully comic scene, the underdog outwits and confuses the rich man much to the delight of Hogan, Josie and Jim Tyrone as well. The fact that Tyrone functions as a member of the audience, hiding inside the house in order to hear the exchange, magnifies the theatricality of a play in which characters play many roles. For example, Josie and her father first spy Tyrone as a 'dead man walking' prior to his appearance on stage; he becomes animated only when he thinks that he is 'onstage' with the Hogans. Josie, too, masquerades as the village slut who has slept with all the neighbouring men, but in fact she is a virgin. Finally, Hogan functions as the 'playwright' within the play, the Irish trickster who seems only to love himself but who actually loves his daughter deeply and contrives circumstances in which she can acknowledge her love for Tyrone and he for her as well. As Josie says of him, there's always a trick within his trick, and the comic scene of Hogan befuddling Harder is just such a ploy.

More importantly, another version of Jamie's story of 'Fat Violet' in *Long Day's Journey Into Night* comes to the stage in the form of Josie Hogan in *A Moon for the Misbegotten*. In Act Four of the earlier play, Jamie tells his brother how he spent the evening at a whorehouse and ended up with the fattest of the prostitutes, whom no one else would hire and who was about to get fired by the madam of the house. 'I like them fat,' says Jamie, 'but not that fat.'[60] Still, he felt sorry for her and hired her anyway and they cried together as he 'confessed' his life story. This, of course, is a comic rendition of the action in the later play and Jim's actions with Josie, who is described in the opening stage directions as '*so oversize for a woman that she is almost a freak*'.[61] At the same time, too, Fat Violet is also an early representation of the 'Blonde Pig' in the later play, another prostitute whom Jim solicited on the train that carried the body of his dead mother back from the west coast. Jim indulged himself with the prostitute for the entire trip in the compartment adjacent to the one carrying his mother. For this action he seeks redemption from Josie, whom he enlists to play the part of his mother, but who evokes his memory of the prostitute as well – the familiar twin images of virgin and whore.

Josie's actions, however, transcend all the easy descriptions of her. Josie loves Jim and she thinks at one point that she can redeem him and that she will take him as her first lover and the love for her lifetime. But the actual romance takes a different turn, because

Jim can only seduce her if she plays the part of the Blonde Pig, a prostitute, and that brief and crude exchange nearly erupts in violent rape before she pulls away and he, too, realizes his mistake. Josie knows, finally, that Jim is past saving, that he cannot or will not be able to accept her love. At that point, she makes a decision to offer Jim the only kind of love that he can accept: she acts the part of his mother and forgives him and holds him as though she were a mother holding her small child. She abandons all her desire for him and her designs on their future and, rather than let him walk away and return to the bars in town and a crowd of strangers, she lets him tell her his sad story as a way of offering him the love and forgiveness that he needs. She has all kinds of love for him, she claims, but this is the greatest of all, she says, 'because it costs so much'.[62] After Jim confesses his guilt and shame, Josie transcends her gendered roles as virgin–whore and mother–lover to perform a selfless and sacrificial act. Josie is healthy and fully capable of sexual and romantic love, but she recognizes Jim's limitations and responds to his needs. Neither idealized nor demonized through her actions, Josie commands this tragedy of sacrificial love: 'A virgin who bears a dead child in the night, and the dawn finds her still a virgin.'[63] Josie did not realize before this night that Tyrone was already dead and that her love, no matter how strong and ardent, could not revive him.

Josie's closing lines confer final grace upon the departed Jim: 'May you have your wish and die in your sleep soon, Jim, darling. May you rest forever in forgiveness and peace.'[64] These same lines bless the end of O'Neill's artistic career as well. It is impossible to see Tyrone struggling to light a match in the middle of the play due to the tremor in his hands without thinking of the degenerative tremor of O'Neill's that ultimately prevented him from writing. In her last book on O'Neill, Doris Alexander titles her chapter on this play 'Epigraph', and says, 'He [O'Neill] certainly was anticipating his own death as a creative artist as he crafted his protagonist's death.'[65] A further rich parallel can be drawn between the end of this play and August Strindberg's *The Ghost Sonata*, one of the last plays of the Swedish playwright, who certainly wrote it with death in mind. O'Neill admired Strindberg more than any other playwright, modelled his themes and dramaturgy after him in many ways, thanked him publicly for his influence in his Nobel acceptance speech and even produced the Strindberg play as the inaugural production of the Experimental Theatre, Inc. in 1924.[66] The conclusion of Strindberg's play strikes the same tone as O'Neill's but is much longer, and it may very well have been on O'Neill's mind when he wrote the last act of his last completed play. In Strindberg's play, the male Student speaks to The Young Lady:

> And you, my darling, you beautiful, innocent, lost soul who suffers for no fault of your own, sleep, sleep a dreamless sleep. And when you wake again ... may you be greeted by a sun that doesn't scorch, in a home without dust, by friends without faults, and by a love without flaw ...[67]

Conclusion

A Moon for the Misbegotten closed during an out-of-town tryout in St Louis in 1947, and O'Neill elected to publish it in book form. He didn't live to see a successful production. Thirty years after O'Neill completed it, José Quintero directed Jason Robards and Colleen Dewhurst in a workshop revival of the play that toured across the country and eventually garnered a nationally-televised broadcast of the staged production. The trio called themselves the 'Resurrection' Company and the production revived the careers of all three artists.[68] Quintero and Robards had previously launched the O'Neill renaissance that began in 1956 with a brilliant revival of *The Iceman Cometh* at the tiny in-the-round space of Circle in the Square Theatre in Greenwich Village, followed by the Broadway and United States premiere of *Long Day's Journey Into Night* in November 1956 at the Helen Hayes Theatre. O'Neill had left instructions for the latter play to remain unpublished for twenty-five years after his death and for it never to be performed. Only three years after his death, however, his wife, Carlotta, granted production rights first to the Royal Dramatic Theatre of Sweden and then to Americans Quintero and his producing partner, Theodore Mann, two virtual unknowns at the time. Ironically, a series of glittering productions resurrected interest in O'Neill, who had himself turned his back on the theatre and preferred the drama as written, as he had written it, to the performances and productions of his plays. Productions in the twenty-first century directed by Doug Hughes, Michael Kahn, Daniel Sullivan and Robert Falls, designed by Santo Loquasto, John Conklin, Bob Crowley, Eugene Lee and Jane Greenwood and performed by Jessica Lange, Eve Best, Vanessa Redgrave, Laurie Metcalf, Cherry Jones, Kevin Spacey, Brian Dennehy, Paul Giamatti, John Douglas Thompson and Nathan Lane ensure that O'Neill remains in public and in the public's consciousness. The struggles of bodies and souls in full view on the stage, as they display a visceral glow with the sweat of heated exchange, concretize the battle between intimacy and denial, and advance the value of love because, in Josie's words, 'it costs so much'.

5

Thornton Wilder: Seeing Beyond Dark Times

Felicia Hardison Londré

The 1940s decade holds some claim to all three of Thornton Wilder's greatest plays. *Our Town* (1938), released as a movie in 1940 and made available for production by community theatres, swept the nation as an affirmation of the American values that bolstered morale at home and on the military fronts. *The Skin of Our Teeth* (1942) drew heavily upon wartime concerns and gave Wilder his 1943 Pulitzer Prize. *The Matchmaker* (1954) was essentially the same play as *The Merchant of Yonkers* (1938), which had lain fallow during the decade, awaiting the right director and the right actress to play Dolly Gallagher Levi. While those three are by far the best known, the most anthologized and – with the possible exception of certain one-acts – most frequently produced of Wilder's plays, the four selected for analysis here more closely fit the decade as a chronological construct while recognizing two relatively less known yet significant works. Besides *Our Town* and *The Skin of Our Teeth*, this chapter examines Wilder's 1942 screenplay *Shadow of a Doubt* and the play that most occupied his thoughts and writing time for long periods during the 1940s: *The Alcestiad*, which finally premiered in 1955.

Although the Second World War dominated public discourse and private anxieties during the first half of the decade of the

1940s, Thornton Wilder managed to meld those concerns with the larger issues that permeate his entire canon: the family as the enduring social unit, a cosmic sense of history, minutiae of existence as a lens on the ideal, and the resilience of the human spirit. The Webb and Gibbs families in *Our Town*, the Antrobus family in *The Skin of Our Teeth*, the Newton family in *Shadow of a Doubt* and the battered family of Alcestis and Admetus all evoke patterns of relationships that remain constant across the centuries. Reflections on the past and the future surface throughout the works, for example: when the denizens of the *Our Town* cemetery 'think only of what's ahead' while it takes 'millions of years' for the speck of light from a star to get to earth;[1] when Mr Antrobus in *The Skin of Our Teeth* recalls his own evolution over 'the last million years', but the Fortune-Teller speaks of how hard it is to know one's own past;[2] when Uncle Charlie in *Shadow of a Doubt* contrasts today's whole 'crooked' world with nostalgia for 'the old times';[3] when Alcestis asks Apollo whether there will be 'grandchildren, and the grandchildren of grandchildren' and he predicts 'beyond all counting'.[4] Small pleasures like shared intimacy at a soda-fountain counter, group singing around a fireplace when it is bitter cold outside, a telegram that satisfies a wish, a bath after a long journey on foot – these and other such telling moments anchor the sense of human solidarity in a world threatened by both natural and man-made disasters. *The Skin of Our Teeth* is permeated with wartime anxieties that were prevalent during its writing and production, but the motif of war surfaces also in the other works, even in *Our Town* where the cemetery holds war dead of the American Revolution and Civil War while the losses to come in the First World War are foreseen by the Stage Manager. In *Shadow of a Doubt* and in *The Alcestiad*, good and innocent people are menaced or harmed by virtually inexplicable outside forces. Awareness of lurking catastrophe underlies any outbreaks of optimism about the future of civilization.

The seriousness of the times and corresponding dark undercurrents in Wilder's writing did not overpower his sense of fun. An example is his playlet *Our Century*, which was performed at New York City's Century Club, as part of its Centennial Celebration, on 26 April 1947, and published that year by the Century Association in 1000 numbered copies – a clothbound edition of only twenty numbered pages. The dominant characters in all three scenes are four self-important club members named Matthew, Mark, Luke and John. Scene One is titled 'The Century Association as Our Sons Imagine It' and shows the four snoozing in their leather chairs after lunch, waking periodically to congratulate themselves on the various ways they 'use their all but unlimited powers for the public good'[5] and finally ringing for the steward to bring drinks. In Scene Two, 'The Century Association as A New Member Imagines It to Be', a younger New Member ventures cautiously into the clubroom. Four Senior Members enter and see the hapless young man. They pointedly discuss past instances of mistakes having been made by the Admission Committee, while the New Member sweats and shreds his handkerchief in agony. The four enlist their steward Thomas to participate in the humiliation, then remove themselves to another room. The New Member finds a revolver and shoots himself. Scene Three, 'The Century Association as Our Wives Imagine It', is partially credited to Henry Clapp Smith; the conceit of this vignette is that the club stewards are complicit in creating alibis for the members to explain their late-evening absences from home. Certainly, these slight sketches echo character elements of George Antrobus and the husband–wife relationship in *The Skin of Our Teeth*. The obliging Thomas who enables the Centurions' worst impulses has his counterpart in Herbie Hawkins of *Shadow of a Doubt*.

Religion held a significant place in most Americans' lives during the 1940s, and certainly Wilder's religious upbringing informed his work even when religious questions were not the focus. In his introduction to *Our Town*, the Stage Manager points out the locations of the various churches, and each act includes the singing of hymns, notably – in each of the three acts – 'Blessed Be the Tie That Binds', a title well calculated – beyond its metaphysical meaning – to evoke a sense of earthly community for a nation soon to unite in great common purpose. *The Skin of Our Teeth* abounds with biblical references: for example, lines from Genesis are quoted during the effort to 'save the human race' at the end of Act One.[6] *Shadow of a Doubt* includes church-related scenes as a motif of community solidarity. In the first act of *The Alcestiad*, Alcestis is convinced that she has a religious vocation and determines that she will be a priestess of Apollo; gradually she realizes that devotion to other human beings can be an equally valid spiritual calling.

The Bible was one of many deeply-engrained sources of ideas and allusions for Wilder. From childhood he read widely with particular emphasis on Greek and Latin classics and on German literature. Soon he was also well versed in Shakespeare, Oscar Wilde, Henrik Ibsen and Bernard Shaw; in American philosophical thought and nineteenth-century novels; in existentialist writers (Kierkegaard, Kafka, Sartre); in French and Italian writing of all genres. He spent long periods immersed in Sir Thomas Browne's *Religio Medici* (1635), in the plays of Lope de Vega and, during the 1940s as a consuming obsession, in James Joyce's 1939 novel *Finnegan's Wake*, which he acknowledged as an inspiration for *The Skin of Our Teeth*. He was also generous about reading works in progress by his friends, among whom Gertrude Stein figured prominently along with many others. Although he was never hesitant about crediting other writers as influences on his own work, Wilder so skilfully threaded literary references into his characteristic style that it can be difficult to pinpoint the homage. As he worked on *Our Town*, Wilder wrote in a September 1937 letter to Stein that 'its third act is based upon your ideas, as on great pillars'; the editors of the published Stein–Wilder correspondence interpret that comment in terms of the epic vision of her 1925 book *The Making of Americans*.[7] Given his acquaintance with French dramatists Jean Cocteau and Jean Giraudoux and director Louis Jouvet, all of whom were associated with 1930s Paris productions that put modern twists on classical myths, it is easy to detect touches of their inspiration in *The Alcestiad*. Alfred Hitchcock marvelled at Wilder's openness to influence during their work together on *Shadow of a Doubt* when Wilder suggested borrowing an idea from an Ernest Hemingway short story.[8]

Even as he integrated the fruits of his wide reading and theatregoing, Thornton Wilder believed that each play should find its own form. His plays of the 1940s offer numerous examples of both his integration of influences and his active experimentation with dramatic technique. As his letters and journal entries attest, his friend Gertrude Stein's iconoclastic thought and expression spurred his own quest for innovation. After Wilder read a draft-in-progress of *Our Town* in 1937 to the invalid playwright Edward Sheldon, whose generous-spirited objectivity aided the many theatre artists who sought him out, Sheldon responded, 'You broke every rule', and went on to laud the play's 'novelty' as actively contributing to its substance.[9] Sheldon similarly served as a sounding board for the 'unorthodox' elements in *The Skin of Our Teeth* as Wilder worked on it in 1941.[10] Conceived as a mix of comedy and human catastrophe that would span millennia from the Ice Age to modern times, *The Skin of Our Teeth* gave free rein to Wilder's 'subconscious' in the creative process,[11] and it must be noted that Sigmund Freud, who befriended Wilder in 1935, had some influence on his thinking about that play. As early as 1939, Wilder wrote in his journal about the difficulty he was having in finding a style for *The Alcestiad* (a struggle that would obsess him throughout the 1940s) and that it would be 'impossible' for him to 'write any play in a realistic setting'.[12] While realism of setting, dialogue, characterization and visual elements is intrinsic to his screenplay for *Shadow of a Doubt*, the action progresses in a manner similar to that of *Our Town*: through the accretion of small details that only gradually add up to a big picture. Indeed, Wilder never restricted his works-in-progress to their original concepts, but allowed them to flower in often surprising ways.

Fifty years after the premiere of *Our Town*, critic William A. Henry III commented that 'In defiance of the 'rules' of drama, Wilder kills off half a dozen characters without offering even one juicy onstage death scene.'[13] Yet Wilder did not shy away from looking squarely at death. The treatment of death in Act Three of *Our Town* serves as the unsparing antidote to the sweetness of many perceptions about the play. *The Skin of Our Teeth* introduces the theme of death from the beginning in Sabina's almost-humorous but soberingly truthful observation, 'In the midst of life we are in the midst of death, a truer word was never said.'[14] *Shadow of a Doubt* builds to a horrifying death struggle. *The Alcestiad* brings Death onto the stage as a character, while the entrance to the underworld may be partially glimpsed in the stage setting. In 1954, as Wilder neared completion of that play, which had taken most of his writing focus throughout the 1940s, he referred to *The Alcestiad* as 'a humdinger – the true extension of the *Our Town* – *Skin* line'.[15] Both Emily's brief return from the grave and Alcestis's being denied a grave demonstrate that death serves humankind positively, as it illuminates meaning in life.

Our Town

The action in *Our Town* is set between 1901 and 1913. American theatregoers in 1938 and throughout the 1940s looked back on that span of years before the outbreak of the First World War (1914–18) in Europe as a period of innocence, opportunity and prosperity. In *Our Town*, most of the characters are insulated by time and place from forebodings about Europe's gathering storm. Keeping the focus on that innocent pre-war era and the apparently idyllic small-town life of Grover's Corners, New Hampshire, allowed depression-weary and war-wary audiences of 1938 to enjoy the play as a vehicle of escapist nostalgia. And yet the play conveys reminders of the world outside the theatre. For example, the eleven-year-old newspaper delivery boy, Joe Crowell, Jr, is scarcely introduced as a character when the Stage Manager tells how the bright lad would get a scholarship to Massachusetts Tech and graduate at the top of the class with plans to be an engineer, but 'the war broke out and he died in France. All that education for nothing.'[16] We learn that Dr Gibbs makes periodic visits to Civil War battlefields, jaunts that satisfy his wanderlust to the extent that he never takes seriously his wife's desire to see Paris. For audiences, of course, her yearning to visit France would seem ironic, given their awareness that only 15 years after the time setting of Act One the land of her dreams would be consumed in mud and blood.

At a time when Broadway theatres had voluminous red plush curtains to mask each show's elaborate stage setting that would be dramatically revealed after the auditorium lights had dimmed, the half-lit bare stage on view to theatregoers at *Our Town*'s New York opening on 4 February 1938 must have seemed like a provocation, if not an ironic commentary on the Depression. Commercial theatre had never been so denatured as when the Stage Manager sauntered on and added a modicum of visual interest with his placement of a table and three chairs at each side of the stage. Functioning as both friendly guide and omniscient narrator, the Stage Manager (played by the folksy character actor Frank Craven) then proceeded to describe the layout of the town, to identify the spaces demarcated by the tables and chairs as the homes of Doc Gibbs and Editor Webb and their families, and to evoke the town's past, present and future. He mentions, for example, that the first automobile would 'come along in about five years – belonged to Banker Cartwright, our richest citizen ... lives in the big white house up on the hill'.[17] No Cartwright appears in the cast of *Our Town*, but the local financial dynasty looms as a constant presence, perhaps deriving from Wilder's awareness that money matters were never far from American minds in 1938. The Stage Manager points out that Cartwrights are among the earliest residents of the Grover's Corners cemetery, and Cartwrights currently own the town's lucrative blanket-making factory. Even little Rebecca Gibbs claims in Act One that what she loves most in the world is money.[18]

Act One serves largely for exposition and immersion in the theatrical conventions. Audiences needed a little transition time to adjust to the invisible props, pantomimed actions like lighting a stove and preparing a meal or delivering milk from a horse-drawn wagon, and the down-homey Stage Manager's godlike orchestration of information and stage activity. Reviewer Brooks Atkinson acknowledged that while 'the form is strange', the minimalism actually opened the way for 'the quintessence of acting'.[19] The Stage Manager gives us snippets from the town's early morning activities, additional data about the town with questions from plants in the audience, and then he skips to afternoon when school gets out. Sixteen-year-old, baseball-obsessed George Gibbs speaks briefly to Emily Webb on their way home from school; her pride in her academic accomplishments presages that of Gladys in *The Skin of Our Teeth* and perhaps even that of little Ann Newton in *Shadow of a Doubt*. In a brief mother–daughter sequence, Emily seeks her mother's affirmation that she is pretty, but gets only, 'You're pretty enough for all normal purposes.'[20]

The Stage Manager's so-called 'Babylon' speech marks the transition to evening on this introductory day (7 May 1901) in the life of the town and also evokes the grand sweep of human endeavour. While we have few records from the huge civilization of ancient Babylon, he says, we know that 'families sat down to supper ... and the smoke went up the chimney – same as here'.[21] With reference to a new Cartwright bank under construction, he muses about what items should go into the cornerstone so that people 'a thousand years from now' will know how we lived in this place and time. The inclusion of 'a copy of this play' (along with the Bible, Shakespeare's plays and the United States Constitution) might be Wilder's deft, subtle homage to Italian playwright Luigi

Pirandello, 'whose plays I adore',[22] and the self-referential theatricality in *Six Characters in Search of an Author*, which had profoundly affected Wilder when he saw the original production in Rome in 1920. *Our Town*'s moonlit evening sequence alternates between the children at their homework and the choir practice conducted by Simon Stimson, an organist, at the Congregational Church. One of the iconic images for *Our Town* is that of the two ladders from which George and Emily look out the second-storey windows of their bedrooms and consult on a maths problem. Outside in the moonlight after choir practice, Mrs Gibbs, Mrs Webb and Mrs Soames comment on the choir director Simon Stimson's drinking problem. Dr Gibbs later explains it to his wife, 'Some people ain't made for small-town life.'[23] Certainly, there is some unrevealed mystery about the character's 'troubles',[24] which have traditionally been explained as the frustration of the artist in a town where there is no interest in high culture. However, Kenneth Elliott argues plausibly in an essay on Stimson as an outsider that he represents the male homosexual in an era when the only way out of the closet was suicide.[25] Walking somewhat unsteadily home from choir practice, Stimson does not return Mr Webb's greeting, and Constable Warren cannot see 'how that's goin' to end'.[26] Counterbalancing the street sequence's hint of tarnish on *Our Town*'s idyllic image are the memorable Act One curtain lines delivered by Rebecca Gibbs when she tells her big brother George about the letter her friend Jane received with the envelope address expanded all the way to 'the Mind of God'.[27]

Act Two is set three years later (on 7 July 1904) and is called 'Love and Marriage'.[28] Over simultaneous breakfasts in the Gibbs and Webb kitchens, the talk centres on George and Emily's wedding day. George goes to the back door of the Webb house 'to see my girl',[29] but Mrs Webb reminds him that 'the groom can't see his bride on his wedding day, not until he sees her in church'.[30] Wilder had learned about that superstition only in 1935 when his brother Amos Niven Wilder had married, and he would use it again in *The Alcestiad*.[31] Invited to sit down for coffee while Mrs Webb goes to keep Emily out of sight, George faces his future father-in-law in an initially awkward conversation that opens up compellingly. The Stage Manager interrupts the scene to take us back to the beginning of George and Emily's understanding that they were meant 'to spend a lifetime together'.[32] Just as the two separate ladders epitomize each teen's individual development in Act One, the placement of a board across the backs of two chairs to represent a drugstore soda-fountain counter in Act Two allows a visual statement of maturing empathy as they sit side by side, facing outward together. The sweetness and reticence of their conversation, followed by George's embarrassment at not having the money at hand to pay for their strawberry ice-cream sodas, make the scene one of the most beloved in all of American dramatic literature. The wedding occupies the remainder of the act. The Stage Manager performs as the minister and reminds us that weddings are witnessed by 'millions' of ancestors. He also cautions that 'even at a good wedding there's a lot of confusion way down deep in people's minds and we thought that ought to be in our play, too'.[33] Wilder specifies 'an abrupt change of approach' in this scene[34] as we hear the unspoken thoughts of some characters, including George and Emily, who each enact a separate moment of misgiving before going up the aisle. But the wedding proceeds, with its all-important musical accompaniments. The act closes on a high note of happiness, two-thirds of the way through the play, just as most lives achieve fulfilment around two-thirds through the journey.

During intermission before Act Three the stage is rearranged. Rows of chairs are placed to represent graves in the cemetery, occupied by those who died during the nine years since the wedding. Seated there are Mrs Gibbs and Simon Stimson, among others. The Stage Manager's introductory remarks progress from what has changed in Grover's Corners during those nine years to a larger vision of time and space represented by the cemetery and then to what may be 'eternal about every human being'.[35] Only very gradually does the subsequent conversation between undertaker Joe Stoddard and a former Grover's Corners citizen, Sam Craig, hint at whose funeral we are to see today: 'a young person', one who died in childbirth, 'another pretty bad blow' for Doc Gibbs. From her grave, Mrs Gibbs identifies the newcomer to the graveyard as 'my daughter-in-law, Emily Webb'.[36] It is a poignant theatrical effect when Emily in a white dress emerges from the cluster of black-clad mourners with their black umbrellas; she slowly crosses to sit on the empty chair next to that of Mrs Gibbs. As she updates her mother-in-law on the family, her tone begins to acquire the emotional detachment of the dead, and she realizes that 'live people don't understand'; they are 'troubled' and 'in the dark'.[37] But suddenly she realizes also that it is possible to go back and relive past times. Mrs Gibbs and Mrs Soames counsel against it, but Emily chooses to return to her 12th birthday, 11 February 1899. The lights brighten on half of the stage where Emily sees and hears the long-ago activity of a snowy morning on Main Street. In the kitchen, Emily marvels at how young and beautiful her parents were. But then, 'It goes so fast. We don't have time to look at one another ... Do any human beings ever realize life while they live it? – every, every minute?'[38] She returns to her grave, accepting the great chasm between the 'ignorance and blindness'[39] of the living and the peaceful fixity of the afterlife. Night falls. George Gibbs comes and prostrates himself on Emily's grave. The Stage Manager evokes the passing of time and bids the audience good night.

In Wilder's own words, 'the central theme of the play' asks, 'What is the relation between the countless "unimportant" details of our daily life, on the one hand, and the great perspectives of time, social history, and current religious ideas, on the other?'[40] *Our Town* was inspired partly by the New England villages he came to love during his summers at the MacDowell Colony and by archaeological excavations he had seen in Rome. Thus he focused on fragments to reconstruct 'the life of a village against the life of the stars'.[41] His awareness that he was 'writing the most beautiful little play you can imagine' is expressed in a letter dated 13 September 1937 to Gertrude Stein and Alice Toklas.[42] During rehearsals, however, he deplored director Jed Harris's deletions of grittier elements, a skewing that Wilder feared would sentimentalize the text. Harris, a brilliant director and notoriously unpleasant personality, certainly played a major role in giving Wilder his first Broadway success, yet the difficult process yielded three somewhat different published versions of the play, as meticulously analysed by Park Bucker,[43] which leave some latitude for interpretation. Over the decades since the 1938 premiere, the play has largely been regarded as 'sweet, sentimental, nostalgic, and funny', but critic William A. Henry III cautioned in 1988 that seeing the play in those terms limits appreciation for a work that remains 'groundbreakingly unconventional in form and chafingly unsettling in its view of human nature'.[44] Twenty-one years after that, director David Cromer mined the darker veins and brought new directorial insights in a 2009 production at New York City's Barrow Street

Theatre that 'made something so new out of so familiar a play ... without doing violence to the original' by making the first two acts apparently artless, as if occurring on a blurred continuum from the street life of the audience;[45] but Emily's Act Three revisiting of the past was staged with the surprise revelation of an utterly naturalistic kitchen and a wealth of turn-of-the-century period details in the costumes, in the setting and even in the aroma of coffee and bacon. Brilliantly the sequence conveyed to jaded twenty-first-century theatregoers Wilder's concept akin to what we would call 'mindfulness': being aware of the present moment as it is lived.

Our Town is often signalled as the most-produced of the great American classic dramas; indeed, it is said that there is a performance of *Our Town* somewhere in the world every day of the year. The original production ran for 336 performances and toured extensively. With the release of amateur production rights in 1939, the play became a staple of community theatres everywhere. One of the early productions, at Kansas City's Resident Theater from 1 to 22 May 1939, featured the great Walter Hampden as guest artist to play the Stage Manager.[46] The 1940 movie produced by Sol Lesser (for which Wilder contributed to the screenplay) earned an Academy Award nomination for Best Picture and uplifted the spirits of audiences across America. The influence of *Our Town* extended even to the musical comedy and to its most successful team, Richard Rodgers and Oscar Hammerstein II, as Terry Teachout noted in his review of a revival of their 1947 musical *Allegro*:

> The first production, designed by Jo Mielziner, made use of near-abstract sets, a drastic departure from traditional musical-comedy practice, and the book, which Hammerstein wrote from scratch instead of adapting it from a familiar source, was very closely influenced by Thornton Wilder's 'Our Town,' which in 1947 was still by a long shot the most dramaturgically radical American play ever to have opened on Broadway.[47]

A chamber opera version of *Our Town* composed by Ned Rorem, with a libretto by J. D. McClatchey, premiered in 2006.

The Skin of Our Teeth

When Wilder began work on *The Skin of Our Teeth* in June 1940, the Second World War was raging in Europe, and Japanese military expansion had destabilized Asia. Backed by American public opinion, the United States had declared its neutrality in 1939. Given his own forebodings of catastrophe, Wilder originally titled his new play *The Ends of the Worlds*.[48] Ultimately, he took the play's title from the Bible's Book of Job, 19.20: 'My bone cleaveth to my skin and to my flesh, and I am escaped with the skin of my teeth.'[49] Again taking the long view of humanity as in *Our Town*, Wilder set out to write a comedy about civilization's eternal struggle to survive. Again he particularized a huge subject by focusing on the travails of a single family. Quite possibly Wilder's inspiration for the Antrobus family may be traced back to a Roman excavation he visited in 1920. There he saw, beneath a traffic-choked modern street, a first-century tomb with depictions of the Aurelius family; there were parents and children going about their daily lives almost a thousand years earlier.[50] From the Aurcliuses to today's Joneses or Antrobuses, countless generations of families have repeated similar patterns of work, play, relationships and rituals. Wilder's purpose was both to spoof those notions and to convey the wonderment of it all.

The Skin of Our Teeth opens with a pastiche of newsreels that regularly preceded feature films at 1940s movie theatres. This one juxtaposes an event of world importance – that the sun rose this morning – with such trivia as a wedding ring found by the theatre's cleaning ladies; the ring is inscribed 'To Eva from Adam. Genesis II:18'.[51] The news announcer mentions a wall of ice rumoured to be moving south, then proceeds to detailed introductions of Mr George Antrobus, inventor of the wheel; his wife Maggie, who invented the apron; their children Henry and Gladys; and their maid Lily Sabina. The wedding ring leitmotiv will recur in subsequent action to hint that Mr and Mrs Antrobus might also be identified as Adam and Eve; indeed, Mr Antrobus apparently had been a gardener (in Eden?), but left under ambiguous circumstances. Sabina dusts the furniture and delivers expository information interlarded with dire pronouncements as the very walls of the house sag and right themselves. She drops the first hint that Henry is actually the biblical Cain who killed his brother Abel; indeed, we learn later that he bears the mark of Cain on his forehead. Then – in one of Wilder's echoes of Pirandello – Sabina breaks character and tells the audience about her frustration with this play. The pet dinosaur and mammoth slip into the house to escape the increasing cold outside. When Mr Antrobus returns home from a long day of inventing the wheel and finishing the alphabet, he tells his wife that the roads are clogged with people fleeing the encroaching ice. Suddenly there are people seeking refuge in the Antrobus home. The language in this sequence – 'I wonder if you have a piece of bread or something that you could spare'; 'There are some tramps knocking at the back door'[52] – surely brought back memories of the Great Depression that everyone in the audience had so recently endured. And when Sabina again breaks character to tell the audience, 'Ladies and gentlemen! Don't take this play serious. The world's not coming to an end. You know it's not,'[53] surely this was Wilder's tongue-in-cheek allusion to the mass panic that ensued on 30 October 1938 as a reaction to the CBS radio broadcast of Orson Welles's adaptation of *The War of the Worlds*. Over the objections of Mrs Antrobus, who fears there will not be enough food for her children when the advancing wall of ice cuts them off, Mr Antrobus invites the refugees into the home. There are nine elderly sisters, the Muses. The blind beggar Homer speaks in Greek to his own guitar accompaniment. Judge Moses recites in Hebrew. Meanwhile Henry has gone out to play with the new wheel and 'has thrown a stone again'[54] and apparently killed the boy next door. At this news, Mr Antrobus is ready to give up. It is the wife and mother who keeps humanity going in spite of errant offspring, volcanoes, a plague of grasshoppers, earthquakes and now this Ice Age. The refugees sing together in the background while Mrs Antrobus jollies her family back to survival mode. Sabina closes the act by asking the audience to hand their chairs up to the stage for use as firewood to 'save the human race'.[55]

Act Two is set on the boardwalk in Atlantic City, New Jersey, where the Ancient and Honorable Order of Mammals, Subdivision Humans, is holding a convention to celebrate its 600,000th anniversary. In an opening scene before the curtain, it is announced that Mr George Antrobus has been elected president. He addresses the assembly, rejoicing in the extinction of the dinosaur and the retreat of the ice. He pronounces 'the watchword for the future: Enjoy Yourselves'.[56] His comments on the election process pointedly satirize the free-wheeling, often raucous, nature of American presidential campaigns in any decade. Mrs Antrobus gets her moment in the spotlight as first lady; she anticipates the upcoming 5,000th anniversary of her wedding to Mr Antrobus and recalls the long-ago era of activism when women struggled to win the institution of marriage: 'at last we women got the ring'. Her watchword for the year, in contrast to that of her husband, is 'Save the Family'.[57] The radio broadcast concludes with the announcement that President Antrobus had judged the beauty contest and awarded the title of Miss Atlantic City 1942 to Miss Lily-Sabina Fairweather.

The curtain opens to reveal a row of boardwalk shops: saltwater taffy, a fortune teller, a bingo parlour, a Turkish bath. Rising from the orchestra pit is a post to which black disks will be added periodically throughout the act to signal increasingly ominous weather: 'One of those black disks means bad weather; two means storm; three means hurricane; and four means the end of the world.'[58] Sabina is now hostess of the Bingo Parlour, and she enlists Esmeralda the Fortune Teller to help in her plan to 'take President Antrobus away from that wife of his. Then I'll take every man away from his wife.'[59] The Fortune Teller addresses the audience, predicting 'shameful things' to be followed by the deluge and once again the narrow escape of some remnant of civilization.[60] Meanwhile, Henry Antrobus is misbehaving and refuses to give up his slingshot to his father; his mother settles for allowing him to put it in his pocket. Mr Antrobus declares, 'I wash my hands of you.'[61] Mrs Antrobus recognizes Miss Atlantic City 1942 as her former maid Sabina, but Mr Antrobus defends Sabina as a high-principled college graduate. After Mrs Antrobus and the children leave, allowing Mr Antrobus to compose himself for his radio address, Sabina works her wiles in a clever scene that playfully draws upon movie clichés of the period. Moreover, the actress again breaks character, refusing to perform dialogue that might wound some tender sensibilities in the audience. Sabina summarizes the omitted sequence – Mr Antobus will leave his wife for her – and then she lures him into her cabana. The remainder of the act intertwines with accelerating urgency the countdown to Mr Antrobus's 'most important broadcast of the year',[62] his clumsy declaration to his obdurate wife that he is ending their marriage, problems with both

Henry and Gladys, and the impending end-of-the-world storm. The Fortune Teller finally insists that he take his family along with two of each kind of animal onto the boat at the end of the pier. Despite the urgency, Mrs Antrobus refuses to board without Henry. Desperately, she calls for 'Cain', and he rushes in, saying 'I didn't think you wanted me.'[63] In the final seconds, Sabina appeals to Mrs Antrobus and is allowed to come along, since there will be work for her to do. Thus Mr and Mrs Antrobus – Adam and Eve – are transmuted into Noah and his wife – with the opportunity to build a new world.

The farrago of ideas and allusions in Act Two brought confused reactions from audiences.[64] Along with the carnival atmosphere that suggests a civilization abandoned to self-indulgent pleasure-seeking, there are psychological insights about the dizzying nature of power, about the raising of children, about social conventions, and notably there is Mrs Antrobus's speech about women. Indeed, Wilder's early work on the play coincided with several of his journal entries reflecting upon representations of women on the stage. He wrote on 29 October 1940 that 'Woman lives in our minds under two aspects.' The first is the 'untouchable' woman who serves as the buttress of social conventions like marriage, virtue, law and custom.[65] This certainly describes Mrs Antrobus with her implacable devotion to her children and her mission in life across the eons: 'I keep the home going.'[66] The second – represented by Sabina – is 'the accessible, even – in spite of the mask of decorum and dignity-indignity – *inviting*'.[67] Both representations are complicated by the fact that 'a woman appearing on the stage pretending to be someone else in a world all pretense, is revealing herself as Womankind', or in other words, on the stage '*a* woman is so quickly All Women'.[68] Wilder's wrestling with these ideas is reified in the play when Miss Somerset, the actress playing Sabina, separates herself from the character Sabina to point up a distinction between herself and a character who epitomizes the second perception of women. Lily Sabina's name evokes both the vixenish Lilith of rabbinical tradition and the Sabine women who were abducted by Romans; indeed, it still rankles Mrs Antrobus that 'Mr. Antrobus raped you home from your Sabine hills.'[69] Sabina refers to herself as 'a girl like I', and audiences of 1942 would have recognized the epithet from Anita Loos's 1925 international bestseller *Gentlemen Prefer Blondes*. Thus, the character is a mix of various kinds of 'other woman': the floozy, the gold-digger, the vamp, the kept woman, the wholesome pin-up girl, the honest girl with seductive allure and perhaps a heart of gold. Girlhood seems to be a different matter for Wilder, as he tends to fall back on certain qualities in his portrayals of young Emily Webb (in Act One of *Our Town*) and Gladys Antrobus. Both girls adore their fathers. Emily believes hers to be 'perfect' and cherishes having been '*your* girl'.[70] Gladys wants to get her father's attention by reciting a Longfellow poem in Act One,[71] and in Act Two shows off rote knowledge about the ocean.[72] The eighteen-year-old Young Charlie in *Shadow of a Doubt* tries to hold her father to higher standards, and she can sound rather like Emily: 'How wonderfully things work out in the world, Mama!'[73] The women are indeed the bearers of optimism in difficult times.

A war has just ended when Act Three of *The Skin of Our Teeth* begins, and the Antrobus home has taken a beating since Act One. Scarcely has Sabina entered when the Stage Manager halts the play to tell the audience that seven actors needed for the end of this act seem to have come down with food poisoning. Fortunately, there are some volunteers who can step in but they will need to rehearse the sequence. The author's idea is 'to show the hours of the night passing by' over the heads of the family reunited in their house; furthermore, each hour is a philosopher: 'Eleven o'clock, for instance, is Aristotle. And nine o'clock is Spinoza.'[74] Each one speaks a snippet of philosophy that together evoke a cosmic wealth of thought about the human condition. And then Sabina begins Act Three again. Mrs Antrobus and Gladys (holding a baby of unmentioned origin) emerge from a trapdoor. Sabina takes charge of putting the house in order for the men's return from the war. Henry arrives, sullen and primed for a father–son conflict, but soon falls asleep. When Mr Antrobus returns home and sees his son, he takes out his revolver. In the ensuing confrontation, Henry is to be played 'as a representation of strong unreconciled evil'.[75] Mr Antrobus knows that Henry will thwart his dreams for peacetime and yet he attempts reconciliation. Henry will have none of it and is about to attack his father physically when Sabina stops the scene, because 'last night you almost strangled him. You became a regular savage.'[76] The actor playing Henry breaks down and confesses his personal resentments. Sabina comforts him and exits with him, as Mr and Mrs Antrobus get back into the play. Their conversation is all about how to pull themselves back together after what they and the world have been through. Their attitudes are hardened and practical, disillusioned and aware of struggles ahead. There is no sugarcoating of the realities that Americans were facing in 1942. What permits the play to end on a hopeful note is the survival of the words in books by thinkers from all ages. The scene that was rehearsed at the beginning of Act Three is now played out, and this time the quotations are not abridged. The ideas resonate powerfully. But midnight brings a blackout, followed by a return to Sabina speaking her opening lines from Act One. The circular construction makes the point about the eternal cycles of human error and striving. Yes, there will be new disasters, new wars. Somehow, almost miraculously, the human race survives to try again.

Shadow of a Doubt

While the credits on the 1943 Alfred Hitchcock movie *Shadow of a Doubt*[77] list 'Thornton Wilder, Sally Benson, Alma Reville' as authors of the screenplay based upon an original story by Gordon McDonell, a comparison of the screenplay as Wilder left it and the film itself demonstrates that it was, as Wilder later claimed, about 80 per cent his own work.[78] This is corroborated by Max Alvarez's invaluable study, which traces the creative process from the McDonell treatment to the story outline by Hitchcock's wife Alma Reville and on through the five weeks (21 May until Wilder reported for military training on 27 June 1942) during which director Alfred Hitchcock and screenwriter Thornton Wilder met daily to go over what Wilder had written. Alvarez examines the three surviving drafts completed by Wilder and analyses subsequent changes by Hitchcock or by Sally Benson, who was hired after Wilder's departure to add a lighter – even comedic – touch.[79] Alvarez concludes that Wilder's wartime writing had taken a darker-than-usual turn and that the differences between Wilder's script and the released film 'are more a matter of tone and technique than content'.[80] The published screenplay text, prepared by J. D. McClatchy from a typescript in the Beinecke Library[81] for the 2007 Library of America edition of Wilder's *Collected Plays &*

Writings on Theater, is the basis for most of the comments here, with only occasional reference to the movie itself.

The opening scene, set in a working-class New Jersey rooming house, establishes what will be a contrast with the idyllic community of Santa Rosa, California, where most of the story occurs. The well-dressed Uncle Charlie (played by Joseph Cotten) lies on his bed, enigmatically unresponsive as his landlady chatters about two men who had come looking for him. He abruptly leaves the rooming house, evades the two men on the street and telegraphs his sister in Santa Rosa that he is coming for a visit. Visually echoing Uncle Charlie, eighteen-year-old Charlie Newton (played by Teresa Wright) lies broodingly on her bed at home in Santa Rosa. She tells her father that the family's standards have deteriorated: he reads 'trashy mystery magazines'; her mother 'doesn't take care of her looks anymore'; her little brother Roger is acquiring his father's bad table manners.[82] Young Charlie decides to telegraph her Uncle Charlie and ask him to 'come and shake us all up'.[83] When she learns that Uncle Charlie has already telegraphed news of his visit, Young Charlie expresses an idea she will reiterate more explicitly in subsequent action: she and Uncle Charlie, for whom she is named, have a special twin-like bond that may even give them something like mental telepathy.[84]

On the train, Uncle Charlie (or Charles Oakley), who was called Mr Spencer at the rooming house, travels as Mr Otis, 'an awful sick man'.[85] His penchant for using aliases (notably 'Chapman O'Higgins', as his sister later recalls) will be a factor in tying him to a criminal past. While the family waits at the station, Young Charlie expresses a premonition: 'Papa, I have a funny feeling that now that it's really coming, maybe this isn't what I wanted after all.'[86] The family dynamics at the dinner table that evening show Uncle Charlie easily dominating with the smooth charm of a sociopath. He spins a tale about yachts and distributes gifts, but becomes uneasy at the mention of 'The Merry Widow Waltz'. Little by little over the following days, Young Charlie begins to see that there is something unnerving about her adored Uncle Charlie. The attractive young detective, Jack Graham, who alerts her that her uncle might be a person of interest to the police, agrees that if an arrest should be warranted he will do it in some other town to spare the family. Indeed, Mrs Newton has blossomed since her brother's arrival, so Young Charlie keeps her new awareness to herself – even after she finds a newspaper article about 'the Merry Widow murderer' whose latest victim had the same initials as those on the ring Uncle Charlie had given her.

In the second family dinner scene, there is an undercurrent of wariness between the two Charlies. Uncle Charlie's advice to his sister on how to conquer her fright when she introduces him at the women's club uses words that might apply to the mental process for committing a murder, while his handling of the wine bottle reifies that subtext:

> First, prepare your speech or make your plan, – whatever it is – thoroughly. Then don't think about it again. Nothing in the world is difficult if you just fix your will on it. Do it!! – but don't let your imagination fool with it beforehand, or afterwards. *(He now is rubbing the neck of the bottle with a rotary motion and pulling at cork.)* No, just take it for what it's worth. Realize that it'll all be over in a few moments. Don't keep turning it over in your mind. Soon it'll be in the past – and you'll be thinking of other things. There! Like that! *(He pulls the cork. Young Charlie has been watching his hands with fascinated horror. She shuts her eyes, but recovers herself.)*[87]

Almost immediately Uncle Charlie segues into what is surely his most arresting and revealing speech in the film – about wealthy, middle-aged widows flaunting their diamonds and leading 'vapid, useless lives'.[88] Only Young Charlie seems attuned to the cold heartlessness of his words. However, it is ostensibly her father's obsession with crime magazines that impels her to leave the table. Her father and his friend Herbie Hawkins (played by Hume Cronyn) endlessly analyse evidence of foul deeds while remaining virtually oblivious toward those closest to them. Uncle Charlie follows Young Charlie on the street, but she tries to ignore him and bumps into the town policeman, who calls her by name. The sequence is somewhat reminiscent of that in *Our Town* between Constable Warren, Mr Webb and Simon Stimson;[89] it certainly underscores the small-town friendliness of Santa Rosa. Uncle Charlie forces Young Charlie into a garish neon-lighted bar so they can talk. The bar seems like an aberration in the charming community: a scenic metaphor for the corruption of innocence. In their conversation there, Uncle Charlie deploys several of the classic techniques of the sociopath (superficial charm, narcissism, preying on women of character, lying, rapid improvisation of stories or explanations, attempts to elicit pity, lack of conscience, absence of empathy, discontent with the world in which the disordered personality seeks acceptance)[90] while his confused victim struggles to reconcile her longstanding good opinion of him against what the evidence says about him. Young Charlie reveals that she knows everything but has told no one. She implores Uncle Charlie to go away before he is found out, which would break her mother's heart.

A bright Sunday morning with church bells temporarily releases the tension. The detectives are leaving to pursue new cases in other towns since they believe that 'the Merry Widow murderer' was captured in Maine. Jack Graham tells Young Charlie he will return to marry her, while she suppresses the impulse to share what she has learned about Uncle Charlie. She is not so reticent with Uncle Charlie himself, to the point that she tells him, 'Go away or I'll kill you myself – that's what happens to a person who has to live near you.'[91] The double meaning of her line is clear, referring both to the women who were murdered and to her own newly-ignited capacity for murderous intent. The evening of Uncle Charlie's speech is punctuated by his attempt to murder Young Charlie by asphyxiation in the garage. She in turn uses the ring engraved with initials of a murdered woman to make it clear that she will denounce him if he doesn't leave. Although he had been talking about settling down in Santa Rosa, Uncle Charlie now announces that he has been called away and will leave on the early morning train. The train sequence that climaxes the screenplay shows that even as Uncle Charlie and Young Charlie struggle in his attempt to throw her from the moving train, she cannot believe that he would murder her. She, like other victims of sociopaths and indeed like 1940s movie audiences, could not fathom the empathic void that was so charmingly masked to delude her; nor could she conceive that he had never felt any warmth toward her or anyone. Although the movie suggests that Uncle Charlie's fall from the train is the lucky result of Young Charlie's struggle to keep her footing, Wilder's screenplay makes it clear that Young Charlie takes the initiative to 'give her uncle a tremendous push'.[92] The final scene, outside the church during the funeral at which Uncle Charlie is mourned as the town's generous benefactor, Jack Graham reassures Young Charlie that the world's badness can be kept in check by 'a lot of watching'.⁹³ It is not as upbeat a curtain line as one might wish in terms of having put the evil to rest and promising a future for the couple. On the other hand, Jack Graham's honest refusal to sugarcoat conditions testifies to his respect for her intelligence as well as the author's deference to wartime realities faced by the 1943 movie audience.

In the context of the times, Uncle Charlie might be said to represent the Nazi menace, just as Hitler initially somehow lulled the Allied powers into concessions and appeasement. However, the 1940s was a decade of breakthroughs in psychiatric studies of psychopathy, with Hervey M. Cleckley's long-in-print *The Mask of Sanity* (1941) alerting Americans to characteristics of psychopathic or sociopathic personalities as well as their skill in concealing it. Given his friendship with Sigmund Freud, Thornton Wilder surely drew upon such studies. Uncle Charlie falls into a long line of dramatic characters lacking in conscience – Iago in *Othello*, Jean in *Miss Julie*, Regina in *The Little Foxes*, Natasha in *Three Sisters* – not to mention historical figures like Gabriele D'Annunzio. However, moviegoers simply took *Shadow of a Doubt* on its own terms as a thriller that reinforced family and community values. Alfred Hitchcock himself sometimes referred to it as his favourite of his own films, one he remembered nostalgically for the pleasure of working with Thornton Wilder as well as for the aesthetic satisfaction of casting his characteristic macabre shadow over simplistic perceptions of *Our Town*.

The Alcestiad

The classical Greek myth of Alcestis held a fixed place in Thornton Wilder's consciousness from childhood, according to his sister Isabel. Alcestis figured as 'the haunting shadow of a play that would take years to write'.⁹⁴ Indeed, Penelope Niven's biography of Wilder traces that subject's recurring insistence, even as he worked on the plays and novels that are now more closely tied to his reputation. Although its stage production and publication did not come until later, *The Alcestiad* undoubtedly belongs to the 1940s. Isabel Wilder recalled that her brother was devastated by the loss of the manuscript of his play-in-progress which he had carried abroad in his military kit in 1943. Even as he awaited his discharge from the US Army Air Corps in 1945, he began afresh to immerse himself in research on classical Greece and to draft a new version of his play, most of which he did that year.[95] By 1950, according to Niven, 'his search for innovative literary forms led him to revisit his own portfolio of work for characters and themes, as well as to reread Kafka, Goethe, and Kierkegaard. As he sought the cutting edge in form and style, he turned back to Euripides and the distant past for inspiration for characters and themes.'[96] Wilder used Euripides' basic plot for Act Two of his three-act play, but altered details that changed motivations and meanings; he was never satisfied that he had achieved the best linguistic style for the dialogue. The play's premiere at the Edinburgh Festival on 22 August 1955 drew lukewarm to negative reviews,[97] but translated into German, it triumphed in Zurich (with 30 curtain calls!) on 27 June 1957[98] and in Vienna on 5 November 1957.[99] An opera version composed by Louise Talma premiered in Frankfurt, Germany, on 1 March 1962 and won a 20-minute ovation from the audience.[100] Only after the posthumous publication of *The Alcestiad* along with the companion afterpiece *The Drunken Sisters* in 1978 did the play begin to figure fully in the Thornton Wilder canon.

In his 'Notes on *The Alcestiad*', Wilder described his play as 'a comedy about the extreme difficulty of any dialogue between heaven and earth'.[101] For the comedic approach, knowing Greek and Latin mythology as he did, Wilder had no end of examples of things going badly when gods meddle in human affairs. Given his Puritan heritage and frequent return to religious themes, the description certainly refers also to the mystery of the relationship between the human and the divine. Given the darker turn evidenced in Wilder's outlook in the second half of the 1940s,[102] there is considerable latitude for interpretation of *The Alcestiad*. Both Mr Antrobus and Uncle Charlie had been tempted to just 'give up' rather than start afresh.[103] That might also be what Alcestis has come to at the end of Act Three – unless she represents a kind of transcendence. Wilder sometimes echoed Chekhov's notion that the writer's job is to ask the right questions, not answer them.[104]

Each of the three acts of *The Alcestiad* 'begins at dawn and ends at sunset of the same day'[105] and is set in the rear court of the royal palace of Thessaly, from which a path leads down to a spring and to the door to the underworld. Act One begins, like the opening of

Euripides's *Alcestis*, with a dialogue between Apollo (god of light, reason and healing) and Death.[106] But the remainder of Wilder's first act occurs on the day set for the king's wedding to Alcestis. It was Apollo who had appeared to King Admetus in a dream to teach him how to win Alcestis. Many renowned heroes had courted her and scarcely survived the test, but only Admetus returned to try a second time and so won the hand of the headstrong daughter of Pelias. But now, while admitting that she loves Admetus, Alcestis prepares to flee to Delphi to become a priestess of Apollo. The timely arrival of the prophet Teiresias (portrayed as a senile clownish figure) brings a message from Delphi: Zeus, the father of the gods, has commanded that his son Apollo descend from Mount Olympus to live as a man among men for one year. Apollo will inhabit the body of one of the four herdsmen outside the palace gates and serve Admetus. Alcestis questions the First Herdsman in an effort to learn 'the meaning of our life',[107] but he can only speculate, stressing awareness of the great gulf between gods and men. Admetus, having learned that Alcestis wants to run away from their marriage, joins her on the palace steps and tells her she is free to go. In that pivotal moment – strongly echoing the same situation in Ibsen's *The Lady from the Sea* (when Dr Wangel declares his wife Ellida free to choose to follow the hypnotic Stranger) – Alcestis (like Ellida) makes the choice to remain earthbound in ordinary marriage.[108]

Twelve years have passed when Act Two of *The Alcestiad* begins. The Watchman explains that Admetus is dying of a wound he received when one of the four Herdsmen accidentally stabbed him. Nobody knows whether Apollo actually dwelt in the body of one of those Herdsman for the first year or whether he still does, perhaps even in the remorseful Herdsman who brought this suffering to the household. A message from Delphi states that Admetus may live if someone else will die in his place. The Watchman, the Herdsman and the nurse Aglaia readily volunteer, but Alcestis calmly persuades them that it must be she, and she commands them to say nothing about it to the king.[109] In Euripides's *Alcestis*, Admetus actively solicits potential substitutes for his death, but Wilder kept Admetus oblivious of the sacrifice to be made for him. With the news that their friend Hercules is about to pay a visit, Alcestis orders that Admetus be carried out onto the palace steps where he can greet Hercules. As husband

and wife converse, his pain dissipates while she becomes progressively weakened. The poignancy of their exiting into the palace together turns instantly to mirth with the entrance of the drunken, boisterous, boastful Hercules. Aglaia stoically welcomes Hercules. Then, coming from his wife's deathbed, Admetus nobly puts on a show of hospitality. When Hercules finally learns the truth, he confesses a secret shame to Admetus: once long ago he had tried to violate Alcestis and fortunately another god rescued her; Alcestis not only forgave Hercules and never spoke of his crime but always regarded him lovingly. Calling to Apollo for help, Hercules vows to venture down to the underworld and bring back Alcestis. The act ends with Alcestis groping her way from below to Admetus's arms. It appears that the tragedy has been averted and that the good couple's domestic happiness will continue. But this is a false hope and temporary respite, not unlike Europe's 18 years between world wars.

In Act Three another twelve years have passed, bringing great changes to Thessaly. Alcestis, a ragged crone, serves the tyrant King Agis and is reviled by the new Watchman, who points to her as the cause of the plague in the land. Her husband Admetus and two of their children are dead. Apollo tells Death why he has allowed this 'ruin and havoc' to come to people he loved: only when 'death plays a large role' are stories remembered.[110] Two young men enter the courtyard, one bent on revenge, the other seeking to establish justice. When Alcestis and her son Epimenes finally recognize each other, she warns him to leave quickly or he will be killed. Townspeople approach the palace seeking relief from the plague, and Agis tries to deflect blame onto Alcestis. She explains the pestilence as the gods' way of leading people to see and understand. She stops her son Epimenes from killing Agis. Stricken by the news that his daughter Laodamia has died of the plague, Agis finally hears what Alcestis has tried to teach him: that only by returning to his own kingdom, leaving Epimenes to rule Thessaly, can Agis give meaning to his daughter's short life. Alcestis reflects on 'all the dead ... all those millions lie imploring us to show them that their lives were not empty and foolish',[111] and one hears in those words an evocation of the lives lost in the two world wars. The play ends with Apollo leading Alcestis to his sacred grove where she will spend eternity without a grave. Her mood is accepting yet her dialogue suggests also that her memories are evaporating, not unlike what happens to the water-sprite in *Ondine* (1938) by Wilder's friend Jean Giraudoux. The one certainty that is acknowledged by Apollo – predictably one of Thornton Wilder's constant themes – is that the human race will continue.

Conclusion

Besides the four works covered here, Lt Colonel Thornton Wilder followed his discharge from the United States Army Air Corps with projects like his continuing close study of Lope de Vega's vast dramatic canon, acting in productions of his own plays (Stage Manager, Mr Antrobus), lecturing abroad, translating Jean-Paul Sartre's *Morts sans sépulture* for Off-Broadway production as *The Victors* (1948), his novel *The Ides of March* (1948) and significant work on *The Emporium*, a play that never came to fruition, although scenes from that work-in-progress have been published.[112] Yale University awarded him an honorary doctorate in 1947, followed by honorary degrees from New York University and Kenyon College in 1949. He lectured at several universities in Germany in 1948 and considered it a crowning achievement when he was invited to deliver a lecture at the three-week Goethe Bicentennial Convocation attended by 2,000 people in Aspen in 1949. 'Nobody ever loved anybody like I love Goethe', he wrote to his brother.[113] Moreover, he translated Dr Albert Schweitzer's lecture from the German and José Ortega y Gasset's lecture from the Spanish. It was indeed a productive and rewarding decade for Thornton Wilder.

6

Tennessee Williams: Experimentation and the 'Great American Play'

Thomas Keith

Tennessee Williams's career as a playwright began in 1940 with high hopes for the Theatre Guild's Broadway-bound production of his first professionally produced play, *Battle of Angels*, which closed after two weeks of a disastrous out-of-town tryout in Boston. That inauspicious beginning prefaced a lustrous career. To understand how Tennessee Williams came to write plays that changed American theatre, it is helpful to examine his progression as an artist, his theatrical instincts and the creative and commercial forces that shaped two of the three plays on which his reputation is primarily built, *The Glass Menagerie* (1945) and *A Streetcar Named Desire* (1947), both written and produced on Broadway in the 1940s. The third in the trio of his greatest critical and commercial successes, *Cat on a Hot Tin Roof*, opened on Broadway in 1955.

As it turns out, there were three other full-length plays by Tennessee Williams produced in the 1940s: *You Touched Me!* (adapted from a short story by D. H. Lawrence), co-authored with his friend Donald Windham, which opened at the Cleveland Play House in October 1943; *Stairs to the Roof*, Williams's attempt to synthesize his lyric style with socially conscious theatre, opened at the Pasadena Playhouse in February 1947; and *Summer and Smoke*, which, following the triumphs of *The Glass Menagerie* and *A Streetcar Named Desire*, opened on Broadway to disappointing reviews in 1948.

Williams's first play, a one-act called *Beauty is the Word*, was written for a contest at the University of Missouri, Columbia, when he was a freshman there in 1930. After being pulled out of college by his father for failing the Reserve Officers Training Corps (ROTC) course, Williams put in his time at the International Shoe Company for nearly three years, performing mindless work until he collapsed from exhaustion in 1935 and was sent to Memphis for the summer to live with his maternal grandparents, the Reverend and Mrs Walter Dakin. Upon his return to St Louis, Williams audited classes (and later enrolled) at Washington University, where he met the poets Clark Mills McBurney and William Jay Smith. They maintained their own private three-member poetry club for several years.

During the decade of the 1930s, Williams wrote nearly two dozen one-act plays that are now published, and drafted parts of dozens more. He referred to his early one-acts as 'fantasies', according to Smith, and they tend to focus on male–female relationships in urban settings with modern concerns that ranged from impending war to sexual freedom to urban violence to politics.[1] The influence of cinema is vivid in these plays, recognizable in the dialogue, the plots and the stock character types – swells, gangsters, showgirls, molls and Steinbeckian farmers. And yet, Williams was already displaying his inclination toward theatrical experimentation, as evidenced in some early one-acts written in the form of dream plays, polemics, dance plays and historical fables.

While the playwright was deeply influenced by the works of Edgar Allan Poe and Walt Whitman, as well as playwrights Henrik Ibsen, August Strindberg, Shakespeare and Federico Garcia Lorca, it is likely that American playwright Eugene O'Neill, American poet Hart Crane, English novelist D. H. Lawrence and Russian dramatist Anton Pavlovich Chekhov had the greatest influence on Williams's writing. Not only did Williams study O'Neill in college and attend productions of O'Neill plays, but after a certain point Williams considered him his competition. What Williams may have taken most from O'Neill was the relentless pursuit of experimentation. Williams was keenly aware that O'Neill had opened doors to potential ways a story could be told in American theatre. Hart Crane (with whom Williams most identified as a poet) and Williams shared similar personal and family backgrounds. Williams wrote that Crane's poetry 'touched fire that burned [him] alive'.[2] In both works, the personal becomes the universal through mythic imagery and lyricism. In the prose of D. H. Lawrence, Williams discovered freedom to identify the sensual and the sexual and to liberate them. He joined Lawrence's celebration of the animal passions of humanity, exposing both the joy and brutality. The influence of Chekhov can readily be found in *The Glass Menagerie*, which resembles *The Seagull* in its focus on the characters of an artistic son and devoted mother who cannot communicate with each other. Likewise, Blanche DuBois in *A Streetcar Named Desire* and Madame Ranevsky in *The Cherry Orchard* both face the loss of a refined way of life and a culture rapidly disappearing, and each finds herself in direct opposition to a coarse and dynamic male adversary in the persons of, respectively, Stanley Kowalski and Yermolay Lopakhin. Williams was also deeply influenced by Chekhov's use of subtext; by necessitating emotional or physical action concurrent with the text, he created plays in which traditional plot was present but did not dominate. Rather, it was driven by the internal lives of the characters.

In the autumn of 1936, Williams wrote a one-act play that concerns a young painter and his actress wife whose denial of their squalid living conditions becomes a game that helps them avoid facing their failed ambitions. Melodramatic and often humorous, *The Magic Tower* contains agile dialogue and emotional depth. It won first prize in a contest with an amateur group just outside of St Louis, in Webster Groves, and led Williams to Willard Holland, a St Louis director and head of a local labour theatre group called the Mummers. Williams's poet friend Clark Mills McBurney brought Williams to Holland's attention, and Holland asked Williams to write a curtain raiser for the Mummers' upcoming production of Irwin Shaw's anti-war play *Bury the Dead*. Not much is known about that curtain raiser, *Headlines*, except that it was brief and that it involved, according to William Jay Smith, posting and projecting various contemporary headlines from newspapers (possibly pre-dating Hallie Flanagan's Living Newspaper plays from 1937) while actors crisscrossed the stage acting them out.

Early full-length plays

When Holland requested a full-length play, Williams gave him *Candles to the Sun*, a labour play he had been drafting since 1935, about the working conditions of Alabama coal miners; the Mummers produced it on 18 and 19 March 1937. In the way that young painters study and initially imitate the great masters, in his first three full-length plays, Williams absorbed the influences of playwrights of the 1930s. The demand for social justice and ambitious use of phonetic speech and jargon in *Candles to the Sun* appear to be inspired in part by Clifford Odets. The play received positive reviews from the local press, including Colvin McPherson of the *St Louis Post-Dispatch*: 'It stands on its own feet. Its characters are genuine, its dialogue of a type that must have been uttered in the author's presence, its appeal in the theater widespread.'[3] Given that observation, the fact that Williams had neither been to Alabama nor met a miner testifies to his dramatic promise. In November 1937, the Mummers produced *The Fugitive Kind*, Williams's second full-length play, set in a St Louis flophouse populated by radicals, writers, artists, mobsters and hobos, all caught up in the economics of the Great Depression. *The Fugitive Kind* reveals some of Williams's expressionistic instincts in a stage direction describing a shift in lighting from realistic to red and shadowy when the mood becomes '*predominantly lyrical*' and the '*realistic details are lost*'.[4] Williams described his third full-length play, *Not About Nightingales*, as the most violent and horrific play he ever wrote. Prompted by a newspaper article about prisoners in Pennsylvania who were roasted alive in a boiler room used for punishment, *Not About Nightingales* owes much to prison films of the 1930s, especially *The Big House* (1930), which also has a main character named Butch and dramatizes a prison strike. The play is notable for its use of an announcer and title for each 'episode' of its three acts, for a dream sequence between one of the main characters and his girlfriend, for a sympathetic African-American character named Queenie who is understood to be homosexual and for an expressionistic, chanted hunger strike. *Not About Nightingales* was not produced during the playwright's lifetime but, after a 1998 London premiere, it opened on Broadway nearly 60 years after it was written, and was nominated for a Tony Award for best play of the 1999–2000 season.

Williams began classes at the University of Iowa in the fall of 1937 and studied playwriting under Professor Edward Charles Mabie. There Williams looked beyond traditional theatre history to contemporary American theatre: experimental work by Eugene O'Neill and Elmer Rice, the poetic plays of Maxwell Anderson and commercial successes by Thornton Wilder and William Saroyan. School papers from this period give clues to his knowledge of theatre as well as his influences: 'Shaw's *Candida*', 'Some Representative Plays of O'Neill and a Discussion of his Art' and 'Birth of Art (Anton Chekhov and the New Theatre)'.[5] There Williams wrote his fourth full-length play in which he began, for the first time, to write about his own life – not about coal miners, stock film characters, Depression-era radicals or striking prisoners, but about people from small towns in Mississippi. *Spring Storm* takes place in the fictional Mississippi Delta town of Port Tyler, an undisguised stand-in for the town of Clarksdale where Williams spent much of his childhood, including summers with his grandparents after his family left Mississippi for St Louis in 1918. The Delta – its locations, culture, people – was the cradle of Williams's imagination and creativity, to which he returned time and time again. The Critchfield family is the fictional counterpart to the wealthy Coutrere family of Clarksdale upon whom Williams drew for nearly every one of his Delta plays. The Critchfield home is dominated by the portrait of a Civil War hero-ancestor that brings the concerns of the old South into the world of 1937, when the play takes place. With *Spring Storm*, Williams began to explore themes of Southern identity, nonconformity, class distinctions and the desire to escape constraints, whether personal, sensual or artistic.

As early as 1938, Williams began to experiment with writing a 'Great American Play', just as writers of the previous generation – Sinclair Lewis, Thomas Wolfe, F. Scott Fitzgerald, Ernest Hemingway, and others – were determined to write the 'Great American Novel'. Williams's impulse to write an epic story during this period is evident in multiple drafts of titles housed at the University of Texas's Harry Ransom Humanities Research Center (HRC) in Austin: these include *The Spinning Song*, *The Paper Lantern: A Dance Play for Martha Graham* and *Daughter of the American Revolution*. In these unrealized works Williams tried out themes and scenarios that later found their way, albeit transformed, into *The Glass Menagerie* and *A Streetcar Named Desire*. Some deal with generational dislocation in the modern world. Williams also grappled with issues of race and with slavery's traumatic aftermath on the country, with African-Americans whose lives were destroyed and with the bond of brother and sister relationships. Most are set in a mythical Southern locale called Blue Mountain where, among other things, women are left waiting for men who will never return. The narrator of the draft play *Daughter of the American Revolution* – indisputably a precursor to the character of Tom in *The Glass Menagerie* – begins the play by announcing to the audience, 'In the beginning there was high adventure for the Wingfields, and they were equal to it. / The continents of America were baptized in their blood.'[6]

After his graduation from the University of Iowa in the spring of 1938, Williams set off to begin life as a writer in New Orleans, away from his family, and entered a playwriting contest sponsored by the Group Theatre in New York. To qualify, the entrants had to be under 25, but Williams was 27. So he changed his birth year on the entry form from 1911 to 1914 and changed his name from Thomas Lanier Williams to Tennessee Williams. Just for good measure, he mailed the plays from Memphis, using his grandparents' return address. His first seven weeks in New Orleans, from 28 December 1938 to 18 February 1939, exposed Williams to the bohemian world that he felt was his home, opened him up sexually and began his lifelong wanderlust. On a jaunt to California he received word that the Group Theatre had awarded him an 'Honorable Mention' and a prize of $100 for the selection of one-act plays he had submitted. This put his name in the New York papers, and shortly thereafter, theatrical agents began to contact him. He signed with agent Audrey Wood, and their 30-year working relationship became one of the best known in American theatre history.

Battle of Angels

Having a New York agent changed everything for Williams, and he began to think about success in the commercial theatre as a more immediate possibility. By late 1939 he had received a grant of $1,000 from the Rockefeller Foundation and had completed the first draft of *Figures in Flames*, the play that would eventually become *Battle of Angels*. By early 1940, Williams and a young playwright named Arthur Miller were taking a playwriting class from John Gassner and Theresa Helburn at the Dramatic Workshop wing of the New School for Social Research, of which Erwin Piscator was the director. Gassner convinced Lawrence Langner and Theresa Helburn, directors of the prestigious Theatre Guild, to look at the play. On 14 March, 1940, Williams wrote optimistically to Wood, 'I *do* think this play is *Commercial*! – Capital 'C' as in CASH!'[7]

Battle of Angels takes place in a small, insular and racist Mississippi town (another stand-in for Clarksdale). A young man of 30, an attractive stranger with a guitar and a snakeskin jacket, arrives and, like a character D. H. Lawrence might have admired, ignites the sexual and spiritual passions of the three women who live there as outsiders themselves: the wife of the town sheriff, Vee; the wife of the town's dry goods store owner, Myra; and the daughter of the town's richest family, Sandra. For Williams, the play was a cry of freedom against the restraints of a narrow-minded world and he packed it with nearly every image and theme in his then and future arsenal. In an 'Imaginary Interview' with himself written prior to the 1957 Broadway premiere of *Orpheus Descending*, his revised version of *Battle of Angels*, Williams wrote that the play possessed a theme, found as variations in nearly all of his writing, which he identified as a prayer for 'more tolerance and respect for the wild and lyric impulses that the human heart feels and so often is forced to repress in order to avoid social censure and worse'.[8] It was a risky move on the part of the Theatre Guild to sign up the unfinished script of an unknown playwright and plan to open it on Broadway. As Williams later wrote of his producers, 'they took it for granted that I was an accomplished playwright ... They had no idea how dazed and stymied I was by the rush of events'.[9] Following the casting of film star Miriam Hopkins in the lead role, the headline in *Variety* (30 October 1940) read, 'HOPKINS MAY PLAY HILLBILLY'S "ANGELS"'.[10]

The schedule was for *Battle of Angels* to open out-of-town in New Haven, Connecticut, on 27 December 1940, transfer to Boston with a 30 December opening for a two-week run, transfer directly to Washington, DC, for another week and then move to Broadway. The Theatre Guild decided to cancel the New Haven appearance and go directly to Boston where the production became one of the most famous fiascos in twentieth-century theatre history. As Williams described that opening night in various essays, it was an unmitigated disaster – the play was not appreciated by the conservative Boston audience; moreover, the smoke pots used to create the effect of a fire at the end of the play were out of control and the theatre filled with smoke. The *Boston Globe* reported that 'the play gives the audience a sensation of having been dunked in mire'.[11] In the *Herald*, Alexander Williams wrote, 'there is ... something that will irritate any customer'.[12] There was a ray of hope from Elinor Hughes at the *Boston Herald*, who speculated that with experience Williams might 'add craftsmanship to imagination and produce important work'.[13] In the *Boston Post*, Eliot Norton even praised Williams's talent as 'most interesting'.[14] Following complaints from angry patrons that 'a picture of Christ was being torn up', a Boston City Council member who had not seen the play described *Battle of Angels* as 'putrid', and demanded that 'the police should arrest the persons responsible for bringing shows of that type to Boston'.[15] A week after the opening, Boston's City Censor, John Spencer, found the play to be 'indecent and improper' as well as 'lascivious and immoral', and demanded changes to the script.[16] The Theatre Guild agreed to make the censor's changes, then announced that the show would close after the Boston run, cancelling the Washington tryout and Broadway opening.

In late 1941, Williams proposed that Erwin Piscator direct *Battle of Angels* at the New School's experimental Dramatic Workshop. Piscator was a German director who had made his name in the 1920s by developing aggressively-polemical, episodically-constructed productions. Piscator valued anything that pulled the audience out of their comfort zone and reminded them they were participating in a live event. He used bare stages rigged with scaffolding for abrupt shifts of level in place and time, and he developed the use of slides, film and projections to comment on the action. One of Piscator's assistants at his theatre in Berlin was young Bertolt Brecht, who took from his work with Piscator much of his concept of Epic (or Dialectic, as he later termed it) Theatre. Williams sent two copies of *Battle of Angels* to his agent in November 1941: 'I am also mailing you for PISCATOR ... I have heard that Piscator intends to put his actors on flying trapezes in his next production, (Joke). – Any trial production would be a good thing.'[17] Piscator was interested in producing *Battle of*

Angels; however, his interest in playing the role of tutor, mentor or guru to Williams did not suit the up-and-coming playwright. Piscator insisted that the play serve as a teaching tool, suggesting that the prologue and epilogue feature 'sociological instruction' to be given by the character of the African-American Conjure Man.[18] In reaction to a laundry list of rewrite demands from Piscator, Williams wrote to his family on 6 March, 1942, 'while I haven't satisfied Piscator's absurd demands with 'Angels', he is going to have a trial reading of the play by actors before an invited audience which may result in attracting other producers'.[19] According to Williams, Piscator called *Battle of Angels* a fascist play and, even after Williams rewrote it substantially, described the characters as 'selfishly pursuing their little personal ends and aims in life with a ruthless disregard for the wrongs and sufferings of the world around them'.[20] In a letter to Audrey Wood, Williams commented, 'A man that lacking in humor is not for me to deal with!' According to Donald Windham, Williams was angry with Piscator for rewriting *Battle of Angels* 'with scissors' and 'cutting up the speeches and giving them to different characters, and ... planning to present it as a political document on life in the South'.[21] Williams withdrew his support for a production at the New School.

Stairs to the Roof

From the time he first began writing plays in the 1930s, Williams wrote multiple plays, one-acts, stories and poems at the same time. In a 1998 essay, 'Advice on the Art of Writing Short Stories', Chilean novelist Roberto Bolaño advised: '1) Never tackle stories one by one. Really, if you tackle them one by one you could be writing the same story until the day you die. 2) It's best to write stories three at a time, or five at a time. If you've got the energy, write them nine at time, or fifteen at a time.'[22] Williams and Bolaño may have shared common sense or perhaps a creative intelligence. After Williams's mother bought him a used Underwood typewriter in 1924, there were very few days in his life when he did not write. At any given time he was working on up to half a dozen stories, up to ten plays and often a poem or two. Evidence of this habit of overlapping can be found in his journals, his letters and various notes and jottings. Stories and plays that were developed simultaneously will routinely share motifs, ideas, character names and, in some drafts, plot points, linked by an invisible web of inspiration. Writing was an appetite that Williams satisfied like nothing else. The bibliographies of Williams's work are long. Four major American archives are bursting with his drafts, fragments and completed manuscripts. Following the long trail of drafts that lead to any play by Tennessee Williams, one can find the nascent attempts and notes, unfinished drafts, fragments, variant titles, one-act versions, multiple drafts and sometimes poems.

For most of the time he was composing *Battle of Angels*, Williams was also revising several drafts of an expressionistic play called *Stairs to the Roof*. He laboured on it after the dismal failure of *Battle of Angels*, with the hope that it would be the commercial Broadway success he wanted. Germs for *Stairs to the Roof* are found in his short stories 'The Swan', 'Stairs to the Roof' and 'The Earth is a Wheel in a Great Big Gambling Casino'. Williams used his three years working in the International Shoe Company as fodder for this drama about the dehumanization of the individual in a highly industrialized society. Woven into the story of the unhappy plant worker Benjamin Murphy – a role he dedicated to the actor Burgess Meredith – who craves a life beyond the suffocating confines of the factory is a love story: Murphy escapes with a young woman known only as 'Girl' into a city park where, after encountering a circus troupe acting out a Beauty and the Beast pantomime, they experience a night of romance. Inspired, Murphy returns to the factory and rallies the workers to take a hidden stairway to the roof where a *deus ex machina* in the person of a Mister E. points the way for Murphy and the Girl to colonize a distant star, and for the audience he points the way to the millennium. While influenced to a great extent by Elmer Rice (Williams imbues *Stairs to the Roof* with the robotic and impersonal setting of *The Adding Machine*), the play is also shaped by Williams's response to the exuberant optimism of William Saroyan. Combine those aspects with the politically-driven theme and the quasi-science-fiction elements and it is quite a jumble of ideas and styles. In a letter to Audrey Wood on 5 July 1940, Williams wrote, 'I'm getting back to work on my new play "Stairs to the Roof" – It doesn't have the strong sex theme but I think is a more serious, artistic piece of drama than "B.A.".'[23] Williams mused to Lawrence

Langner in a 23 July 1940 letter that if someone else were writing *Stairs to the Roof*, it might turn out to be 'the "great American drama" – there is so much amplitude in the theme'.[24] *Stairs to the Roof* was given a full production at the Pasadena Playhouse in 1947, but remained unpublished until 2000.

The Glass Menagerie

Throughout the same years that Williams was rewriting *Battle of Angels* and revising full-length drafts of *Stairs to the Roof*, he was also working on something more personal and elusive, which propelled him through multiple incarnations, motifs, genres and themes; he wanted to write about his sister, Rose Isabelle Williams. Two years older than her brother, Rose was so inseparable from Tom when they were children and young adults that they were often referred to as 'the twins'. Each was the sanctuary for the other in a house torn by marital strife. Their mother, Edwina Williams, was controlling, extremely verbal and, according to biographer John Lahr, frigid; she had a profound effect on how her two oldest children saw the world. Their father, Cornelius Coffin Williams, a Southerner from Tennessee, was a travelling salesman, a drinker, a gambler, sometimes a brawler. During the first ten years of the Williams' marriage, Edwina and her parents took care of the children while Cornelius was primarily on the road. Once both parents were living under the same roof in St Louis, the small skirmishes and squalls of their marriage became continual blow-ups and clashes that made their home a battlefield and drew Rose and Tom even closer together. While Tom Williams was by nature a shy boy and was considered a sissy by his father, a debilitating childhood illness added to Tom's sense of vulnerability and his reliance on his sister. Rose, on the other hand, went through much of her adolescence as an outgoing and charming girl but by her late teens began to show signs of emotional distress, depression and eventually mental illness. At the age of twenty-seven, Rose was diagnosed with schizophrenia and institutionalized. Williams was traumatized by his sister's torment and by losing his best friend, and he was deeply afraid of suffering the same fate.

Williams's earliest attempts to portray his sister in drama and stories may have begun in 1935 with the short story 'Blue

Roses'. However, from the time of Rose's admission to a mental hospital, Williams was always working on at least one but usually multiple short stories and one-acts about her: *The Family Pew*, *The Preacher's Daughter*, 'Miss Rose and the Grocery Clerk', 'The Lost Girl' and 'The Resemblance Between a Violin Case and a Coffin'. Williams's attempt to write an epic American play and his desire to dramatize the life of his sister merged in a play he worked on during this same period called *The Spinning Song*, which portrays 'the disintegration of a southern family through adultery, incest, murder and mental fragility'.[25] In many ways, *The Spinning Song* holds the seeds of both *The Glass Menagerie* and *A Streetcar Named Desire*. Like *Spring Storm*, it reaches back to the Civil War era, but then it accelerates to the present where a couple are in perpetual conflict, their shy daughter unable to find a husband and their son yearning to escape the family and find adventure. In a journal entry dated 25 February 1942, Williams wrote, 'I have just finished writing "The Spinning Song" a play suggested by my sister's tragedy.'[26] In one draft fragment, a character named Blanche lives on a plantation, Belle-reve, with her two children while her husband lives in New Orleans. In another, a mother discusses whether or not her daughter Ariadne can stay on the plantation, following her diagnosis of dementia praecox (schizophrenia).

True to his lifelong habit of working on multiple projects simultaneously, Williams also began collaborating with his friend Donald Windham in the spring of 1942 on dramatizing the D. H. Lawrence short story *You Touched Me!* Later that year, some offshoots of *The Spinning Song* – including the one-acts and drafts *Hawk's Daughter*, *The Front Porch Girl*, *If You Breathe It Breaks*, *Carolers Our Candle*, *Summer at the Lake* and *Sacre du Printemps* – evolved into various rough drafts of a generational family play titled *The Gentleman Caller*. Meanwhile, in April 1943, Audrey Wood secured Williams a six-month contract as a scriptwriter at Metro Goldwyn Mayer Studios in Hollywood. It was the largest salary Williams had yet received, $250 per week, and he dove into his assignments with gusto. Quickly, he found out he did not fit well with the on-demand nature of the job nor the kinds of projects which he was given, so he began drafting a screen treatment of *The Gentleman Caller*, which MGM rejected. Unhappy with his work, the studio decided to put Williams on 'hiatus' for the rest of his contract. Until the end of October he remained on salary with MGM while he continued to work on his own material. Returning to *The Gentleman Caller* as a play, this time Williams shaped it as 'a sentimental family portrait'.[27] The shift may have been due to the rejection by MGM, but it was more likely because his mother had authorized a pre-frontal lobotomy for Rose in early 1943. Williams did not find out the exact details until that spring, but he was horrified and it became a psychic wound that found its way into his writing for the rest of his life. It also changed the way he sought to tell his sister's story.

Eddie Dowling was an actor/manager of the kind that had been around since the nineteenth century – he was a showman who bought plays as vehicles he could direct, star in, tour with, and on which he could make a profit. When Audrey Wood sent Dowling the script for *The Gentleman Caller*, he signed on a first-time producer, Louis Singer, with the caveat that Singer not read the script until the play opened. Next, Dowling began to court the actress Laurette Taylor to play the role of the mother. Considered one of the greatest actresses of her generation, Taylor had been a star on Broadway since 1908, most famously as the ingénue in *Peg o' My Heart* (1912), a sentimental Irish comedy written by her husband, J. Hartley Manners. After Manners's death in 1928, Taylor turned to alcohol, and her heavy drinking made her a liability; she had not worked in five years. By September of 1944, the play was called *The Fiddle in the Wings*, but it was soon titled *The Glass Menagerie*, and was a much different play from *The Spinning Song*, *The Gentleman Caller* or any of the plays from which it sprang. It was now ostensibly a simple domestic story of a woman and her two children surviving the end of the Great Depression. It is famous for being Williams's most autobiographical play, which perhaps it is, but it is autobiography transformed by drama and distance into something quite different from the events in Williams's life that inspired it.

At a meeting with his publisher, James Laughlin, in the late 1970s, Williams responded to an observation about the 'experimental quality' of some of his later plays that he was and had always been an '*experimental* playwright'.[28] It was an argument Williams had been making from the time of his first great successes in the 1940s, though it usually fell on deaf ears. Some of Williams's experimental instincts came from his innate theatrical sensibility and his passion for the cinema. Other influences were the playwrights and poets he most admired, his teachers, Edward Charles Mabie and John Gassner. And there was Erwin Piscator. As much contact as Williams had with Piscator, it has not been fully documented whether or not the techniques Piscator championed, which are also found to varying degrees in *The Glass Menagerie*, *A Streetcar Named Desire* and *Summer and Smoke*, came immediately from the German director. Scholar John Willett indicates with confidence that *The Glass Menagerie*'s 'narrator and projections ... clearly reflect Piscator's methods'.[29] Speaking to a group of Dramatic Workshop alumni in 1950, Piscator lamented that his work had not produced a 'vanguard army of political theaters across America', and he complained that former students – Tennessee Williams, among others – had failed him in that regard.[30] Something critical Williams may have learned from his encounters with Piscator was what he did *not* want to emulate as a playwright. It may have been in response to Piscator that Williams learned to reject the impulse to be directly or aggressively political, polemic or pedagogical in his plays. Initially, Williams had inclined to explore social issues through his dramas but it was not until *The Glass Menagerie* that he let go of that tendency. It may have even been the lesson learned with *Stairs to the Roof*, which was running in its workshop production in Pasadena while *The Glass Menagerie* and *You Touched Me!* were on Broadway in 1945. In his programme note to the 1947 Pasadena revival, Williams confessed that he did not feel apologetic about *Stairs to the Roof*, though he did refer to the passion of the main character as 'sometimes sophomoric' and qualified that observation by asking the playgoer to respect its 'purity of feeling' and 'honest concern' for the basic problem[s] of mankind.[31] Williams essentially abandoned *Stairs to the Roof* after that, except for mentioning it in an occasional essay. And he never returned to the text to either revise it or even to clean it up for publication. He not only rejected the polemic but went to the other end of the spectrum.

Dedicated to ambiguity for most of his writing career, Williams embraced the complexity of life, a value that appears for the first time in *The Glass Menagerie* and most powerfully in *A Streetcar Named Desire*. In a 1962 interview, Williams addressed the issue: '[T]he thing that I've always pushed in my writing – that I've always felt was needed to be said over and over – [is] that human relations are terrifyingly ambiguous. If you write a character that isn't ambiguous you are writing a false character, not a true one.'[32] Williams's use of ambiguity opens up multiple possibilities, double-meanings and uncertainty – it is what makes his writing modern. Inherent to ambiguity in drama is the anti-Aristotelian, anti-polemical approach of neither wrapping up the action neatly nor sending the audience home with a message. Williams proved the value of ambiguity in *The Glass Menagerie*, while solidifying some of his convictions about what makes dynamic and fluid theatre that can 'find a closer approach, a more vivid and penetrating and vivid expression of things as they are'.[33] Many of the more experimental and expressionistic aspects of Williams's working script were cut from the original production, muted, ignored or even rewritten. Dowling removed some of Williams's expressionistic elements and even added a curtain line that Williams detested, 'Here's where my memory stops and your imagination begins', which was actually printed in the first acting edition of the play.[34]

Though Williams never wrote a formal manifesto about theatre, throughout his life he drafted statements, notes, essays and random thoughts that were pointed in that direction. His 'Production Notes' for the published editions of *The Glass Menagerie* are the closest he came to such a manifesto; therein he sets out his ideas about what he calls the 'plastic theatre' and introduces the reader to his original concepts for the play's production. Even before *The Glass Menagerie*, Williams was thinking these things through on paper. After a screening of Sergei Eisenstein's film *Alexander Nevsky* in September 1943, Williams wrote a response in which he pleads for the fluidity and sculptural abilities of film to be translated into the staging of plays: 'The influence of modern music and surreal art, both present in this film masterpiece, could be used as powerfully in a poetic stage play.'[35] Another jotting, from March 1943, seems to be a kind of draft introduction to *The Gentleman Caller*; Williams wrote that the play was 'a general plea for a theatre based on <u>truth</u>. The settings in this play, like those in Stairs to the Roof, are better done by suggestion than carried out in detail. Because of the brevity and rapidity of the scenes, a spot-light technique is indicated.'[36] In his 'Production Notes' for *The Glass Menagerie*, Williams focuses initially on his belief that realism is not the best way to discover 'truth, life, or reality', which he feels are best represented through transformation. He calls for 'a new plastic theatre' to take the place of 'realistic conventions',[37] and then proceeds to describe how the screen device, the music and the lighting, as he originally envisioned them, serve as plastic elements that can lift a static play into the realm of living theatrical experience and thereby deepen the audience's understanding. Williams's use of the word 'plastic' can be understood as 'sculptural'; his principle is in essence that the playwright's responsibility goes beyond the words, and must incorporate music, sound, light, settings – what he also calls 'extra-literary accent[s]' – and their strategic use within the physical environment to reach those moments of 'truth' which elevate one's experience seeing a play.[38] Williams later stated in his 'Production Notes' that he did not regret Eddie Dowling's cutting of the 'images and titles' that Williams wanted projected above the stage, the screen devices that are called 'legends' in the body of the play. However, by describing them in detail in the published script, Williams made plain his hope that future productions would incorporate them: 'The legend or image upon the screen will strengthen the effect of what is merely allusion in the writing and allow the primary point to be made more simply and lightly than if the entire responsibility were on the spoken lines.'[39] Most of the other elements Williams describes were maintained in the original production, and can be found in both the acting and trade editions of the script. Set designer Jo Mielziner credited to the author the use of a transparent fourth wall and the gauze curtains that separate the various playing spaces. Williams collaborated on nine Broadway productions with Mielziner, who appreciated Williams's sculptural and theatrical sense from their first work together on *The Glass Menagerie*. Mielziner later wrote that 'Even as an inexperienced young writer, Tennessee Williams revealed a strong instinct for the visual qualities of the theatre. If he had written plays in the days before the technical development of translucent and transparent scenery, I believe he would have invented it.'[40]

Williams compares the music that underscores much of the action in *The Glass Menagerie*, the 'recurring tune' as he calls it, to circus music heard in the distance, 'weaving in and out of your preoccupied consciousness'. And it is indeed the subconscious he wishes to reach with his 'non-realistic' devices – there is always a taut balance in Williams's plays between his ideas about what is expressionistic in the plastic elements versus the dialogue, which has often been described as 'lyric realism'. For example,

Williams indicates the use of a technique that could be identified as Brechtian – though Williams, as well as Brecht, may well have been influenced by Piscator in this regard – when he designates distinct theme music for different characters, to be played under certain dialogue for cinematic effect. He also does this by directing incongruous lighting effects onto Laura when she is outside of a realistic scene being played, 'in contradistinction to the apparent center'.[41] In Scene Five of the play, Amanda and Laura are clearing the table, 'their movements formalized almost as a dance or ritual, their moving forms as pale and silent as moths',[42] when Tom walks past them to the fire escape, initiating with his mother what is understood as realistic dialogue.

Most of the time this balance between the presentational and the realistic is low-key, even discreet, but there are times when Williams arranges the non-verbal action in such a specific way that it cannot be ignored without ignoring the character relationships or the feeling of the moment. One such instance comes in stage directions at the very end of the play when it is revealed that the Gentleman Caller, Jim, is unavailable, already engaged to a girl named Betty. Amanda's hopes dashed, her son about to leave the family in the dark (literally), and unable to believe that her son didn't already know Jim was spoken for, she begins to rail at Tom. The argument rapidly escalates to a shouting match that drives him out of the apartment. As soon as Tom exits onto the fire escape – with the slamming of a door, the smashing of a glass, a scream from Laura, the moon breaking through storm clouds, and loud music from across the alley – Williams implements a different kind of presentational technique by choreographing a pantomime to run simultaneously with Tom's final speech to the audience. The playwright explains that what is happening inside the Wingfield apartment is now seen by the audience 'as though through soundproof glass',[43] so the actions that follow are part of a dumb show in counterpoint to Tom's monologue. Her face hidden by her hair until the final moments, Laura is 'huddled' on the sofa, comforted by her mother who, Williams tells us, 'has dignity and tragic beauty' now that we can't hear her speech.[44] The gestures Amanda uses to console her daughter are described as 'slow and graceful, almost dancelike' before she glances at her husband's picture above the mantelpiece and exits, leaving Laura alone. The action is timed so that Laura blows out the candles as Tom tells her to do so, ending the play.[45]

From the beginning of the play the audience knows that Tom will leave; the narrative is *his* memories, provided entirely by him, that constitute this memory play. Up until the very last moment he decides what the audience will or will not discover about the Wingfield family. To ignore this final orchestration of grief, pity and dignity from mother and daughter, intertwined with the guilt, regret and longing of son, is to omit a visceral and subconscious depth that Tom's monologue does not possess without it. And with it – this ballet of sorrow – the feelings that are generated supersede plot or theme. What happens to these characters is ambiguous; nothing is tied up and no message is given except, perhaps, the information that the world is now lit by lightning, instead of by candles.

When *The Glass Menagerie* opened in Chicago on 26 December 1944, there was a blizzard in the city that lasted for several weeks. To understand what was new and different about the play, it is worthwhile to consider the response of the most prominent critics who saw it on that first snowy night. Claudia Cassidy, who remained a fixture in Chicago theatre for another 40 years, caught the theatrical power of *The Glass Menagerie* in the first paragraph of her review: 'It comes alive in theater terms of words, motion, lighting, and music ... it reaches out tentacles, first tentative, then gripping, and you are caught in its spell.'[46] Ashton Stevens, who had been reviewing plays for the Hearst newspapers in New York and Chicago for 50 years, saw and reviewed everyone from James O'Neill to Eleonora Duse to Sara Bernhardt. In his review he recounts major plot points, extols Jo Mielziner's designs as 'a new note in the poetics of the modern stagery', singles out Laurette Taylor for special praise, admires Dowling's performance and direction, and describes the play's structure as 'a series of dramatic sketches', comparing the narrator (Tom) to the narrator in the Moscow Art Theatre's production of *The Brothers Karamazov*. Then, after all his attempts to convey its power, Stevens indicates that he has never before seen a play like *The Glass Menagerie*. Calling it 'a beautiful and mystically vivid play', 'lovely', 'original', having the 'courage of true poetry couched in colloquial prose' and 'eerie and earthy' at the same time, Stevens later explains that the mother and daughter are left alone at the end 'as Life sometimes does leave women and the Stage hardly ever'.[47] He then writes, 'The play leaves you in the air. But I like this air. It is rare, rich.

It is the only air in which a woman so powerfully enchanting as Laurette Taylor's Mother could have her being.'[48] To accept the ethereal emotional power of a play while allowing for such ambiguity of plot was an exceptional response by a major critic and is an indication of how unique *The Glass Menagerie* was, even prior to its Broadway opening the following March.

To further understand what was new about *The Glass Menagerie* when it appeared on Broadway, the observations of Williams's contemporary Arthur Miller are discerning. Miller regarded *The Glass Menagerie* as 'a triumph of fragility', and remembered that seeing it in the context of commercial Broadway plays of the period 'was like stumbling on a flower in a junkyard'.[49] Miller felt that the job of playwrights at that time was akin to engineers and architects, 'structure and its problems taking first place in all consideration of the art'.[50] But Williams was a different kind of American playwright for Miller because, instead of focusing first on plot, it is character and language that largely drive the action of *The Glass Menagerie*, modest and Chekhovian as it may be. Miller recognized that Williams's radical breakthrough with *The Glass Menagerie* was because of 'his rhapsodic insistence that form serve his utterance rather than dominating and cramping it'.[51] Miller further asserted that in Williams's embrace of eloquence, feeling and equivocation, 'he wanted not to approve or disapprove but to touch the germ of life and celebrate it with verbal beauty'.[52] That Williams succeeded on Miller's terms is corroborated by the perpetual and deep-seated place the play has held in the American theatre and in the American psyche.

Summer and Smoke

In the spring of 1945, not long after *The Glass Menagerie* opened on Broadway, Williams began drafting a play he called *A Chart of Anatomy*, the roots of which can be traced to the short stories 'Bobo' (1941) and 'The Yellow Bird' (1945).[53] *Summer and Smoke* (the eventual title) represents a continuation of his desire to both put his 'sister on paper'[54] and to make himself 'a post-war writer'[55] with his experimentation; Williams keenly understood the challenge to bring psychological truth to the repressed Mississippi

Delta spinster Alma Winemiller and still expand and explore his range of theatrical expression. With *Summer and Smoke*, more than for any play of the 1940s, Williams felt tremendous pressure to succeed, to rekindle the accolades he generated with *The Glass Menagerie*. He was dogged by the feeling that he had a potentially great play in the making for which he could not find the theatrical engine of the story. He kept rewriting and revising almost continuously for nearly three years. Some of the draft titles include *The Bird Girl in His Arms*, *Fiddler's Green*, *The Good Time House*, *The Room is Cold*, *Scenes of a Magic Lantern*, *Portrait With a Parasol* and *World of Light and Shadow*.[56]

For most of the summer of 1946, Williams shared a house on Nantucket Island with Carson McCullers; she was adapting her novel *The Member of the Wedding* into a play and Williams was working almost fanatically on *Summer and Smoke*. Consistent with a story that takes place at the time of the First World War, Williams's drafts from that summer incorporate aspects of silent film – cinematic techniques being among Williams's elements of plastic theatre, as often used by Piscator. Draft fragments for silent film scenes are extant, such as Alma calling the police on the Buchanans, Alma assisting John as he inoculates field workers, and an argument between John and his father.[57] Many of the silent film descriptions come with a caption for the key image, much like those used by Piscator and Brecht, to accentuate the primary event of a scene. Also found in these drafts are the incorporation of direct address, live narration over silent film, combinations of silent film and silent stage action, and live vocal effects such as disembodied female voices that compliment Alma after she sings in the bandshell.[58]

After labouring for nearly three months, Williams wrote to Audrey Wood on 29 August 1946, 'I hope that you were able to feel in the play a sort of Gothic quality – spiritually romantic – which I wanted to create. It is hard to use such stuff in a modern play for a modern audience, but I feel it is valid.' Then, bringing up the cinematic techniques, he writes, 'I also hope you will feel that it might be practicable to actually combine the silent film sequences (perhaps 16MM) with the stage scenes.'[59] Williams continued to believe in the viability of the film sequences when he wrote to director Margo Jones on 17 October 1946: '[N]ow I'm going whole hog and making them [the silent film sequences] an integral part of the script. I know it can be done, the question is – Will anybody do it?'[60] Yet, on 19 November 1946, Williams told Jones that he had decided to dispense with the film sequences because, 'I'm afraid they would break the poetic unity'.[61] Williams did not discard his vision of a Gothic quality for *Summer and Smoke*, which is evident in the 'Author's Production Notes' to the published version of the play. He draws attention to the sky and the design of the Episcopal Rectory and the Buchanan home. Describing the sky as a 'pure and intense blue' of the kind found in Renaissance paintings, Williams calls for an 'American Gothic design', and asks that the architecture be barely suggested by fragments and outlines of rooms and roof, only what was necessary to show doorways and stairs, or hang the chart of anatomy. To convey the feeling of this 'see-through' set, Williams suggests that studying *Conversation among the Ruins*, by the Italian painter Giorgio de Chirico, is helpful to create the fragmentary spirit of the design. Sparse, doleful and surreal, de Chirico's painting supports the dichotomy between the poetic and idiomatic quality of Williams's dialogue and his inclination to shape a presentational theatre experience.[62]

A diary entry from Sunday, 1 December 1946, shows Williams unhappy with the play: 'Still here, still working on "Chart." Sometimes it seems just a grade or two superior to a radio soap-opera. I have committed some astonishing lapses of taste in this play.'[63] Writing to James Laughlin on 9 April 1947, two years after he began writing *Summer and Smoke*, Williams was dismayed that the play was a disappointment and yet he felt that 'eventually something might work out of it. The basic conception was very pure and different from anything else I have tried. It was built around an argument over the existence of a "human soul" but that got pretty thoroughly lost in a narrative that somehow slipped to the level of magazine fiction, or worse.'[64] To some extent Williams may have been right; the characters, their virtues and vices, and their relationships in *Summer and Smoke*, are so formally composed, and sometimes narrowly rendered, that there may be insufficient room left for complexity or ambiguity.

In spite of the playwright's doubts, early in 1947, Margo Jones read a draft version of *Summer and Smoke* and pressed Williams to let her direct the play at her recently opened regional theatre, Dallas '47. The play premiered with Jones directing at the Gulf Oil

Playhouse, Dallas, on 8 July 1947 (prior to the Broadway opening of *A Streetcar Named Desire* on 3 December of that same year). The production was poorly received and did not fare much better when it opened on Broadway in 1948. During rehearsals for the Broadway run, Williams was in Europe writing a new version of the play he called *The Eccentricities of a Nightingale* – in which he restored sections he had cut for the Dallas production and removed the overly-broad Mexican characters – but he arrived too late for the new script to replace *Summer and Smoke*, so he put his revision away. *The Eccentricities of a Nightingale* was published in 1965 and it opened on Broadway in 1976.

A Streetcar Named Desire

With his next major work, Williams continued to explore the plastic elements of theatre-making, though *A Streetcar Named Desire* was material of much greater intensity and potential danger. He still wanted to write, even contingently, about the tragedy of his sister Rose, and he also wanted to return to the generational and epic scope he had tried out with *The Spinning Song*, *Daughter of the American Revolution* and others. The genesis of *A Streetcar Named Desire* was a single image of a woman seated, looking out of a window at the moon, waiting for a man who would never show up. Based on that image, in December 1944, Williams wrote one scene of a play titled *Blanche's Chair in the Moon*. He later told an interviewer that the ideas he came up with in that first draft initially terrified him so much he did not want to return to the material. Later draft titles show the playwright's evolution in theme and protagonist: *The Passion of a Moth*, *Go, Said the Bird*, *The Moth*, *The Primary Colors*, *Electric Avenue*, *The Paper Lantern* and *The Poker Night*. Over time the action moved from Chicago to New Orleans, the Shannon sisters became the DuBois sisters and Ralph became Stanley. In a one-act version called *Interior: Panic*, Williams experimented with Blanche's interior voice being heard by the audience. This was likely a direct influence of O'Neill's experiment with audible subtext in *Strange Interlude*; writing to his grandfather on 31 January 1929 about a production of O'Neill's play in St Louis, Williams noted: 'Its unusual feature is that all the actors speak their thoughts, showing decided difference between what people <u>say</u> to others and what they <u>think</u> in reality.'[65]

When a script was complete, Audrey Wood sent *A Streetcar Named Desire* to another inexperienced producer, though this time one who was much more savvy, with financial connections in Hollywood, Irene Mayer Selznick. Compared to Margaret Webster (who had directed *Battle of Angels*), Eddie Dowling (*The Glass Menagerie*) and Margo Jones (*Summer and Smoke*), Elia Kazan proved to be quite a different director as collaborator. Having reached a high point in his career – his power so great that he was the first director to have his name appear above the title of a play – Kazan was Williams's first choice to direct *A Streetcar Named Desire*. Kazan, for his part, had great admiration for Williams and was honoured by the invitation. Before everyone was signed on, however, there was some negotiating at hand due to some rightly perceived resistance on the part of Kazan. It turned out he had wanted to produce the play himself and was balking at the selection of Selznick. Williams didn't know the details of Kazan's reservations when he wrote to him on 19 April 1947 from New Orleans hoping to clear up any misconceptions and explain his intentions in the play. Williams took care to paint a picture of a world in which 'there are no "good" or "bad" people', only those whose vision of other people is so hindered by a layered fog of ego and misunderstanding that 'nobody sees anybody <u>truly</u>'.[66] Williams went on to describe the way people fail to see one another through the multiple layers of distortion created by flaws in each person's ego. He then discussed getting to the truth through transformation in drama – impartially rendering characters who can be seen for who they really are by the audience, if not by one another, so that their tragedy becomes self-evident to the viewer 'through the detached eye of art'.[67] In presenting this case for ambiguity and complexity, Williams even pointed out that when writing a play to 'score a certain point' – harking back to his polemical and pedagogic plays prior to *The Glass Menagerie* – the play's 'fidelity to life may suffer'.[68] And finally, Williams responded to a question Kazan had asked about what an audience should feel for Blanche with an answer that was unequivocal: 'It is a tragedy with the classic aim of producing a katharsis of pity and terror.'[69] Kazan felt that the letter helped to clarify his grasp of *A Streetcar Named Desire* and inspired him further to take up the challenge of directing it. Williams's letter also embodies what the playwright succeeded in creating with *A Streetcar Named Desire*, a modern tragedy without a hero or a villain; each protagonist is also an antagonist, and so instead of a hero's journey, we are offered rather a raw and painful view of human misunderstanding.

In *A Streetcar Named Desire*, as in *The Glass Menagerie*, there is something significant to be lost if one rejects or ignores the non-literary elements in Williams's stage directions, and the final scene of *Streetcar* is a masterful example of what can be gained. After Blanche delivers her famous line, 'Whoever you are – I have always depended on the kindness of strangers,'[70] and disappears around the corner with the doctor and matron, the poker players are standing in the kitchen, Stella is crouched at the bottom of the fire escape shouting her sister's name and Eunice is higher up on the fire escape holding the Kowalski's newborn baby. Williams has Eunice bring the baby, wrapped in a pale blue blanket, down to a sobbing Stella, who takes the child. Eunice goes into the kitchen where the men are seating themselves around the table again as Stanley goes out and stands looking at his wife and child. As Stella surrenders to weeping with 'inhuman abandon',[71] Stanley speaks soothing endearments to her while he kneels closer to her and 'his fingers find the opening of her blouse'. Stella's 'luxurious' sobbing begins to fade as the sounds of the 'blue piano' and a muted trumpet rise and fill the theatre, but not before Steve is heard to say, 'This game is seven-card stud,'[72] and the curtain descends. Creating a stage picture composed of clear and simple actions, using minimal dialogue, Williams leaves another play in the air. Change his stage directions or dialogue, ignore the fingers that find the blouse, and the play will not be the same. As Williams has written this ending, the audience has beheld a scene of pity and terror and yet cannot be sure of Blanche's fate, nor what Stella or Stanley will do. But there is one certainty they are given: that life will go on.

Conclusion

While some of the initial reviews were mixed, *A Streetcar Named Desire* was a phenomenon – considered by many to indeed be the 'Great American Play' – that changed the American theatre and the ways in which American playwrights write their plays. If experimental seems an overstatement, in Williams's eyes it was not. In his masterpieces, *The Glass Menagerie*, *A Streetcar Named Desire* and *Cat on a Hot Tin Roof*, along with the rest of his massive body of theatre work – thirty-three full-length plays and over seventy-five one-acts – there is always some attempt to create a poetic expression of truth, life or reality through the transformational power of theatre.

7

Arthur Miller: The Individual and Social Responsibility

Valleri Robinson

In the opening episode of Arthur Miller's novel *Focus* (1945), the white, middle-class protagonist, Mr Newman, ignores the cries for help of a woman he assumes to be Puerto Rican, reasoning that 'she could take care of herself'.[1] And, besides, he wasn't wearing his slippers, 'so he could not be expected to go outside and stop this'.[2] Throughout the novel, Newman conforms in order to maintain his status within his own racial and class group. He ignores the activities of the racist and anti-Semitic group in his neighbourhood until he is mistaken as Jewish. After losing his job and withstanding a violent attack, Newman finally takes action against the Christian Front by reporting its members to the authorities.

In this novel, set only a few years prior to its publication, Miller uses historical events and figures and distinctively American social and economic contexts to explore an individual's growing consciousness of his relationship to the common good. As long as Newman remains concerned about his own wealth and well-being and that of his family, he doesn't exercise social responsibility or act to protect those outside of his perceived group, and the violence escalates around him. The novel established the key problems Miller would probe over the next decade in his dramas. Like the novel, *All My Sons*, *Death of a Salesman*, his adaptation of Ibsen's *Enemy of the People* and *The Crucible* all examine economic and social pressures to conform as well as tensions between protecting or advancing the family and fighting for social justice.

All My Sons

In 1947, Arthur Miller emerged as a significant voice in the American theatre when he won the New York Drama Critics' Circle Award for Best Play, edging out Eugene O'Neill by eight votes. Miller's socially conscious play, *All My Sons*, prevailed over O'Neill's *The Iceman Cometh* in a run-off vote. The New York critics, though acknowledging the play's shortcomings, found that *All My Sons* offered a direct and honest criticism of American individualism, and it demonstrated dramatic craftsmanship. In the increasingly constrictive American Cold War climate, the critics viewed Miller's examination of a fundamental American principle, the drive for personal wealth, and his critique of American capitalism and business ethics, as courageous and important.

Miller based his play on the 1943 charges brought against the Wright Aeronautical Corporation of Lockland, Ohio, accused of selling defective airplane parts to the United States government. The company allegedly falsified test reports intended to verify the effectiveness of the materials and influenced the Army Air Forces's inspection process through coercion.[3] The post-war period revealed a number of failed management practices during wartime production, and Miller set out to explore the pressures that would lead to such failures. He heightened the story dramatically by casting it as a moral or ethical failure. Through his lead character, Joe Keller, the owner of a plant that sold cracked airplane cylinder heads to the government, Miller suggests that such action had been prompted by an American ethos that values individual over communal success. Throughout the play, Keller masks his guilt for the deaths of twenty-one pilots and excuses his actions as necessary to protect his own family and the company he had built to ensure their financial comfort. Under pressure to produce as many parts as possible and afraid of losing the government contracts, Keller had enabled his manager to sell the faulty parts. In addition to this ethical lapse, he blamed his business partner, who ended up with a lengthy jail sentence. Keller's actions, those prior to the play's stage action as well as those in the play, are all tied to ensuring the success and financial security of his own sons.

In the opening sequence of the play, Miller establishes that the family enjoys the comfort of an upper middle-class existence. They live in an expensive home with a well-manicured lawn. Keller is especially proud to have earned enough money to hire a maid, so his wife, Kate, 'would take it easy'.[4] But the luxuries are superficial: it is the maid's day off and Keller still has to take out the garbage. His blue-collar roots are exposed in spite of himself. Additionally, on the green, well-maintained suburban lawn lies a fallen apple tree. The tree had recently been planted in memory of the Kellers' son Larry, an Army Air Corps pilot who is still missing in action. The tree lying in the back yard disrupts the superficial perfection of the setting. The opening scene predicts the unravelling of Keller's comfortable life and worldview.

Act One also establishes a false sense of community. At the beginning of the play, Keller sits in the sun reading the want ads in the Sunday paper, more curious about what people want to buy than about news events. His neighbour Jim, a doctor, reads the paper at a table nearby. Another neighbour, Frank, wanders by and engages Keller and Jim in light conversation. The neighbours' wives join the group intermittently, bringing a sense of a dynamic, interconnected community atmosphere. It appears to be a safe, comfortable, supportive community. There are suggestions, though, of the community's instability when Keller references Jim's home as a place where a 'happy family' used to live, which raises a question about why a happy family would move away from such a stable environment. Later in the play, it is revealed that Jim's house used to belong to Keller's partner, the father of Ann Deever, Larry's former fiancée, who has just arrived to visit Keller's son Chris. Keller's actions uprooted the community when he condemned his neighbour, who is now in prison. Although it first appears as a tight-knit community, the neighbours, especially Jim and his wife Sue, are resentful about what they perceive as Keller's false innocence, and they merely pretend to trust him.

Keller's wife Kate tries to uphold an image of Keller, though she is clearly concerned that others still judge him guilty. Keller had spent time in the penitentiary prior to the opening of the play, but he explains that after he was exonerated and had re-established his wealth, the neighbourhood grew to respect him again. It becomes clear, though, that the neighbours and his partner's children doubt his innocence and distrust him. All the relationships beyond the familial relations are disingenuous, the play suggests, because American social life has been built around the needs and success of the family and not the broader community. This mirrors Keller's willingness to let his friend, neighbour and colleague pay the price for his own wrongdoing.

Keller's son Chris highlights this theme in the play. Although he, too, wants to grow wealth for his future wife and family, Chris desires a society in which group interests outweigh individual interests. In a long monologue to Ann, he explains the wondrous bond that developed among the men in his army company. He says that they felt a sense of responsibility to others, and their individual lives were less important than the group: 'it seemed to me that one new thing was made. A kind of – responsibility. Man for man.'[5] This feeling he developed for his company also awakened his social consciousness concerning American labour practices and materialist forces. He tells Ann that upon returning to the States and falling back into the patterns of the American 'rat-race' he 'felt wrong to be alive, to open the bank-book, to drive the new car, to see the new refrigerator'.[6] He stresses the importance of understanding how these material goods came to be and to know where the money came from; otherwise, he argues, 'there's blood on it'.[7] That is, he stresses the significance of understanding the labour processes in this increasingly consumerist society as a means of contributing to the social, not just to the personal, good. This monologue communicates Miller's worldview and critique of American materialism with its pressure to avoid failure at all costs. The idea gets further articulated in the final acts of the play.

Near the end of Act Two, Keller's guilt is established when Kate accidentally undermines his alibi. Chris begins to suspect his father's guilt and demands the truth. In his monologue that follows, Keller describes the extreme pressure he felt to produce: 'I'm in business, a man is in business; a hundred and twenty cracked, you're out of business ... You lay forty years into a business and they knock you out in five minutes, what could I do, let them take forty years, let them take my life away?'⁸ Chris attacks his father's inability to see beyond the business and his own financial security and that of his children to the people who would be harmed, the unseen individual victims of American manufacturing.

Like the title character in Bertolt Brecht's *Mother Courage* (1939), Keller begins to understand that he has profited from the war at the cost of his own children, not just the invisible others. He learns in the last act of the play that Larry had killed himself upon discovering that his father's company had been responsible for the deaths of the 21 pilots. Only with this revelation does Keller understand the broader implication of his actions: 'I think to him they were all my sons. And I guess they were, I guess they were.'⁹ Chris finds himself in an ethical dilemma but decides to report his father to the authorities, viewing his familial ties as less significant than his responsibility to the greater community. Keller, though, goes inside the home and takes his own life. This act frees Chris from the shame of his father's wrongful deeds and achieves a sense of justice.

The idea of justice is developed throughout the play and is determined by an individual's value system. Miller uses the metaphor of prison with increasing force throughout the play. It is first introduced in the opening moments of the action, when Keller teases a neighbourhood boy about having a jail inside his home. Kate admonishes him for this joke, as she tries to separate the family from Keller's time in prison and to re-establish the veneer of respectability. Prison is again invoked with reference to Ann's father, who continues to serve his sentence though Keller was released. The younger characters begin to wonder whether Ann's father had been wrongfully convicted for Keller's crime. In the play's economy, the question of justice raised by Ann's brother, and later by Chris, must be answered. Chris decides that the socially responsible action is to turn in his father to the authorities. But Keller committed the crime of selling the faulty parts because he believed it would protect his sons, and going to prison would only further damage his son. Justice demands that the perpetrator pay a price for his crime, but time in prison would not balance the crime dramaturgically. In the context of the play, Keller's suicide would truly rebalance the world and enable its new economy to emerge. Because his act takes place inside the home, the symbol of prosperity, it may be understood that the home had indeed been a prison for Keller. He had bought into an American ethos that had imprisoned him, so his death in this space symbolically reveals how he had always been trapped. His suicide enables the next generation to move beyond those materialist confines.

All My Sons created a stir even before it opened at the Coronet Theatre on Broadway on 29 January 1947. Advertised as a work to be presented by Harold Clurman, Elia Kazan and Walter Fried, well-known members of the disbanded Group Theatre, *All My Sons* was anticipated in the theatre community as a revival of character-driven social drama. Although the rehearsal process caused a few bruises among the partners, the production, directed by Kazan and designed by Mordecai Gorelik, highlighted the strengths of the play. The skilled cast included Ed Begley as Keller, Arthur Kennedy as Chris, the Belasco-era star Beth Merrill as Kate, Lois Wheeler as Ann and Karl Malden as George. Critics raved about the inspired, vigorous and balanced ensemble performance. Among the original reviewers, William Hawkins and Howard Barnes highlighted the role of Kate as a central character, while Richard Watts Jr and Robert Coleman focused on Chris; others analysed strengths and weaknesses of the script.[10]

One of the play's most ardent critics, Claudia Cassidy of the *Chicago Daily Tribune*, challenged the New York Drama Critics for rewarding the play for its ideas rather than for its craftsmanship. A drama critic whose insights aided many mid-century American playwrights in their development, Cassidy astutely critiqued Miller's unwieldy and unfocused structure, the lack of character development and motivation, and the contrived nature of the plot. Although Cassidy did not highlight these specific aspects of Miller's dramatic writing, two key moments exemplify Miller's underdeveloped sophistication in motivating events in the play. Firstly, Kate's slip regarding Joe's health, when she tells George that Joe had not been sick in 15 years, seems inconsistent in a character whose sole focus has been guarding her husband's secret and protecting his reputation. Secondly, Miller's use of the well-made play device of a revelation of a secret through a letter indicates his reliance on outdated dramaturgical shorthand. The plot can only be resolved when Ann produces the letter she has kept secret for several years. The revelation of Larry's suicide motivates the crisis and Keller's suicide.[11]

In addition to criticisms of the play's dramaturgy, the play soon came under fire as 'party line propaganda'.[12] Following a protest by the national commander of the Catholic War Veterans, the United States Army review board determined that the play, 'which had been procured for production' in Japan and Germany, was unsuitable for production in occupied countries including Germany, Austria, Japan and Korea.[13] Though this pronouncement never amounted to a ban, it reveals the post-war emergence of an American Cold War culture concerned with how artists represented capitalism. While Miller certainly was familiar with anti-leftist dogma from his days as a writer for the Federal Theatre Project, this controversy placed him at the centre of debates about censorship. Brooks Atkinson, one of the play's greatest critical supporters, responded to the attacks on Miller in an essay titled 'Mare's-Nest Inquiries: Searching "All My Sons" for Hidden Motives' in the *New York Times* on 7 September 1947, which questioned a growing decline in 'tolerance and flexibility' as suggested by attacks on Miller and his play. Atkinson argues eloquently against the outcries of those 'working in the direction of censorship and restriction' by noting the demonstrated ills of censorship in the Soviet Union. He doesn't defend Miller against claims of presenting a communist point of view, but writes to defend free expression. 'As the country is now constituted, people are entitled to have an opinion and express it,'[14] he writes, defending both Miller and his accusers. Atkinson's fears of rising American censorship would be borne out later, again touching on Miller and the artists closest to him.

All My Sons later provided fodder for the House of Representatives Committee on Un-American Activities (HUAC), when Arthur Miller was brought to testify in 1956 in relation to investigations of unauthorized uses of United States passports. The committee questioned Miller about his support for communist organizations and his participation with the Civil Rights Congress, which had attacked the FBI and called for the abolition of the Smith Act (used to condemn the Hollywood Ten), the Internal Security Act and HUAC itself. The committee attempted to build a case against Miller's communist sympathies centring on his activities with various organizations in 1947. That year, his play *All My Sons* had been celebrated in the communist newspaper the *Daily Worker*, and Miller had sponsored an effort to send a production of the play to the World Youth Festival in Prague, Czechoslovakia. When government funding was denied to the artists involved in the production, Miller had signed a plea, urging the government to reconsider its decision and provide transportation for the participants.[15] As he had done in the past, in 1947 Miller was heavily involved in defending civil liberties, as it had become clear through attacks on his play that external pressures to silence dissent were escalating.

Although *All My Sons* lacks the dramaturgical sophistication of Miller's later plays, it began to outline some of the major themes and an approach to character development and conflict that would dominate his later work. Social pressures and expectations drive the action of many of his literary characters in their individual pursuit of happiness and success, which in the earlier works is defined by access to material wealth. Throughout the 1940s, Miller explored the impact of wartime and post-war American social, economic and political life on an individual's character and psychology, determined by his tenuous relationship to the community and his marketability. Although Miller portrayed strong women in his plays of this period, he tended to focus on the factors that determine the moral and ethical attitudes and actions of white, middle-class American males.

Death of a Salesman

Miller's next play concentrated on the psychology of a contemporary, aging American working man, drawing upon studies in psychology and sociology published during the period. Erich Fromm's *Man for Himself: An Inquiry into the Psychology of Ethics* (1947) outlines a distinctive, emergent personality type, which Fromm and his protégé David Riesman viewed as especially American. Fromm, an extremely popular German émigré author and a founding member of the Frankfurt School,[16] defined the 'marketing orientation' as characteristic of a personality type emergent in modern, capitalist, service-oriented cultures in which an individual begins to view himself as a commodity. One's personality, especially likability, becomes more valuable than one's skill or ability to produce.[17] Fromm writes:

> Since modern man experiences himself both as the seller and as the commodity to be sold on the market, his self-esteem depends

on conditions beyond his control. If he is 'successful,' he is valuable; if he is not, he is worthless. The degree of insecurity which results from this orientation can hardly be overestimated. If one feels that one's own value is not constituted primarily by the human qualities one possesses, but by one's success on a competitive market with ever-changing conditions, one's self-esteem is bound to be shaky and in constant need of confirmation of others ... If the vicissitudes of the market are the judges of one's value, the sense of dignity and pride is destroyed.[18]

Fromm and Riesman's *Lonely Crowd: A Study of the Changing American Character* (1950) discusses a process of alienation characterized by anxiety and instability, by which an individual faces the decline of his exchange value. Such studies strikingly designate a character type under consideration in Miller's *Death of a Salesman* (1949). In fact, the 'marketing orientation' as described by Fromm manifests itself in a psychology in which physical exhaustion and constant mental adjustment generate instability. Miller's *Death of a Salesman* depicts such a psychology in both content and form.

Under the influence of Fritz Lang's film *The Testament of Dr. Mabuse* and Tennessee Williams's *A Streetcar Named Desire*,[19] Miller felt liberated to depict with dramaturgical complexity and nuance the salesman's alienation and mental collapse in an increasingly competitive American marketplace. The setting and non-linear development reveal the interior as well as exterior workings of Willy Loman's world. Miller represents Loman's internalization of the constant external pressure of the shifting socio-economic landscape as the salesman, in his final decline, struggles to negotiate a world he no longer understands.

That urban America was changing to become more competitive and less forgiving is demonstrated throughout the play. It is first seen in Miller's opening description of the setting. A romantic flute melody is disrupted as the curtain rises to reveal Willy Loman's house. 'We are aware of towering, angular shapes behind it, surrounding it on all sides.'[20] A small piece of sky indicated by a blue light falls on the house, but 'the surrounding area shows an angry glow of orange'.[21] During the first act, the audience learns that the home used to be surrounded by trees and open space for planting a vegetable garden, but increasing development has limited sunlight and potential for growth. The rapid urbanization of the city and the competition that inevitably accompanies the population growth, depicted in a harrowing, expressionistic manner, is suffocating Loman. 'There's not a breath of fresh air in the neighborhood,' Loman complains.[22] That urbanization creates unusual pressure on Loman parallels the findings in Fromm's and Riesman's studies about the development of externally-focused personality traits. In modern, competitive, urban settings with expanding populations like New York City, they argue, individuals develop their identities in relation to how others perceive them. One's individuality is subsumed by mass culture and a need to please; 'the need to be liked' directs and guides his or her actions.[23] In the opening scene of the play, Willy Loman rails against urbanization: 'There's more people! That's what's ruining this country! Population is getting out of control. The competition is maddening! Smell the stink from that apartment house! And another one on the other side.'[24] In conversation with leading 1940s sociologists, Miller depicts the tragic stakes for an individual trapped in this emerging, competitive culture.

Miller establishes at the outset that his salesman's ability to navigate the new environment has led to his exhaustion and mental instability. The physically and mentally exhausted sixty-year-old Willy Loman enters the house with a sample case and suitcase, signs of his life as a travelling salesman. 'If old man Wagner was alive, I'd a been in charge of New York now!'[25] Willy has worked loyally as a salesman for his company for many years, as a travelling east coast representative. The audience soon discovers that his new boss, old man Wagner's son, has recently taken him off his salary and placed him on commission only, increasing the pressure on him. The once-successful Willy believes in an old system by which a company rewards its long-time employees; however, the new business model destroys its workers when their exchange value has declined. Willy regards the passing era nostalgically, as a time when an individual, an internally-driven man, was able to control his own fate. His flashback encounters with his self-made brother Ben, who purportedly became rich in the African diamond industry, represent Willy's view of this former culture in its most distorted, blinding light. Ben has taken a risk and, through the exploitation of others, built his own company, while Willy has been risk averse and subordinate to the demands of Wagner's company. Miller seems to suggest that because Willy so admires Ben, an exploitative colonialist who appears movie-star-like in Willy's visions, he is unable to understand his own exploitation by old Wagner, blinded as he is by his dream for material success and status. Miller critiques both the old and new systems as exploitative, but myths of the old system foster the emerging system which locks the urban middle class into a cycle of debt built on dreams of home-ownership and new material necessities such as cars and appliances.

Tension is set up between a rural, natural, thriving environment and the oppressive urban scene. In the former, individuals build and nurture with their hands. Loman's son Biff loves the freedom of working outdoors on a farm or cattle ranch, where a person's value is based on useful labour. He describes the work and landscape poetically, and he finds the work pleasurable. However, he has internalized his father's value system, in which material success and status prove a person's worth, though he doesn't agree with it. At the outset of the play, Biff has returned home feeling frustrated by his wasted life, and the audience learns that Biff and Willy have had a terrible argument the night before. Willy cannot understand why Biff, 'a young man with such – personal attractiveness', has gotten lost in the world.[26] Because Biff was so popular in high school, Willy expects he could have been very successful in business. Throughout the play, Willy maintains this hope, even as Biff explains his failures. In the fraught urban setting, Biff's ethical life, like that of his father, rests on pretence and falsehood. Additionally, Biff has a background of stealing: stealing balls from the sporting goods store where he worked, lumber from a lumberyard, and finally, a fountain pen when he goes to ask for a loan to start his own sporting goods store. Denied an opportunity to meet with his former boss, Biff steals the man's pen. These seemingly random actions reveal Biff's understanding of the competitive system's emphasis on material objects. Without any rank or status, Biff can only undermine his superior by undermining his material wealth, no matter how slightly.

As with *All My Sons*, *Death of a Salesman* really turns on the intergenerational conflict between a father and son. The sons in both cases have challenged the socio-economic and moral/ethical belief systems of the fathers. Neither Chris in *All My Sons* nor Biff in *Death of a Salesman* understands or condones the actions of their fathers, and their own actions undermine their fathers' values. Chris departs from his father's unethical business practices, and Biff's faith in his father's value system is shattered when he discovers his father is having an affair with a woman in Boston. Up to that point, as presented in flashbacks, the teenage Biff admired his father. However, the affair revealed the façade of Willy's self-presentation. 'You fake! You phony little fake! You fake!' he shouts at his father.[27] He loses faith in his father's authenticity and influence with the revelation that his character was determined by a desire for approval and status, which drove him to constantly reinvent himself and present himself in the most favourable light. If he were truly powerful and important, as Biff sees it, Willy would not need to have an affair to assert his masculinity.

Willy's other son, Happy, has fallen into a similar life pattern as his father, but he has self-awareness about his limitations within the economic system. 'All I can do now is wait for the merchandise manager to die,' he confesses to Biff.[28] Even if he could be promoted, he understands that the trappings of wealth don't lead to happiness or comfort. 'I don't know what the hell I'm workin' for … I think of the rent I'm paying. And it's crazy. But then, it's what I always wanted. My own apartment, a car, and plenty of women.'[29] With his father and Biff, who once dominated his environment as a high school athlete, as models, Happy has viewed independence, the ability to support himself financially and his physical potency as the markers of manhood. He has come to understand the emptiness and limitations of such markers. He articulates his disgruntlement at work in terms of masculinity, especially physical prowess. 'Sometimes I want to just rip my clothes off in the middle of the store and outbox the goddam merchandise manager. I mean I can outbox, outrun, and outlift anybody in that store, and I have to take orders from those common, petty sons-of-bitches …'[30] Following his father's path, he can never assert his masculinity in the workplace, so he does so privately. Like Willy, he uses his false confidence to seduce women, including the fiancée of his superior, as a means of asserting power and importance. Unable to achieve dominance in the workplace governed by men, it is in relation to women, depicted as commodities, that both Biff and Happy assert their manhood. In reference to some women with whom he and Biff have spent the evening in Act One, Happy says, 'I get that anytime I want, Biff. Whenever I feel disgusted.'[31] Because he understands the frustrations of the service industry, and how it emasculates middle-class men, Happy has become a peacemaker for Willy and quickly tells him what Happy believes he needs to hear to maintain his illusion of status and power, at work and at home. Like Kate in *All My Sons*, Willy's wife Linda fully devotes herself to her husband, defending him and gently guiding his actions. Both women maintain the status quo. From Willy's flashback of his missed opportunity to set out on the business venture with his brother, it is clear that Linda discouraged him from taking huge risks. She preferred stability and the steady acquisition of a home and the slow accumulation of status she believed awaited Willy. Arguing against Ben's proffered dream of wealth in Alaska, she says, 'You're well liked, and the boys love you, and some day – *to Ben* – why, old man Wagner told him just the other day that if he keeps it up he'll be a member of the firm ...'[32] Even when Willy commits suicide in the final act, Linda cannot understand how he would take such an action when they had just sent the final mortgage payment. For her, this demonstrated an achievement, even if it wasn't on a grand scale, and suggested an easing of the financial burdens of the past. Although she knows that Willy has not always been direct and honest with her, and that his commissions have been decreasing and that he has been borrowing money to cover it up, she helps him maintain the illusion that he continues to support her and have influence in the business world. Willy's affair, while it reveals his desire for status and potency, also provides an escape from the constraints of middle-class domesticity, which Linda upholds. His affair symbolizes a rupture in the illusion of the American dream as it is tied to the sustenance of a middle-class nuclear family and finds parallels in the broken appliances and faulty cars. The tension between Biff and Willy escalates in regard to Linda, whom Biff defends when Willy raises his voice to her. Biff doesn't divulge information about the affair he discovered, but he centres his anger on Willy's disregard for her. Linda acknowledges that Willy never became a great success but continues to grant him respect and to build his confidence. In doing so, she inadvertently increases Willy's pressure to exert his authority, feign importance and prove his worth to his sons.

Although Linda cannot grasp Willy's suicide, it remains consistent with Willy's desire to prove his value in the world. He has assessed his worth on his ability to sell himself, and the steady decline of his influence and likability decreases his value as a man.

He not only views the world in terms of what people think of him but also in terms of what his sons think of him. He desires not only the respect of his sons, particularly Biff whom he has failed, but he wants them to like him. In his worldview, likability is the most marketable commodity and leads to self-worth and economic and social advantage. Willy's association of likability with self-worth becomes clear in the exchange with Biff that leads to the father's suicide. Following a day of failed attempts to ensure their financial futures, Biff explodes to his father about the pretence and 'hot air' that has compensated for genuine success and authentic character. 'I am not a leader of me, Willy, and neither are you,' Biff famously remarks. 'You were never anything but a hard-working drummer who landed in the ash can like all the rest of them!' Exhausted by his outburst, Biff sobs, 'Will you take that phony dream and burn it before something happens?' Before going to his upstairs bedroom, he tells his father that he will leave the next day. Willy's reaction to Biff's meltdown is most telling: '*after a long pause, astonished, elated*: Isn't that – isn't that remarkable? Biff – he likes me!'[33] When the others have gone to bed, Willy remains alone and wonders about Biff's love for him, 'Isn't that a remarkable thing? Ben, he'll worship me for it.'[34] A horrifying moment follows in which '*sounds, faces, voices, seem to be swarming in upon him*'.[35] Willy Loman darts out of the house. The sounds of frenzied and crashing music signify his suicidal car wreck. The escalation of his resolve to maintain his son's love accompanied by the panicked and threatening sounds swirling around him reveal the latent insecurity of the salesman, that is, the once upwardly-mobile, middle-class man in the post-war American landscape.

Still considered by many the greatest play ever written by an American, *Death of a Salesman* struck a chord and captured an emergent American mentality. Miller's depiction of Willy Loman's anxiety portrayed the effect of the service economy in an increasingly oppressive urban environment described the following year by sociologist David Riesman. Riesman, in his *The Lonely Crowd*, argued that Americans were so obsessed with affability that their minds worked like radars, absorbing input from so many sources, trying to adapt to the changing demands of consumerism in order to constantly sell themselves. Both Miller and Riesman, like Fromm before them, presented the mental collapse brought about by such constant social pressures. The sociologists viewed this as uniquely

American at the time, as the American service economy developed more rapidly than other areas did.

Miller could not have predicted the phenomenal success of the play and the way it catapulted him into the American artistic and literary élite. Directed by Elia Kazan and produced by Walter Fried and Kermit Bloomgarden, the play opened on Broadway at the Morosco Theatre on 12 February 1949. Jo Mielziner, the set and lighting designer, visually evoked the harrowing world of Willy Loman's mind, building on principles of constructivist and expressionist design. Lee J. Cobb, an unlikely choice with his physically powerful build, premiered the title role with great success, sympathetically and tenderly revealing the mental and physical deterioration of the character. Critics acclaimed Kazan's ability to create a balanced ensemble and draw out the poetic elements of Miller's play. They praised Miller's ability to develop a tragedy from the life of a middle-class American salesman. The play ran for over two years on Broadway, with 742 performances, and received the Tony Award for Best Play and the Pulitzer Prize for Drama.

Only the communist *Daily Forward*, it seemed, found issue with the play. Unable to assess the rich critique of the American socio-economic landscape in the play, the reviewer had hoped to see a more direct attack on American capitalism, such as he had found in *All My Sons*. Miller's critique of the organization of American life in *Death of a Salesman* is much more subtle than his overt criticisms in the earlier play. In an interview with Fredric Wertham of the *New York Times*, Miller explained that one of the key elements of Loman's discontent and displacement was his separation from the means of production. Biff 'insists that his future stability and sanity lie in production, in achieving a connection with the creation of things rather than by manipulation of things'.[36] Others wrote about Miller's critique of modern materialist society, but most critics agreed with Brooks Atkinson that 'Mr. Miller is not writing about ideas but about human beings.'[37] The human beings existed in a distinctively American context that didn't undermine the play's ability to transcend geographical boundaries. One London critic wrote that 'Willy Loman, a man who goes about the sale of merchandise with a mystical fervor as if he were a priest of a new religion, is not immediately recognizable or familiar here,'[38] but the play proved successful in London and elsewhere and continues to be widely produced.

The Crucible

In both *Death of a Salesman* and *All My Sons*, Miller meditates on the relationship between the individual and the group in modern, democratic, capitalist America. Willy Loman sought constant approval from the crowd, whereas Keller acted independently only to be criticized by his son for selfish individualism and lack of concern for the group. For Chris, the welfare of the group outweighs individual success. Miller, though, also studied the problem of an individual withstanding the pressures of the crowd-turned-mob. He first explored the theme on a large scale in his novel *Focus* (1945), which follows the apathetically racist Mr Newman on his path to social enlightenment and his individual fight for social justice against the rising tide of American wartime anti-Semitism.[39] In his adaptation of Ibsen's *An Enemy of the People* (1950), Miller further explored the social, ethical and economic dilemmas of the individual of conviction who becomes overwhelmed by a self-righteous crowd. 'It is an enduring theme,' Miller wrote in his preface to the adaptation, 'because there never was, nor will there ever be, an organized society able to countenance calmly the individual who insists that he is right while the vast majority is absolutely wrong.'[40] Ibsen's vilified Dr Stockmann stands against his entire Norwegian town when he reveals that the hot springs, which provide the livelihood for the residents, are contaminated, and he recommends costly restructuring of the system to protect tourists and locals. Miller felt the play addressed a critical problem in American political and social life of the period. 'Simply, it is the question of whether the democratic guarantees protecting political minorities ought to be set aside in times of crisis.'[41] Miller referred primarily to the escalating Cold War frenzy that gave increasing power to the House Un-American Activities Committee (HUAC), whose investigations throughout the 1940s the communist press compared to the Salem witch trials of 1692.

HUAC was initiated in 1938 to investigate subversive activity in the United States. Almost immediately, the committee's leadership created intense fear and anxiety about communism and associated many politically left organizations and individuals with communist plots to undermine democracy and capitalism. Although the committee was often derided and mocked by the politically moderate and by the left for 'shotgun accusations' and irresponsible and unfair claims, the committee's scope and power grew throughout the 1940s.[42] As noted, in 1947, following the hearings that led to the blacklisting of the Hollywood Ten, a group of screenwriters and directors who refused to provide testimony about American communist organizations during their HUAC hearings, Arthur Miller joined others in attacking HUAC and the Alien Registration Act of 1940. With the rise of McCarthyism in the early 1950s,[43] Miller became increasingly concerned that Cold War anxiety and fear suppressed individual expression and the voices of any political minorities. In his testimony before the committee in 1956, Miller noted that he had written two short plays dealing with HUAC directly and had begun thinking about his play about the Salem witch trials as early as 1938. Comparisons between HUAC investigations and hearings and the Salem witch trials were common. US Representative Thomas H. Elliot of Massachusetts referred to the 'witch hunts' of the committee in a 1942 House debate on the continuance of the committee. When asked by the committee about the relationship between his 1953 play *The Crucible* and HUAC, Miller commented, 'The comparison is inevitable, sir.'[44]

In his autobiography, Miller recounts his decision to write the play as well as the events that shaped his perspective. Just before leaving for Salem to conduct research on the trials, he received a call from Elia Kazan, his close artistic ally and friend. Miller stopped to visit Kazan on his way to Salem, and Kazan told him about his decision to testify before the committee and provide information in order to stabilize his emerging film career. Kazan's wife, Molly, who had been such an advocate for Miller's work, charged Miller with being out of touch with the post-war American climate when he told them about his idea for a play based on the Salem witch trials that were widely associated with McCarthyism.[45] The incident aroused a sense of deep despair for Miller as he felt sadness about the inevitable loss of friendships and feeling of community that the new climate produced.

The Crucible, Miller notes in his foreword, is based on historical detail. He used trial transcripts and other documents to develop his understanding of the events, though he embellished somewhat as he wrote. He captured the archaic dialect recorded in the documents to ground the work in historical specificity. Although

Miller hoped to speak broadly to the types of circumstances that give rise to panic and distrust so severe that rationality itself is lost, his attention to historical circumstances grounds the play in rich realism that distinguishes the stark, oppressive New England town. Miller's interest in the political and economic circumstances that enabled the panic outweighs his interest in individual characters, so he wrote the play in a way that allowed him to reveal the broad community that surrounds his key figure, John Proctor, a farmer who becomes ensnared in a multidirectional web of deceit and power. The figures of authority in the play, including the reverend, the judge of the makeshift court and the authority on witchcraft, all work to suppress and maintain Salem's theocracy. In his extensive and detailed introductory notes, Miller writes, 'The witch-hunt was a perverse manifestation of the panic which set in among all classes when the balance began to turn toward greater individual freedom.'[46] The play depicts the attempt to express individual belief and action in the face of a reactionary 'autocracy by consent'.[47] In light of the vast extermination of Jews in Europe and the rise of McCarthyism, the play calls for resistance and individual action against social systems built on 'the idea of exclusion and prohibition'.[48]

The play opens in the home of Reverend Parris, the leading authority figure, who was both respected and feared by the town's residents. Parris prays at his sick daughter's bedside. He had recently caught his daughter and niece, along with other girls, dancing and running naked in the woods, and he suspects an invasion of the demonic. In his first action of the play, Parris denies his slave, Tituba, entry into his daughter's bedroom. This denial symbolically represents the fear of otherness, particularly represented by her blackness, as tied to contamination and the demonic. Miller wrote in his autobiography that in his research he had discovered in testimonies about witchcraft that 'the Devil himself ... was almost always a black man in a white community', and in Salem, the most convincing testimony had been Tituba's confession, because it aligned with pre-established fear of blackness.[49] By the end of Act One, Tituba confesses to collusion with the Devil, after being threatened with being whipped to death or hanged. Her confession of conversing with the Devil enables her to arouse fear in Parris ('Oh, how many times he bid me kill you, Mr. Parris!'[50]) and unravel the white community that has oppressed her ('Look! I have *white* people belong to me'[51]) even as she saves herself. In this confession, she undermines the power structure with a vengeance.

The first act establishes the conflicts that drive the play forward and introduces an array of characters who represent the dynamic in the contained, restrictive environment. Rumours of witchcraft have been spreading in the town following the strange illness that has overtaken a few of the resident girls. Mrs Ann Putnam had sent her daughter to Tituba to conjure her recently dead sister, and the girl now at home behaves strangely. Parris's own daughter has become ill after dancing naked around a fire with Putnam's daughter and her cousin Abigail. Parris had sent for a specialist in the demonic arts, Reverend John Hale, as a precaution, but fearful of losing the parish and his reputation, Parris initially denies the possibility of witchcraft in the community. When Reverend Hale begins to press Abigail about the events in the woods, she accuses Tituba of controlling her with demonic powers, though it is clear that Abigail invents this to save herself. Abigail, recently dismissed from service in John Proctor's home when his wife discovered that they had an affair, begins to view these accusations as a source of power. With Hale's authority supporting the claims, Parris joins the fight against sorcery and witchcraft, which, according to Tituba's confession, has overtaken the town. In this first act, Miller hoped to demonstrate the way a toxic mix of the fear of losing power, desire for containment, long-standing resentments and pressure on the powerless can arouse irrational anxiety and thoughtless action with inhumane consequences in a society.

Act Two takes place late in the evening in the home of John and Elizabeth Proctor, whose strained relationship is apparent in their uneasy physical interaction. Their young servant, Mary Warren, returns from Salem, announcing that 39 women have been arrested on charges of witchcraft and that one has been condemned to hang after refusing to confess. Proctor threatens Mary with a whipping for going to Salem without his approval, but to his dismay Mary responds, 'I'm – I am an official of the court now.'[52] With her newfound power, Mary forcefully stands up to him. Proctor questions the authority of the court proceedings and the newly created legal establishment. Like the HUAC committee, whose power was questioned in two Supreme Court cases in 1947, the legal infrastructure of the Salem trials is revealed to be dubiously constituted and overreaching. Although Proctor attempts to withstand the force of this new authority, which has been justified by Reverend Hale's pronouncement of witchcraft, he cannot protect Elizabeth against charges that Abigail has made against her. Proctor destroys the warrant for her arrest, challenges the veracity of the accuser and physically bars the deputies from taking her, but Elizabeth leaves, in chains, with the men. Reverend Hale begins to show signs of disbelief in the girls' accusations, but he realizes he has gone too far and cannot easily reverse the legal process. As the scene closes, Proctor attacks Hale for cowardice and violently insists that Mary Warren tell the truth in court. She cries, 'I cannot, I cannot, I cannot', knowing that the girls will turn against her and attack her if she does. Importantly, Act Two demonstrates the strength of the accuser over the accused and the difficulty of resistance in politically extremist societies.

Miller wrote in a note in Act One, 'Political opposition, thereby, is given an inhumane overlay which then justifies the abrogation of all normally applied customs of civilized intercourse.' Clearly referencing McCarthyism as well as the Salem trials, he also observed that '[a] political policy is equated with moral right, and all opposition to it with diabolical malevolence'.[53] As his wife is charged, Proctor shouts, 'Is the accuser always holy now?'[54] The question reveals an underlying problem of the HUAC proceedings, which gave such weight to the accusation that many leftists were associated with acts of subversion and treason regardless of their innocence or guilt. Miller understood the limits of the comparison of the HUAC hearings and the Salem witch trials. There really were American communists who had spied or associated with the Communist International, primarily in the 1930s, whose intent was the construction of worldwide communism that would require the overthrow of the current American structure of government. There were no actual witches in Salem.[55] Nevertheless, Miller's interest is less about the existence of dangerous and even diabolical elements, but about the way in which their existence or perceived existence was used to justify unfair legal proceedings that destroyed the lives of innocents.

Act Three of *The Crucible* homes in on the legal proceedings. The act introduces Judge Hathorne and Deputy Governor Danforth, both self-righteous, threatening and impatient authorities abusing their power in the name of holiness and justice. Miller's decision to represent both the Judge and the Deputy Governor, rather than just a single authority, reveals the ways in which the judicial and legislative powers collude to enforce the moral ideology. They work as a committee, but with one voice. Hathorne submits to the will of Danforth, the true authority in the play. In the act, Proctor confesses that he had an affair with Abigail and explains that vengeance is the cause of her accusation against his wife. Elizabeth, without knowing Proctor confessed this, hides this information from Danforth to protect her husband's reputation. The act ends in a frenzy of performance by the girls, enflamed by representatives of the state, the court and the Church, as the teenagers now charge Proctor himself. In the final moments of the scene, Reverend Hale denounces the court proceedings.

It is in the final act of the play, set in a jail cell moments before John Proctor is scheduled to be hanged, that Miller's thesis becomes clear. Encouraged by his wife and the authorities of the court, Proctor agrees to give a confession. Unlike the others who refused to confess and died as martyrs, Proctor believes his sin of adultery has tainted him. 'I cannot mount the gibbet like a saint. It is a fraud. I am not that man,' he tells Elizabeth.[56] After confessing to Danforth, though, he refuses to name the names of others in spite of Danforth's threats. 'I can speak my own sins; I cannot judge another.'[57] Parris convinces Danforth that Proctor's testimony and signature alone will influence the town to have faith in the court proceedings, so Danforth relents as Proctor signs the document. After signing, though, Proctor refuses to give the paper to Danforth and finally destroys it, unwilling to be used to reinforce the proceedings and mar his name. In a rage, Danforth calls for Proctor and the others to be hanged. As they are escorted out, a drum roll rises and Hale pleads with Elizabeth to go to Proctor and change his mind. Having been kissed passionately by Proctor after he absolved himself, Elizabeth stands firmly: 'He have his goodness now. God forbid I take it from him!'[58] Even as Hale weeps frantically, 'the new sun is pouring upon her face'.[59] Proctor's courageous action, not that of the morally righteous but of the socially convicted, stands as the significant event of the play. Miller, writing in his autobiography about his desire to finish the Salem play that he had begun many years earlier, stated, 'The longer I worked the more certain I felt that as improbable as it might seem, there were moments when an individual conscience was all there was that could keep the world from falling.'[60]

Proctor's defiant action, like Stockmann's in Miller's adaptation of Ibsen and Newman's in Miller's novel *Focus*, stood as examples of Miller's belief in an individual's capacity to resist the corruption and power of the mob to ensure hope for a more just and equitable future society.

Because of his strained relations with Kazan, Miller sought a new director to stage *The Crucible*. A colleague recommended long-time Broadway director Jed Harris, well known for his successful productions of modern plays. Miller felt that the strong-willed, domineering director misunderstood the play, and the producer Kermit Bloomgarden fired the director shortly before the opening. This mismatch led to a moderately successful production that *New York Times* critic Brooks Atkinson found 'overwrought' and a little emotionally 'tiresome'. Drawn to the theme and parallels between HUAC and the 1692 trials, he found the play itself 'gripping' and 'exciting' but not warm.[61] He felt that Miller's focus on the social structures and mob hysteria left little room for individual character development, though he complimented the performances of Arthur Kennedy as Proctor and Beatrice Straight as Elizabeth. The critic for the *Washington Post*, Richard L. Coe, criticized the Washington production of the play, less loudly staged by Elliott Silverman, along similar terms. In his memoir, Miller expressed discontent with the early productions and their reviews, but he understood the play's power after watching one audience at the initial production stand silently with their heads bowed for several minutes after Proctor leaves to be executed. 'The Rosenbergs were at that moment being electrocuted in Sing Sing ... The play then became an act of resistance' for the cast.[62]

Although the first production of the play was not entirely commercially or critically successful, according to Miller, the play became his most produced play, nationally and internationally, because of its stance on resistance.[63] Two years after writing the play, when Miller was called to testify before the House Un-American Activities Committee, like Proctor, he admitted to his own associations, but refused to condemn others by naming names. In spite of the contemporary resonance with McCarthyism, the play came to reference the rise of tyranny and political suppression more generally. As suggested by his thoughts about the play decades after he wrote it, it is clear that Miller continued to believe in the power of individual conviction and resistance to authority.

Conclusion

As Miller's work of the late 1940s and early 1950s indicates, his force as a playwright aligned him with socially-committed playwrights such as the twentieth-century Yiddish playwright Jacob Gordin, as well as Clifford Odets, John Howard Lawson, Lillian Hellman and, more recently, Tony Kushner. His plays captured the social, economic and political pressures of the post-war years that encouraged individuals to conform to dominant American values. His critiques exposed the dehumanizing systems of power that suppress individual moral action while revealing the capacity for pathos and resistance. At a time when many writers and intellectuals were overcome with an existential sense of hopelessness and meaninglessness, Miller depicted the potential of individual conscience and social responsibility. Concerned that contemporary society had left individuals adrift, he continued to advocate for ethical, social, economic and legal systems that offered citizens dignity, justice and a right to free political expression.

Afterword

Felicia Hardison Londré

The major plays of Eugene O'Neill, Thornton Wilder, Tennessee Williams and Arthur Miller from the 1940s remain timeless classics of the American drama. These four writers were indeed the first truly great American dramatists, and few playwrights of later generations have risen to join their pantheon, perhaps only Edward Albee and August Wilson. What elevates a playwright to classic status beyond the dozens of dramatists whose work we now find exciting? The viability of the works on page and stage these many decades after they first provoked and captivated audiences testifies to their illumination of something about human nature and relationships that is not fully contained by their historical context. Their specificity tempered by all-too-human ambiguity gives rise to their universality. The greatness of the individual plays covered in this book is further enhanced by each playwright's overall *oeuvre* in which those masterpieces are embedded. A prolific playwright is one who enjoys the scope for a learning curve, including failures. Moreover, all four pushed the boundaries of dramatic form as then understood and accepted. The fact that Thornton Wilder did not write as prolifically for the stage as did the other three may account for his omission from Thomas Keith's assessment in his Foreword to *Tennessee Williams and Europe*, wherein he notes that in 1983, when Williams died, he and Arthur Miller constituted the supporting sides of the triumvirate of best American playwrights with Eugene O'Neill at the apex.[1] It's a valid image and yet we find also a niche in it for Wilder's *Our Town*.

Eugene O'Neill

When Eugene O'Neill died in 1953, he had not had a Broadway premiere since *The Iceman Cometh* in 1946. *A Moon for the Misbegotten* was produced by the Theatre Guild and toured to four Midwestern cities in the spring of 1947, but did not reach New York. In the 1950s, Williams and Miller had moved to the forefront of theatrical recognition while O'Neill's glory was fading – until his widow Carlotta Monterey began releasing work that O'Neill had withheld. The dates by which the late plays were completed, as provided by Robert M. Dowling,[2] long precede their stage premieres. *Long Day's Journey Into Night*, written in 1941, premiered first in Stockholm, Sweden, and then at New York's Helen Hayes Theatre on 7 November 1956 under the direction of Jose Quintero. This masterpiece of personal revelation in dramatic form reignited appreciation for O'Neill, and Monterey subsequently released *A Touch of the Poet*, written in 1942 and premiered on 2 October 1958, directed by Harold Clurman. In 1964, the one-act *Hughie*, written in 1941, premiered at the Royale Theatre under the direction of José Quintero. *More Stately Mansions*, written in 1939, had its Broadway premiere on 31 October 1967, directed by José Quintero. And yet, the following decades saw O'Neill's plays more frequently analysed by scholars as dramatic literature than produced on stage. Finally, the new century has brought a resurgence of interest in the plays as viable works of theatre. Paralleling the renewed popularity of O'Neill's work on stage has been the rediscovery of his contemporary Susan Glaspell. Both careers began with one-act plays staged by the Provincetown Players in 1916, and it is an ongoing question whether she influenced him or vice versa; some have detected interesting similarities between her expressionist play *The Verge* (1921) and his *Strange Interlude* (1927). Among more recent playwrights, Tracy Letts has had his play *August: Osage County* (2007) compared to O'Neill's work.

Since the turn of the millennium, O'Neill's plays have attracted outstanding actors of the English-speaking stage: Brian Dennehy, Philip Seymour Hoffman, Vanessa Redgrave, Kevin Spacey, Nathan Lane and others. The Eugene O'Neill Society meets in locales that were important in the dramatist's life – Nanjing, China (1988), Bermuda (1999), Tours, France (2003), Provincetown,

Massachusetts (2005), Danville, California (2008), Greenwich Village, New York City (2013), New London, Connecticut (2014), Galway, Ireland (2017) – and publishes *The Eugene O'Neill Review*.

Thornton Wilder

Two novels and a play constitute Thornton Wilder's major work after the 1940s. The novels, surely his best, are *The Eighth Day* (1967) and *Theophilus North* (1973). The latter has been successfully dramatized by Matthew Burnett (Samuel French, 2003). Wilder's comedy *The Matchmaker* (1955), which evolved out of his earlier play *The Merchant of Yonkers*, may be best known in its musical comedy version *Hello, Dolly!* (1964). The 1980s and 1990s saw publication of his journals, his letters, his interviews and a wealth of new scholarship devoted to him. Several biographies were published, but all were surpassed by the definitive *Thornton Wilder: A Life* (2012) by Penelope Niven. The Thornton Wilder Society publishes an annual newsletter and has held two international conferences: at the College of New Jersey (2008) and at Salve Regina University, Newport, Rhode Island (2015). *Our Town* remains a favourite on stage, both professionally and in academic theatres and among amateurs, all over the world. Director David Cromer's fresh approach to the play – basically a modern uncovering of its innate theatricality – has garnered accolades wherever he has staged it: New York, Kansas City, London and elsewhere.

Because *The Skin of Our Teeth* is a challenging play to produce, it reaches the stage only infrequently; like Tennessee Williams's *Camino Real*, it can be perplexing yet rewarding for those who tackle it. Given the troubled state of the world in 2016, *The Skin of Our Teeth* is ripe for a renaissance on stage. Lincoln Konkle has shown how Wilder's work was affected by the lingering effects of the Second World War that fused with his latent Puritan ideology.[3] Whether on the scale of the individual or of civilization itself, the recurring pattern is one of stepping to the brink of annihilation but somehow surviving to endure a new round of struggles. Over the decades, Americans have tended to read that pattern optimistically as one of survival against the odds. Only in recent years has there been a tendency to see the pattern in Wilder's plays and novels as a dire warning that catastrophe is always lurking around the next corner. But, of course, some calculated latitude for ambiguity has always been a mark of a great writer.

Tennessee Williams

Williams never rested on his laurels after his successes of the 1940s. When he took up his writing each day, he could always go to any of several works in progress. Major plays of subsequent decades include *The Rose Tattoo* (1951), *Camino Real* (1953), *Cat on a Hot Tin Roof* (1955), *Suddenly Last Summer* (1958), *Sweet Bird of Youth* (1959), *The Night of the Iguana* (1961), *Small Craft Warnings* (1972) and *Out Cry* (1973). Less-known late plays plus numerous earlier works have been unearthed and published in recent years. Sadly, the decade after Williams's death in 1983 saw a virtual stranglehold on publications and productions of his plays due to his literary executor's disastrous caprices; that saga is detailed in John Lahr's *Tennessee Williams: Mad Pilgrimage of the Flesh* (2014) and in Lahr's earlier *New Yorker* article on the subject (19 December 1994). The death of Maria St Just in 1994 enabled Lyle Leverich at last to publish his long-delayed biography, *Tom: The Unknown Tennessee Williams* (1995), which Williams had authorized; and suddenly the plays were again gracing world stages. Tennessee Williams's plays have found particular favour in French translation, thanks in part to their many successful motion picture versions. Johnny Hallyday's 1985 song 'Quelque chose de Tennessee' has remained at the top of the popular singer's repertoire since he introduced it. Annual festivals and conferences celebrating Williams's work are held in Provincetown and in New Orleans. His influence on subsequent generations of playwrights is endless, as shown in Philip C. Kolin's *The Influence of Tennessee Williams* (2008).

Arthur Miller

Arthur Miller lived long enough to see his writing and his social activism celebrated internationally. Just as Tennessee Williams was loved in France and Thornton Wilder's plays found special favour on German-language stages, so Arthur Miller was the darling of British theatre. Miller's friend and biographer Christopher Bigsby of the University of East Anglia has published numerous important studies of Miller's work. When he died on 10 February 2005 at his home in Roxbury, Connecticut, he was excited about the prospect of Brian Dennehy playing Willy Loman in a London production that May. His later plays include *Incident at Vichy* (1964), *After the Fall* (1964), *The Price* (1968), *The Creation of the World and Other Business* (1972), *The Archbishop's Ceiling* (1977), *The American Clock* (1980), *The Ride Down Mount Morgan* (1991) and *Broken Glass* (1994). He also wrote collections of short stories and essays, his memoir *Timebends* (1987) and the screenplay for *The Misfits*, a 1961 movie directed by John Huston and starring his second wife, Marilyn Monroe. In 1965 he was elected president of the international PEN organization. In 1983, Miller travelled to Beijing to direct *Death of a Salesman* in Chinese, starring Ying Ruocheng. Among his many recognitions were the lifetime achievement honours at the Kennedy Center in Washington, DC (1984).

Documents

For Such is the Ruling of Broadway
Ann Crisp

Ann Crisp was a senior at Oneonta High School in Oneonta, New York, when she wrote this essay in 1947. At that point, of course, few had yet heard of either Tennessee Williams or Arthur Miller. The original typescript with minor inked corrections by Miss Crisp and additional corrections by her teacher was scanned and provided by her granddaughter Stephanie Demaree with permission from Ann Crisp Demaree. The teacher's handwritten comment on the paper is: 'You have given a very complete treatment of your subject.' The paper is graded A.

Current drama is a huge and vastly interesting field. Authorities often say that a play is judged by its author and cast, as well as its plot. Perhaps this is true when one is picking a play he wishes to see but it is not at all true when one is picking a play he wishes to read. The author is ever important in play choosing – famous playwrights invariably turn out noted plays in rapid succession. This was true in the case of Eugene O'Neill, Moss Hart, and George S. Kaufman. Another guide to play selecting is the awards the play has received – Drama Critics' Award and the Pulitzer Prize are perhaps the best known of these. As the last guide I should choose the play's run on Broadway. Although few people have the same taste, time usually proves the quality product.

The plays which I have read were primarily chosen through the last method. Though some were excellent, others were inclined to be vulgar and without plot. The masters of the current plays are to my mind O'Neill and Steinbeck. These two outshine all others in depth and yet in simplicity of plot, in dramatic climax and in character study. Both Steinbeck's 'Of Mice and Men' and O'Neill's 'Beyond the Horizon' deal with broken unhappy people (farmers in both cases) who try desperately to get ahead, but fail through human weaknesses. Each of these plays received due award. 'Beyond the Horizon' won the Pulitzer Prize for 1919–20 and 'Of Mice and Men' the Drama Critics' Circle Award of 1937 and 1938.

'Our Town' by Thornton Wilder brings something entirely different to the Broadway stage. With a cast of twenty-four principals and twenty-five extras, the play is staged without the aid of scenery. The lighting effect is extremely important and helps to create the desired impressions.

To be a success a play must appeal to the emotions. Comedy has a place of its own in the hearts of theatre goers – especially did the public want a chance to laugh during the past war – it was then that 'Claudia,' 'My Sister Eileen,' 'Arsenic and Old Lace,' 'Junior Miss,' and 'Harvey' were produced. Clifford Goldsmith's 'What a Life,' although not a wartime production was such a success that there is now a radio show solely about the trials and troubles of Henry Aldrich around whom the play was written. 'Harvey,' Mary Chase's imaginary 6-foot-tall white rabbit, has been amusing theatre-goers since 1 November 1944. Cleverly written, impossible, and the winner of the 1944–45 Pulitzer Prize is 'Harvey.'

Broadway has seen few of these outstanding plays in the past three years, strangely enough. John Van Druten's 'The Voice of the Turtle' was quite a let down after reading Goldsmith's 'What a Life' or Day's 'Life with Father.' The drama also seems to lack that little 'something' it had in earlier years. 'Decision' by Edward Chodorov or 'Pick-Up Girl' by Elsa Shelley can hardly be compared with Rostand's 'Cyrano de Bergerac' or O'Neill's 'Emperor Jones.'

Although there have been few play successes in the last few years, the musical comedy has not suffered. 'Oklahoma!,' by Hammerstein and Rodgers, along with 'Bloomer Girl,' 'Carousel,' and 'Annie Get Your Gun' have been tops in box office sales. 'The Late George Apley' by John Marquand and George S. Kaufman added its mark to the successes of 1944 – while it holds to ridicule the Bostonian primness, there is a quirk of lightness about it that relaxes as well as amuses the reader.

Elmer Rice tried in his play, 'Dream Girl,' to catch something of the differentness and audience appeal that Moss Hart caught in 'Lady in the Dark.' Mr. Rice was not so successful as was Hart, even with Betty Field in the title role. 'Dream Girl' was supposedly a comedy, yet I failed to see anything funny about a girl who spends her time pretending.

One of the most famous contemporary playwrights is Lillian Hellman. 'Watch on the Rhine,' 'The Children's Hour,' and 'The Little Foxes' are three of her best known works. 'The Searching Wind' is her last and seems to be as popular as any done in the Hellman style. Few authors obtain the intensity and audience-moving effect that Miss Hellman does.

Modern plays often deal with social injustice or expose an existing evil. Most of Galsworthy's works are of the nature of a reform. 'Strife,' for example, presented the social wrong doing of the capitalists against the laborites. Many of John Galsworthy's works deal with the class distinction as he sees it in England.

'Deep Are the Roots' presents to the public the racial problem. Although the action takes place in the deep south, the question is by no means limited to that section of the country. O'Neill's 'All God's Chillun Got Wings,' presents the same problem perhaps in a more skillful way than does 'Deep Are the Roots.'

Edward Chodorov's 'Decision' exposes the threat of fascism in the United States. It takes a small town and makes a startling sensation out of something that could never have happened. At the same time this no doubt left its mark in the minds of the theatre-going public, showing them that there is always a threat of dictatorship if you let someone think for you.

Another play written solely to point out existing evil is 'Pick-Up Girl' by Elsa Shelley. The juvenile delinquency of the so-called 'victory girl' during World War II encouraged Elsa Shelley to write this. The whole play is staged in a courtroom and Elizabeth Collins is the character being tried. The play was cheap, vulgar, and it presented only the case without trying to find the cure.

When one looks back at the so-called field of dream, he wonders what there is about the fairly simple story that causes it to influence lives of millions of people – these same people are willing to spend hard-earned money on plays that are often second-rate and have a 'B' cast. Is it a form of momentary escape? Is it a pleasure to vicariously have excitement that might never otherwise be obtained?

When in 1945 'Tobacco Road' had broken all records with its 3,192 performances and 'Life with Father' had 2,362 performances to its credit, then was $4,000,000 advanced for twenty-eight new Broadway hits. During those war years there was more theatre-going, more demand for new as well as for the time-proven old plays. People wanted something to make them relax, to take their minds away from their troubles, to challenge them. The theatre seemed to do all of this. This year we have had several new plays staged on Broadway. Eugene O'Neill has made a comeback with his 'The Iceman Cometh.' True to O'Neill's style the play is a long one, taking several hours of the afternoon, a dinner recess, and well into the night for its production.

Broadway has known great authors, great plays, and great actors. It has been the pattern of showmanship for the world. John Galsworthy, Maxwell Anderson, and Eugene O'Neill have seen most of their plays Broadway successes. 'You Can't Take It With You,' 'The Old Maid,' and 'Strange Interlude' are all products of the Broadway stage. Giving the audience tops in performance are John, Ethel, and Lionel Barrymore, Katharine Cornell, and Maurice Evans.

Few of the plays which I read had the strangeness or the moral teaching values that are to be found in 'Susan and God' by Rachel Crothers. The character study is exceptionally good. The way she depicts the broken home of the Trexels, the drunkenness of Barrie Trexel, the husband, and the human erring of Susan make for an enjoyable play.

Plays have come and gone. Styles of plays have changed in the same way as the styles of women's dresses. Although we didn't realize it at the time, these plays, more often movies to us, have a definite effect upon our standards, morale, and outlook upon general life. Galsworthy's 'Strife' certainly gave the common people something to think about. The oppression of labor by capital is seldom found to such a great degree today.

Yes, the drama does play its part in the daily lives of the citizens of the world. It influences both in a good and bad way the every day living of the individual to a very great extent. Drama will continue and the number of theatre-goers will increase – for such is the ruling of Broadway.

Plays

Clarence Day	Life with Father
John Galsworthy	Strife
Edmond Rostand	Cyrano de Bergerac
Eugene O'Neill	Beyond the Horizon
	The Emperor Jones
Lindsay & Crouse	The State of the Union
Moss Hart	Winged Victory
Edward Chodorov	Decision
John Van Druten	The Voice of the Turtle
Elsa Shelley	Pick-Up Girl
John Steinbeck	Of Mice and Men
Thornton Wilder	Our Town
Rachel Crothers	Susan and God
Clifford Goldsmith	What a Life
Lillian Hellman	The Little Foxes
D'Useau & Gow	Deep Are the Roots
John Marquand and George S. Kaufman	The Late George Apley
Mary Chase	Harvey
Elmer Rice	Dream Girl

Collecting Eugene O'Neill

Lamar Lentz

In high school, theatre history and the literature of theatre were more compelling to me than acting and technical arts of drama. My best efforts were in the area of playwriting and I strongly favoured American playwrights. As a freshman in the Department of Drama at the University of Texas at Austin in 1969, I chose theatre history as my stated major. After securing a part-time job in the Hoblitzelle Theatre Arts Library in the Harry Ransom Center, I was exposed to the world of rare books, manuscripts, original scene designs and theatre memorabilia as diverse as dance, circus, and industrial design (Norman Bel Geddes). Dr. W. H. Crain, director of the Hoblitzelle Theatre Arts Library, was also the primary patron of the collection.

Through Dr. Crain, and as a student worker in the library, I catalogued and arranged a host of old and new materials for the collection. From Dr. Crain, I learned of the rarity of items related to Eugene O'Neill and particularly of the rarity of O'Neill signatures. Given my interest in rare books and collections, Dr. Crain suggested I consider collecting signed editions of Eugene O'Neill plays. I stored the idea away as I pursued my studies and began my professional career in the field of rare books and museum collections. Dr. Crain remained a friend, and whenever I was in Austin I would visit the theatre arts collection. By 1978 the idea of my collecting items related to Eugene O'Neill was about to become a reality.

A conversation with Dr. Crain led to my discovery of Richard Stoddard's Performing Arts Books in New York. It was then a thriving book store on East 10th Street. I have the carbon of the letter to Richard Stoddard that I wrote on 2 February 1978, seeking a signed photograph of Eugene O'Neill. He replied that signed photographs were rare, but he would be glad to look for one for me and the search might take some time. He did offer me a one-line note signed by O'Neill to Oliver Sayler, from 1923, which I immediately acquired. This was my introduction to other materials signed by O'Neill. Stoddard invited me visit his shop if I were ever in New York. On my first visit to the shop in 1979, I was amazed to see a pastel of Eugene O'Neill, done from life, in Provincetown in 1920 by Leo Mielziner, the father of Jo Mielziner. After many starts and stops, I was able to borrow the money to acquire the pastel, and the journey of my Eugene O'Neill collection began.

My association with Richard Stoddard and his shop was a catalyst for the growth of my collection. In a letter dated 13 May 1980, he offered me a copy of Jennifer McCabe Atkinson's *Eugene O'Neill: A Descriptive Bibliography* (1974). This became my greatest source of information for assembling my collection. With the help of the Stoddard shop, I began collecting first trade editions, signed editions, and selected theatre programs from first productions of O'Neill plays. Through the Stoddard shop I acquired some remarkable items: four costume designs for the opera *The Emperor Jones*, rendered by Jo Mielziner, along with his personal copy of the play (Number 175 of 750). I was also able to acquire a few books that had been in the library of Eugene O'Neill. Another treasure is a Theatre Guild program for *Strange Interlude* at the Quincy Theatre in Quincy, Massachusetts, where it opened on 30 September 1929, following the Broadway run. Quincy, a suburb of Boston, welcomed the production after Boston's mayor banned it, and Quincy restaurant owner Howard Johnson famously built his chain on income he earned during *Strange Interlude*'s dinner break. The back cover of the program has a map showing places to eat near the theatre.

The search for some works began in the 1980s and continued until recently. As a native Texan, I was keen to obtain a copy of 'Eugene O'Neill and the Senator from Texas.' One hundred copies were signed by Senator Mayfield and published by Yale in 1961. The search took me to Washington D.C. where a representative of the Mayfield family informed me that most of the copies were still in the Mayfield home, and they were not receptive to parting with any of the copies. I continued to search until 1998 when I put my O'Neill collecting on hold in order to pursue a graduate degree in art history. It was the same year that Richard Stoddard's Performing Arts Books sent me one of their last handlists, #75. The shop, which had enriched my collection so greatly, went to an on-line format. One of the last major pieces I acquired from the shop was a portrait by Leo Mielziner of the artist George Bellows. Bellows had been a roommate of O'Neill for a time in New York. So after collecting O'Neill for twenty years, I locked up the entire collection in my bookcase and went on leave.

I had not thought of O'Neill or the collection again until I received an invitation from Kate Pogue to talk about my O'Neill collection for the annual Theatre Forum at the Round Top Festival Institute where I have been Director of Library and Museum Collections since 1976. I got out the collection and my worn copy of Atkinson and begin to take stock again. I decided to try to complete the collection, and the second voyage of the adventure was launched. What a difference fifteen years had made in the rare book and materials market! I found that Richard Stoddard Performing Arts Books no longer had an open shop but still existed on the internet. I contacted Richard Stoddard about the task. He was delighted but was no longer dealing in editions but concentrating on programs. His advice was to fill in the gaps by going to AbeBooks and Ebay, all online. There were some great things still available but most would not equal the condition of my earlier acquisitions. I went forward nonetheless, realizing how time had passed. I also found that there were still some materials and signed works by Carlotta Monterey and O'Neill family friends, Fania Marinoff and Carl van Vechten. So I began to broaden the scope of the collection and found a greater number of inscribed pieces from O'Neill's circle. I am still happily filling in the gaps from time to time. The search is easier from the computer screen but not quite as interesting to me. I miss holding a book in my hand before I purchase it, and I miss the one-on-one communication with book dealers and other collectors. What a difference nearly forty years of collecting Eugene O'Neill has made!

Acting in *The Skin of Our Teeth* with Helen Hayes

Hank Whittemore

One spring afternoon long ago, the cast and crew for a production of *The Skin of Our Teeth* sat in a large college auditorium in the midwest, anxiously awaiting the arrival of Helen Hayes. We had been anticipating this moment for some months – first during the wintertime, after we had auditioned and won our roles, then during the several weeks of rehearsal until now, just a few days before the run would begin. It was the spring of 1960 and I was in freshman year at the University of Notre Dame in Indiana; we were facing the stage at nearby St. Mary's College, where the First Lady of the American Theatre was about to join us. In my imagination Hayes would be a goddess, riding in her golden chariot in blinding splendor.

Our director had given us certain limited information. The play, by Thornton Wilder, had opened on Broadway in November 1942 amid World War II. Heading the cast had been Florence Eldridge and Fredric March as Mrs. and Mrs. Antrobus (Adam and Eve), with Tallulah Bankhead as Sabina, their seductively attractive maid *a.k.a.* the Other Woman. The revival in 1955 starred Helen Hayes and George Abbott as the First Couple of the human race, with Mary Martin completing the age-old triangle. The world-renowned actress whom we were about to meet had played her role on Broadway, for goodness sake! She had recreated it for a television adaptation (Producers' Showcase) and had played the part most recently in Paris. All this was guaranteed to further strain our nerves. There in the otherwise empty auditorium, however, we chatted it up, joked and laughed, trying to stay loose, when a little lady in a long brown coat and a kerchief on her head must have slipped in, through one of the side doors, and stood there quietly waiting until someone recognized her. Then came a flurry of greetings before the director told us what we already knew, that here in the flesh was Helen Hayes. We applauded, of course, and she said a few kind words – she was glad to be here, glad to meet us – while my attention wandered over to the very talented professional actress who, all during rehearsals, had 'filled in' the role of Mrs. Antrobus until our guest star could arrive at the last moment and take her place.

I began to feel sorry for the woman, whom I had come to know and respect. She was very believable on stage, I felt, and wondered how even Miss Hayes could be more effective in the role – especially now that she turned out to be this rather tiny, fragile-seeming woman, in her sixtieth year, who conveyed none of the dynamic presence I had been expecting. To this point our production had been going along just fine, I thought, so what more can she bring to the role of Mrs. Antrobus? What possibly could be missing that our 'stand-in' had failed to deliver?

We were scheduled to have our first full dress rehearsal a few nights later. This afternoon Hayes wanted to immediately run through two different scenes; then, over the next two days, we would take her through the entire blocking we had learned, and she would adjust accordingly. In a friendly manner, she made it plain that she had come to work. My own role was that of Henry Antrobus, *a.k.a.* Cain, so it was never far from my mind that Hayes and I were going to be mother and son on stage.

First she wanted to try the long scene early in Act One with just Sabina and Mrs. Antrobus in the family living room. The rest of us remained seated in the auditorium. We were about to get our very first glimpse of her actually rehearsing on stage. They began toward the end of Sabina's monologue, as the pretty maid strutted around in her short skirt, swirling her feather duster and assuring us, '*We came through the depression by the skin of our teeth – that's true! – and one more tight squeeze like that and where will we be?*'

Enter Mrs. Antrobus. In she came, wearing a frumpy dress but no longer the coat, looking all around as if to register and memorize everything in the room, one item at a time. This so-called 'little old lady' seemed to grow a few inches taller as something caught her attention and she snapped, with matter-of-fact crispness, '*Sabina, you've let the fire go out.*' We had never laughed at that line before, but now we let out a collective guffaw. She already had our attention. She was talking and listening but also busily inspecting this or that, very specifically, and before long she was standing at the window with a watering can. Off and on she turned her head to Sabina, but then, continuing to speak, she pointed the spout sharply downward toward the window sill to water the plant. And as she did, we gasped!

Yes, without warning we shared a sudden, loud intake of breath. It was a moment of surprise and wonder that I had never experienced and did not fully comprehend. In the years ever since I have thought it must have been the unexpectedness of the gesture, which Miss Hayes seemed to produce with utter spontaneity – even though she must have executed that simple stage business over and over, with one watering can or another, from New York to Paris and elsewhere, before landing here on this college stage in Indiana! Whatever the case, the gesture was new to us, and it knocked the air from our lungs.

Helen Hayes was giving us some acting tips, if we could only translate them correctly. What, exactly, was the meaning of that gasp? What was the lesson?

Next she wanted to run through the opening scene of Act Two, when she and her husband George Antrobus would address the crowd from the Boardwalk of Atlantic City. As our director had blocked it, they would sit together on a bench, with the curtain closed behind them, and address the audience as though speaking to the crowd on the beach. First Mr. Antrobus would stand and tell his '*fellow mammals, fellow vertebrates and fellow humans*' all about the progress that the human race had made, since the beginning of the world up to now; then he would sit back down while his wife stood and delivered a speech of her own.

Again we watched the run-through; and this time, without our knowing it until the night of the full dress rehearsal, she gave us a demonstration of what *not* to do. The actor playing Mr. Antrobus rose to his feet while Hayes, wearing a wide-brimmed beach hat, twisted her face sideways and upward to watch him as he spoke. After a few lines, to our surprise, she twitched her face a little in reaction and the hat fell over her eyes! As she reached up to adjust it, we laughed, realizing we had never laughed at that point. All through her husband's prepared speech, according to lines of the play, Mrs. Antrobus kept feeding him lines until she finally snapped, '*George, sit down!*'

We trained our eyes on this fascinating woman who was able to keep us laughing while stealing every moment of the scene for herself. She had kept her attention upon him, her expressions continually changing in reaction, sending us into fits of hilarity. Now, after Mr. Antrobus sat back down and Hayes finally stood, she continued to draw our full attention as if he was invisible. We giggled all through the delivery of her own speech; only later would we realize that this would turn out to be yet another lesson.

Over the next two days we took her through the blocking of all three acts. She knew the role but worked hard, making notes in her script and learning all the physical moves we had practiced during the previous weeks. Whenever I wasn't on stage I would sneak into the auditorium to watch again, then race back to the wings to make my entrances. When it came time for the dress rehearsal, in front of an invited audience of some three hundred students, it might as well have been our opening night.

Standing in the wings, usually at stage right, I caught as many of her scenes as possible while also waiting for my cues. The audience gave her a big ovation when she made her first entrance, of course, and after that she was a constant delight to watch and listen to. My time on stage began near the end of Act One, with several others onstage, and it seemed to go by in a flash. Before long I was standing again in the wings, this time as far downstage as I could get, to catch the Boardwalk speeches at the opening of Act Two; and now came the next half of the lesson.

The lines were the same but all else changed. Now, when Mr. Antrobus rose from the bench, Hayes fixed her attention on him and hung on his every word. Yes, once again the wide-brimmed hat tipped over and she had to fix it, getting her huge laugh, but this time her focus was such that the actor got all the responses he could have expected and more. He got laughs where he had never gotten them before; never had he been so good in this speech.

Then he sat back down and it was her turn. This time she stood and summoned some new energy and delivered a knockout, blowing the house down! Right there in the wings it became clear to me that Helen Hayes had developed the ability to 'take it away' from another actor and to 'give it back' to the same fellow player whenever she chose. She had the power to make you virtually disappear or to make you the focus of all attention. The stage, with everything and everybody in it, was under her control; and I must have sensed that it all had to do with some intense, moment-to-moment concentration or focus that she had made an automatic part of her. Now, however, we come to the reason I am telling this story in the first place, to the experience that has lodged in the brain as a special memory – a moment in my own acting life that would never be duplicated.

As the 'end of the world' approached in the second act, in the form of the hurricane and the oncoming Great Flood, I stood backstage as usual and waited for my cue to enter stage right. Behind me hung a huge, dark, rectangular sheet of heavy tin, with a stagehand waiting next to it. At a certain point the atmosphere would grow dark amid the storm clouds and howling wind, and Mrs. Antrobus would appear as she climbed up through a trap door downstage centre, holding a lantern and gazing around the empty, darkening boardwalk. Once on her feet, she would call for me ('*Henry!*') several times before resorting to her son's real name ('*Cain! Cain!*'), at which point the stagehand would smash a mallet against the tin sheet, creating a booming blast of thunder – my cue to race onstage crying, '*Here I am, Mama*' and run into her arms.

All that had gone smoothly and effectively during our previous rehearsals with the professional actress as Mrs. Antrobus. She had done this scene particularly well, I thought, which made me wonder how the great lady from Broadway and Hollywood could do much better with it. Hayes had quickly picked up on the various ways in which the director had blocked this scene; he had taken her through the paces with me; but we had never *acted* it together. Now, with an audience out there, we were about to go through it for real. I thought: How much differently can it go?

Let me tell it from here in the present tense:

As I wait in the wings, the activity on stage amid the hurricane grows ever more chaotic. Members of the Antrobus family are racing around to collect pairs of animals and shoo them up a ramp to the boat (Noah's Ark), while Mrs. Antrobus wanders through the turmoil saying, '*I can't find Henry,*' then calling out, '*Hennrry!*' She rushes offstage again as more chaos follows – the pier is going to break away any moment, they have to hurry, and now they disappear as the stage darkens. It's the proverbial lull before the storm and all grows quiet. Slowly the trap door downstage centre begins to open. I am watching, trying not to breathe too loudly, as it flips up all the way and – yes, a light appears, and we see a little elderly hand holding a lighted lantern. The hand stops moving upward; it aims the yellow light this way, that way, as if looking all around. The lantern has come alive.

Now Helen Hayes continues to move upward. With the light leading, she rises all the way, stepping onto the stage. She lets the trap door swing down and close itself shut beside her feet. So there she is, holding out the lantern with an outstretched arm, searching all around, worried, a mother desperate to find her child. I am fascinated, mesmerized, to the point of virtually forgetting that, in fact, I am supposed to be that very child for whom she is so desperately searching. Already this is different from any other time I've waited here for my entrance, palpably different. It feels as though she is sending out a wave of unfolding fear, a genuine concern that is morphing into a mother's terror, straining to see what she cannot see.

From somewhere offstage, Mr. Antrobus calls to her: '*Come on, now, Maggie – the pier's going to break any minute.*'

'*I'm not going a step without Henry,*' she says, now utterly alone. She holds up the lantern and calls sternly and loudly into the wind: '*Henry!*'

She waits and I wait with her. I am expecting her to get on with it, to give me my cue, but first she almost sings the name in a high voice, as if calling into the valley of a vast mountain range:

'*Hennnnn-rrrry!*'

More silence, as if we are waiting for an echo of her voice.

And finally she utters my real name, in what sounds like a gravelly male voice: '*Cain!*'

More silence.

I am ready.

On the verge.

Now it begins with a long low rumble from the deepest part of this little woman's insides, from some unknown invisible place

within, and it comes out with such overwhelming force that she might be summoning the Devil himself:
'CAIN!'
That's my cue, all right, but I can't move.
I am stuck there.
Now comes the crashing boom of that tin sheet right behind me, a blast of sound that seems to shake the earth itself and my own body with it.
Trembling, I start forward to rush onto the stage, only to find my knees buckling and dropping me straight down to the floor! Instead of moving forward on two feet I crash down to my knees and begin to crawl onto the stage toward Miss Hayes. She appears startled, concerned, confused; but this is the real full dress rehearsal and she, in response to what I am doing, is bending all the way down to her own knees to greet me. So I crawl and crawl and reach out, shouting, '*Here I am, Mama*,' now collapsing into her arms. At this moment she is, in fact, my mother, patting me on my head and back, now looking straight into my eyes and whispering fiercely, '*Thank God*,' her arms shaking as she hugs me and I tell her, '*I didn't think you wanted me*' and break into sobs on her shoulder.

Before I can realize what is taking place, she finds the physical strength to lift me to my feet, telling me to come quickly to the ramp so we can get into the boat. We make our way as the conventioneers at Atlantic City are dancing and marching and acting wildly, even as the world is ending. They jeer at the Fortune Teller, who tells them that they have had their chance, have had their day, and have lost – while even now, we members of the Antrobus family are venturing forth to make 'a new world.'

And so ends the second act, as I wander away backstage by myself, not quite sure of what just occurred.

It would happen that way during all the other performances – well, almost the same way, because from then on I did manage to prevent my knees from buckling and dropping me to the floor. Otherwise the feelings were the same and, over and over, I did burst into tears. I felt, during those brief moments on stage with Helen Hayes, that she really did care for me as a mother would care for her son.

All I understood at the time is that it certainly felt as though something enormous had happened in my life. I knew it would be important to remember the experience and, if possible, learn its meaning. Whether I have done so, however, is no longer the point; what counts for me is that this elusive lesson, whatever it was at the time, has remained alive for me from then to now.

Tennessee Williams in Ptown: The 1940s and Now

David Kaplan

David Kaplan, Curator of the Provincetown Tennessee Williams Theater Festival, wrote portions of this essay for the 2015 festival catalogue; that essay is included in Tenn Years: Tennessee Williams on Stage *(2015).*

In late June of 1940, Tennessee Williams arrived in Provincetown, Massachusetts, a New England fishing village at the farthest reach of Cape Cod, a long and narrow peninsula curled sixty-five miles out into the Atlantic Ocean. Ptown, as it is familiarly called, had been successfully countering a decline in its fishing industry since the mid-1930s by touting to tourists that Provincetown was where the Pilgrims from the Mayflower first came ashore in America. In 1940, 3,500 people lived in Ptown in winter; that same year, 100,000 people visited between July 4th and Labor Day in early September.[1]

Williams was twenty-nine in 1940 when he arrived for a summer at the Cape ingrained with the polite manners and mellifluous accent of his Mississippi Delta small-town upbringing, tempered by a profound sense of loss he took on after his family moved, when he was eight,[2] to what seemed to him the cold-hearted midwestern city of St. Louis. Just before New Year's Day 1939, he discovered a way of life to his liking in the freewheeling French Quarter of New Orleans. Seven weeks later, he left there for Laguna Beach, California, then Taos, New Mexico, then Manhattan. In the summer of 1940 he was brown-haired, brown-eyed, tanned, and, aside from a cataract clouding his left eye, fit. He swam every day in the curl of the bay or off the rougher Atlantic side of the Cape. Ptown was a conveniently short ferry trip from Boston, where prestigious producers, the Theatre Guild, planned to stage in the fall a full-length play he had written, *Battle of Angels*. A run after that was planned for Broadway. As Williams readied for *Battle*, he drafted another full-length play, *Stairs to the Roof*, in which a spaceship landed on top of a St. Louis shirt factory. His 1940 plans evolved in unintended ways. *Battle of Angels* was condemned by critics in Boston who were outraged by its equation of sex with salvation. The Theatre Guild opted out of a New York run. *Stairs to the Roof* led to a dead-end after the Pasadena Playhouse presented it in 1947. The play would receive its next professional production in 2014.

In the summer of 1941 Williams returned to write in Ptown, and again in 1944. In early September 1944, while living in a dune shack with the poet Harold Norse, Williams finished a draft of *The Glass Menagerie*. By late December, *Menagerie* opened in Chicago; by March of 1945, despite critical skepticism in New York, *Menagerie* was a Broadway hit. In 1947 Williams had the funds to rent a two-bedroom cottage on the eastern outskirts of Provincetown. There he refined two full-length plays, changing their titles. *Chart of Anatomy*, set in the Mississippi Delta, became *Summer and Smoke* for a production that August in Texas. *The Poker Night*, set in New Orleans, would arrive on Broadway as *A Streetcar Named Desire*. Its critical and commercial success would redefine Williams's life. Late in the 1947 season in Ptown, Williams began the first notes for *The Night of the Iguana*. During all four of his summers at the Cape, he wrote short stories and poems, exploring themes he would develop in plays, among them *Suddenly Last Summer*. If his idyllic childhood in Mississippi, subsequent misery in St. Louis, and revitalizing joy in New Orleans can be thought of as the light of his inspiration, we might think of that light refracted in Provincetown as if through a prism. Something happened his first summer there that changed his life.

Williams fell in love in Provincetown in the summer of 1940.[3] When the affair ended – it lasted less than six weeks – he began to sketch dialogue for a new play, *The Parade*, recording, as best he could, his infatuation for a beautiful young man, a dancer named Kip Kiernan, who rejected him. Dissatisfied with the sketch – in later years he would claim he was too angry to be fair to the characters – Williams ripped the pages out of his notebook. Not even that gesture turned out as intended. A thoughtful friend kept the cast-off pages. In 1960, they were returned to Williams.[4] In 1962, at the time *Night of the Iguana* was running on Broadway, he began to refine the Provincetown sketch into a Chekhovian one-act of unfulfilled longing: longing for love, for fame, for artistic achievement. *The Parade* ends the way the first act of Chekhov's *Seagull* ends, with two people, young and old, watching the summer sun set over water, in *Seagull* a lake, in *The Parade*, the Ptown Bay.

The central character of *The Parade* is a twenty-nine-year-old Southern-born playwright named Don, living suspended in what he calls the golden bubble of August weather in Ptown, hoping a play he has written will find enough favour with the Theatre Guild to make it to Broadway. Don is in love with a younger man, a dancer who claims to be straight. The parade of the title is Don's sense that love is just around the corner, but will never arrive for him. Like Laura in Williams's *Glass Menagerie*, listening to music spill from the paradise of a dance hall she will never visit, Don imagines he hears the trumpets and bells of a parade: signs that love is approaching, but headed to someone else, not to him. A worldly teen-ager from New York, Miriam, is hopelessly in love with Don, as much as he is in love with the dancer. Being gay, being straight, being a man or woman, love is the same: human. As Miriam says to Don: to be gay (she says *queer*) is as normal as a duck's egg. At the time, it was illegal in American and English theatres to present queer as normal. Williams could have had little expectation of a performance.

By 1980, when he was sixty-nine, Williams conceived a new full-length play set in Provincetown, *Something Cloudy, Something Clear*. The title refers to the author's eyes – one with a cataract, one without – but the title also refers to the intermittent vision of the author, cloudy and clear when experiencing what happened in Provincetown, cloudy and clear when remembering it. Williams evokes onstage the multiplicity of vision that derives from experience: the double-exposure of present and past. In *Something Cloudy*, the young southern playwright is named August. He lives in a Ptown dune shack, which was true in 1944, not 1940, waiting for Broadway producers to like his new play enough to present it in New York. He is in love with a younger dancer, named Kip, who is shadowed by a young woman named Clare. August knows what happens after the action of the play ends: Kip and Clare will both die young, which was true for Kip Kiernan, who died at twenty-six. Conflating his four summers at the Cape, Williams included visions of Frank Merlo, whom he met there in 1947, and who lived with Williams for nearly fourteen years. As in his *Memoir*, written in 1975, Williams swings the action of *Something Cloudy*, without warning, between the author at the moment of remembering and a younger self involved in what's happening in the present moment on stage. Williams imagined Henry Fonda, who was seventy-five in 1980, playing the role of the intermittently 29-year-old August.[5]

In earlier plays written by Williams, memory softens and exalts. 'Being a memory play,' says Tom, the narrator of *The Glass Menagerie*, 'it is by nature sentimental.' In *Something Cloudy, Something Clear*, Clare directly asks: 'Are you cruel, August?' and the playwright answers 'I'd rather be cruel than sentimental.' *Something Cloudy, Something Clear* is often cruel. One is reminded of *Miss Julie* and August Strindberg, not just August in Ptown. Williams's play borrows Strindberg's vision that people are either vampires or vampires' victims. The would-be Broadway producers in *Something Cloudy, Something Clear* force rewrites and try to get away without paying for them; the playwright forces them to play fair. Sex, straight or gay, is enforced blackmail. Fame and charm are weapons, brute force gets what it wants, talent is fierce. Kip and Clare try to feed off the playwright, mistakenly thinking him rich; the playwright instead feeds off them by turning Kip and Clare into his subject matter. Kip submits to August, not rape so much as survival tactics for all parties concerned. The play ends with August watching a comet race among the stars, and the older, remembering playwright, quoting the German poet Rilke, weighs the value of a beautiful face against the value of the eternal sky.

The Parade and *Something Cloudy, Something Clear* clearly demonstrate that Williams's insights into the transitory nature of love and youth were reinforced by his experience of living in Provincetown – and the force of his memory recalling that experience. In 2006 in Provincetown, in the last week of September, the Provincetown Tennessee Williams Theater Festival began a mission to share Williams's insights and experiences by presenting performances of what Williams wrote. In the ten seasons since 2006, fifty-eight plays by Williams have been produced by the Festival during the last week of September. Theatre companies from Hong Kong, New Zealand, South Africa, Portugal, Italy, and

England have shared interpretations of Williams's writing, as have theatre artists from New York, Chicago, New Orleans, Boston, Los Angeles, Albuquerque, New Orleans, Minneapolis, and ensembles from Mississippi to Maine. *The Parade* had its world premiere at the Festival in 2006. Ten other one-act plays by Williams have received their first performances at the Festival. *The Pronoun 'I'*, written around 1975, and *Sun Burst*, written around 1980, premiered in 2007; *Green Eyes*, written in 1970, and *The Dog Enchanted by the Divine View*, a 1948 precursor to *The Rose Tattoo*, premiered 2008; the down and dirty *Remarkable Rooming-House of Madame LeMonde*, written in 1982, and the mini-tragedy of *The Enemy: Time*, a 1955 sketch for *Sweet Bird of Youth*, premiered 2009; *American Gothic*, written circa 1938, premiered 2010; *Once in a Lifetime*, written circa 1938, premiered 2011; *Curtains for the Gentleman*, written 1936, premiered 2013; and *Aimez-Vous Ionesco?* written circa 1982, premiered 2015.[6] Well-known plays – *The Glass Menagerie*, *A Streetcar Named Desire*, *Suddenly Last Summer*, for example – have also been presented at the Provincetown Festival, along with plays by Williams that had not been seen on a stage in decades, including a production of his first play *Cairo! Shanghai! Bombay!* for the first time since it was shown in a Memphis, Tennessee, rose garden in 1935.

The range of the Festival's productions has reinforced the continuity of Williams's craft and concerns throughout the decades of his writing. For Festival audiences, the fourth-wall-shattering Kabuki stagehands in *The Milk Train Doesn't Stop Here Anymore* (1964) are in a line with the projections and fourth-wall-shattering direct address of *The Glass Menagerie* (1945). The disorienting timeshifts in *Something Cloudy, Something Clear* (1981), within the context of Williams's writing as a whole, evoke the same simultaneity of past and present as the disorienting phantasmagoria of Blanche's hallucinations in *A Streetcar Named Desire* (1947). Departures from conventional theatre at the festival in Provincetown parallel Williams's theatre-going in 1940s Provincetown. The one play we know he saw there was Eugene O'Neill's *Diff'rent*, in which an eccentric spinster makes a decision that ruins her life. Written in 1920, it was performed in 1940 at the Artists' Theatre, which opened after the Playhouse on the Wharf burned down in February of that year. Other than *Diff'rent*, Williams seems to have kept himself apart from what had become a summer stock theatre scene. The days of the Provincetown Players and its challenging new plays were over. Eugene O'Neill, who arrived at the Cape in 1916, spent his last summer there in 1922.[7]

Williams socialized in Ptown in the company of the artists' community, which dated back to 1899, when painters, attracted by light bouncing over the water and sand, came to Cape Cod to practice French Impressionist techniques of working in the open air. In the 1930s, émigré European artists arrived at the Cape, among them Georg Grosz, Chaim Gross, Max Ernst (briefly), Pavel Tchelitchew, and the influential expressionist German painter, Hans Hofmann, who opened up a school to teach composition and a theory of opposing hot and cold colour. Williams socialized with the Hofmann crowd. Kip, the dancer he was in love with, and Joe Hazan, the friend who saved the pages of *The Parade*, were both models for the Hofmann school, as was the radical performance artist, Valeska Gert, someone Williams knew from Manhattan. His Manhattan acquaintances studying with Hofmann included his close friend, the sculptor/painter Fritz Bultman, and Lee Krasner, who was dating Jackson Pollock (who did not study with Hofmann). Through Krasner, Williams met and was befriended by Pollock. According to Williams's *Memoir*, at a picnic in the dunes with Krasner and Pollock, Kip arrived by bicycle to end his affair with the infatuated playwright.[8] Though Williams omits artists in his plays set in Provincetown, the art circles made an impact. Williams wrote 'An Appreciation of Hans Hofmann,' published in 1948, and directly mentions Hofmann's colour theory in his novel *Moise and the World of Reason* (1975) and in the play *The Day on Which a Man Dies* (1960), which has as its central metaphor the making of abstract paintings in the manner of Pollock as a form of rebellion from figurative art parallel to Williams's rebellion from kitchen-sink realism. Valeska appears, thinly disguised as *The Gnädiges Fraulein* in the play of the same name, snatching up dead fish on the beach of Key West and eating them raw as she was said to have done in Provincetown. As was true for the Provincetown Players for whom Eugene O'Neill wrote in 1916, the non-conventional artists' community Williams knew attracted like-minded writers, actors, musicians, and political radicals.

Since the days of the first artists' colony it had been understood in Provincetown that pushing boundaries in writing and painting means pushing boundaries of identity and social liberties, including the open sexuality that offended in 1940. According to the 2010 US census, Provincetown has the highest per capita gay population in the United States.[9] Performed in Provincetown, Williams's celebrations of sexuality are political, metaphoric, and enjoyed. Being queer, in any sense of the word, has a history in Provincetown that dates back to right after the Pilgrims abandoned the place and those who would escape Puritanism crept back. The tip of the Cape was too far away from Boston for the sheriff to come regularly. It's still too far away for the sheriffs of good taste.

What helped and encouraged Tennessee Williams when he was living in Provincetown for four summers in the 1940s continues to help and encourage the festival held in his honor there the last week of September. A hundred theatre artists a year are donated by inns and homeowners in town, maintaining the tradition of the fishermen who gave Williams fish and potatoes in the summer of 1944 when he was noticeably thinner. Most of the performance venues are free. Plays by Williams have been performed in Provincetown's storefronts, bars, churches, theatres, hotel rooms, private homes, and gardens. The seasonality of the Cape heightens the drama of outdoor performances suspended in the golden bubble of a sunny day in September. In 2011, the year of Williams's centennial, *Something Cloudy, Something Clear* was performed in a tent with clear plastic sides so actors could be seen entering from and dancing on the beach. In 2015, the play was performed on the beach, where an audience sat watching as the sun set over the vast flats exposed by low tide.

The liminality of the land at the tip of the Cape is literal: the sand crumbles into the sea. At evening the horizon blurs, the colours of the sky and sea merge, the eye crosses easily over sea to sky and back again. Williams's plays have in common a similar crossing over (and back) between the physical world to the world of the spirit. This is expressed by the setting sun in *The Parade*, by the time shifts of *Something Cloudy, Something Clear*, by a rebellious suicidal artist walking through curtains of paper in *The Day on Which a Man Dies*, by taking a ride off the highway in *Battle of Angels*. All of these are voyages to another way of seeing, being, loving, thinking. That it is possible to travel to and from another world is suggested by the mix of people one meets walking up and down the narrow Provincetown streets. When Williams was there, tanned fishermen and artists, pale Yankees, German émigrés tourists from New York and Boston, sailors from the naval base and drag queens – even in the 1940s – shared the town. Their paths were not so separate as in Mississippi, where Williams was born, with its state-enforced segregation of black and white. In Provincetown, as in New Orleans, the city of *laissez les bons temps rouler*, there's mingling. Within sight of the bay through which the Pilgrims walked ashore from the *Mayflower*, in Provincetown, as in Mississippi or in New Orleans, the intensity of the present moment is enhanced by one's sense of the past. What – and why – Williams wrote in Provincetown in the 1940s resounds there still.

Arthur Miller in Brooklyn Heights, 1940–1956

Stephen Marino

One hundred years ago, on 17 October 1915, Arthur Miller was delivered to the world in an apartment on 45 West 110th Street in Manhattan. As he sucked in his first breaths, the air of New York City filled the fiber of his being. The Miller centennial year invites us to examine just how much Miller's formative years growing up in Manhattan and Brooklyn and his years living in Brooklyn Heights stimulated his writing. Arthur Miller used his native New York City and its surrounding environs as the central focus of many of his major dramas and fiction. Miller transformed the defining experiences of his youth and early adulthood formed primarily on the streets and in the neighborhoods of the New York boroughs of Manhattan and Brooklyn. He created a dramatic landscape where his characters encounter New York City's indigenous twentieth-century cultures, and its ethnic, religious, and economic issues.

Miller placed nine of his major plays in New York: *Death of a Salesman*, *A Memory of Two Mondays*, *A View From the Bridge*, *After the Fall*, *The Price*, *The American Clock*, *The Ride Down Mt. Morgan*, *Broken Glass*, *Mr. Peter's Connections*. All have settings in which the characters' interactions with the cityscape significantly impact the narratives. Much of the action of Miller's only novel, *Focus*, occurs in the borough of Queens, where Miller shows parochial religious, ethnic, and racial prejudices, mirroring the same prejudices in the workplace in Manhattan. In addition, most of Miller's short stories use New York settings that are vital to the main characters' conflicts. His novella, *Homely Girl, A Life*, creates a sweeping landscape of time and emotion in Manhattan. In many interviews and articles and in his autobiography *Timebends*, Arthur Miller details the significant events for him as a boy growing up in Manhattan and Brooklyn in the 1920s and 1930s and as a young husband, father, and playwright in Brooklyn Heights in the 1940s and early 1950s. During Miller's childhood, his parents and siblings lived in upper-middle-class splendor on West 110th Street in Manhattan, in a large apartment overlooking Central Park. The family owned a chauffeur-driven, seven-passenger 'National' automobile and a summer bungalow on the beach in Far Rockaway. However, hard times came for them. Following the financial collapse of his factory, Miller's father Isadore moved his family to Brooklyn when Arthur was thirteen. This was clearly a step down, as the family relocated to a little six-room house on East Third Street in the Midwood section of the borough. There, Miller shared a bedroom with his maternal grandfather.[1]

Arthur Miller often describes the Brooklyn of his youth as if it were a rural, frontier outpost. In *The American Clock*, a play that partly chronicles his family's downfall during the Depression, the sisters Rose and Fanny (characters based on Miller's own mother and aunt) argue over their father's objections to moving to Brooklyn. Fanny says: 'And what is he going to do with himself in Brooklyn? He never liked the country.'[2] This description of Brooklyn as 'the country' typifies an attitude towards the borough in the 1920s and 1930s – a point of view that impressed Miller so much he would later use it in *Death of a Salesman*. For despite the borough's size and population (when Brooklyn joined New York in 1898, it had been the fourth largest city in the country with a population of 1.1 million), surprisingly many areas remained relatively rural even as the infrastructure of the city – streets, trolley, bus, subway and elevated train lines – was being built. And life in an 'outer' borough like Brooklyn greatly contrasted with life in Manhattan, what people then (and now) called 'the city.' In a piece he wrote in 1955 for *Holiday* magazine, 'A Boy Grew in Brooklyn,' Miller described the Midwood section of thirty years earlier:

As a flat forest of great elms through which ran the elevated Culver Line to Coney Island, two and a half miles distant ... Children going to school in those days could be watched from the back porch and kept in view for nearly a mile. There were streets, of course, but the few houses had well-trodden trails running out their back doors which connected with each other and must have looked from the air like a cross section of a mole run; these trails were much more used than streets, which were as unpaved as any in the Wild West and just as muddy.[3]

Today, Miller's boyhood home looks much as it did then. East Third Street is a few blocks from the wide boulevard known as Ocean Parkway. This famous Brooklyn street traverses the borough with its terminus, as the name indicates, at the Atlantic Ocean. In *Timebends* Miller recollects how as a young boy he worked for a bakery; one cold winter morning his bicycle toppled over on the icy road, spilling bagels, rolls, and breads over this six-lane parkway.[4] In *Broken Glass*, Dr. Harry Hyman rode his horse on the bridle paths – now pedestrian walkways – which formerly lined this boulevard.

Driving down Ocean Parkway through the Midwood section gives a clear sense of how much Miller used Brooklyn in his work, especially in *Death of a Salesman*. The elevated line still runs parallel to the wide parkway where grand brick houses of the wealthier Brooklyn residents stand. These single-family homes are shadowed by the larger apartment buildings that were constructed during the rapid growth of Brooklyn in the era between the world wars, when Miller witnessed the borough's quick and dramatic change to the wholly urban environment of today. The side streets off Ocean Parkway are occupied by many of the same small wood frame houses that dominated the neighborhood when Miller lived there, interspersed with the more recently-built brick apartment buildings. The block of East Third Street also is the same as when young Miller played football and baseball there – a dead-end street in what is technically the 'Gravesend' section of the borough, an appropriate name for both the street and the cemetery that lies beyond the baseball field at its north end. You can still see and hear, as young Arthur did, the 'el' train heading south towards Coney Island and north towards Manhattan. Miller's house, number 1350, sits two-thirds of the way down the dead end on the left side and one can see how it served a pivotal role in the formation of Miller's artistic life. What is particularly striking about Miller's block is how powerfully it evokes *Death of a Salesman*. The houses resemble Willy's and Charley's houses with the 'bricks and windows, windows and bricks' of apartment buildings lurking over them. Across from Miller's boyhood home is the house where his cousin Jean and her husband Moe lived with his mother. Miller used it as the setting for his most autobiographical short story, 'The 1928 Buick.' Equally compelling are the homes (two blocks away on East Fifth) of Manny Newman and Lee Balsam, Miller's salesmen uncles, who had moved their families to Brooklyn after World War I, a decade before his own family's move. The Newman–Balsam connected houses are still flanked by four other pairs, a line of little wooden homes with flat roofs and three-step stoops. Beyond their backyards, on the next block, loom larger apartment houses.

After Miller graduated from the University of Michigan in 1938 and he married Mary Slattery, the couple lived from 1940 to 1956 in various apartments and homes in Brooklyn Heights, which Miller describes in *Timebends* as a 'quiet, leafy village.'[5] Miller's dramatic vision congealed in Brooklyn Heights. He moved into the neighborhood as an unknown, aspiring writer and left as one of the most famous literary, political, and social figures in America. Miller's dramatic reputation rests upon the four tragedies he produced between 1947 and 1956, *All My Sons*, *Death of a Salesman*, *The Crucible*, and *A View From the Bridge*, the period he was living in Brooklyn Heights. Brooklyn Heights is a national historic district that had a reputation in the early nineteenth century as New York's first suburb. Pre-Civil War homes there are carefully preserved, designated as protected structures. But Brooklyn Heights in the 1930s, 1940s and 1950s had a downtrodden reputation, and consequently was a haven for artists and writers including Thomas Wolfe, Henry Miller, Richard Wright, W. H. Auden, Norman Mailer, Truman Capote, and Carson McCullers. As Miller said, 'There were a lot of boarded up houses, especially along Columbia Heights.'[6] And: 'Brooklyn Heights in the 40s was the cheapest place you could live in New York City.'[7] Today, the downtown Brooklyn Civic Centre has exploded with condos and towering office buildings. In 2004, when Miller attended the Arthur Miller Conference at St. Francis College and was asked how he felt upon returning home to Brooklyn, he quipped, 'I don't recognize it. It looks like Philadelphia.'[8] He further noted, 'I would get lost here and I used to walk these streets all the time. It got much richer, it seems to me. I wasn't there today, but I can't imagine anything is boarded up now.'[9] Despite Miller's reaction to the physical changes in his Brooklyn Heights neighborhood, all of the residences where he lived in 1940s and 1950s survive. Miller would recognize the houses of his Brooklyn neighborhood

Miller and wife Mary Slattery lived in five residences between 1940 and 1956. Their first Brooklyn Heights residence was at 62 Montague Street, in an ornate apartment building constructed in 1885 as a luxury multi-family residence, which the owners called 'French Flats.' Round rooms, towers, and cupolas distinguish the Queen Anne-style building. The couple lived in a seven-room apartment that he shared with her roommates, an arrangement that seems unusual for newlyweds. Miller recalled: 'It was about $80 a month for the whole apartment.'[10] Money was a pressing concern for the struggling writer throughout these early years. But Mary and Arthur had an untypical marriage from the start. In *Timebends*, he relates that they had been married for little more than week when he went off for a few weeks on a freighter to visit gulf ports and learn more about ships at sea for a play he had outlined about Germans in the South Pacific. Miller admits that he had a 'divided desire for settled order and lust for experience.'[11] Perhaps this unsettled feeling in Miller, coupled with his financial concerns, was part of the reason he moved frequently during the fifteen years he lived in Brooklyn Heights. It was when the couple lived at 62 Montague Street that Miller started writing radio plays and his first version of *The Man Who Had All the Luck*.

In 1941, the Millers moved from Montague Street to 18 Schermerhorn Street, one of the first Brooklyn Heights single-family homes to be remodeled and converted into apartments. Norman Rosten, a friend of Miller's from the University of Michigan, also lived in the building. Miller explained:

> My first apartment was on Schermerhorn Street after I got married and that was a newly remodeled brownstone building. Nobody had ever lived in this apartment before and it was a living room, and a kitchen and a bedroom – beautiful. It went right through the building. And that cost $35 a month. Now

even then, elsewhere you'd have to pay double that, and a lot of writers and artists moved to Brooklyn Heights because of that, because it was cheap. But it was also beautiful.[12]

Miller's apartment window looked out on the backyard of a mosque. 'I used to sit and watch the Moslems holding services,' Miller wrote. 'They had a real Moorish garden symmetrically planted with curving lines of white stones laid out in the earth, and they would sit in white robes – twenty or thirty of them, eating at a long table, and served by their women who wore the flowing purple and rose togas of the East.'[13] During this time, Miller worked in the Brooklyn Navy Yard and he also wrote half-hour radio plays for DuPont's *Cavalcade of America*, for the Columbia Workshop, and for U.S. Steel. These radio plays exhibit themes that are evident in later Miller masterpieces. For example, in the radio playlet *The Pussycat and the Expert Plumber Who Was a Man*, one character states: 'The one thing a man fears next to death is the loss of his good name. Man is evil in his own eyes, my friends, worthless, and the only way he can find respect for himself is by getting other people to say he's a nice fellow.' This proclamation foreshadows similar cries by such Miller characters as Willy Loman, John Proctor, and Eddie Carbone, who value the worth of their names in the eyes of the world.[14] In early 1943, Miller left the Navy Yard to conduct research for a screenplay, *The Story of G.I. Joe*, that he adapted from American war reporter Ernie Pyle's columns. In *Timebends*, he explains that he took the assignment because he was lured by the $750 a week salary.[15] Miller used his research for a book of reportage called *Situation Normal* (1944), his first published book, in which he tried to see among soldiers a higher purpose about the aims of World War II. He also wrote his first Broadway play, *The Man Who Had All the Luck*, while living on Schermerhorn Street. .

In 1944, the Millers moved again, to a duplex apartment at 102 Pierrepont Street. As Miller remembered it: 'The rooms were very dark – wood-paneled. It had been a very elaborate home. We never could see anything. Norman Mailer lived upstairs, but much of the time he was away at war.'[16] In *Timebends*, Miller recalls that one afternoon he intervened in a hallway argument between Mailer and a woman. Mailer later approached Miller on the street, introduced himself, and having apparently seen *All My Sons*, proclaimed, 'I could write a play like that.' Miller laughed at Mailer's bravado.[17] In a 1963 interview with *The Brooklyn Heights Press*, Mailer was asked about the period when he and Miller lived in the same building. 'We didn't know each other then,' said Mailer, with a broad smile. 'We used to pass each other on the stairs and each would think "That guy doesn't have much!"'[18] Miller's children – Jane (1944) and Robert (1947) – were born while the family lived there. In that residence also, Miller suffered the disappointment of a Broadway flop (*The Man Who Had All the Luck*), wrote *Focus*, and enjoyed his first Broadway hit: *All My Sons*.

With the success of *All My Sons*, Miller realized how 'the word *royalty* took on a more exact meaning.'[19] The play, and film rights that Miller sold, gave him financial and artistic freedom. Although the idealist in Miller vowed never to change his lifestyle, he reasoned that it made little sense for his family to stay in the small apartment on Pierrepont Street. In 1947, Miller purchased his first home, 31 Grace Court, near the steep hill that at that time led down to the East River. The home contained two duplex apartments; the Miller family occupied the upper floor while the lower floor was rented to the previous tenants, Mr. and Mrs. Henry Davenport; he was president of the Brooklyn Savings Bank. In *Timebends*, Miller details the extravagant lifestyle of the Davenports, but rails at their complaints about problems with the apartment. Miller disliked being a landlord and wanted to sell the house.[20] But he judged that he would need another hit play and more money to do so. With his royalties, Miller had also purchased a country home on over three hundred acres in Roxbury, Connecticut.

While Miller lived on Grace Court, he conceived and completed his masterpiece *Death of a Salesman*, although he actually wrote the first draft of the play in the studio he built near his Connecticut country house.[21] Miller also wrote his version of Henrik Ibsen's *Enemy of the People* on Grace Court, and the long gestation of *A View From Bridge* (detailed below) began while Miller resided there. During this time, Miller also traveled to Hollywood with the director Elia Kazan to promote a film titled *The Hook*. While there, Kazan introduced Miller to Marilyn Monroe, and this marked the start of their relationship. In 1951, Miller, the reluctant landlord, finally sold that home. It was purchased anonymously through an agent for the African American historian W. E. B. DuBois – unable to find a home to rent as he was hounded by the FBI for his vocal membership in the Communist Party – but finally able to purchase Miller's Grace Court home.

The home that Miller bought at 155 Willow Street in 1951 is considered a Brooklyn Heights architectural gem, one of three Federal-style brick row-houses that are among the oldest in the neighborhood, having been built in the 1820s. These houses also played a distinct role in the American Civil War as havens on the Underground Railroad. A plaque at 157 Willow Street explains that the homes had underground storage space to hide runaway slaves as they escaped northward to Canada. In *Timebends*, Miller relates how he spruced up the house, installing a subfloor and cork floor in the entrance hallway and built conveniences in the kitchen.[22] But he also details how he performed these acts as duty because, torn by attraction to Monroe, he felt his marriage to Mary was floundering. Miller's Willow Street home is located one block from the famous Brooklyn Promenade (which Miller called 'the Esplanade'). It sits atop a hill on which two levels of the Brooklyn–Queens Expressway are built. During Miller's residence there, the highway had not been constructed, and a steep hill inclined to the East River, where the Brooklyn docks were located. Here is a breath-taking view of lower Manhattan across the East River. From this vantage, you can see the Brooklyn Bridge, the Brooklyn Navy Yard, the Statue of Liberty, Ellis Island, and the docks and piers of Red Hook that Miller used in *A View From the Bridge*. Miller remembered:

> Before the esplanade was built, the promenade there, and you looked down on the docks where ships were still being loaded and unloaded, and there were longshoremen bars down there. It was a whole life going on at the edge of the river. Later it dried up because of the container ships that didn't require so many longshoremen, but it was an interesting place to live. Out of that came *A View from the Bridge* because I got to know some of the people down there.[23]

While Miller lived on Willow Street, he wrote *The Crucible* after researching the trial transcripts in Salem.

Miller also wrote the one-act version of *A View From the Bridge*, and no play better illustrates the effect of Miller's years in Brooklyn Heights. After his success with *All My Sons*, Miller became intrigued by the Italian immigrant society of the Brooklyn docks. He had noticed graffiti dotting the walls and sidewalks around the piers at the foot of the neighborhood. The graffiti asked in Italian: 'Dove Pete Panto?' This translates as: 'Where is Pete Panto?' The message also appeared on subway stations and on office buildings at the Court Street Civic Center in downtown Brooklyn. Miller learned from newspaper coverage that Pete Panto was a young longshoreman who had challenged the powerful Mafia leadership of the seaman's union and had mysteriously disappeared, effectively ending the threat he posed to the union's corruption. Miller wanted to write about the tragic ending of this heroic man. He began researching the criminal underworld of the Brooklyn docksides, visiting the piers and attempting to learn the truth behind Panto's fate. However, Miller was stymied by the intimidated silence of the longshoremen who feared to speak out against their bosses. Miller unexpectedly received a phone call from Mitch Berenson, a union organizer, and Vinny Longhi, a lawyer, who were attempting to continue Pete Panto's resistance to the longshoremen union's power structure. After Miller offered to write about their efforts, they enabled him to enter the mysterious under belly of this corrupt world. He learned about the lives and culture of the longshoremen, many of whom he befriended, often visiting their homes in their Red Hook neighborhood, south of Brooklyn Heights. Miller absorbed the roots of the Sicilian society and came to understand the cultural connection between the American immigrants and their native land. During this time, Longhi told Miller the story of another longshoreman who had informed to the Immigration Bureau on his cousins, two brothers who were related to him and living illegally in his house. The longshoreman's betrayal, intended to break up a relationship between his niece and one of the brothers, made him a pariah in his neighborhood, and he was reportedly killed by one of the brothers. Miller was awed by what seemed almost the work of fate. He fiddled with a screenplay about the story, but soon became consumed with writing *Death of a Salesman* in 1948 and with its production in 1949.

After the success of *Death of a Salesman*, Miller wrote the screenplay, *The Hook*, about his experience on the docks. Then he returned to the tale of the Italian longshoreman who had snitched on his relatives, working for several months on a play then titled *An Italian Tragedy*, before abandoning it again. It was not until 1954 after the controversial run of *The Crucible* that Miller would complete the play now called *A View From the Bridge*. The title refers to the famous Brooklyn Bridge that spans the East River between Manhattan and Brooklyn at the foot of Brooklyn Heights. At this time, Miller also was interested in further exploring the themes of betrayal, informing, and adultery, as he had done in *The Crucible*. By the time he was writing the one-act version of *A View From the Bridge*, Miller had embarked on his affair with Marilyn Monroe, was about to divorce his wife, and was becoming a target of the House Un-American Activities Committee (HUAC), as his friends and colleagues had.[24] Miller had the opportunity to revise the play in 1956, a tumultuous year for him: he committed to Monroe and spent six weeks in April in Nevada to establish residency for a 'quickie' divorce. After the divorce filing, Miller had his celebrated hearing before HUAC, after which he and Monroe married in late June; then the famous couple flew to England where Monroe was to star with Laurence Olivier in a film, *The Prince and the Showgirl*, and where Miller revised *A View From the Bridge* into a two-act for the London production. After 1956, Miller would never again live in Brooklyn.

A Retrospective of Influence

Thomas D. Pawley III

Thomas Désiré Pawley III, Curators' Distinguished Professor Emeritus of Speech and Theatre, Lincoln University, earned his MA and PhD at the University of Iowa, where his first year as a graduate student coincided with Tom (later 'Tennessee') Williams's one year there, 1937–8. Although Tom Williams played a black preacher (cast for his Southern accent) in one of Tom Pawley's plays, Pawley could not claim Williams as a friend, because even the cafeteria was segregated at Iowa. Pawley's later play that he mentions in this retrospective, The Tumult and the Shouting (1964), *is published in* Black Theatre USA: 1935–Today, *edited by James V. Hatch and Ted Shine.*

As a playwright, I was intrigued by the plays in which a principal character functioned as a part of the dramatic action while frequently commenting upon it, as in *Our Town*, *The Glass*

Menagerie, and *Death of a Salesman*. I use this technique in *The Tumult and the Shouting*, in which the narrator opens and closes the play. Two plays from the decade, *The Iceman Cometh* and *The Glass Menagerie*, inform my discussion of race in the essays 'Where the Streetcar Doesn't Run' and 'Eugene O'Neill and American Race Relations.'[1]

A high point in my career as a director was a summer theatre production of *A Streetcar Named Desire* – the first, I am advised, by an African American theatre group at a time when directors at neighboring institutions were afraid to produce it. Our repertory at Lincoln University during my tenure has included all of the major plays of the 1940s by Tennessee Williams and Arthur Miller as well as Thornton Wilder's *Our Town*, but none from that decade by Eugene O'Neill. My production of his earlier play *The Emperor Jones* was greeted by a dead silence at the curtain.

As a theatregoer, I will never forget the production of *Death of a Salesman* which I attended in Chicago many years ago. I was one of the last patrons to leave the theatre, having been so moved by the final scene, which for me had the emotional overtones of these immortal lines:

... Good night, sweet prince,
And flights of angels sing thee to thy rest.

NOTES

1 Introduction to the 1940s

1. For example, Wilder wrote to his brother and sister from Vienna on 22 September 1935, 'Just a word to you before the war breaks out ... I guess there's going to be a war soon. Italy had 500,000 men in manoevres in their northernmost mountains when I was there ...': Thornton Wilder, *The Selected Letters of Thornton Wilder*, ed. Robin G. Wilder and Jackson R. Bryer (New York: Harper Perennial, 2008), 299.

2. Time-Life Books, *This Fabulous Century*, Vol. 5: 1940–50 (New York: Time-Life Books, 1969), 22.

3. Ronald Allen Goldberg, *America in the Forties*, Foreword by John Robert Greene (Syracuse, NY: Syracuse University Press, 2012), 25.

4. Alan Saunders, *George C. Marshall: A General for Peace* (New York: Facts on File, 1996), 69.

5. George Catlett Marshall appears on the cover of *Time* magazines dated 29 January 1940, 19 October 1942, 3 January 1944, 10 March 1947 and 5 January 1948. Those chosen as *Time*'s Man of the Year during the 1940s are Joseph Stalin (1939 and 1942), Winston Churchill (1940 and 1949), Franklin Delano Roosevelt (1941), George C. Marshall (1943 and 1947), Dwight D. Eisenhower (1944), Harry Truman (1945 and 1948) and James F. Byrnes (1946).

6. 'U.S. at War: The General', *Time*, 3 January 1944, 16, 17, 18.

7. 'Foreign Relations: The Year of Decision', *Time*, 5 January 1948, 18, 19.

8. Goldberg, 130, 126.

9. Writing about leaders of the decade is a slippery slope, because so many are deserving of recognition. Among those who made

exceptional contributions is General Henry H. 'Hap' Arnold, a five-star general of the US Army who commanded the Army Air Forces during the war and might be called the father of the US Air Force (USAF). James F. Byrnes was a brilliant politician who served in all three branches of government during the 1940s: as US senator from South Carolina, Supreme Court Justice and Secretary of State under President Truman; in the 1950s Byrnes served as governor of his state. In the arts, certain trailblazers not mentioned elsewhere in the chapter must be signalled: Martha Graham, John Cage and Jackson Pollock for, respectively, modern dance, music and painting.

10 Norman Polmar and Thomas B. Allen, *World War II: The Encyclopedia of the War Years 1941–1945* (Mineola, NY: Dover Publications, 2012), 439–40.

11 William S. Graebner, *The Age of Doubt: American Thought and Culture in the 1940s* (Boston: Twayne Publishers, 1991), 31.

12 Robert Sickels, *The 1940s* (Westport, CT: Greenwood Press, 2004), 13.

13 Priscilla Hardison with Anne Wormser, *The Suzy-Q* (Boston: Houghton-Mifflin, 1943), vi. See also Caroline Iverson, '"Suzy-Q," Fightingest Flying Fortress', *Life* 14 (3) (18 January 1943): 82, 83. Also Capt. Albert T. Nice, 'If You Knew Suzy As I Knew Suzy', *Skyways* 2, no. 3 (March 1943): 27.

14 G. Kurt Piehler, ed., *The United States in World War II: A Documentary Reader* (Malden MA: Wiley-Blackwell, 2013), 239.

15 Goldberg, 30–1.

16 Piehler, 97.

17 JoAnn Olian, ed. and Introduction, *Everyday Fashions of the Forties: As Pictured in Sears Catalogs* (New York: Dover, 1992), v.

18 Herbert G. Goldman, *Jolson: The Legend Comes to* Life (New York: Oxford University Press, 1988), 98, 262–5. Frank Coffey, with Special Foreword by Bob Hope, *Always Home: 50 Years of the USO: The Official Photographic History* (Washington, DC: Brassey's, 1991), 55. Contrary to popular perception, Al Jolson abandoned the use of blackface long before some others did. Stars who still occasionally employed that show business convention as late as the 1940s included Eddie Cantor, Bing Crosby and Judy Garland. Jolson was a career-long champion of black artists, including Noble Sissle and Eubie Blake, Cab Calloway and Garland Anderson. The African-American architect Paul Revere Williams designed Jolson's tomb and memorial shrine in Hillside Memorial Park, Culver City, California.

19 Meghan K. Winchell, *Good Girls, Good Food, Good Fun: The Story of USO Hostesse During World War II* (Chapel Hill: University of North Carolina Press, 2008), 2–3.
20 Gary L. Bloomfield and Stacie L. Shain, with Arlen C. Davidson, *Duty, Honor, Applause: America's Entertainers in World War II* (Guilford, CT: Lyons Press, 2004), 148–51.
21 The essay 'My America' was originally published in the *Journal of Educational Sociology* 16 (February 1943): 334–6. It is reprinted in Piehler, 222–3.
22 Molly Guptill Manning, *When Books Went to War: The Stories That Helped Us Win World War II* (Boston: Houghton Mifflin Harcourt, 2015), xv, 111. An appendix lists the titles and authors of all Armed Services editions, the most popular of which was *A Tree Grows in Brooklyn* (1943) by Betty Smith, number 117 of December 1943's Series D (105).
23 Sickels, 22.
24 Sylvia Lovegren, *Fashionable Food: Seven Decades of Food Fads* (New York: Macmillan, 1995), 139.
25 Sickels, 104–5.
26 Michael Wallis, *Route 66: The Mother Road* (New York: St Martin's Griffin, 2001), 268.
27 Graebner, 6, 59, 71.
28 Susan Jonas and Marilyn Nissenson, *Going Going Gone: Vanishing Americana* (San Francisco: Chronicle Books, 1998), 146, 140.
29 Sickels, 158.
30 Ibid., 155–80.
31 Ellen Stern, *The Very Best from Hallmark: Greeting Cards Through the Years* (New York: Harry N. Abrams, Inc.), 9.
32 James Fisher, *Al Jolson: A Bio-Bibliography* (Westport, CT: Greenwood Press, 1994), 168–72.
33 Sickels, 190, 237.
34 Bloomfield and Shain, 282.
35 Mark Harris, *Five Came Back* (New York: Penguin Press, 2014), 172–3.
36 Gorton Carruth, *The Encyclopedia of American Facts and Dates*, 9th edn (New York: HarperCollins Publishers, 1993), 535.
37 Jonas and Nissenson, 57.

38 Ian Gordon, *Comic Strips and Consumer Culture 1890–1945* (Washington, DC: Smithsonian Institution Press, 1998), 137.
39 Wade Laboissoniere, *Blueprints of Fashion: Home Sewing Patterns of the 1940s*, rev. 2nd edn (Atglen, PA: Schiffer Publishing, 2009), 6.
40 Time-Life Books, 54.
41 Sources for this listing are: Carruth; Sickels; Time-Life; Vincent DePaul Lupiano and Ken W. Sayers, *It Was a Very Good Year: A Cultural History of the United States from 1776 to the Present* (Holbrook, MA: Bob Adams, 1994); James Trager, *The People's Chronology: A Year-by-Year Record of Human Events from Prehistory to the Present*, rev. and upd. edn (New York: Henry Holt, 1992).
42 Hervey Cleckley, *The Mask of Sanity: An Attempt to Reinterpret the So-Called Psychopathic Personality* (St Louis: C.V. Mosby Company, 1941).
43 Greg Behrman, *The Most Noble Adventure* (New York: Free Press, 2007), 19.
44 Ibid., 232.

2 American Theatre in the 1940s

1 The 27 June 2013 issue of *Entertainment Weekly* published its list of 'The 50 Best Plays of the Past 100 Years', not limited to English-language plays but strongly tilted that way. The American plays of the 1940s on that list, with their placings, are: 1. *Death of a Salesman*, 2. *A Streetcar Named Desire*, 4. *Long Day's Journey Into Night*, 10. *Our Town*, 12. *The Glass Menagerie* and 16. *The Iceman Cometh*; selection and ranking criteria are not specified. These same titles appear regularly on most lists of ten titles that were submitted by readers to the online Pittsburgh post-gazette.com and published on 23 January 2004 (http://old.post-gazette.com/ae/20040122tens012fnp9.asp [accessed 31 July 2015]). In 2008, Goodreads invited reader response and published a slightly evolving list of 100 ranked 'Best American Plays', which included the following from the decade: 1. *A Streetcar Named Desire*, 2. *The Crucible*, 3. *Death of a Salesman*, 4. *The Glass Menagerie*, 7. *Our Town*, 8. *Long Day's Journey Into Night*, 15. *Arsenic and Old Lace*, 16. *All My Sons*, 23. *The Iceman Cometh*, 31. *Harvey* and 42. *The Skin of Our Teeth* (http://www.goodreads.com/list/show/37.Best_American_Plays

[accessed 31 July 2015]). One of the most credible such lists, in terms of specifics on how the rankings were determined, was assembled by the *Denver Post* theatre critic John Moore in 2010, although it must be noted that the 177 voters were almost all theatre professionals. A list of the voters and the 263 rank-ordered titles they submitted was posted on 14 February 2010, with updated data on the top ten posted on 17 February 2010: 1. *Death of a Salesman*, 3. *A Streetcar Named Desire*, 4. *Long Day's Journey Into Night*, 6. *Our Town*, 7. *The Glass Menagerie* and 9. *The Crucible* (http://www.denverpost.com/theater/ci_14397304 and http://www.denverpost.com/ci_143853617source=infinite [both accessed on 31 July 2015]). The latter article reports that playwright Tony Kushner signals *Salesman*, *Streetcar* and *Journey* as 'the unquestionable big three' of American playwriting. *Wall Street Journal* theatre critic Terry Teachout has frequently written of the seminal status of *Our Town* and *The Glass Menagerie* in American drama. In his article, 'Sightings: He's Got a Little List' (*Wall Street Journal*, 15 May 2010, W9), Teachout relayed playwright David Mamet's 'top ten' list: 1. *Our Town*, 4. *A Streetcar Named Desire* and 5. *All My Sons*.

2 'Foreign Relations: The Year of Decision', *Time*, 5 January 1948, 21.

3 Don B. Wilmeth and Christopher Bigsby, *The Cambridge History of American Theatre*, Vol. II: 1870–1945 (Cambridge: Cambridge University Press, 1999), 357.

4 Albert Wertheim, *Staging the War: American Drama and World War II* (Bloomington: Indiana University Press, 2004), xi.

5 Ibid., *Staging the War*, 5.

6 John O'Connor and Lorraine Brown, eds, *Free, Adult, Uncensored: The Living History of the Federal Theatre Project*, Foreword by John Houseman (Washington, DC: New Republic Books, 1978), 59–61.

7 Gene Brown, *Show Time: A Chronology of Broadway and the Theatre from Its Beginnings to the Present* (New York: Macmillan, 1997), 124.

8 Jane De Hart Mathews, *The Federal Theatre, 1935–1939: Plays, Relief, and Politics* (New York: Octagon Books, 1980), 209.

9 The saga of the Dies Committee investigations, like that of the later investigations, is a complex one. Mathews' analysis, pp. 198–235, offers a carefully balanced view.

10 Penelope Niven, *Thornton Wilder: A Life*, Foreword by Edward Albee (New York: Harper Perennial, 2012), 453.

11 Howard Blue, *Words at War: World War II Era Radio Drama and the Postwar Broadcasting Industry Blacklist* (Lanham, MD: Scarecrow Press, 2002), 79–82.
12 Norman Corwin, 'The Sovereign Word: Some Notes on Radio Drama', *Theatre Arts* XXIV 2 (February 1940): 130.
13 Ibid., 131–3.
14 Blue, *Words at War*, 161–3.
15 Ibid., 164–6.
16 Ibid., 167–8.
17 Ibid., 100.
18 Ibid., 155.
19 Brown, *Show Time*, 141–97.
20 Gerald Bordman, *American Theatre: A Chronicle of Comedy and Drama, 1930–1969* (New York: Oxford University Press, 1996), 193, 181.
21 Doris E. Abramson, *Negro Playwrights in the American Theatre, 1925–1959* (New York: Columbia University Press, 1969), 92–3.
22 Glenda F. Gill, *No Surrender! No Retreat! African American Pioneer Performers of Twentieth-Century American Theater* (New York: St Martin's Press, 2000), 118.
23 Errol G. Hill and James V. Hatch, *A History of African American Theatre* (Cambridge: Cambridge University Press, 2003), 356.
24 Ibid., 348–9.
25 James Fisher, *Al Jolson: A Bio-Bibliography* (Westport, CT: Greenwood Press, 1994), 26, 79–81. About touring, Gertrude Lawrence told an interviewer in 1943 that 'you're not a star until you get that feeling for the road – that sense of belonging to it. Stars don't shine merely over Broadway you know' (quoted in McClung, *Lady in the Dark*, 135).
26 Brown, *Show Time*, 141.
27 Bruce D. McClung, *Lady in the Dark: Biography of a Musical* (New York: Oxford University Press, 2007), 155.
28 Brown, *Show Time*, 147.
29 McClung, *Lady in the Dark*, 149–53.
30 Ibid., xv.
31 Gerald Bordman, *American Musical Theatre: A Chronicle*, 3rd edn (Oxford: Oxford University Press, 2001), 577.

32 McClung, quoting *Variety*, *Lady in the Dark*, 112–13.
33 McClung, *Lady in the Dark*, 123.
34 Ibid., 135.
35 Ibid., 148.
36 Ibid., 33.
37 'Gertie the Great', *Time*, 3 February 1941, http://content.time.com/time/magazine/article/0,9171,765235,00.html (accessed 31 July 2015).
38 Richard Stoddard Aldrich, *Gertrude Lawrence as Mrs. A: An Intimate Biography of the Great Star* (New York: Greystone Press, 1954), 73.
39 Ibid., 75.
40 McClung, *Lady in the Dark*, 105.
41 Ibid., 118, 221.
42 Aldrich, *Gertrude Lawrence*, 154.
43 McClung, *Lady in the Dark*, 138.
44 Ibid., 158.
45 Ibid., 122.
46 The seven women were Rachel Crothers, Louise Closser Hale, Dorothy Donnelly, Josephine Hull, Minnie Dupree, Bessie Tyree and Louise Drew. Isabelle Stevenson and Roy A. Somlyo, *The Tony Award: A Complete Listing of Winners and Nominees of the American Theatre Wing's Tony Award with a History of the American Theatre Wing* (Portsmouth, NH: Heinemann, 2001), ix.
47 Stevenson and Somlyo, *The Tony Awards*, x.
48 Ibid., xi.
49 Brown, *Show Time*, 156.
50 Stevenson and Somlyo, *The Tony Awards*, xii–xiii.
51 'Stage Folk S.R.O. for Canteen Task', *New York Times*, 18 February 1942, 14.
52 Stevenson and Somlyo, *The Tony Awards*, xi.
53 Brown, *Show Time*, 150; Meghan K. Winchell, *Good Girls, Good Food, Good Fun: The Story of the USO Hostesses During World War II* (Chapel Hill: University of North Carolina Press, 2008), 53–6, 64–5.
54 Hill and Hatch, *A History*, 336.
55 'Stage Door Canteen: One of the Town's Better Institutions

Celebrates an Anniversary', *New York Times*, 28 February 1943, X1.
56 McClung, *Lady in the Dark*, 121.
57 Stevenson and Somlyo, *The Tony Awards*, xi; Brown, *Show Time*, 150.
58 Maxene Andrews and Bill Gilbert, *Over Here, Over There: The Andrews Sisters and the USO Stars in World War II* (New York: Zebra Books, Kensington Publishing Co., 1993), 83–6.
59 Gary L. Bloomfield and Stacie L. Shain, with Arlen C. Davidson, *Duty, Honor, Applause: America's Entertainers in World War II* (Guilford, CT: Lyons Press, 2004), 148–9; Andrews, *Over Here*, 84.
60 'Canteen Closing Oct. 28', *New York Times*, 20 October 1945, 11.
61 'Stage Door Canteen Comes to Its End: Host to Millions in Allied Armed Services', *New York Times*, 29 October 1945, 21.
62 Frank Coffey, *Always Home: 50 Years of the USO: The Official Photographic History*, with Special Foreword by Bob Hope (Washington, DC: Brassey's (US), 1991), 3.
63 Andrews, *Over Here*, 84.
64 Coffey, *Always Home*, 5.
65 Ibid., 6.
66 Lynn O'Neal Heberling, *Soldiers in Greasepaint: USO Camp Shows, Inc. During World War II* (PhD diss., Kent State University, 1989), 48.
67 Heberling, *Soldiers in Greasepaint*, 81; Coffey, *Always Home*, 25.
68 Julia M. H. Carson, *Home Away from Home: The Story of the USO* (New York: Harper & Brothers, 1946), 111.
69 Ibid., 112.
70 Andrews, *Over Here*, 197.
71 Andrews, *Over Here*, 197; Coffey, *Always Home*, 25–6.
72 Hill and Hatch, *A History*, 136.
73 Heberling, *Soldiers in Greasepaint*, 93–4.
74 'Stock for the Boys at Front is Planned', *New York Times*, 16 February 1944, 15; 'Stage Stars Leave for Overseas Tour', *New York Times*, 7 August 1944, 9.
75 Brooks Atkinson, *Broadway*, rev. edn (New York: Macmillan Publishing Co., 1974), 396.

76 Coffey, *Always Home*, ix.
77 Terry Teachout, 'Bard of the Electric Ear', *About Last Night: An Arts Journal Blog* (8 November 2004), www.artsjournal.com/aboutlastnight/2004/11/tt-bard-of-the-elecric-ear.html (accessed 31 July 2015).
78 Blue, *Words at War*, 149.
79 Ibid., 337, quoting Philip Hamburger, 'Profiles: The Odyssey of the Oblong Blur', *New Yorker*, 5 April 1947, 36.
80 Blue, *Words at War*, 184.
81 Ibid., 188.
82 Ray Barfield, *Listening to Radio, 1920–1950*, Foreword by M. Thomas Inge (Westport, CT: Praeger, 1996), 25.
83 McClung, *Lady in the Dark*, 156.
84 Martha Dreiblatt, 'Words on the Theatre and War', *New York Times*, 16 May 1943, X1, X2.
85 Bordman, *American Musical*, 583.
86 Ethan Mordden, *Beautiful Mornin': The Broadway Musical in the 1940s* (Oxford: Oxford University Press, 1999), 3, 71–3.
87 Ibid., 102.
88 David Leopold, *Irving Berlin's Show Business* (New York: Harry N. Abrams, 2005), 149.
89 Ibid., 153.
90 Alan Anderson, *The Songwriter Goes to War: The Story of Irving Berlin's World War II All-Army Production of This Is the Army*, Foreword by Mary Ellin Barrett (Pompton Plains, NJ: Limelight Editions, 2004), xvi.
91 Quoted in Anderson, *Songwriter*, x.
92 Leopold, *Irving Berlin's*, 155.
93 Anderson, *Songwriter*, 79–81.
94 Ibid., 69.
95 Ibid., 90.
96 Ibid., 110.
97 Ibid., 118.
98 Ibid., 127.
99 Ibid., 312.
100 Ibid., 315.

101 John Lahr, 'The Theatre: O.K. Chorale', *New Yorker*, 1 April 2002, 84.
102 Frederick Nolan, *The Sound of Their Music: The Story of Rodgers and Hammerstein* (New York: Applause Theatre and Cinema Books, 2002), 7.
103 Denny Martin Flinn, *Musical! A Grand Tour* (New York: Schirmer Books, 1997), 229.
104 Quoted in Max Wilk, *OK! The Story of Oklahoma!* (New York: Grove Press, 1993), 73.
105 Wilk, *OK!*, 74–7.
106 Ibid., 86.
107 Ibid., 99.
108 Ibid., 105.
109 Ibid., 118–21.
110 Ibid., 152–3.
111 Ibid., 192.
112 Ibid., 200–3.
113 Nolan, *The Sound of Their Music*, 25.
114 Wilk, *OK!*, 239.
115 Nolan, *The Sound of Their Music*, 24.
116 Martin Duberman, 'Robeson and *Othello*', in *Paul Robeson: Artist and Citizen*, ed. and Introduction by Jeffrey C. Stewart (New Brunswick: Rutgers University Press, 1998), 131.
117 Susan Spector, 'Margaret Webster's *Othello*: The Principal Players Versus the Director', *Theatre History Studies* VI (1986): 98.
118 Martin Bauml Duberman, *Paul Robeson: A Biography* (New York: Ballentine Books, 1989), 265.
119 Ibid., 275.
120 Spector, 'Margaret Webster's', 105.
121 Duberman, *Paul Robeson*, 277.
122 Spector, 'Margaret Webster's', 105–6.
123 Ibid., 106–7.
124 Virginia Mason Vaughan, *Othello: A Contextual History* (Cambridge: Cambridge University Press, 1994), 196.
125 Duberman, *Paul Robson*, 289–90.
126 Spector, 'Margaret Webster's', 108.

127 Abramson, *Negro Playwrights*, 189.
128 Hill and Hatch, *A History*, 531; James V. Hatch, *Sorrow Is the Only Faithful One: The Life of Owen Dodson*, Foreword by Arnold Rampersand (Urbana: University of Illinois Press, 1995), 112–15.
129 Emmanuel S. Nelson, ed., *African American Dramatists: An A-to-Z Guide* (Westport, CT: Greenwood Press, 2004), 141.
130 Mona Z. Smith, *Becoming Something: The Story of Canada Lee* (New York: Faber and Faber, 2004), 170–3.
131 Marvin McAllister, *Whiting Up: Whiteface Minstrels & Stage Europeans in African American Performance* (Chapel Hill: University of North Carolina Press, 2011), 143.
132 Quoted in McAllister, *Whiting Up*, from the *Daily Worker* (25 September 1946); see also Smith, *Becoming Something*, 223.
133 Brown, *Show Time*, 153.
134 Ibid., 171.
135 Ibid., 174–5.
136 Ibid., 178.
137 Ibid., 173.
138 Ibid., 175.
139 Ibid., 173.
140 Flinn, *Musical!*, 234.
141 Rosamond Gilder, Hermine Rich Isaacs, Robert M. MacGregor and Edward Reed, eds, *Theatre Arts Anthology: A Record and a Prophecy* (New York: Theatre Arts Books, 1950), 209–21.
142 Flinn, *Musical!*, 213.
143 Mordden, *Beautiful Mornin'*, 125.
144 Agnes de Mille, *Martha: The Life and Work of Martha Graham* (New York: Random House, 1991), 262.
145 'The Tributary Theatre', *Theatre Arts* XXIV 2 (February 1940): 147.
146 Ibid., 147–8.
147 Gilder et al., *Theatre Arts Anthology*, 502–4.
148 'Tributary Theatre Directory', *Theatre Arts* XXX 7 (July 1946): 423–9.
149 Jeffrey Ullom, *America's First Regional Theatre: The Cleveland Playhouse and Its Search for a Home* (New York: Palgrave Macmillan, 2014), 106–9.

150 Julius Novick, *Beyond Broadway: The Quest for Permanent Theatres* (New York: Hill & Wang, 1968), 70.
151 Ibid., 38.
152 Felix Sper, *From Native Roots: A Panorama of Our Regional Drama* (Caldwell, ID: Caxton Printers, 1948).
153 William Leonard, ed., *Chicago Stagebill Yearbook 1947* (Chicago: Chicago Stagebill, 1947), 13.
154 Ibid., 15.
155 Chris Jones, *Bigger, Brighter, Louder: 150 Years of Chicago Theater as Seen by* Chicago Tribune *Critics* (Chicago: University of Chicago Press, 2013), 97.
156 Ibid., 107.
157 Flinn, *Musical!*, 213.
158 Robert A. Schanke, *Shattered Applause: The Eva Le Gallienne Story* (New York: Barricade Books, 1992), 284–6.
159 Margaret Webster, *Don't Put Your Daughter on the Stage* (New York: Alfred A. Knopf, 1972), 170.
160 Helen Sheehy, *Margo: The Life and Theatre of Margo Jones* (Dallas: Southern Methodist University Press, 1989), 248.

3 Introducing the Playwrights

1 Penelope Niven, *Thornton Wilder: A Life* (New York: Harper Perennial, 2012), 294.
2 Ibid., 356–7.
3 Robert M. Dowling, *Eugene O'Neill: A Life in Four Acts* (New Haven, CT: Yale University Press, 2014), 50.
4 Niven, 118, 458.
5 Ibid., 486.
6 John S. Bak, *Tennessee Williams: A Literary Life* (New York: Palgrave Macmillan, 2013), 21.
7 Christopher Bigsby, *Arthur Miller 1915–1962* (London: Phoenix, 2009), 14.
8 According to Martin Gottfried, *Arthur Miller: His Life and Work* (Cambridge, MA: Da Capo Press, 2003), 'Miller would cite the Wall Street crash and its aftermath as the formative event in his life'. Gottfried also cites his sister Joan: 'Arthur carries scars from

that time ... It is a memory, in his nerves, and in his muscles, that he just can't get rid of' (15). Bigsby notes that 'the Depression taught him that no system was reliable, that everything could disappear' (40).

9   Bigsby, 69.
10 Enoch Brater, *Arthur Miller: A Playwright's Life and Works* (New York: Thames and Hudson, 2005), notes the interesting coincidence that Tennessee Williams was also working on a reform-minded prison drama, *Not About Nightingales*, at the same time (27).
11 Bigsby, 197–9.

4 Eugene O'Neill: Love and Loss of the Soul

1   Carlotta Monterey, O'Neill's third wife, renovated the home the couple named Tao House (the Right Way) to facilitate her husband's playwriting. Located in Danville, California, the home is now a National Historic Site run by the National Park Service.
2   See Travis Bogard, *Contour in Time*, rev. edn (New York: Oxford University Press, 1988), 366–412. Of this unfinished opus, Bogard claimed, 'Had he completed his work, it might well have provided the only lasting crown of the theatre in the 1930's, indeed he might again have changed the course of American drama, as he had in the 1920's' (368).
3   See Virginia Floyd, *Eugene O'Neill at Work* (New York: Frederick Ungar, 1981), 260–97. Floyd's study makes a thorough examination and analysis of O'Neill's work diaries.
4   *Selected Letters of Eugene O'Neill*, ed. Travis Bogard and Jackson R. Bryer (New Haven, CT: Yale University Press, 1988; New York: Limelight, 1994), 490.
5   See Robert M. Dowling, *Eugene O'Neill: A Life in Four Acts* (New Haven, CT: Yale University Press, 2014), 473–4. A new autopsy performed almost 50 years after O'Neill's death determined the cause of his tremor as 'late-onset spinal cerebellar atrophy'.
6   *Selected Letters*, 493, 509, 526.
7   *Beyond the Horizon* (1920), *'Anna Christie'* (1922) and *Strange*

Interlude (1928) won Pulitzer Prizes. *The Hairy Ape, The Emperor Jones, Desire Under the Elms* and *Mourning Becomes Electra* remain part of the modern repertory today.

8   The Group Theatre heralded the arrival of Odets in the 1930s. *The Glass Menagerie*, Williams's first success, premiered in 1945. Miller's *All My Sons* won the Drama Desk Award as Best Play in 1946 over *The Iceman Cometh*.

9   Dowling, *Eugene O'Neill*, 448–9.

10 John S. Wilson, 'O'Neill on the World and *The Iceman*', in *Conversations with Eugene O'Neill*, ed. Mark W. Estrin (Jackson: University Press of Mississippi, 1990), 164–5. Reprinted from *PM*, 3 September 1946.

11 See William Davies King, 'Historical and Critical Perspectives', in *Long Day's Journey Into Night*, by Eugene O'Neill, critical edn, ed. William Davies King (New Haven, CT: Yale University Press, 2014), 198–224.

12 Eugene O'Neill, *Complete Plays 1932–1943*, ed. Travis Bogard (New York: Library of America, 1988), 195. This three-volume set commemorates the centenary of O'Neill's birth with excellent notes and contains all his plays except the early autobiographical one-act *Exorcism*, produced in 1919, but only recently published (*New Yorker*, 2011; Yale, 2012). All citations from the plays come from the Library of America edition.

13 O'Neill, *Complete Plays 1932–1943*, 195, 205.

14 O'Neill, *Complete Plays 1913–1920*, 573.

15 O'Neill, *Complete Plays 1932–1943*, 196.

16 Ibid., 213.

17 Ibid., 275–6.

18 A *shebeen*, an Irish word meaning 'illicit whiskey', is an establishment that serves alcohol without a license.

19 O'Neill, *Complete Plays 1932–1943*, 281.

20 Ibid., 237.

21 Louis Sheaffer, *O'Neill: Son and Artist*, vol. 2 (Boston: Little, Brown, 1973; New York: Cooper Square Press, 2002), 531.

22 Dowling, *Eugene O'Neill*, 414.

23 O'Neill, *Complete Plays 1932–1943*, 196.

24 Ibid., 262–3.

25 O'Neill, *Complete Plays 1920–1931*, 528.

26 Wilson, 'O'Neill on the World and *The Iceman*', in *Conversations with Eugene O'Neill*, 165.
27 See Bette Mandl, 'Absence as Presence: The Second Sex in *The Iceman Cometh*', *Eugene O'Neill Newsletter* 6, no. 2 (Summer–Fall 1982), http://www.eoneill.com/library/newsletter/vi_2/vi-2d.htm (accessed 18 November 2014). My interest focuses on how the male characters construct the absent females to suit their purposes. Not surprisingly, Rosa Parritt, discussed by two men who were close to her, emerges as the most complex female character.
28 Mt. 25.6 (King James Version).
29 Mt. 25.13 (KJV).
30 O'Neill, *Complete Plays 1932–1943*, 700.
31 George Jean Nathan, 'Eugene O'Neill after Twelve Years', *Conversations with Eugene O'Neill*, 179. Reprinted from *American Mercury* 63 (October 1946).
32 *Selected Letters*, 531. *Hughie* (1942) is the only play that O'Neill completed in this proposed series, but it provides an excellent example of the technique the playwright describes.
33 O'Neill, *Complete Plays 1932–1943*, 639.
34 Ibid., 674.
35 Ibid., 637.
36 Ibid., 769–70.
37 See Steven F. Bloom, '"The Mad Scene: Enter Ophelia!": O'Neill's Use of the Delayed Entrance in *Long Day's Journey Into Night*', *Eugene O'Neill Review* 26 (2004): 226–38. Although all four of the Tyrones compel attention, Bloom argues convincingly for the centrality of Mary.
38 O'Neill, *Complete Plays 1932–1943*, 757.
39 Ibid., 749.
40 The living room in the play matches almost exactly the O'Neill family summer home in New London, Connecticut, known as 'Monte Cristo Cottage', named after the play and role that made actor James O'Neill a fortune. Named a National Historic Landmark in 1971, the house is currently owned and operated by the Eugene O'Neill Theater Center in nearby Waterford, Connecticut.
41 O'Neill, *Complete Plays 1932–1943*, 719.
42 Ibid., 760.
43 Ibid., 773.

44 Ibid., 801.
45 Michael Manheim, *Eugene O'Neill's New Language of Kinship* (Syracuse, NY: Syracuse University Press, 1982).
46 O'Neill, *Complete Plays 1932–1943*, 764.
47 Ibid., 775.
48 Ibid., 801.
49 Ibid., 800–1.
50 Quoted in Dowling, *Eugene O'Neill*, 385.
51 O'Neill, *Complete Plays 1932–1943*, 826.
52 Ibid., 827.
53 Ibid., 828.
54 Ibid., 828.
55 See Stephen A. Black, *Eugene O'Neill: Beyond Mourning and Tragedy* (New Haven, CT: Yale University Press, 1999), 37–58. Black provides an outstanding psychological profile of Jamie and contrasts his development with that of his younger brother.
56 O'Neill, *Complete Plays 1932–1943*, 714.
57 Matthew H. Wikander, 'O'Neill and the Cult of Sincerity', in *The Cambridge Companion to Eugene O'Neill*, ed. Michael Manheim (New York: Cambridge University Press, 1998), 217–35.
58 Steven F. Bloom, *Student Companion to Eugene O'Neill* (Westport, CT: Greenwood Press, 2007), 167.
59 Harder and Harker are amalgamations of Standard Oil magnate and philanthropist Edward S. Harkness. In a delicious irony, the Eugene O'Neill Theater Center in Waterford, CT, is built on land once owned by Harkness and is adjacent to Harkness State Park.
60 O'Neill, *Complete Plays 1932–1943*, 816.
61 Ibid., 857.
62 Ibid., 927.
63 Ibid., 936.
64 Ibid., 946.
65 Doris Alexander, *Eugene O'Neill's Last Plays: Separating Art from Autobiography* (Athens, GA: University of Georgia Press, 2005), 163. Alexander, unlike me, sees Tyrone as the protagonist.
66 See Zander Brietzke, 'O'Neill and the Nobel', in *Critical Insights: Eugene O'Neill*, ed. Steven F. Bloom (Ipswich, MA: Salem Press, 2012), 222–37.

67 August Strindberg, *The Ghost Sonata*, *Selected Plays: August Strindberg*, vol. 2, trans. Evert Sprinchorn (1986; Minneapolis: University of Minnesota Press, 2012), 404–5.

68 Barbara Gelb, 'A Theatrical History', preface to *A Moon for the Misbegotten* by Eugene O'Neill (1952; New York: Vintage Books, 1974).

5 Thornton Wilder: Seeing Beyond Dark Times

1 Thornton Wilder, *Three Plays: Our Town, The Skin of Our Teeth, and The Matchmaker* (New York: Harper Perennial Modern Classics, 2006), 101, 112.

2 Ibid., 172, 179.

3 Thornton Wilder, *Thornton Wilder: Collected Plays & Writings on Theater* (New York: Library of America, 2007), 746, 748.

4 Ibid., 429.

5 Thornton Wilder, *Our Century: A Play in Three Scenes* (New York: Century Association, 1947), 3.

6 Wilder, *Three Plays*, 168.

7 Gertrude Stein, *The Letters of Gertrude Stein & Thornton Wilder*, ed. Edward M. Burns and Ulla E. Dydo with William Rice (New Haven, CT: Yale University Press, 1996), 175–6.

8 Max Alvarez, 'Hitchcock and Wilder: Writing and Rewriting *Shadow of a Doubt*', in *Thornton Wilder: New Perspectives*, ed. Jackson R. Bryer and Lincoln Konkle (Evanston, IL: Northwestern University Press, 2013), 306.

9 Eric Wollencott Barnes, *The Man Who Lived Twice: The Biography of Edward Sheldon*, with introductory chapter by Anne Morrow Lindbergh (New York: Charles Scribner's Sons, 1956), 220.

10 Ibid., 221.

11 Penelope Niven, *Thornton Wilder: A Life*, Foreword by Edward Albee (New York: Harper Perennial, 2013), 491–3.

12 Thornton Wilder, *The Journals of Thornton Wilder 1939–1961*, selected and ed. Donald Gallup (New Haven, CT: Yale University Press, 1985), 1.

13 William A. Henry III, 'Theater: Scraping Away the Sentiment in *Our Town*', *Time*, 4 January 1988, 171.
14 Wilder, *Three Plays*, 124.
15 J. D. McClatchey, 'Chronology', *Thornton Wilder: Collected Plays and Writings on Theater* (New York: Library of America, 2007), 831.
16 Wilder, *Three Plays*, 11.
17 Ibid., 7.
18 Ibid., 8, 17, 18.
19 Brooks Atkinson, 'Our Town', *New York Times*, 5 February 1938, 18.
20 Wilder, *Three Plays*, 34.
21 Ibid., 34–5.
22 Niven, 192.
23 Wilder, *Three Plays*, 43.
24 Ibid., 41.
25 Kenneth Elliott, 'The Outsider: Contextualizing Simon Stimson in *Our Town*', in *Thornton Wilder: New Perspectives*, ed. Jackson R. Bryer and Lincoln Konkle (Evanston, IL: Northwestern University Press, 2013), 121–31.
26 Wilder, *Three Plays*, 46.
27 Ibid., 48.
28 Ibid., 50.
29 Ibid., 59.
30 Ibid.
31 Wilder, *Collected Plays*, 384.
32 Wilder, *Three Plays*, 64.
33 Wilder, *Our Town*, 77.
34 Thornton Wilder, '"Our Town": Some Suggestions for the Director', *Thornton Wilder: Collected Plays, & Writings on Theater* (New York: Library of America, 2007), 661.
35 Wilder, *Three Plays*, 90.
36 Ibid., 94.
37 Ibid., 98–9.
38 Ibid., 110.
39 Ibid., 111.

40 Thornton Wilder, 'A Preface for "Our Town"', *Thornton Wilder: Collected Plays & Writings on Theater* (New York: Library of America, 2007), 657.
41 Wilder, 'A Preface', *Collected Plays*, 659.
42 Stein, *The Letters*, 175.
43 Park Bucker, 'Wearing Down "The Edge of Boldness": Wilder's Evolving Values and Stagecraft in the Three Published Versions and Prompt Script of *Our Town*', in *Thornton Wilder: New Perspectives*, ed. Jackson R. Bryer and Lincoln Konkle (Evanston, IL: Northwestern University Press, 2013), 132–53.
44 Henry, 171.
45 Terry Teachout, 'The Genius of David Cromer', *Wall Street Journal*, 27 February 2009, W7.
46 Richard N. Piland, *The Illustrated History of the Resident Theater, Kansas City, Missouri, 1932–1983*, with a Foreword by Dr. Glenn Q. Pierce (Fairfield, OH: Personalized Research, 2011), 29–30.
47 Terry Teachout, 'Sentimental Journey: *Allegro*', *Wall Street Journal*, 28 November 2014, D8.
48 Niven, 491.
49 Job 19.20, King James Bible (Grand Rapids, MI: Zondervan, 2002), 348.
50 Niven, 185.
51 Wilder, *Three Plays*, 122.
52 Ibid., 150–1.
53 Ibid., 152.
54 Ibid., 161.
55 Ibid., 168.
56 Ibid., 172.
57 Ibid., 175.
58 Ibid., 189.
59 Ibid., 178.
60 Ibid., 180.
61 Ibid., 183.
62 Ibid., 202.
63 Ibid., 212.
64 See, for example, Lewis Nichols, 'Thornton Wilder', *New York Times*, 3 January 1943. Nichols, having written enthusiastically

about the play in his *New York Times* review of the opening (19 November 1942, 29), now reported a range of responses to the production, from heated discussion to demands for return of the ticket price. The *New York Times* critical summaries from London (W. A. Darlington, 27 May 1945) and Dublin (Hugh Smith, 18 November 1945) found the play ill-suited for those who are 'too logical' or too intellectual.

65 Wilder, *The Journals*, 25.
66 Wilder, *Three Plays*, 132.
67 Wilder, *The Journals*, 25.
68 Ibid., 24.
69 Wilder, *Three Plays*, 131.
70 Ibid., 68, 81.
71 Ibid., 164–5.
72 Ibid., 190.
73 Wilder, *Collected Plays*, 745.
74 Wilder, *Three Plays*, 219.
75 Ibid., 235.
76 Ibid., 237.
77 *Shadow of a Doubt*, prod. Jack H. Skirball, dir. Alfred Hitchcock, Universal Studios, 1942, Universal DVD video 28313.
78 Alvarez, 'Hitchcock and Wilder', 300.
79 Ibid., 307.
80 Ibid., 329.
81 J. D. McClatchy, 'Note on the Texts', *Thornton Wilder: Collected Plays & Writings on Theater* (New York: Library of America, 2007), 839.
82 Wilder, *Collected Plays*, 737–8.
83 Ibid., 738.
84 Young Charlie's name also echoes the Wilder family's nickname for Thornton's younger sibling Charlotte (Niven, 59).
85 Wilder, *Collected Plays*, 741.
86 Ibid., 742.
87 Ibid., 781.
88 Ibid., 782.
89 Wilder, *Three Plays*, 46–7.

90 Studies of sociopathic personalities include Robert D. Hare, PhD, *Without Conscience: The Disturbing World of the Psychopaths Among Us* (New York: Guilford Press, 1999); Martha Stout, *The Sociopath Next Door: The Ruthless Versus the Rest of Us* (New York: Three River Press, 2005); Dr Jane M. McGregor and Tim McGregor, *The Empathy Trap: Understanding Antisocial Personalities* (London: Sheldon Press, 2013).

91 Wilder, *Collected Plays*, 804.

92 Ibid., 815.

93 Ibid., 817.

94 Isabel Wilder, 'Foreword', *The Alcestiad or A Life in the Sun: A Play in Three Acts with a Satyr Play The Drunken Sisters* by Thornton Wilder (New York: Harper & Row, 1977), ix.

95 Ibid., xii.

96 Niven, 605.

97 'Cloudy Opening For "Life In Sun"', *New York Times*, 24 August 1955, 24.

98 'Wilder's "Alcestiad" Cheered in Zurich', *New York Times*, 29 June 1957, 11.

99 'Vienna Hails Wilder Play', *New York Times*, 6 November 1957, 43.

100 Paul Moor, 'Louise Talma's "The Alcestiad" In Premiere at Frankfurt Opera', *New York Times*, 2 March 1962, 25.

101 Thornton Wilder, 'Notes On "The Alcestiad"', *Thornton Wilder: Collected Plays & Writings on Theater* (New York: Library of America, 2007), 690.

102 Lincoln Konkle, *Thornton Wilder and the Puritan Narrative Tradition* (Columbia: University of Missouri Press, 2006), 174–7.

103 Wilder, *Three Plays*, 162, 241; Wilder, *Collected Plays*, 790.

104 For example, in a letter to John A. Townley, dated 6 March 1928, Wilder wrote: 'Chekhov said: "The business of literature is not to answer questions, but to state them fairly"', *The Selected Letters of Thornton Wilder*, ed. Robin G. Wilder and Jackson R. Bryer (New York: Harper Perennial, 2008), 226.

105 Wilder, *Collected Plays*, 371.

106 In the opening speech of Euripides's *Alcestis*, Apollo relates his backstory: how he tricked the Fates to save the life of Admetus, but that backfired when he had to send 'in his place another corpse' (Euripides, *Alcestis; Medea; Hippolytus*, trans. Diane

260 NOTES

Arnson Svarlien (Indianapolis: Hackett Publishing Company, 2007, 3)). Thornton Wilder saved that backstory for his satyr play *The Drunken Sister* (*Thornton Wilder: Collected Plays & Writings on Theater*, New York: Library of America, 2007, 435–43).

107 Wilder, *Collected Plays*, 385.

108 Interestingly, the scene also calls to mind Isabelle's choice in the final scene of Jean Giraudoux's *Intermezzo* (1933) between the romantic spectre and the prosaic Inspector of Weights and Measure.

109 This is one of Wilder's significant departures from the character dynamics in Euripides's *Alcestis*, in which Admetus actively seeks someone to die in his place and acquiesces when Alcestis volunteers.

110 Wilder, *Collected Plays*, 414.

111 Ibid., 420.

112 Wilder, *Collected Plays*, 462–95; Wilder, *The Journals*, 295ff.

113 Niven, 600–1.

6 Tennessee Williams: Experimentation and 'The Great American Play'

1 William Jay Smith, *My Friend Tom: The Poet-Playwright Tennessee Williams* (Jackson and London: University Press of Mississippi, 2011), 33.

2 Tennessee Williams, *Memoirs*, intro. by John Waters (New York: New Directions, 2006), 250.

3 Lyle Leverich, *Tom: The Unknown Tennessee Williams* (London: W.W. Norton, 1995), 208.

4 Tennessee Williams, *Fugitive Kind*, edited, intro. by Allean Hale (New York: New Directions, 2001), 3.

5 Tennessee Williams, *New Selected Essays: Where I Live*, ed. John S. Bak (New York: New Directions, 2009), ix.

6 Tennessee Williams, unpublished draft fragment from *Daughter of the American Revolution* (Austin: Harry Ransom Humanities Research Center (HRC), University of Texas, Austin, n.d.).

7 Tennessee Williams, *Selected Letters of Tennessee Williams, Volume I*, ed. Albert J. Devlin and Nancy Tischler (New York: New Directions, 2000), 239.

8   Tennessee Williams, unpublished manuscript, 'Imaginary Interview' (Austin: Harry Ransom Humanities Research Center (HRC), University of Texas, Austin, n.d.), 3.
9   Williams, *Essays*, 19.
10 John Lahr, *Tennessee Williams: Mad Pilgrimage of the Flesh* (New York and London: W. W. Norton, 2014), 23.
11 Leverich, *Tom*, 393.
12 Richard F. Leavitt, *The World of Tennessee Williams* (London: W. H. Allen, 1978), 46.
13 Claudia Wilsch Case, 'Battle in Boston: Tennessee Williams' First Professional Production', in *Tenn at One Hundred*, ed. David Kaplan (East Brunswick, NJ: Hansen Publishing Group, 2011), 54–5.
14 Case, 'Battle', 55–6.
16 Ibid., 56.
17 Williams, *Letters V. I*, 358.
18 Case, 'Battle', 297.
19 Williams, *Letters V. I*, 374.
20 Ibid., 387.
21 Donald Windham, *Tennessee Williams' Letters to Donald Windham, 1940–1965* (New York: Holt, Rinehart and Winston, 1977), 24.
22 Roberto Bolaño, *Between Parentheses: Essays, Articles, and Speeches, 1998–2003* (New York: New Directions, 2011), 350.
23 Williams, *Letters V. I*, 256.
24 Ibid., 259.
25 Tennessee Williams, *Notebooks*, ed. Margaret Bradham Thornton (New Haven, CT, and London: Yale University Press, 2006), 386.
26 Ibid., 281.
27 Tennessee Williams, unpublished letter to James Laughlin, 25 September 1944 (Cambridge, MA: Houghton Library, Harvard University).
28 Ian S. MacNiven, *'Literchoor Is My Beat': A Life of James Laughlin, Publisher of New Directions* (New York: Farrar, Straus and Giroux, 2014), 352–3.
29 John Willett, *The Theatre of Erwin Piscator* (New York: Holmes & Meier, 1979), 166.
30 Judith Malina, *The Piscator Notebook* (London and New York: Routledge, 2012), 169.

31 Tennessee Williams, *Stairs to the Roof*, edited, intro. by Allean Hale (New York: New Directions, 2000), 101.
32 Albert J. Devlin, ed., *Conversations with Tennessee Williams* (Jackson and London: University Press of Mississippi, 1986), 98.
33 Tennessee Williams, *The Glass Menagerie*, intro. by Tony Kushner (New York: New Directions, 2011), 53.
34 John S. Bak, *Tennessee Williams: A Literary Life* (London: Palgrave Macmillan, 2013), 109.
35 Unpublished, HRC, n.d.
36 Unpublished, HRC, March 1943.
37 Williams, *Menagerie*, 53
38 Ibid., 53–5.
39 Ibid., 54.
40 Jo Mielziner, *Designing for the Theatre: A Memoir and a Portfolio* (New York: Bramhall House, 1965), 124.
41 Williams, *Menagerie*, 55.
42 Ibid., 89.
43 Ibid., 145.
44 Ibid., 145.
45 Ibid., 145.
46 Margaret A. Van Antwerp and Sally Johns, *Dictionary of Literary Biography, Volume Four, Tennessee Williams* (Detroit: Bruccoli, Clark & Gale Research, 1984), 61.
47 David Kaplan, 'Rescuing *The Glass Menagerie*', in *Tenn at One Hundred*, ed. David Kaplan (East Brunswick, NJ: Hansen Publishing Group, 2011), 68–70.
48 Ibid., 70.
49 Arthur Miller, 'Regarding *Streetcar*', in Tennessee Williams, *A Streetcar Named Desire* (New York: New Directions, 2004), x.
50 Ibid., x.
51 Williams, *Notebooks*, xiv.
52 Ibid.
53 Tennessee Williams, *Selected Letters of Tennessee Williams, Volume II*, ed. Albert J. Devlin and Nancy Tischler (New York: New Directions, 2004), 28.
54 Williams, *Letters V. I*, 527.
55 Williams, unpublished essay, HRC, n.d.

56	Williams, unpublished notes, HRC, n.d.
57	Williams, *Notebooks*, 446.
58	Williams, unpublished notes, HRC, n.d.
59	Williams, *Letters V. II*, 62.
60	Williams, *Notebooks*, 446.
61	Ibid., 446.
62	Tennessee Williams, *Summer and Smoke*, in *The Theatre of Tennessee Williams Volume II* (New York: New Directions, 1971), 119–20.
63	Williams, *Notebooks*, 449.
64	Williams, *Letters V. II*, 93.
65	Williams, *Letters V. I*, 25.
66	Williams, *Letters V. II*, 96.
67	Ibid., 97.
68	Ibid.
69	Ibid.
70	Tennessee Williams, *A Streetcar Named Desire*, intro. by Arthur Miller (New York: New Directions, 2004), 178.
71	Ibid., 59.
72	Ibid.

7 Arthur Miller: The Individual and Social Responsibility

1	Arthur Miller, *Focus* (New York: Reynal and Hitchcock, 1945), 3.
2	Ibid., 2.
3	Brooks Atkinson, 'Mare's-Nest Inquiries: Searching "All My Sons" for Hidden Motives', *New York Times*, 7 September 1947, X1; Proquest Historical Newspapers.
4	Arthur Miller, *Collected Plays, 1944–1961* (New York: The Library of America, 2006), 99.
5	Ibid., 115.
6	Ibid.
7	Ibid.
8	Ibid., 145–6.

9 Ibid., 157.
10 *New York Theatre Critics' Reviews 1947* VIII (1) (week of 3 February 1947), 475–8.
11 Claudia Cassidy, '"All My Sons" Is Called More Earnest than Able', *Chicago Daily Tribune*, 23 November 1947, F2; Proquest Historical Newspapers. See also Chris Jones, *Bigger, Brighter, Louder: 150 Years of Chicago Theater as Seen by Chicago Tribune Critics* (Chicago: University of Chicago Press, 2013), 109–16.
12 'CWV Chief Protests "All My Sons" Plans', *New York Times*, 12 August 1947, 26; Proquest Historical Newspapers.
13 'CWV Chief Protests'. Also Sam Zolotow, '"All My Sons" Out as Overseas Play', *New York Times*, 12 August 1947, 13; Proquest Historical Newspapers.
14 Brooks Atkinson, 'Mare's-Nest Inquiries: Searching 'All My Sons' for Hidden Motives', *New York Times*, 7 September 1947, X1; Proquest Historical Newspapers.
15 'Miller Fails in Plea: *All My Sons* Falls Short in Aims for Prague Festival', *New York Times*, 11 June 11 1947, 33; Proquest Historical Newspapers.
16 The Frankfurt School was founded in Frankfurt, Germany, in 1923. It refers to a group of philosophers, psychoanalysts, economists and social critics who developed theories of civil society that built upon the works of Hegel, Marx and Freud, among others.
17 Erich Fromm, *Man for Himself: An Inquiry into the Psychology of Ethics* (New York: Rinehart and Company, 1947), 69–70.
18 Ibid., 72.
19 Arthur Miller, *Timebends* (New York: Grove Press, 1987), 177–85.
20 Miller, *Collected Plays*, 161.
21 Ibid.
22 Ibid., 165.
23 David Riesman, *The Lonely Crowd: A Study of the Changing American Character* (New Haven, CT: Yale University Press, 1950), 23.
24 Miller, *Collected Plays*, 166.
25 Ibid., 163.
26 Ibid., 165.
27 Ibid., 242.

28   Ibid., 170.
29   Ibid.
30   Ibid.
31   Ibid., 171.
32   Ibid., 216.
33   Ibid., 251.
34   Ibid., 253.
35   Ibid., 253–4.
36   Fredric Wertham, 'Let the Salesman Beware: A Dialogue', *New York Times*, 15 May 1949, BR4; ProQuest Historical Newspapers.
37   Brooks Atkinson, 'Death of a Salesman: Arthur Miller Tragedy of an Ordinary Man', *New York Times*, 20 February 1949, X1; ProQuest Historical Newspapers.
38   W. A. Darlington, 'London Sees Miller's Death of a Salesman', *New York Times*, 7 August 1949, X1; ProQuest Historical Newspapers.
39   Miller explicitly references the popular radio programme of Father Charles E. Coughlin, who supported the establishment of the Christian Front, an increasingly violent militia that harassed American Jews in the early years of the Second World War. Arthur Miller, *Focus* (New York: Reynal and Hitchcock, 1945), 128.
40   Miller, *Collected Plays*, 262.
41   Ibid.
42   Roscoe Drummond, 'Noted House Committee Dims Klieg Lights', *Christian Science Monitor*, 11 May 1949, 1.
43   McCarthyism refers to the period (1950–6) when, under the leadership of Senator Joseph McCarthy, the Government Committee on Operations of the Senate intensified Cold War American fear of communism by accusing without evidence or probable cause numerous individuals and dissidents of subversion or treason.
44   Hearings before the Committee on Un-American Activities, House of Representatives, Eighty-Fourth Congress, June 14 and 21, 1956.
45   Miller, *Timebends*, 134–5.
46   Miller, *Collected Plays*, 350.
47   Ibid., 348.
48   Miller, *Collected Plays*, 350.

49 Miller, *Timebends*, 340.
50 Miller, *Collected Plays*, 381.
51 Ibid., 382.
52 Ibid., 391.
53 Ibid., 372.
54 Ibid., 404.
55 This view was expressed by Miller in his introductory notes and his autobiography as well as by Brooks Atkinson in the first *New York Times* review of the play: 'The Crucible: Arthur Miller's Dramatization of the Salem Witch Trial in 1692', 1 February 1953), X1; ProQuest Historical Newspapers.
56 Miller, *Collected Plays*, 447.
57 Ibid., 451.
58 Ibid., 454.
59 Ibid., 454.
60 Miller, *Timebends*, 342.
61 Brooks Atkinson, 'The Crucible: Arthur Miller's Dramatization of the Salem Witch Trial in 1692', *New York Times*, 1 February 1953, X1; ProQuest Historical Newspapers.
62 Miller, *Timebends*, 347.
63 Ibid., 348.

Afterword

1 Thomas Keith, 'Foreword', *Tennessee Williams and Europe*, ed. by John S. Bak (Amsterdam: Rodopi, 2014), xvii.
2 Robert M. Dowling, *Eugene O'Neill: A Life in Four Acts* (New Haven, CT: Yale University Press, 2014), 489.
3 Lincoln Konkle, *Thornton Wilder and the Puritan Narrative Tradition* (Columbia: University of Missouri Press, 2006), 174–201.

Documents

Tennessee Williams in Ptown: The 1940s and Now

1   The Provincetown *Advocate*, 1936–45.
2   Thomas Keith, 'Chronology', in *Tennessee Williams: Mad Pilgrimage of the Flesh* by John Lahr (New York: Norton, 2014).
3   Lyle Leverich, *Tom: The Unknown Tennessee Williams* (New York: Crown Publishers, 1995).
4   Conversation with Joe Hazan, New York, August 2006. See also Andreas Brown letter, 19 February 1962, mentioned by Leverich.
5   Dotson Rader, *Cry of the Heart* (New York: Doubleday, 1985).
6   David Kaplan, *Tenn Years* (East Brunswick, NJ: Hansen Publishing Group, 2015).
7   Robert M. Dowling, *Critical Companion to Eugene O'Neill: A Literary Reference to his Life and Work* (New York: Facts On File, 2009).
8   David Kaplan, *Tennessee Williams in Provincetown* (East Brunswick, NJ: Hansen Publishing Group, 2006). See also Leverich.
9   Analysing the 2010 Census data, the UCLA Williams Institute of Law (the name is a coincidence) announced Provincetown has 163 same-sex couples per 1,000 households. By comparison, Manhattan only has 19.3 gay couples per 1,000 households.

Arthur Miller in Brooklyn Heights, 1940–1956

1   Some of the previous material appeared in Stephen Marino, 'Touring Arthur Miller's Brooklyn', *The Arthur Miller Society Newsletter* 11 (June 1005): 8–12.
2   Arthur Miller, *Two Plays:* The Archbishop's Ceiling *and* The American Clock (New York: Grove Press, 1989), 110.
3   Arthur Miller, 'A Boy Grew in Brooklyn', *Holiday* 17 (March 1955): 54. Some of the previous material appeared in Stephen

Marino, '"It's Brooklyn, I know, but we hunt too": The Image of the Borough in *Death of a Salesman*', in *'The Salesman Has A Birthday': Essays Celebrating the Fiftieth Anniversary of Arthur Miller's* Death of a Salesman (Lanham, MD: University Press of America, 2000).

4 Arthur Miller, *Timebends, A Life* (New York: Grove Press, 1987), 107–8.
5 Ibid., 70.
6 Arthur Miller, interviewed by Christopher Bigsby, 'A Final Conversation with Arthur Miller', *The Arthur Miller Journal* 1, no. 1 (Spring 2006): 61.
7 Ibid., 65.
8 Ibid., 61.
9 Ibid., 65.
10 'He Was No Misfit in Brooklyn', *On This Day in History: October 17, Brooklyn Daily Eagle*, published online, 17 October 2006.
11 Miller, *Timebends*, 70.
12 Miller interviewed by Bigsby, 65.
13 *Brooklyn Daily Eagle*.
14 Stephen Marino, 'Arthur Miller', *Twentieth-Century American Dramatists: Fourth Series*, Dictionary of Literary Biography, Vol. 266, ed. Christopher J. Wheatley (Detroit: Gale, 2003), 189.
15 Miller, *Timebends*, 277.
16 *Brooklyn Daily Eagle*.
17 Miller, *Timebends*, 139.
18 *Brooklyn Daily Eagle*.
19 Miller, *Timebends*, 141.
20 Ibid., 143.
21 Ibid., 182–4.
22 Ibid., 328.
23 Miller interviewed by Bigsby, 65.
24 Some of the previous material is adapted from Stephen Marino, 'Commentary', in *Arthur Miller, A View From the Bridge*, with commentary and notes Stephen Marino (London: Methuen Drama, 2010).

A Retrospective of Influence

1   Thomas D. Pawley, 'Where the Streetcar Doesn't Run: The Black World of Tennessee Williams', *Journal of American Drama and Theatre* 14, no. 3 (2002): 18–33; 'Eugene O'Neill and American Race Relations', *Journal of American Drama and Theatre* 9 (1997): 66–89.

Bibliography

1 Introduction to the 1940s

Behrman, Greg. *The Most Noble Adventure: The Marshall Plan and How America Helped Rebuild Europe*. New York: Free Press, 2007.

Belasco, Warren James. *Americans on the Road: From Autocamp to Motel, 1910–1945*. Baltimore: Johns Hopkins University Press, 1979.

Bloomfield, Gary L. and Stacie L. Shain, with Arlen C. Davidson. *Duty, Honor, Applause: America's Entertainers in World War II*. Guilford, CT: Lyons Press, 2004.

Brookeman, Christopher. *American Culture and Society since the 1930s*. New York: Schocken Books, 1984.

Burnes, Brian. *The Ike Files: Mementos of the Man and His Era*. Kansas City: Kansas City Star Books, 2008.

Carruth, Gorton. *The Encyclopedia of American Facts and Dates*, 9th edition, fully revised. New York: HarperCollins Publishers, 1993.

Cleckley, Hervey. *The Mask of Sanity: An Attempt to Reinterpret the So-Called Psychopathic Personality*. St Louis: C.V. Mosby Company, 1941.

Coffey, Frank. *Always Home: 50 Years of the USO: The Official Photographic History*, Special Foreword by Bob Hope. Washington, DC: Brassey's (US), 1991.

Cooke, James J. *American Girls, Beer, and Glenn Miller: GI Morale in World War II*. Columbia: University of Missouri Press, 2012.

Dirix, Emmanuelle and Charlotte Fiell. *1940s Fashions: The Definitive Sourcebook*. London: Carlton Publishing Group, 2013.

Endres, Kathleen L. *Rosie the Rubber Worker: Women Workers in Akron's Rubber Factories During World War II*. Kent, OH: Kent State University Press, 2000.

Feininger, Andreas, *New York in the Forties*, with text by John von Hartz. New York: Dover Publications, 1978.

Finder, Harry, ed. with Giles Harvey. *The 40s: The Story of a Decade: The New Yorker*. New York: Random House, 2014.

Fisher, James. *Al Jolson: A Bio-Bibliography*. Westport, CT: Greenwood Press, 1994.

Friess, Steve. 'When "Holocaust" Became "The Holocaust"', *The New*

Republic, 17 May 2015, https://newrepublic.com/article/121807/when-holocaust-became-holocaust (accessed 17 March 2016).

Fromm, Erich. *Escape from Freedom*. New York: Holt, Rinehart and Winston, 1941.

Garraty, John A. and Jerome L. Sternstein. *Encyclopedia of American Biography*, 2nd edition. New York: HarperCollins, 1996.

Goldberg, Ronald Allen. *America in the Forties*. Syracuse, NY: Syracuse University Press, 2012.

Gordon, Ian. *Comic Strips and Consumer Culture 1890–1945*. Washington, DC: Smithsonian Institution Press, 1998.

Graebner, William S. *The Age of Doubt: American Thought and Culture in the 1940s*. Boston: Twayne, 1991.

Hardison, Priscilla, with Anne Wormser. *The Suzy-Q*. Boston: Houghton Mifflin, 1943.

Harris, Mark. *Five Came Back: A Story of Hollywood and the Second World War*. New York: Penguin Press, 2014.

Higham, Charles and Joel Greenberg. *Hollywood in the Forties*. New York: Paperback Library, 1970.

Iverson, Caroline. "'Suzy-Q,' Fightingest Flying Fortress', *Life* 14 (3) (18 January 1943): 82–92.

Jonas, Susan and Marilyn Nissenson. *Going Going Gone: Vanishing Americana*. San Francisco: Chronicle Books, 1998.

Jones, John Bush. *The Songs That Fought the War: Popular Music and the Home Front, 1939–1945*. Waltham, MA: Brandeis University Press, 2006.

Karash, Julius A. and Rick Montgomery. *TWA: Kansas City's Hometown Airline*. Kansas City: Kansas City Star Books, 2001.

Kinn, Gail and Jim Piazza. *The Academy Awards: The Complete Unofficial History*. New York: Black Dog & Leventhal Publishers, 2004.

Kismaric, Carole and Marvin Heiferman. *Growing Up with Dick and Jane*, Preface by Bob Keeshan, creator of *Captain Kangaroo*. New York: Collins Publishers, 1996.

Laboissonniere, Wade. *Blueprints of Fashion: Home Sewing Patterns of the 1940s*, rev. 2nd edition. Atglen, PA: Schiffer Publishing, 2009.

Lescott, James. *The Forties in Pictures*. Bath, UK: Parragon Books, 2007.

Leuchtenburg, William E. *A Troubled Feast: American Society Since 1945*, updated edition. Glenview, IL: Scott, Foresman and Co., 1983.

Lovegren, Sylvia. *Fashionable Food: Seven Decades of Food Fads*. New York: Macmillan, 1995.

Lupiano, Vincent DePaul and Ken W. Sayers. *It Was a Very Good Year: A Cultural History of the United States from 1776 to the Present*. Holbrook, MA: Bob Adams, Inc., 1994.

Manning, Molly Guptill. *When Books Went to War: The Stories That Helped Us Win World War II*. Boston: Houghton Mifflin Harcourt, 2014.

Marshall, George Catlett. *The Papers of George Catlett Marshall*, Volume 2: 'We Cannot Delay' July 1, 1939–December 6, 1941, ed. Larry I. Bland, Sharon R. Ritenour and Clarence E. Wunderlin, Jr. Baltimore: Johns Hopkins University Press, 1986.

Marshall, George Catlett. *The Papers of George Catlett Marshall*, Volume 3: 'The Right Man for the Job' December 7, 1941–May 31, 1943, ed. Larry J. Bland and Sharon Ritenour Stevens. Baltimore: Johns Hopkins University Press, 1991.

Mauldin, Bill. *Willie and Joe: Back Home*, ed. Todd DePastino. Seattle: Fantagraphics Books, 2011.

Morgan, Henry, ed. *Decade of Crisis: Milestones of History 11*. New York: Newsweek Books, 1975.

The New Yorker. *The 40s: The Story of a Decade*, ed. Henry Finder with Giles Harvey, Introduction by David Remnick. New York: Random House, 2014.

Nice, Capt Albert T. 'If You Knew Suzy As I Knew Suzy', *Skyways* 2 (3) (March 1943): 27.

Olian, JoAnn, ed. and Introduction. *Everyday Fashions of the Forties: As Pictured in Sears Catalogs*. New York: Dover Publications, 1992.

Piehler, G. Kurt, ed. *The United States in World War II: A Documentary Reader*. Malden, MA: Wiley-Blackwell, 2013.

Polmar, Norman and Thomas B. Allen. *World War II: The Encyclopedia of the War Years 1941–1945*. Mineola, NY: Dover Publications, 2012.

Riesman, David, with Nathan Glazer and Reuel Denney. *The Lonely Crowd: A Study of the Changing American Character*. New Haven, CT: Yale University Press, 1950.

Rose, Jonathan. *The Literary Churchill: Author, Reader, Actor*. New Haven, CT: Yale University Press, 2014.

Rottman, Gordon. *US Army Air Force (2)*. Oxford: Osprey Publishing, 2002.

Saunders, Alan. *George C. Marshall: A General for Peace*. New York: Facts on File, 1996.

Sickels, Robert, *The 1940s*. Westport, CT: Greenwood Press, 2004.

Snyder, Timothy. 'Holocaust: The Ignored Reality', *The New York Review*, 16 July 2009, http://www.nybooks.com/articles/2009/07/16/holocaust-the-ignored-reality/ (accessed 17 March 2016).

Stern, Ellen. *The Very Best from Hallmark: Greeting Cards through the Years*. New York: Harry N. Abrams, 1988.

Time-Life Books. *This Fabulous Century, Volume V: 1940–1950*. New York: Time-Life Books, 1969.

Trager, James. *The People's Chronology: A Year-by-Year Record of Human Events from Prehistory to the Present*, revised and updated edition. New York: Henry Holt, 1992.
Van Gelder, Lawrence. *Ike: A Soldier's Crusade.* New York: Universal Publishing, 1969.
Walford, Jonathan, *Forties Fashion: From Siren Suits to the New Look.* London: Thames and Hudson, 2011.
Walker, Brian. *The Comics: The Complete Collection.* New York: Abrams, 2011.
Wallis, Michael. *Route 66: The Mother Road.* New York: St Martin's Griffin, 2001.
Winchell, Meghan K. *Good Girls, Good Food, Good Fun: The Story of USO Hostesses During World War II.* Chapel Hill: University of North Carolina Press, 2008.

2 American Theatre in the 1940s

Abramson, Doris E. *Negro Playwrights in the American Theatre 1925–1959.* New York: Columbia University Press, 1969.
Adler, Stella, *Stella Adler on America's Master Playwrights*, ed. and commentary by Barry Paris. New York: Alfred A. Knopf, 2012.
Adler, Thomas P. *Mirror on the Stage: The Pulitzer Plays as an Approach to American Drama.* West Lafayette, IN: Purdue University Press, 1987.
Aldrich, Richard Stoddard. *Gertrude Lawrence as Mrs. A.: An Intimate Biography of the Great Star.* New York: Greystone Press, 1954.
Anderson, Alan. *The Songwriter Goes to War: The Story of Irving Berlin's World War II All-Army Production of* This Is the Army, Foreword by Mary Ellin Barrett. Pompton Plains, NJ: Limelight Editions, 2004.
Anderson, Arthur. *Let's Pretend: A History of Radio's Best Loved Children's Show by a Longtime Cast Member*, Foreword by Norman Corwin. Jefferson, NC: McFarland, 1994.
Anderson, Maxwell. *Off Broadway: Essays about the Theater.* New York: William Sloane Associates, 1947.
Andrews, Maxene and Bill Gilbert. *Over Here, Over There: The Andrews Sisters and the USO Stars in World War II.* New York: Zebra Books, Kensington Publishing Co., 1993.
Atkinson, Brooks. *Broadway*, revised edition. New York: Macmillan, 1974.

Barfield, Ray. *Listening to Radio, 1920–1950*, Foreword by M. Thomas Inge. Westport, CT: Praeger, 1996.

Barranger, Milly S. *Unfriendly Witnesses: Gender, Theater, and Film in the McCarthy Era*. Carbondale: Southern Illinois University Press, 2008.

Berlin, Irving. *The Complete Lyrics of Irving Berlin*, ed. Robert Kimball and Linda Emmet. New York: Alfred A. Knopf, 2001.

Bigsby, C. W. E. *A Critical Introduction to Twentieth-Century American Drama*, Vol. One: 1900–40. Cambridge: Cambridge University Press, 1982.

Bloomfield, Gary L. and Stacie L. Shain, with Arlen C. Davidson. *Duty, Honor, Applause: America's Entertainers in World War II*. Guilford, CT: Lyons Press, 2004.

Blue, Howard. *Words at War: World War II Era Radio Drama and the Postwar Broadcasting Industry Blacklist*. Lanham, MD: Scarecrow Press, 2002.

Bonin, Jane F. *Prize-Winning American Drama: A Bibliographical and Descriptive Guide*. Metuchen, NJ: Scarecrow Press, 1973.

Bordman, Gerald. *American Theatre: A Chronicle of Comedy and Drama, 1930–1969*. New York: Oxford University Press, 1996.

Bordman, Gerald. *American Musical Theatre: A Chronicle*, 3rd edition. Oxford: Oxford University Press, 2001.

Bronner, Edwin J. *The Encyclopedia of the American Theatre 1900–1975*. San Diego: A.S. Barnes and Co., 1980.

Brown, Gene. *Show Time: A Chronology of Broadway and the Theatre from Its Beginnings to the Present*. New York: Macmillan, 1997.

Carson, Julia M. H. *Home Away from Home: The Story of the USO*. New York: Harper and Brothers, 1946.

Christiansen, Richard. *A Theater of Our Own: A History and a Memoir of 1,001 Nights in Chicago*. Evanston, IL: Northwestern University Press, 2004.

Coffey, Frank. *Always Home: 50 Years of the USO: The Official Photographic History*, Special Foreword by Bob Hope. Washington, DC: Brassey's (US), 1991.

Corwin, Norman. 'The Sovereign Word: Some Notes on Radio Drama', *Theatre Arts* XXIV 2 (February 1940): 130–6.

Corwin, Norman. *On a Note of Triumph*. New York: Simon and Schuster, 1945.

Csida, Joseph and June Bundy Csida. *American Entertainment: A Unique History of Popular Show Business*. New York: A Billboard Book, 1978.

Davis, Walter A. *Get the Guests: Psychoanalysis, Modern American Drama, and the Audience*. Madison: University of Wisconsin Press, 1994.

De Mille, Agnes. *Lizzie Borden: A Dance of Death*. Boston: An Atlantic Monthly Press Book (Little, Brown and Co.), 1968.

De Mille, Agnes. *Martha: The Life and Work of Martha Graham*. New York: Random House, 1991.

Dreiblatt, Martha. 'Words on the Theatre and War', *New York Times*, 16 May 1943, X1–X2.

Duberman, Martin Bauml. *Paul Robeson: A Biography*. New York: Ballantine Books, 1989.

Duberman, Martin Bauml. 'Robeson and *Othello*', in *Paul Robson: Artist and Citizen*, ed. and Introduction by Jeffrey C. Stewart, 123–33. New Brunswick, NJ: Rutgers University Press, 1998.

Fisher, James. *Al Jolson: A Bio-Bibliography*. Westport, CT: Greenwood Press, 1994.

Flinn, Denny Martin. *Musical! A Grand Tour*. New York: Schirmer Books, 1997.

Gilder, Rosamond, Hermine Rich Isaacs, Robert M. MacGregor and Edward Reed, eds *Theatre Arts Anthology: A Record and a Prophecy*. New York: Theatre Arts Books, 1950.

Gill, Glenda E. *No Surrender! No Retreat! African American Pioneer Performers of Twentieth-Century American Theater*. New York: St Martin's Press, 2000.

Hanff, Helene. *Underfoot in Show Business*. New York: Penguin Books, 1981.

Hatch, James V. *Sorrow Is the Only Faithful One: The Life of Owen Dodson*, Foreword by Arnold Rampersand. Urbana: University of Illinois Press, 1995.

Heberling, Lynn O'Neal. *Soldiers in Greasepaint: USO-Camp Shows, Inc., During World War II*. PhD dissertation, Kent State University, 1989.

Hill, Errol. *Shakespeare in Sable: A History of Black Shakespearean Actors*. Amherst: University of Massachusetts Press, 1986.

Hill, Errol G. and James V. Hatch. *A History of African American Theatre*. Cambridge: Cambridge University Press, 2003.

Jones, Chris. *Bigger, Brighter, Louder: 150 Years of Chicago Theater as Seen by* Chicago Tribune *Critics*. Chicago: University of Chicago Press, 2013.

Lahr, John. 'The Theatre: O.K. Chorale', *The New Yorker*, 1 April 2002, 84–6.

Leonard, William, ed. *Chicago Stagebill Yearbook 1947*. Chicago: Chicago Stagebill, 1947.

Leopold, David. *Irving Berlin's Show Business*. New York: Harry N. Abrams, 2005.

Mathews, Jane De Hart. *The Federal Theatre, 1935–1939: Plays, Relief, and Politics*. New York: Octagon Books, 1980.
McAllister, Marvin. *Whiting Up: Whiteface Minstrels & Stage Europeans in African American Performance*. Chapel Hill: University of North Carolina Press, 2011.
McClung, Bruce D. *Lady in the Dark: Biography of a Musical*. New York: Oxford University Press, 2007.
Mordden, Ethan. *Beautiful Mornin': The Broadway Musical in the 1940s*. Oxford: Oxford University Press, 1999.
Mordden, Ethan. *All That Glittered: The Golden Age of Drama on Broadway, 1919–1959*. New York: St Martin's Press, 2007.
Mullenbach, Cheryl. *Double Victory: How African American Women Broke Race and Gender Barriers to Help Win World War II*. Chicago: Chicago Review Press, 2013.
Nadel, Norman. *A Pictorial History of the Theatre Guild*, Introduction by Brooks Atkinson, special material Lawrence Langner and Armina Marshall. New York: Crown Publishers, 1969.
Nathan, George Jean. *The Entertainment of a Nation or Three-Sheets in the Wind*. New York: Alfred A. Knopf, 1942.
Nelson, Emmanuel S., ed. *African American Dramatists: A Z-to-Z Guide*. Westport, CT: Greenwood Press, 2004.
Nolan, Frederick. *The Sound of Their Music: The Story of Rodgers and Hammerstein*. New York: Applause Theatre & Cinema Books, 2002.
Novick, Julius. *Beyond Broadway: The Quest for Permanent Theatres*. New York: Hill and Wang, 1968.
O'Connor, John and Lorraine Brown, eds *Free, Adult, Uncensored: The Living History of the Federal Theatre Project*, Foreword by John Houseman. Washington, DC: New Republic Books, 1978.
Schanke, Robert A. *Shattered Applause: The Eva Le Gallienne Story*, Foreword by May Sarton. New York: Barricade Books Inc., 1992.
Sheehy, Helen. *Margo: The Life and Theatre of Margo Jones*. Dallas: Southern Methodist University Press, 1989.
Smiley, Sam. *The Drama of Attack: Didactic Plays of the American Depression*. Columbia: University of Missouri Press, 1972.
Smith, Mona Z. *Becoming Something: The Story of Canada Lee*. New York: Faber and Faber, Inc., 2004.
Spector, Susan. 'Margaret Webster's *Othello*; The Principal Players Versus the Direrctor', *Theatre History Studies* VI (1986): 93–108.
Sper, Felix. *From Native Roots: A Panorama of Our Regional Drama*. Caldwell, ID: Caxton Printers, 1948.
Sporn, Paul. *Against Itself: The Federal Theater and Writers' Projects in the Midwest*. Detroit: Wayne State University Press, 1995.
Stevenson, Isabelle and Roy A. Somlyo. *The Tony Award: A Complete*

Listing of Winners and Nominees of the American Theatre Wing's Tony Award, with a History of the American Theatre Wing. Portsmouth, NH: Heinemann, 2001.

Stewart, Jeffrey C., ed. and Introduction. *Paul Robson: Artist and Citizen.* New Brunswick, NJ: Rutgers University Press, 1998.

Teachout, Terry. 'Bard of the Electric Ear', *About Last Night: An Arts Journal Blog*, 8 November 2004, http://www.artsjournal.com/aboutlastnight/2004/11/tt-bard-of-the-electric-ear.html (accessed 17 September 2015).

Teachout, Terry. 'He's Got a Little List: What Plays does David Mamet Like Best – and Why?', *Wall Street Journal*, 15 May 2010, http://www.wsj.com/articles/SB10001424052748704635204575242163033076720 (accessed 31 July 2015).

Toohey, John L. *A History of the Pulitzer Prize Plays.* New York: Citadel Press, 1967.

Ullom, Jeffrey. *America's First Regional Theatre: The Cleveland Playhouse and Its Search for a Home.* New York: Palgrave Macmillan, 2014.

Vaughan, Virginia Mason. *Othello: A Contextual History.* Cambridge: Cambridge University Press, 1994.

Webster, Margaret. *Don't Put Your Daughter on the Stage.* New York: Alfred A. Knopf, 1972.

Wertheim, Albert. *Staging the War: American Drama and World War II.* Bloomington: Indiana University Press, 2004.

Wilk, Max. *OK! The Story of Oklahoma!* New York: Grove Press, 1993.

Wilmeth, Don B. and Christopher Bigsby, eds *The Cambridge History of American Theatre*, Volume II: 1870–1945. Cambridge: Cambridge University Press, 1999.

4 Eugene O'Neill: Love and Loss of the Soul

Plays

O'Neill, Eugene. *Complete Plays 1913–1920*, ed. Travis Bogard. New York: Library of America, 1988a.

O'Neill, Eugene. *Complete Plays 1920–1931*, ed. Travis Bogard. New York: Library of America, 1988b.

O'Neill, Eugene. *Complete Plays 1932–1943*, ed. Travis Bogard. New York: Library of America, 1988c.

Recommended books and articles

Bogard, Travis. *'From the Silence of Tao House': Essays about Eugene & Carlotta O'Neill and the Tao House Plays*. Danville, CA: Eugene O'Neill Foundation, Tao House, 1993.

Brietzke, Zander. *The Aesthetics of Failure: Dynamic Structure in the Plays of Eugene O'Neill*. Jefferson, NC: McFarland, 2001.

Bryer, Jackson R. and Robert M. Dowling, eds *Eugene O'Neill: The Contemporary Reviews*. New York: Cambridge University Press, 2014.

Diggins, John Patrick. *Eugene O'Neill's America: Desire Under Democracy*. Chicago: University of Chicago Press, 2007.

Dowling, Robert M. *Eugene O'Neill: A Life in Four Acts*. New Haven, CT: Yale University Press, 2014.

Dubost, Thierry. *Struggle, Defeat or Rebirth: Eugene O'Neill's Vision of Humanity*. Jefferson, NC: McFarland and Co., 1997.

Manheim, Michael, ed. *The Cambridge Companion to Eugene O'Neill*. New York: Cambridge University Press, 1988.

Pawley, Thomas. 'Eugene O'Neill and American Race Relations', *Journal of American Drama and Theatre* 9 (1997): 66–89.

5 Thornton Wilder: Seeing Beyond Dark Times

Plays and other writing

Wilder, Thornton. *Our Century: A Play in Three Scenes*. Century Association, 1947.

Wilder, Thornton. *The Journals of Thornton Wilder, 1939–1961*, selected and ed. Donald Gallup. New Haven, CT: Yale University Press, 1985.

Wilder, Thornton. *Three Plays*, with a new Foreword by John Guare. New York: Harper Perennial, 2006.

Wilder, Thornton. *Collected Plays & Writings on Theater*, ed. J. D. McClatchey. New York: Library of America, 2007.

Wilder, Thornton. *The Selected Letters of Thornton Wilder*, ed. Robin G. Wilder and Jackson R. Bryer. New York: Harper Perennial, 2008.

Recommended books and articles

Barnes, Eric Wollencott. *The Man Who Lived Twice: The Biography of Edward Sheldon*. New York: Charles Scribner's Sons, 1956.

Bryer, Jackson R., ed. *Conversations with Thornton Wilder*. Jackson: University Press of Mississippi, 1992.

Bryer, Jackson R. and Lincoln Konkle, eds *Thornton Wilder: New Perspectives*. Evanston, IL: Northwestern University Press, 2013.

Bucker, Park. 'Wearing Down "The Edge of Boldness": Wilder's Evolving Values and Stagecraft in the Three Published Versions and Prompt Script of *Our Town*', in *Thornton Wilder: New Perspectives*, ed. Jackson R. Bryer and Lincoln Konkle, 132–53. Evanston, IL: Northwestern University Press, 2013.

De Koster, Katie, ed. *Readings on Thornton Wilder*. San Diego: Greenhaven Press, 1998.

Elliott, Kenneth. 'The Outsider: Contextualizing Simon Stimson in *Our Town*', in *Thornton Wilder: New Perspectives*, ed. Jackson R. Bryer and Lincoln Konkle, 121–31. Evanston, IL: Northwestern University Press, 2013.

Goldstone, Richard H. *Thornton Wilder: An Intimate Portrait*. New York: E. P. Dutton, 1975.

Harrison, Gilbert A. *The Enthusiast: A Life of Thornton Wilder*. New Haven, CT: Ticknor and Fields, 1983.

Henry, William A., III. 'Theater: Scraping Away the Sentiment in *Our Town*', *Time*, 4 January 1988, 171.

Konkle, Lincoln. *Thornton Wilder and the Puritan Narrative Tradition*. Columbia: University of Missouri Press, 2006.

Niven, Penelope. *Thornton Wilder: A Life*. New York: Harper Perennial, 2013.

Piland, Richard N. *The Illustrated History of the Resident Theatre, Kansas City, Missouri, 1932–1983*, Foreword by Glenn Q. Pierce. Fairfield, OH: Personalized Research, 2011.

Simon, Linda. *Thornton Wilder: His World*. Garden City, NY: Doubleday, 1979.

Stein, Gertrude and Thornton Wilder. *The Letters of Gertrude Stein and Thornton Wilder*, ed. Edward M. Burns and Ulla E. Dydo with William Rice. New Haven, CT: Yale University Press, 1996.

Wheatley, Christopher J. *Thornton Wilder & Amos Wilder: Writing Religion in Twentieth Century America*. Notre Dame, IN: University of Notre Dame Press, 2011.

Wilder, Amos Niven. *Thornton Wilder and His Public*. Philadelphia: Fortress Press, 1980.

Wilder, Isabel. 'Foreword', in Thornton Wilder, *The Alcestiad or A Life in the Sun: A Play in Three Acts with a Satyr Play The Drunken Sisters*, ix–xxi. New York: Harper and Row, 1977.

6 Tennessee Williams: Experimentation and 'The Great American Play'

Plays and other writing

Tennessee, Williams. *Not About Nightingales*, ed. and Introduction by Allean Hale. New York: New Directions, 1998.

Tennessee, Williams. *Spring Storm*, ed. and Introduction by Dan Isaac. New York: New Directions, 1999.

Tennessee, Williams. *Plays: 1937–1955*, ed. Mel Gussow and Kenneth Holditch. New York: Library of America, 2000a.

Tennessee, Williams. *Plays: 1957–1980*, ed. Mel Gussow and Kenneth Holditch. New York: Library of America, 2000b.

Tennessee, Williams. *Selected Letters of Tennessee Williams, Volume I*, ed. Albert J. Devlin and Nancy Tischler. New York: New Directions, 2000c.

Tennessee, Williams. *Stairs to the Roof*, ed. and Introduction by Allean Hale. New York: New Directions, 2000d.

Tennessee, Williams. *Fugitive Kind*, ed. and Introduction by Allean Hale. New York: New Directions, 2001.

Tennessee, Williams. *Candles to the Sun*, ed. and Introduction by Dan Isaac. New York: New Directions, 2004a.

Tennessee, Williams. *Selected Letters of Tennessee Williams, Volume II*, ed. Albert J. Devlin and Nancy Tischler. New York: New Directions, 2004b.

Tennessee, Williams. *A Streetcar Named Desire*, Introduction by Arthur Miller. New York: New Directions, 2004c.

Tennessee, Williams. *Mister Paradise and Other One-Act Plays*, ed. and notes by Nicholas Moschovakis and David Roessel. New York: New Directions, 2005.

Tennessee, Williams. *Memoirs*. New York: New Directions, 2006a.

Tennessee, Williams. *Notebooks*, ed. Margaret Bradham Thornton. New Haven, CT, and London: Yale University Press, 2006b.

Tennessee, Williams. *New Selected Essays: Where I Live*, ed. John S. Bak. New York: New Directions, 2009.

Tennessee, Williams. *The Glass Menagerie*, Introduction by Tony Kushner. New York: New Directions, 2011a.

Tennessee, Williams. *The Magic Tower and Other One-Act Plays*, ed. and notes Thomas Keith. New York: New Directions, 2011b.

Recommended books and articles

Bak, John S., ed. *Tennessee Williams and Europe: Intercultural Encounters, Transatlantic Exchanges*. Amsterdam: Rodopi, 2011.

Bak, John S. *Tennessee Williams: A Literary Life*. New York: Palgrave Macmillan, 2013.

Barranger, Milly S. *Audrey Wood and the Playwrights*. New York: Palgrave Macmillan, 2013.

Case, Claudia Wilsch. 'Battle in Boston: Tennessee Williams' First Professional Production', in *Tenn at One Hundred*, ed. David Kaplan. East Brunswick, NJ: Hansen Publishing Group, 2011.

Devlin, Albert J., ed. *Conversations with Tennessee Williams*. Jackson and London: University Press of Mississippi, 1986.

Kaplan, David. 'Rescuing *The Glass Menagerie*', in *Tenn at One Hundred*, ed. David Kaplan. East Brunswick, NJ: Hansen Publishing Group, 2011.

Kazan, Elia. *The Selected Letters of Elia Kazan*, ed. Albert J. Devlin with Marlene J. Devlin. New York: Knopf, 2014.

Kolin, Philip C. *Williams: A Streetcar Named Desire*. Cambridge: Cambridge University Press, 1999.

Kolin, Philip C., ed. *The Tennessee Williams Encyclopedia*. Westport, CT: Greenwood Press, 2004.

Kolin, Philip C., *The Influence of Tennessee Williams: Essays on Fifteen American Playwrights*. Jefferson, NC: McFarland and Co., 2008.

Lahr, John. *Tennessee Williams: Mad Pilgrimage of the Flesh*. New York and London: W.W. Norton, 2014.

Leverich, Lyle. *Tom: The Unknown Tennessee Williams*. London: W. W. Norton, 1995.

Ley-Piscator, Maria. *The Piscator Experiment*. New York: James H. Heineman, 1967.

Londré, Felicia Hardison. *Tennessee Williams*. New York: Frederick Ungar, 1979.

MacNiven, Ian S. *'Literchoor Is My Beat': A Life of James Laughlin, Publisher of New Directions*. New York: Farrar, Straus and Giroux, 2014.

Malina, Judith. *The Piscator Notebook*. London and New York: Routledge, 2012.

Mielziner, Jo. *Designing for the Theatre: A Memoir and a Portfolio*. New York: Bramhall House, 1965.

Miller, Arthur. 'Regarding *Streetcar*', in Tennessee Williams, *A Streetcar Named Desire*. New York: New Directions, 2004.
Murphy, Brenda. *The Theatre of Tennessee Williams*. London: Bloomsbury, 2014.
Pawley, Thomas D. 'Where the Streetcar Doesn't Run: The Black World of Tennessee Williams', *Journal of American Drama and Theatre* 14 (3) (2002): 18–33.
Roudané, Matthew C., ed. *The Cambridge Companion to Tennessee Williams*. Cambridge: Cambridge University Press, 1997.
Smith, William Jay. *My Friend Tom: The Poet-Playwright Tennessee Williams*. Jackson and London: University Press of Mississippi, 2011.
Van Antwerp, Margaret A. and Sally Johns. *Dictionary of Literary Biography, Volume Four, Tennessee Williams*. Detroit: Bruccoli Clark and Gale Research, 1984.
Voss, Ralph S., ed. *Magical Muse: Millennial Essays on Tennessee Williams*. Tuscaloosa: University of Alabama Press, 2002.
Willett, John. *The Theatre of Erwin Piscator*. New York: Holmes and Meier, 1979.
Windham, Donald. *Tennessee Williams' Letters to Donald Windham 1940–1965*. New York: Holt, Rinehart and Winston, 1977.

7 Arthur Miller: The Individual and Social Responsibility

Plays and other writing

Miller, Arthur. 'A Boy Grew in Brooklyn', *Holiday* 17 (March 1955): 54+.
Miller, Arthur. *Focus*, with Introduction by author. New York: Penguin Books, 1984.
Miller, Arthur. *Timebends, A Life*. New York: Grove Press, 1987.
Miller, Arthur. *Two Plays: The Archbishop's Ceiling* and *The American Clock*, with introduction by author. New York: Grove Press, 1989.
Miller, Arthur. *Echoes Down the Corridor: Collected Essays 1944–2000*, ed. Steven R. Centola. New York: Penguin Books, 2001.
Miller, Arthur. *Collected Plays 1944–1961*, ed. Tony Kushner. New York: Library of America, 2006.
Miller, Arthur. 'A Final Conversation with Arthur Miller', interviewed by Christopher Bigsby, *The Arthur Miller Journal* 1 (1) (Spring 2006): 61–77.

Miller, Arthur. *Arthur Miller Plays: Six*, with Introduction by Enoch Brater. London: Methuen Drama, 2009.

Recommended books

Bigsby, Christopher, ed. *Arthur Miller and Company*. London: Methuen Drama in association with The Arthur Miller Centre for American Studies, 1990.

Bigsby, Christopher, ed. *The Cambridge Companion to Arthur Miller*. Cambridge: Cambridge University Press, 1999.

Bigsby, Christopher. *Arthur Miller, 1915–1962*. London: Phoenix, 2009.

Brater, Enoch. *Arthur Miller: A Playwright's Life and Works*. London: Thames and Hudson, 2005a.

Brater, Enoch. *Arthur Miller's America: Theater & Culture in a Time of Change*. Ann Arbor: University of Michigan Press, 2005b.

Brater, Enoch, ed. *A Student Handbook to the Plays of Arthur Miller*. London: Bloomsbury, 2013.

Gottfried, Martin. *Arthur Miller: His Life and Work*. Cambridge, MA: Da Capo Press, 1994.

'He Was No Misfit in Brooklyn', *On This Day in History: October 17*. *Brooklyn Eagle*, published online, 17 October 2006.

Mailer, Norman. 'Interview', *Brooklyn Heights Press*, 30 September 1982.

Marino, Stephen. '"It's Brooklyn, I know, but we hunt too": The Image of the Borough in *Death of a Salesman*', in *'The Salesman Has a Birthday': Essays Celebrating the Fiftieth Anniversary of Arthur Miller's* Death of a Salesman. Lanham, MD: University Press of America, 2000.

Marino, Stephen. 'Touring Arthur Miller's Brooklyn', *The Arthur Miller Society Newsletter* 11 (June 2005): 8–12.

Marino, Stephen. 'Commentary', in *Arthur Miller, A View From the Bridge*, with commentary and notes by Stephen Marino. London: Methuen Drama, 2010.

Wheatley, Christopher J., ed. *Twentieth-Century American Dramatists: Fourth Series, Dictionary of Literary Biography*, Vol. 266. Detroit: Gale, 2003.

Documents

Pawley, Thomas, 'The Tumult and the Shouting', in *Black Theater USA: Forty-Five Plays by Black Americans 1847–1974*, ed. James V. Hatch, with Ted Shine, consultant, 475–513. New York: Free Press, 1974.

Reardon, William R. and Thomas D. Pawley, eds *The Black Teacher and the Dramatic Arts: A Dialogue, Bibliography, and Anthology*. Westport, CT: Negro Universities Press, 1970.

INDEX

1930s 1, 5, 19, 99
   theatre 37–42, 66
   timeline 2–4

Abbott, George 62, 78, 82–3, 214
Abie's Irish Rose (play, Anne
   Nichols) 46
Academy Award 25, 75, 135
acting 214–21
Actors' Equity Association (*aka*
   Equity) 45, 55, 74
Actors Studio 84
Acuff, Roy 22
The Adding Machine (play, Elmer
   Rice) 160
advertising 11, 18, 19–20, 24, 28
African Americans 8, 9, 15, 21,
   30, 44–5, 53, 56, 62, 64–5,
   70–4, 79, 92, 96, 107,
   154, 156, 159, 234, 238,
   240 n.18, 250 n.9 *see also*
   segregation/desegregation
agriculture 13
Aherne, Brian 56
Akins, Zoe 60
Albee, Edward 201
Aldrich, Richard Stoddard 50
Alexander, Doris 122
Allen, Vera 51, 52
Alvarez, Max 141
American Academy, Rome 94
American Ballet Theatre 80
American Expeditionary Forces
   (AEF) 4, 7

American Negro Theatre (ANT)
   45, 60
American Repertory Theatre 84
American Theatre Wing 14, 51–6,
   75
Anderson, Alan 64–6
Anderson, Judith 47, 53, 76
Anderson, Marian 9
Anderson, Maxwell 38, 39, 42,
   47, 59, 60, 74, 76, 78, 155,
   210
   Anne of the Thousand Days
     76
   Candle in the Wind 47
   High Tor 39, 42
   Lost in the Stars 78
   Winterset 38
   see also *Joan of Lorraine*
Andrews sisters (Maxene, Patty
   and LaVerne) 22, 51, 54–6
Anna Lucasta (play, Philip
   Yordan) 45, 60
anti-Semitism 2, 12, 13, 100, 177,
   192, 265 n.39
Antoinette Perry Award (Tony)
   52, 75, 76, 83, 84, 154,
   191
Arlen, Harold 60, 61, 63
Army Emergency Relief Fund 64,
   65
Arnold, Henry H. 'Hap' 240 n.9
Arsenic and Old Lace (play,
   Joseph Kesselring) 46, 81,
   208

Ashcroft, Peggy 70
Astaire, Fred 55
athletics 29, 31, 98
Atkinson, Brooks 52, 56, 131, 183, 191, 198
Atkinson, Jennifer McCabe 212
Atlantic 4, 221
Atomic Energy Commission (AEC) 7, 12, 32
atoms/atomic energy 6, 10, 11–12
  see also bombs
Atwater, Edith 51
Auden, W. H. 31, 231
August: Osage County (play, Tracy Letts) 202
Australia 10
Austria 3, 183
automobiles 17–18, 21, 26
Autry, Gene 22
Avery, Tex 26
aviation 1, 12, 26–7, 29, 30, 178
awards 39, 52, 75, 99, 207
  American Women's Voluntary Services recognition 51
  Avery Hopwood Award 99
  Clarence Derwent Award 45
  see also Academy Award; Antoinette Perry (Tony) Award; New York Drama Critics' Circle Award; Nobel Prize; Pulitzer Prize
Ayers, Lemuel 68

baby boom 16
Bak, John S. 96
Baker, George Pierce 80, 91
Balanchine, George 31, 44
Ball, Lucille 24
Ballard, Lucinda 76
Ballet Russe de Monte Carlo 31, 80
Bankhead, Tallulah 214
Barber, Samuel 79

Barnes, Howard 182
Barrett, Mary Ellen 64
Barretts of Wimpole Street, The (play, Rudolf Besier) 56
Barrie, J. M. 84
Barry, Philip 41, 59
Barrymore, Ethel, John, and Lionel 210
Barter Theatre 81–2
Baruch, Bernard M. 32
baseball 24, 29, 30, 230
battleships *see* ships
Begley, Ed 182
Behrman, S. N. 41, 59, 77
Beiswanger, George A. 79
Bel Geddes, Norman *see* Geddes, Norman Bel
Belgium 4
Bellows, George 213
Benson, Sally 47, 141
Benton, Thomas Hart 29
Bergen, Edgar (and Charlie McCarthy) 24, 53, 55
Bergman, Ingrid 75, 76
Berle, Milton 25
Berlin, Germany 32
Berlin, Irving 13, 22, 41, 59, 60, 63–6, 77
  Annie Get Your Gun 22, 77, 208
  As Thousands Cheer 44
  'God Bless America' 22, 63
  Louisiana Purchase 41
  This Is the Army 49, 59, 63–6
  'White Christmas' 22
Bernadotte, Folke 9
Bernhardt, Sarah 168
Bernstein, Leonard 31, 34, 62
Best, Eve 124
Bible 93, 103, 109–10, 113, 127, 131, 136
Bigsby, Christopher 204

INDEX 289

Big White Fog (play, Theodore Ward) 44, 45
blacklist 33 *see also* Hollywood Ten
Blanc, Mel 26
Blithe Spirit (play, Noel Coward) 47, 56
Blitzstein, Marc 41, 78
Bloom, Steven F. 119
Bloomer Girl (musical, Harold Arlen and E. Y. Harburg) 208
Bloomgarden, Kermit 191, 198
Bogart, Humphrey 29
Bolaño, Roberto 159
Bolger, Ray 53
Bolton, Guy 60
bomb 10, 13
  atomic 10, 11–12, 30, 32, 33
books 6, 13, 15, 16, 19, 29, 30, 31, 32, 40, 128, 211–14
  Armed Services Editions 15–16, 241 n.22
Boothe, Clare 39, 41
Bordman, Gerald 49, 60
Borglum, Gutzon 29
Born Yesterday (play, Garson Kanin) 76
Boston 64, 71, 157, 158, 208, 213, 221–2, 225, 227, 228
Boulton, Agnes 92
boxing 29, 93
Boyer, Charles 24
Braham, Horace 59
Brando, Marlon 84
Brecht, Bertolt 158, 167, 170, 181
bridge (card game) 27, 28
Brigadoon (musical, Alan J. Lerner and Frederick Loewe) 75, 78, 80, 83
Britain 4, 5, 6, 10, 50–1, 65, 70, 204

air raids 4, 10
British War Relief Society 50, 52
Broadway 14, 36, 37, 39, 41, 42, 44, 45, 46–7, 48, 49, 50, 53, 56, 58–63, 64, 67, 68, 70, 73, 74–80, 82–5, 100, 130, 151, 152, 157, 160, 164, 169, 172, 182, 191, 198, 201, 202, 207, 208, 210, 214, 218, 222, 223, 224 *see also* musicals
Brooklyn 98–100, 228–37
Brown, John Mason 50
Brown, Lawrence 70
Browne, Theodore 45
Browne, Sir Thomas 128
Bucker, Park 134
Buloff, Joseph 68
Bultman, Fritz 226
Bunche, Ralph 9
Burke, Billie 60
Burnett, Matthew 203
Burns, George 28
Burton, Virginia Lee 19
Bury the Dead (play, Irwin Shaw) 39, 153
Byrnes, James F. 240 n.9

Cabin in the Sky (musical, Vernon Duke and John Latouche) 44
Cabrini, Mother Frances Xavier 30
Cage, John 240 n. 9
Cagney, James 25
Cahn, Sammy 78
Caldecott Medal 19
Caldwell, Erskine 46
Campbell, Dick 56
capitalism 209, 210
Capote, Truman 231
Capp, Al 26
Capra, Frank 25
Carmichael, Hoagy 22

Carnegie, Dale 31
Carnegie, Hattie 48
Carousel 62, 78, 80
Carroll, Paul Vincent 41
Cassidy, Claudia 82, 168, 182
Cassidy, Hopalong 20
Catholicism 30, 87, 90
censorship 158, 183
Central Intelligence Agency (CIA) 32, 33
Chambers, Whittaker 33
Channing, Carol 79
Chaplin, Oona O'Neill 107
Chase, Mary 208, 211
Chekhov, Anton Pavlovich 97, 152, 153, 155, 169, 223, 259 n.104
Cherry Orchard, The (play, Anton Pavlovich Chekhov) 83, 153
Chicago 44, 49, 64, 81, 82, 89, 168, 225, 238
children 16, 17, 18–20
Childress, Alice 73
China 2, 3, 33, 93
Chirico, Giorgio de 171
Chodorov, Jerome 46, 47, 56, 208, 209, 211
Churchill, Winston 6, 32
cigarettes and cigars 28
Citizen Kane (film, Orson Welles) 29
Civic Repertory Theatre 45
civil rights 8, 15, 182
 Fair Employment Practices Committee 15
 see also social activism
Claudia (play, Rose Franken) 46–7, 208
Cleckley, Hervey 32, 145
Cleveland Play House 81, 151
clothing and shoes 13, 14, 20, 21, 27–8, 29

Clurman, Harold 182, 202
Cobb, Lee J. 191
Cocteau, Jean 128
Coe, Richard L. 198
Cohan, George M. 25, 61, 63, 83, 92
Cohn, Harry 68
Cold War 32, 178, 183, 192–3
Cole, Nat King 22
Colefax, Sibyl 93
Coleman, Robert 182
College of Fellows of the American Theatre 45
Comden, Betty 62
comic books and comic strips 26
communism 5, 7, 32, 33, 39, 40, 41, 183, 192–3, 196, 235
community theatre 19, 36, 38, 60, 78, 80, 125, 135
concentration camps 3, 12, 13
Conklin, John 124
consumerism 16–28, 180 *see also* materialism
Copeland, Aaron 80
Cornell, Katharine 42, 53, 56, 75, 76, 95, 210
Corwin, Norman 43, 57
Costain, Thomas B. 30
Cotten, Joseph 142
Count of Monte Cristo, The (play, Alexandre Dumas père) 90, 91
Coward, Noel 47
Cowl, Jane 52, 53
Cradle Will Rock, The (musical, Marc Blitzstein) 40, 41–2
Crain, W. H. 211, 212
Crane, Hart 97, 152, 153
Craven, Frank 130
Crawford, Cheryl 75, 83–4
Cromer, David 134–5, 203
Cronyn, Hume 143
Crosby, Bing 22, 24, 28, 55

Cross, James A. 'Stump' 64
Crothers, Rachel 51–2, 210, 211
Crowley, Bob 124
Cyrano de Bergerac (play,
  Edmond Rostand) 75, 208,
  211
Czechoslovakia 3, 32, 183

Dairy Queen 18
Dakin, Rosina Otte 95, 152
Dakin, Walter 95, 152
dance 21, 31, 79–80
Dark of the Moon (play, Howard
  Richardson and William
  Berney) 60, 76
Da Silva, Howard 68
Davis, Bette 54
Davis, Miles 22
Davis, Ossie 73
Davis, Owen 46
Day, Clarence 208, 211
Daylight savings time 13
death 113, 129, 133–4, 148
Decision (play, Jerome Chodorov)
  208, 209, 211
D-Day 10
Dee, Ruby 73
Deep Are the Roots (play,
  D'Usseau and Gow) 73,
  209, 211
DeMille, Cecil B. 43
Denmark 4
Dennehy, Brian 124, 202, 205
Depression 1, 6, 37, 60, 66, 88,
  97, 98, 130, 137, 154, 155,
  163, 229, 250–1 n.8
Deval, Jacques 39
De Voto, Bernard 31
Dewey, Thomas 8
Dewhurst, Colleen 123
Dick and Jane 19
Dickens, Charles 96
Dies, Martin 41

Dietrich, Marlene 53, 54, 55
Dietz, Howard 60, 62
DiMaggio, Joe 29
directors 82–5, 173
Disney, Walt 25–6
Dixon, Lee 68
Dodson, Owen 73
Doolittle, James 10
Dorsey, Tommy 21
Douglas, William O. 32
Dowling, Eddie 163, 165, 166,
  168, 173
Dowling, Robert M. 91, 202
Drake, Alfred 67, 68
Drama Critics' Circle *see* New
  York Drama Critics' Circle
dream ballet 48–9
Dreiblatt, Martha 58–9
drinking 90, 93, 96, 105, 107,
  110–12, 114–16, 119, 132,
  163, 210, 252 n.18
drive-ins 17–18
drug addiction 90, 114–16
Duberman, Martin 71, 72
DuBois, W. E. B. 234
Duke, Vernon 44, 60, 62
Dunham, Katherine 44, 62, 63,
  79
Dupree, Minnie 51
Duse, Eleonora 168
D'Usseau, Arnaud 73, 211

Edinburgh Festival 146
education 15, 19, 28, 30
Eisenhower, Dwight D. 8–9, 10,
  31, 65
Eisenstein, Sergei 165
Eldridge, Florence 214
Eliot, T. S. 76
Elliot, Thomas H. 193
Elliott, Kenneth 132
Ellington, Duke 21
Emergency Committee of the

Entertainment Industry (ECEI) 74
England *see* Britain
ENIAC 30
Ernst, Max 226
Eugene O'Neill Society 202
Euripides 36, 76, 89, 146, 147, 259–60 nn.106, 109
European Recovery Act *see* Marshall Plan
Evans, Maurice 42, 47, 56, 75, 210
experimentation in dramatic form and staging 128–9, 130–1, 153, 154, 158, 163–4, 165–6, 170, 175, 225
expressionism 92, 154, 165, 166, 186, 202

Fair Deal 8
Falls, Robert 124
Fancy Free (musical, Leonard Bernstein and Jerome Robbins) 62, 79
fascism 2, 40, 41, 43, 209
Fay, Frank 60
Federal Bureau of Investigation (FBI) 183, 234
Federal Theatre Project (FTP) 19, 40–1, 44, 45, 99, 183
Ferrer, José 71–3, 75
Ffolkes, David 76
Field, Betty 209
Fields, Dorothy 61, 62
Fields, Herbert 61, 62
Fields, Joseph 46, 47, 56, 59
Finian's Rainbow (musical, Burton Lane, E. Y. Harburg and Fred Saidy) 77
Finland 4, 47
Finnegan's Wake (novel, James Joyce) 128
First World War 1, 3, 4, 12, 14, 25, 37, 39, 51, 56, 60, 63, 94, 96, 130, 170, 231
Stage Women's War Relief 14, 51
Fitzgerald, F. Scott 155
Flanagan, Hallie 40, 41, 153
Flinn, Denny Martin 67, 78
flying saucers 31
Flynn, Errol 25
Fonda, Henry 76, 224
Fontanne, Lynne 37, 59, 77
food 13, 16–17, 18, 52–3
Ford, John 25
France 2, 3, 4, 9, 10, 14, 47, 51, 92, 96, 130, 202, 204
Frank, Anne 13
Franken, Rose 46
Freedley, Vinton 52
Freedom Train 30
French plays in translation 42, 76, 77 *see also* Giraudoux, Jean; Sartre, Jean-Paul
Freud, Sigmund 48, 93, 129, 145
Fried, Walter 182, 191
Fromm, Erich 184–6, 190
Fuller, Buckminster 29

Galsworthy, John 209, 210, 211
García Lorca, Federico 152
Garde, Betty 68
Garfield, John 54
Garland, Judy 24
Garrett, Oliver H. P. 39
Gassner, John 45, 157, 164
gay *see* homosexuality
Geddes, Norman Bel 211
Gentlemen Prefer Blondes (novel, Anita Loos; play, Loos and John Emerson) 78–9, 80, 139
George Washington Slept Here (play, Kaufman and Hart) 46, 83

Germany 2, 3, 4, 5, 9, 10, 12, 32, 57, 146, 149, 183
Gershwin, George 34
Gershwin, Ira 48
Gert, Valeska 226
Giamatti, Paul 124
Gielgud, John 42
G.I. Bill 15, 17
Gill, Glenda E. 45
Gillespie, Dizzy 21
Gilpin, Charles 92
Giraudoux, Jean 42, 76, 77, 128, 149, 260 n.108
G.I.s 11, 12, 15, 30, 54, 55, 75, 100
Glaspell, Susan 202
Godfrey, Arthur 24
Goethe, Johann Wolfgang von 146, 149
Goetz, Augustus 76
Golden, John 58
Goldsmith, Clifford 208, 211
golf 31
Goodman, Benny 21
Gordin, Jacob 199
Gordon, Max 52, 68, 69
Gordon, Ruth 42, 60, 76, 95
Gorelik, Mordecai 182
Gow, James 73, 211
Grable, Betty 14
Graebner, William S. 11, 19
Graham, Martha 79–80, 155, 240 n.9
Graziano, Rocky 29
Great Gildersleeve see Peary, Harold
Great War *see* First World War
Greek classics 79–80, 89, 93, 94, 128, 137, 145 *see also* Euripides
Green, Adolph 62
Green Grow the Lilacs (play, Lynn Riggs) 66, 67

Green, Paul 42
Greenwood, Jane 124
Grieg, Edvard 61
Gross, Chaim 226
Grosz, Georg 226
Group Theatre 42, 156, 182
Guinan, Texas 89
Gunther, John 31
Guthrie, Woody 22

Hagen, Uta 71–2
Haines, William Wister 76
Hall Johnson Choir 62
Hallmark greeting cards 23
Hallyday, Johnny 204
Hamilton, Patrick 47
Hamlet (play, William Shakespeare) 42, 56, 75, 82, 84, 238
Hammerstein II, Oscar 60, 61, 63, 67, 69
Hampden, Walter 135
Hanna, William and Joseph Barbera. 26
Harburg, E. Y. 'Yip' 46, 60, 61, 77
Hardison, Felix M. 12
Harlem 44, 45
Harriet (play, Florence Ryerson and Colin Clements) 59
Harris, Jed 83, 134, 198
Harris, Sam 83
Hart, Lorenz 42, 46, 61, 67
Hart, Moss 47, 48, 59, 76, 207, 209, 211 *see also* Kaufman and Hart
Harvey (play, Mary Chase) 35, 60, 75, 83, 208
Havoc, June 61, 62
Hawkins, William 182
Hayes, Helen 47, 52, 53, 59, 75, 214–20
Hayward, Leland 84

Hayworth, Rita 14
Hazan, Joe 226
Helburn, Theresa 38, 45, 51, 66–8, 80, 157
Hellman, Lillian 42, 47, 60, 74, 76, 78, 199, 209, 211
  Another Part of the Forest 76
  Children's Hour, The 209
  Little Foxes, The 42, 78, 209, 211
  Searching Wind, The 60, 209
  Watch on the Rhine 47, 209
Hemingway, Ernest 29, 93, 128, 155
Henry III, William A. 129, 134
Hepburn, Katharine 53, 59
Heyward, DuBose and Dorothy 42, 74
High Button Shoes 77–8, 83
Hill, Abram 45
Hiss, Alger 33
Hitchcock, Alfred 74, 89, 128, 141, 145
Hitler, Adolf 2, 3, 9, 37, 39, 40, 43, 145
Hoffman, Philip Seymour 202
Hofmann, Hans 226
Hokinson, Helen 28
Hold on to Your Hats 46
Holland, Willard 153, 154
Hollywood 14, 25, 48, 60, 65, 68, 162, 218, 234
Hollywood Canteen 14, 54
Hollywood Ten 33, 41, 183, 193
Holm, Celeste 61, 68, 69
Holm, Hanya 79
Holocaust 12
home furnishings and appliances 17
homosexuality 48, 87, 132, 154, 223, 227
Hope for a Harvest (play, Sophie Treadwell) 47

Hopkins, Arthur 83
Hopkins, Miriam 157
House Un-American Activities Committee (HUAC) 7, 33, 41, 183, 192, 195, 196, 198, 237
housekeeping (home-making) 16, 18, 19
housing 15, 17
Hope, Bob 14, 55, 56
Hopper, Edward 29
Howard Johnson (restaurants) 213
Howard, Leslie 42
Howard Players 73–4
Howard, Sidney 39
Howdy Doody Show 24
Hughes, Doug 124
Hughes, Elinor 158
Hughes, Langston 15, 78
Hull, Josephine 51, 52
Humphrey, Doris 79
Huston, John 205
Hutchins, Robert Maynard 93, 95
Hutton, Betty 77

Ibsen, Henrik 42, 74, 81, 84, 89, 95, 99, 128, 147, 152, 178, 192, 198, 234 *see also* Miller, Arthur: *An Enemy of the People*
Idiot's Delight (play, Robert Sherwood) 37–8
Inge, William 84
Ingram, Rex 44, 62
internment camps 11
Irish 90, 105, 106, 107, 120, 121, 163
iron curtain 32
isolationism 4, 5, 6, 50
Italy 2, 3, 5, 9, 11, 65
It Can't Happen Here (novel, play, Sinclair Lewis) 40–1

Iwo Jima 10

Jackson, Robert (Supreme Court Justice) 12
Jackson, Shirley 13
James, Henry 76
Japan 2, 3, 4, 5, 6, 9, 10, 183
Japanese-Americans 11
Jeffers, Robinson 76
Jefferson Memorial 29
Jenkins, Kathleen 91
Jewish 3, 9, 12, 87, 177, 194
Joan of Lorraine (play, Maxwell Anderson) 74, 75, 76
Johnson Act 3, 4
Jolson, Al 14, 23–4, 25, 46, 89, 240 n.9
Jones, Cherry 124
Jones, Chris 82
Jones, Margo 81, 170–1, 173
Jones, Robert Edmond 72
Jones, Spike 22
Jory, Victor 75
Jouvet, Louis 128
Joyce, James 128
Junior Miss (play, Chodorov and Fields) 47, 56, 208

Kafka, Franz 128, 146
Kahn, Michael 124
Kai-shek, Chiang 33
Kanin, Fay 76
Kanin, Garson 76
Karloff, Boris 24
Kaufman, George S. 52, 60, 207, 208, 211
Kaufman and Hart 39, 46 *see also George Washington Slept Here*; *The Man Who Came to Dinner*; *You Can't Take It With You*
Kaye, Danny 22, 48
Kaye, Sammy 21

Kazan, Elia 76, 84, 173, 182, 191, 193, 198, 234
Keel, Howard 77
Keith, Thomas 201
Kelly, Paul 76
Kennan, George F. 8, 32
Kennedy, Arthur 198
Kern, Jerome 67
Kesselring, Joseph 46
Kidd, Michael 76
Kierkegaard, Soren 128, 146
Kiernan, Kip 222, 223–4, 226
Kilroy 30
Kingsley, Sidney 59, 76
Kinsey, Alfred C. 31
Kirkland, Jack 46
Kirsten, Dorothy 24
Kiss and Tell (play, F. Hugh Herbert) 59
Kiss Me, Kate (musical, Cole Porter) 76, 78
Koch, Frederick 80
Kolin, Philip C. 204
Konkle, Lincoln 203
Korea 183
Kramer, Hazel 96
Krasna, Norman 60
Krasner, Lee 226
Kubie, Lawrence S. 48
Kummer, Clare 60
Kushner, Tony 199

labour 3, 8, 13–14, 31, 73, 91, 94, 99, 154, 160, 180
Lady in the Dark (musical, Kurt Weill, Ira Gershwin and Moss Hart) 48–50, 53, 83, 209
Lahr, John 66, 161, 204
Laine, Frankie 22
Lamour, Dorothy 24
Lane, Burton 46, 77
Lane, Nathan 124, 202

Lang, Fritz 185
Lange, Jessica 124
Langner, Lawrence 38, 157, 160–1
Late George Apley, The (play, John Marquand and George S. Kaufman) 208, 211
Latino Americans 28, 29–30 *see also* Miranda, Carmen
Latouche, John 44
Laughlin, James 163, 171
Laughton, Charles 24
Laurents, Arthur 76
Lavery, Emmet 76
Lawrence, D. H. 151, 152, 153, 157, 162
Lawrence, Gertrude 48–52, 53, 244 n.25
Lawrence, Jerome and Robert E. Lee 58
Lawson, John Howard 199
Lee, Canada 44, 45, 60, 73–4, 83
Lee, Eugene 124
Le Gallienne, Eva 75, 83–4
Lend-Lease Act 4, 5
LeNoire, Rosetta 60
Lerner, Alan J. 61, 75, 78 *see also* Loewe, Frederick
Lesser, Sol 53, 135
Letts, Tracy 202
Levant, Oscar 24
Leverich, Lyle 204
Levittown 17
Lewis, Sinclair 155 *see also It Can't Happen Here*
Ley, Willy 12
Life with Father (play, Lindsay and Crouse) 41, 46, 208, 210, 211
Lincoln Theatre (Harlem) 44
Lindsay, Howard and Russel Crouse 41, 75
Little Theatre Movement (1920s) 36, 38, 80, 91 *see also* community theatre
Loesser, Frank 21, 22, 78
Loewe, Frederick 61, 75, 78
Logan, Joshua 76, 77, 84
London 191, 204
Looney Tunes *see* Tex Avery
Loos, Anita 78, 139
Lope de Vega, Felix Carpio 128, 149
Loquasto, Santo 124
Louis, Joe 29
Luce, Henry 94
Luhan, Mabel Dodge 93
Lunt, Alfred 37, 53, 59, 77

Mabie, Edward Charles 155, 164
MacArthur, Douglas 8, 10
MacDonald, Betty 30
MacDonald, Golden 19
MacLeish, Archibald 43
McBurney, Clark Mills 97, 152, 153
McCarthy, Charlie *see* Bergen, Edgar
McCarthy, Joseph 33
McCarthyism 41, 193, 194, 196, 198, 265 n.43
McClatchey, J. D. 135, 141
McClintic, Guthrie 56
McCloskey, Robert 19
McClung, Bruce 48, 49, 58
McConnell, Frederic 81
McCullers, Carson 170, 231
McDonald's 18
McDonell, Gordon 141
McKenney, Ruth 46
McPherson, Colvin 154
magazines 26, 229
Mailer, Norman 31, 231, 233–4
Making of Americans, The (book by Gertrude Stein) 128
Malden, Karl 182

Mamba's Daughters (play, DuBose and Dorothy Heyward) 42, 44, 74
Mamoulian, Rouben 68
Manheim, Michael 117
Manners, J. Hartley 163
Mann, Theodore 123
Man Who Came to Dinner, The (play, Kaufman and Hart) 41, 46, 56
Mao, Zedong 33
March, Fredric 75, 214
Margaret Webster Shakespeare Company (Marweb) 84
Marinoff, Fania 214
Marquand, John 208, 211
Marshall, George Catlett 6, 7, 8, 65
Marshall Plan (European Recovery Act) 7, 8, 34
Martin, Mary 61, 77, 78, 214
Marx, Groucho 24
Marx, Harpo 53
Massey, Raymond 52
Matthews, Brander 80
materialism 92, 103, 105, 106, 180, 184, 187, 191
Mauldin, Bill 11
Mayfield, Senator 213
medicine 29, 30, 31
Mellon, Andrew W. 29
Member of the Wedding, The (novel, play, Carson McCullers) 170
mental illness 161
Menuhin, Yehudi 24, 53
Mercer, Johnny 63
Mercury Theatre 42
Meredith, Burgess 160
Merlo, Frank 224
Merman, Ethel 61, 77
Merrill, Beth 182
Metcalf, Laurie 124

Metropolitan Opera House 80
Michener, James A. 31, 78
Mielziner, Jo 135, 166, 191, 212
Mielziner, Leo 212, 213
Mille, Agnes de 31, 61, 68, 76, 79, 80 *see also Oklahoma!*; *Rodeo*
Miller, Arthur 42, 43, 60, 74, 84, 87–9, 97–100, 157, 169, 177–99, 201, 202, 204–5, 207, 228–37
  After the Fall 205, 228
  All My Sons 17, 35, 75, 76, 84, 100, 178–84, 187, 189, 191, 192, 231, 233, 235
  The American Clock 205, 228, 229
  The Archbishop's Ceiling 205
  awards 99, 182, 191, 205
  Broken Glass 205, 228, 230
  Creation of the World and Other Business, The 205
  Crucible, The 178, 192–8, 231, 236, 237
  Death of a Salesman 19, 35, 74, 76, 84, 178, 184–91, 192, 228, 229, 230, 231, 234, 236
  education 98–9
  Enemy of the People, An (adaptation) 178, 192, 234
  Focus (novel) 100, 177, 192, 198, 228, 234
  Great Disobedience, The 99
  Incident at Vichy 205
  Man Who Had All the Luck, The 60, 100, 232, 233, 234
  marriages 89, 99, 205, 231
  Memory of Two Mondays, A 228
  Misfits, The (screenplay) 89, 205
  Mr Peter's Connections 228
  No Villain 99

Price, The 205, 228
Ride Down Mount Morgan, The 205, 228
Situation Normal (nonfiction) 100
Story of G.I. Joe, The (screenplay) 100, 233
They Too Arise 99
Timebends (memoir) 193, 205, 229, 230, 233, 234, 235
View from the Bridge, A 89, 228, 231, 234, 235–7
Miller, Augusta Barnett (Arthur Miller's mother) 98
Miller, Gilbert 52
Miller, Glenn 21
Miller, Isidore (Arthur Miller's father) 98
Miller, Joan (Arthur Miller's sister) 98
Miller, Kermit (Arthur Miller's brother) 98
Miranda, Carmen 27
Miss Julie (play, August Strindberg) 224
Mister Roberts (play, Thomas Heggen and Joshua Logan) 76
Mitchell, Abbie 73
Mitchell, Billy 12
Moeller, Phillip 38
Moffitt, John C. 40
Monroe, Marilyn 89, 205, 234, 235, 237
Monte Cristo Cottage 253 n.40
Monterey, Carlotta 92, 102, 118, 123, 202, 214
Moore, Marian 52
Moorehead, Agnes 43
Mordden, Ethan 61
Moss, Arnold 83
Mother Courage (play, Bertolt Brecht) 181

mothers/motherhood 16, 28, 88, 108, 112–13, 118, 119, 120, 121, 122, 130, 219–20
motion pictures *see* movies
Moscow Art Theatre 168
Mount Palomar 31
Mount Rushmore 29
movies 13, 17, 18, 23, 25–6, 27, 29, 46, 53–4, 65, 68, 77, 89, 97, 125, 136, 138, 141–5, 152, 154, 165, 170
  animated cartoons 23, 26
  documentaries 25
  newsreels 23, 136
Mr. and Mrs. North (play, Owen Davis) 46
Mummers 153, 154
Murrow, Edward R. 10, 57
music 21–2, 31, 67, 98, 166–7
musicals 22, 48–51, 60–2, 76–8, 208 *see also* Berlin, Irving; Lerner and Loewe; *Oklahoma!*; Rodgers and Hammerstein
Mussolini, Benito 2, 9, 37, 39
My Sister Eileen (play, Chodorov and Fields, musical, Leonard Bernstein) 46, 208

Nash, Ogden 61
Nathan, George Jean 111
National Association for the Advancement of Colored People (NAACP) 7, 8, 15
National Gallery of Art 29
Native Son (novel, Richard Wright) 29
Native Son (play, Richard Wright and Paul Green) 45
Nazi 2, 3, 4, 6, 9, 12, 13, 39, 40, 47, 145 *see also* concentration camps

Negro Playwrights Company
  (NPC) 44
Negro Theatre Project 40
New Orleans, Louisiana 81, 221,
  222, 225, 228
New School for Social Research
  45, 74, 157, 158, 159
newspapers 9, 23, 26, 88, 89, 91,
  93, 96, 99, 153, 154, 179
New York Drama Critics' Circle
  38, 182, 207, 208
  awards 38, 39, 42, 47, 59, 75,
  76, 178
New Yorker 28, 46, 47, 57
New York Times 11, 58, 183,
  191, 198
Nichols, Anne 46
Nisei *see* Japanese-Americans
Niven, Penelope 95, 145, 146, 203
Nixon, Richard 33
Nobel Prize 9, 30, 41, 92, 122
Noguchi, Isamu 80
Norse, Harold 222
North Atlantic Treaty
  Organization (NATO) 33
Norton, Eliot 158
Norway 4, 47
Nuremberg War Crimes Trial 12

Oboler, Arch 57
Odets, Clifford 39, 42, 154, 199
Oklahoma! 22, 49, 61, 63,
  66–70, 79, 80, 208 *see also*
  Rodgers and Hammerstein
Old Maid, The (play, Zoe Akins)
  210
O'Neal, Frederick 45, 60
O'Neill, Ella Quinlan 90
O'Neill, Eugene 34, 38, 70, 75,
  77, 87–92, 97, 101–24,
  152, 155, 172, 178, 201–2,
  207, 208, 210, 211–14,
  225, 226, 237–8

Ah! Wilderness 92
All God's Chillun Got Wings
  70, 92, 209
Anna Christie 92
Beyond the Horizon 91, 105,
  208, 211
Bound East for Cardiff 91
children 92
cycle of projected plays 92,
  101–2, 103, 106
Days Without End 102
Desire Under the Elms 92, 103
Diff'rent 225
Dynamo 92
Emperor Jones, The 70, 91,
  92, 208, 211, 212, 238
Great God Brown, The 92,
  108
Hairy Ape, The 91, 92
Hughie 102, 202
Iceman Cometh, The 35, 38,
  75, 77, 92, 101, 102–3,
  109–13, 114, 117, 118, 120,
  123, 178, 201, 210, 238
Long Day's Journey Into Night
  35, 90, 92, 101, 102, 103,
  114–19, 119, 120, 121,
  123, 202
Marco Millions 92, 103
marriages 91, 92 *see also*
  Boulton, Agnes; Jenkins,
  Kathleen; Monterey,
  Carlotta
Moon for the Misbegotten, A
  102, 103, 119–23, 201–2
More Stately Mansions 92,
  106, 109, 202
Mourning Becomes Electra 89,
  92, 118
religion 87, 90
seafaring 91
Strange Interlude 92, 172, 202,
  210, 213

Touch of the Poet, A 92, 102, 104–9, 114, 120, 202
  worldview 91, 103, 104
O'Neill, Eugene, Jr. 92
O'Neill, James 90, 168
O'Neill, James, Jr. 90
O'Neill, Oona *see* Chaplin
135th Street Library Theatre (Harlem) 45
One Touch of Venus (musical, Kurt Weill, S. J. Perlman and Ogden Nash) 49, 61, 80, 83
On Striver's Row (play, Abram Hill) 45
On the Town (musical, Leonard Bernstein, Betty Comden and Adolph Green) 49, 62, 79, 83
On Whitman Avenue (play by Maxine Wood) 73
operetta 61, 62
Ortega y Gasset, José 149
Othello 63, 70–2, 83

Pacific front 4, 5, 6, 10, 11, 51, 56, 65–6, 102
pacifism 37, 47, 171
painting 29, 87, 226
Pal Joey (musical, Rodgers and Hart) 46, 67, 82
Paris, France 3, 54
Parker, Charlie 'Bird' 22
Parker, Dorothy 84
Pasadena Playhouse 81, 152, 161, 164, 222
Paton, Alan
Patrick, John 60
Pearl Harbor 4, 5, 9, 25, 39, 50, 52, 57, 59, 62, 102
Peary, Harold 24
Peg o' My Heart (play, J. Hartley Manners) 163

Pemberton, Brock 52, 54, 83
Pentagon 29
Perlman, S. J. 61
Perry, Antoinette 51, 52, 75, 83
Pershing, John J. 4
Philippines 8, 10, 30, 64, 66
Pick-Up Girl (play, Elsa Shelley) 208, 209, 211
pin-ups 14
Pinza, Ezio 78
Pirandello, Luigi 131–2, 137
Piscator, Erwin 45, 157, 158, 159, 164, 167, 170
Pius XII, Pope 30
Playwrights' Company 47
Poe, Edgar Allan 152
poetry 31, 43, 87, 104, 105, 140, 152, 153, 168
Pogue, Kate 213
Poland 3, 4, 5, 6, 98
Pollock, Jackson 226, 249 n.9
Porter, Cole 22, 42, 60, 61, 76, 78
postal service 23
post-war recovery 6, 32
prison reform 99, 154, 251 n.10
producers 82–5
Provincetown, Massachusetts 91, 212, 221–8
Provincetown Players 91, 202, 226
Provincetown Tennessee Williams Theater Festival 221, 224–5
psychology/psychoanalysis 32, 48, 144, 145, 163, 184–5, 259 n.90
Pulitzer Prize 11, 29, 31, 35, 37, 38, 39, 42, 47, 59, 60, 75, 76, 91, 95, 191, 207, 208
Pyle, Ernie 10–11, 233

queer *see* homosexuality
Quintero, Jose 123, 202

race relations 209 *see also*
    African-American;
    anti-Semitism;
    Japanese-American
race riots 15, 29–30
radio 5, 6, 10, 13, 17, 19–20, 21,
    23–4, 43, 46, 54, 57–8, 59,
    89, 99, 100, 102, 137, 138,
    208, 265 n.39
  Armed Forces Radio Service 58
  Cavalcade of America 43, 100,
    233
  Chaplain Jim 58
  Fall of the City, The
    (Archibald MacLeish) 43
  Let's Pretend 19–20
  Lux Radio Theatre 43
  March of Time, The 43
  War of the Worlds, The 137
  Your Hit Parade 21
  see also Corwin, Norman
Randolph, A. Philip 15
Rasch, Albertina 48, 79
Rathbone, Basil 76
rationing 13, 16, 18, 26
Reagan, Ronald 65
records (phonograph) 21, 70, 72
Red Cross 43, 50, 65
Redgrave, Vanessa 124, 202
Reinhardt, Max 93, 95
Reville, Alma 141
Rice, Elmer 39, 59, 76, 78, 155,
    160, 209
  Adding Machine, The 160
  Dream Girl 76, 209, 211
  Judgment Day 39
  Street Scene 78
Riesman, David 184–6, 190
Riggs, Lynn 66, 81
Rilke, Rainer Maria 224
road *see* touring (theatrical)
Robards, Jason 123
Robbins, Jerome 62, 79

Roberts, Joan 68
Robeson, Paul 15, 63, 70–2, 83,
    92
Robinsin, Bill 'Bojangles' 62
Robinson, Jackie 30
Rockefeller, John D. Jr. 30
Rockwell, Norman 29
Rodeo 31, 80 *see also* Mille,
    Agnes de
Rodgers and Hammerstein 61,
    62, 63, 67, 76, 77, 78, 135,
    208
  Allegro 78, 135
  Carousel 67, 75, 78, 208
  South Pacific 76, 78
  see also Oklahoma!
Rodgers, Richard 60, 67
  with Lorenz Hart 42, 46, 61,
    67
  see also Hammerstein II, Oscar
Rogers, Roy 22
Romberg, Sigmund 62
Rome, Harold 60
Roosevelt, Eleanor 9, 64
Roosevelt, Franklin Delano 5, 6,
    8, 10, 15, 29, 31, 64, 66
Rorem, Ned 135
Rose, Billy 52, 62
Rose McClendon Players 45
Rosenberg, Julius and Ethel 198
Rosenstock, Milton 64
Rosie the Riveter 13–14
Rostand, Edmond 75, 208, 211
Rosten 232
Route 66 18
Rowe, Kenneth T. 99
Royle, Selena 52
Russell, Jane 14
Russia 5, 10 *see also* Union of
    Soviet Socialist Republics

'Sad Sack' 11
Saidy, Fred 77

St. Louis, Missouri 152, 153, 154, 221, 222
Salem witch trials 192–6
Sarnoff, David 24
Saroyan, William 42, 155, 160
Sartre, Jean-Paul 75, 77, 128, 149
Sayler, Oliver 212
Schlesinger, Arthur M. 30
Schweitzer, Albert 149
Scouts, Boy and Girl Scouts of America 64
Second World War 1, 2, 4, 8, 12, 24, 36, 37, 57, 75, 87, 125, 136, 203, 209, 214, 233
 Europe 1, 3–4, 5, 6, 8, 36
 Pacific 3–4, 5, 6, 10, 11
segregation/desegregation 15, 64, 73–4, 79, 228
Selznick, Irene Mayer 85, 173
Shakespeare, William 36, 42, 47, 53, 56, 63, 70–1, 74–5, 78, 81, 83–4, 90, 96, 114, 128, 131, 152
Sharaff, Irene 48
Shaw, George Bernard 36, 75, 81, 84, 128, 155
Shaw, Irwin 39, 153
Sheldon, Edward 93, 128
Shelley, Elsa 208, 209, 211
Sherwood, Robert 37, 39, 47
 Abe Lincoln in Illinois 42
 There Shall Be No Night 47
 see also *Idiot's Delight*
ships 4, 5, 10, 50, 65
Shmoos 26
Shore, Dinah 55
Shubert, Lee 52
Shumlin, Herman 85
Silverman, Elliott 198
Simonson, Lee 38
Sinatra, Frank 21
Singer, Louis 163
Sissle, Noble 56

Six Characters in Search of an Author (play, Luigi Pirandello) 131–2
Skelton, Red 24
Slattery, Mary 99, 231, 232
Slinky 19
Smith, Kate 63
Smith, Lillian and Esther 73
Smith, Oliver 62, 79
Smith, William Jay 97, 152, 153
social issues 87, 99, 154, 158–9, 164, 177–8, 180, 181, 183, 191, 192, 199, 204 see also civil rights
Sondheim, Stephen 57
Song of Norway (musical) 61
songs 12, 13, 18, 21–2, 48, 50, 53, 61, 62, 63, 67, 69, 70, 77, 78, 79, 89, 127, 204
Soviet Union see Union of Soviet Socialist Republics
Spacey, Kevin 124, 202
Spencer, John 158
Sper, Felix 82
Spewak, Sam and Bella 78
Spock, Dr. Benjamin 16
sports see athletics
Stage Door Canteen 14, 22, 52–4
Stage Women's War Relief see First World War
Stalin, Joseph 2, 7, 8, 32, 33
State of the Union, The (play, Howard Lindsay and Russel Crouse) 211
Stars and Stripes 1, 128
Steinbeck, John 29, 39, 47, 152, 208, 211
 Moon Is Down, The 47
 Of Mice and Men 39, 42, 208, 211
Stein, Gertrude 93, 95, 128, 134
Stein, Jules 54

Stevens, Ashton 168
Stevens, Thomas Wood 80
Stoddard, Richard 212, 213
Stone, Ezra 63
Strife (play, John Galsworthy) 209, 210, 211
Strindberg, August 81, 91, 122–3, 152, 224
Styne, Jule 78, 79
suburbs 17, 179
Superman 26
Susan and God (play, Rachel Crothers) 210, 211
Sullivan, Daniel 124
Sweden 202

Taft-Hartey Act 31
Tallchief, Maria 31
Talma, Louise 146
Tandy, Jessica 76
taxes 13
Taylor, Laurette 163, 168–9
Tchelitchew, Pavel 226
Teachout, Terry 57, 135
teenagers 6, 20–2
telephones 23
television 17, 24–5, 42, 215
Tempest, The 83–4
Testament of Dr. Mabuse (film, Fritz Lang) 185
Theatre Arts 43, 79, 80–1
Theatre Guild 37, 38, 47, 66–71, 74, 77, 99, 102, 151, 157, 158, 202, 213, 222, 223
  Guild Theatre 38, 67
This Is the Army (musical, Irving Berlin) 49, 59, 63–6
Thompson, John Douglas 124
Thornton Wilder Society 203
Till the Day I Die (play, Clifford Odets) 39
Time 6, 7, 26, 33, 35, 50, 77, 94
  Man of the Year 6, 239 n.5

Time of Your Life, The (play, William Saroyan) 42
Tobacco Road (play. Jack Kirland) 46, 66, 210
Toklas, Alice B. 134
Tom and Jerry (cartoons) 26
Tony Award *see* Antoinette Perry Award
touring (theatrical) 46, 49, 53, 55, 72, 73–4, 82, 84, 91, 202, 244 n.25
trains 15, 26–7
Traube, Shepard 59
travel 18, 26–7
Treadwell, Sophie 47
Treaty of Versailles 2, 37
tributary theatre 80–2
Truman Doctrine 8, 33
Truman, Harry 6, 8, 10, 11, 15, 30, 33
Tunney, Gene 93

UFO scare 31, 32
Union of Scenic Artists 44
Union of Soviet Socialist Republics (USSR) 2, 3, 8, 32, 33, 182 *see also* Russia
United Nations (UN) 8, 9, 30, 32, 33
United Service Organizations (USO) 8, 14, 51, 52, 54–7
  Camp Shows, Inc. (CSI) 14, 36, 55–6
United States of America 10, 44
  draft 5, 14, 44, 54
  economy 1, 6, 8, 16, 181, 190, 191
  internment camps 11 *see also* Japanese-Americans
  military 4, 5, 7, 100
    Air Force 12
    Army 5, 14. 55, 63, 182

Army Air Corps 12, 146, 179
Army Air Forces 12, 14, 178
Coast Guard 94
desegregation 15
Marines 10, 14
Navy 55, 73
occupation forces 15, 182
public opinion 5, 6
Supreme Court 195
world leadership responsibility 7
United States Constitution 131
university theatre 71, 80–1
urbanization 185–6, 231

V-2 rocket 12
Vance, Nina 81
Van Druten, John 60, 208, 211
Variety 41, 47, 74, 157
Vechten, Carl van 214
The Verge (play, Susan Glaspell) 202
Versailles Treaty *see* Treaty of Versailles
victory in Europe (V-E) Day 10, 66
victory in Japan (V-J) Day 10, 66
Voice of the Turtle, The (play, John Van Druten) 60, 208, 211
Von Braun, Wernher 12
Voscovec, George 83–4

Wager, Charles H. 94
Walt Disney *see* Disney, Walt
war 102, 125–6, 130, 145, 239 n.1
  air 4, 10
  effect on civilian life 1, 6, 13, 102, 208, 210
  plays about 37, 39, 47, 59, 76
  radio drama 57
  sea 4, 10
  see also First World War; Second World War
War Bonds 13, 50, 52
Ward, Theodore 44, 73
Warner Brothers 26
Warren, Robert Penn 30
Washington, DC 29, 64, 74, 157, 205, 213
Waters, Ethel 42, 44, 45, 53, 62
Watkins, Perry 44
Watson, Lucile 51
Watts, Richard, Jr. 50, 182
Webster, Margaret 47, 70–2, 74, 75, 83–4, 173
Weidman, Charles 79
Weill, Kurt 42, 48, 61, 78
Welles, Orson 29, 43, 137
Wertham, Frederick 191
Wertheim, Albert 39, 40
West Side Story 49
What a Life (play, Clifford Goldsmith) 208, 211
Wheeler, Lois 182
White, Jane 73
White, Miles 68, 79
Whitman, Walt 152
Why We Fight see Capra, Frank
Wikander, Matthew 119
Wilde, Oscar 128
Wilder, Amos Parker 93–4
Wilder, Amos Parker, Jr. 93, 132
Wilder, Charlotte 93, 94
Wilder, Isabel 93, 94, 145
Wilder, Isabella Niven 93, 94
Wilder, Janet 93
Wilder, Thornton 1, 34, 42, 59, 83, 87–9, 92–5, 125–49, 155, 201, 203, 204, 208, 211, 214, 237–8
  Alcestiad, The 89, 125, 126, 127, 128, 129, 132, 145–9

INDEX

Bridge of San Luis Rey, The 88, 95
Cabala, The 94
Doll's House, A 42, 95
Drunken Sisters, The 146
Eighth Day, The (novel) 203
foreign languages 92, 93, 95, 146, 149
Happy Journey to Trenton and Camden, The 42
Hello, Dolly! 203
Ides of March, The 149
letters 88, 92, 93, 95, 128
Matchmaker, The 125, 203
Merchant of Yonkers, The 42, 93, 95, 125, 203
military service 87, 91, 94, 141, 149
Our Century 126–7
Our Town 1, 35, 39, 42, 56, 78, 81, 83, 125, 126, 128, 129, 130–5, 140, 143, 145, 201, 203, 208, 211, 237, 238
Rape of Lucrece, The 95
Shadow of a Doubt 125, 126, 127, 128, 129, 131, 140, 141–5
Skin of Our Teeth, The 35, 59, 125, 126, 127, 128, 129, 131, 136–41, 203, 214–20
Theophilus North (novel) 203
Victors, The (translation, Morts sans sépulture) 77, 149
scholarly pursuits 92
travels abroad 1, 88–9, 93, 95
Wilkie, Wendell L. 5
Williams, Alexander 158
Williams, Cornelius Coffin 95, 96, 97, 161
Williams, Edwina Dakin 95–6, 161, 163
Williams, Hank 21

Williams, Rose Isabel 96, 161–3, 172
Williams, Tennessee 34, 36, 42, 48, 74, 75, 84, 87–9, 95–7, 151–75, 201, 202, 207, 221–8, 237–8
1930s 152–6, 226
Battle of Angels 151, 156–9, 161, 173, 222, 227
Beauty Is the Word 152
Cairo! Shanghai! Bombay! 97, 225
Camino Real 203, 204
Candles to the Sun 154
Cat on a Hot Tin Roof 151, 175, 204
Daughter of the American Revolution 156, 172
Day on Which a Man Dies, The 226, 227
Eccentricities of a Nightingale, The 172
Fugitive Kind, The 154
Gentleman Caller, The 162–3, 165
Glass Menagerie, The 35, 60, 75, 82, 84, 151, 151, 153, 155, 156, 161–8, 162, 173, 174, 175, 222, 223, 225, 237, 238
Gnädiges Fraulein 226
Headlines 153
Magic Tower, The 153
Memoir 224, 226
Milk Train Doesn't Stop Here Anymore, The 225
Moise and the World of Reason (novel) 226
Night of the Iguana, The 204, 222, 223
Not About Nightingales 154
Orpheus Descending 89, 157
Out Cry 204

Ozzie 96
Parade, The 222–4, 227
Rose Tattoo, The 204, 225
Small Craft Warnings 204
Something Cloudy, Something Clear 223–4, 225, 227
Southern influences and qualities 95, 155, 156, 159, 221, 237
Spinning Song, The 162, 172
Spring Storm 155, 162
Stairs to the Roof 151, 159–61, 164, 222
Streetcar Named Desire, A 35, 74, 76, 84, 85, 151, 152, 153, 155, 162, 164, 172–4, 185, 222, 225, 238
Suddenly Last Summer 204, 222
Summer and Smoke 152, 169–72, 173, 222, 225
Sweet Bird of Youth 204, 225
travel abroad 96
You Touched Me! 75, 151, 162, 164
Willett, John 164
'Willie and Joe' *see* Mauldin
Wilson, Arthur 'Dooley' 44
Wilson, Perry 73
Wilson, August 201
Winchell, Walter 69
Windham, Donald 75, 151, 159, 162
Winged Victory (play, Moss Hart) 211
Wirich, Jiri 83–4

Wolfe, Thomas 155, 231
women 9, 13–14, 16, 19, 27–8, 49, 61, 111–12, 139–40
  clubs 28
  in military service branches 13–14, 65
  volunteer work 14, 28, 51, 55
  see also clothing and shoes; mothers/motherhood
Wonder Woman 26
Wood, Audrey 156, 157, 159, 160, 162, 163, 170, 173
Wood, Maxine 73
Woollcott, Alexander 93
World War I *see* First World War
World War II *see* Second World War
Wright, Richard 29, 45, 231
Wright, Teresa 142
Wynn, Ed 53

Yeager, Chuck 30
Years Ago (play, Ruth Gordon) 75, 76
Ying Ruocheng 205
You Can't Take It With You (play, Kaufman and Hart) 41, 210
Young Men's Christian Association (YMCA) 14, 54
Yordan, Philip 60

Zaharias, Mildred 'Babe' Didrickson 31
Ziegfeld Theatre 62
zoot suits 28, 29–30
Zorina, Vera 83